Medical Records and the Law

Second Edition

William H. Roach, Jr., M.S., J.D.
Gardner, Carton & Douglas
Chicago, Illinois

and

Aspen Health Law Center
Patricia Younger, J.D.
Cynthia Conner, LL.L.
Kara Kinney Cartwright, J.D.

An Aspen Publication®
Aspen Publishers, Inc.
Gaithersburg, Maryland
1994

This publication is designed to provide accurate and authoritative information in regard to the Subject Matter covered. It is sold with the understanding that the publisher is not engaged in rendering legal, accounting, or other professional service. If legal advice or other expert assistance is required, the service of a competent professional person should be sought. *(From a Declaration of Principles jointly adopted by a Committee of the American Bar Association and a Committee of Publishers and Associations.)*

Library of Congress Cataloging-in-Publication Data
Medical records and the law / William H. Roach, Jr. . . . [et al.]. — 2nd ed.
p. cm.
Rev. ed. of: Medical records and the law / William H. Roach, Jr., Susan N. Chernoff, Carole Lange Esley. 1985.
Includes bibliographical references and index.
ISBN: 0-8342-0317-0
1. Medical records—Law and legislation—United States.
I. Roach, William H. II. Roach, William H. Medical records and the law.
[DNLM: WX 33 AA1 M385 1994]
KF3827.R4R63   1994
344.73'041—dc20
[347.30441]
DNLM/DLC
for Library of Congress
94-3803
CIP

Editorial Resources: Ruth Bloom

Library of Congress Catalog Card Number: 94-3803
ISBN: 0-8342-0317-0

Printed in the United States of America

1 2 3 4 5

Table of Contents

Preface

Medical records and the information they contain play a crucial role in the delivery of all health care services. Specific goals that health care providers set out to achieve when treating patients can be met by ensuring that medical records are accurate and complete. Risk management and quality assurance programs, for example, rely heavily on medical records for information to determine if patient care measures up to specific standards of care and to identify potential risks. A provider's duty to conduct peer review by reviewing the qualifications and performance of medical staff members is also largely dependent on information obtained from medical records. Obtaining payment and/or reimbursement for the health care services rendered requires accurate and current data about the nature of these services and the identity of the recipient. In addition, a medical record is often the single most important document available to a provider in defending against a negligence suit. Finally, the delivery of appropriate and timely medical care to patients would not be possible without adequate medical record documentation.

The role that medical record information plays in the delivery of health care services is increasing as the health care industry undergoes significant transition. With or without federal legislation, health care reform is well underway as a result of consumer/employer demand, state initiatives, and economic necessity. The industry is shifting away from the domination of fee-for-service medicine and acute care facilities toward managed care systems and networks of providers providing a full range of services. With the integration of various categories of health care providers and a greater focus on cost effectiveness has arisen the need to develop new approaches to managing health care information. Experts have predicted that increased automation and widespread access are the two main components of the emerging future in health care information management. Linking various providers, payors, employers, vendors, and support organizations through centralized databases while protecting the confidentiality of the information represents one of the major health care challenges of the next decade.

The second edition of the highly acclaimed *Medical Records and The Law* derives its *raison d'etre* from these trends. The book addresses the fundamental legal issues associated with medical records including contents, retention, authentication, corrections, and destruction, with a focus on current regulatory requirements, case law, and practical advice. Other chapters discuss access to medical records information, liability for improper disclosure of medical record information, and the use of medical records as evidence. Special legal problems such as the documentation of advance directives, inclusion of outside test reports in a medical record, compliance with the federal Emergency Medical Treatment and Active Labor Act (COBRA), child abuse reporting legislation, and the disposition of medical records in a change of ownership or closure, are examined in depth. The complex issues associated with AIDS patients' records, including specific statutory reporting and confidentiality requirements, are analyzed in a chapter entirely dedicated to this subject. Similarly, a new chapter on the legal aspects of computerized medical records has been added to keep pace with the evolution of information management in the health care industry.

The Aspen Health Law Center is grateful to every member of its staff for the patience and dedication they brought to this project. The Center's staff attorneys, Patricia Younger, Kara Kinney Cartwright, and Cynthia Conner, each made significant contributions to the book through their writing and research efforts. Audrey Hudiburgh, the Center's librarian, also devoted many research hours to the project, and Patricia Newcomer, its Administrative Assistant, provided valuable help in compiling the tables and appendixes. We are also grateful to Ruth Bloom, Aspen's Managing Editor in the Books Department, who kept us on schedule and helped us to look good in print. Finally, the Health Law Center would like to thank William Roach and the law firm of Gardner, Carton & Douglas for giving us the opportunity to work on such a distinguished product.

Acknowledgments

Producing the second edition of this book while practicing law full-time proved just as arduous a task as writing the original work. Once again, a team of highly qualified professionals made this edition possible. Susan Chernoff, an extremely knowledgeable and capable health lawyer at Gardner, Carton & Douglas, with the assistance of Marcie Handler, a student in the Loyola University School of Law masters in health law program, researched the recent developments in the law and prepared the initial manuscripts. Cynthia Conner, Patricia Younger, and Kara Kinney Cartwright, attorneys at the Aspen Health Law Center, completed the initial manuscripts and prepared additional chapters on issues of critical importance in the evolving law of medical information. My partner, Adele Waller, an expert on the law governing computerized medical records data, co-authored with the Aspen Health Law Center the chapter concerning use of automated record information.

Our tireless staff at Gardner, Carton & Douglas, Mary Born Wilson, Danielle LaVine, Peggy Jones, and Gwen Brinker, continued throughout to display the understanding, patience, and wisdom required to manage harried attorneys. Our editor, Jack Bruggeman, urged us steadily on with consummate diplomacy. To all these individuals, I am deeply grateful.

William H. Roach, Jr.
Chicago, Illinois

1

Patient Record Requirements

RECORDS THAT MUST BE KEPT

A hospital must maintain a record for each of its patients. This requirement is imposed by state licensure laws, Joint Commission on Accreditation of Healthcare Organizations (Joint Commission) standards, and conditions of participation in federal reimbursement programs. In addition, a small number of judicial opinions have held that, under certain circumstances, a hospital is liable to a patient for failure to maintain a proper record. To avoid civil liability and maintain its license, certification, and accreditation, a hospital therefore must develop and enforce appropriate recordkeeping policies. These policies should set forth clearly the types of information to be included in each record, how long each record must be kept, and proper methods for final destruction of a record.

The medical record consists of four types of data concerning an individual patient: (1) personal, (2) financial, (3) social, and (4) medical.[1] Personal information usually is obtained upon admission and will include name, birth date, sex, marital status, next of kin, occupation, identification of physicians, and other items needed for specific patient identification. Financial data include the name of the patient's employer, health insurance company, types of insurance and policy numbers, Medicare and Medicaid numbers, if any, and other information that will enable the hospital to bill for its services. Social data include the patient's race and ethnic background, family relationships, community activities, and life style. It also includes any court orders or other directions concerning the patient, and other information related to the patient's position in society that may indicate a need for special confidentiality protection.

---

[1]See K. Waters and G. Murphy, *Medical Records in Health Information* (Gaithersburg, Md.: Aspen Publishers, Inc., 1975), 39-95.

Medical data form the patient's clinical record, a continuously maintained history of the treatment provided in the hospital. These data include the patient's chief complaint, medical and family histories, results of physical examinations, planned course of treatment, physicians' diagnosis and therapeutic orders, evidence of informed consent, clinical observations, progress notes made by the medical staff, consultation reports, nursing notes, reports and results of all procedures and tests including pathology and clinical laboratory tests and examinations,[2] operative record, radiology and nuclear medicine examinations and treatment, anesthesia records, other reports generated during the patient's treatment, and conclusions made at the termination of hospitalization.[3] Medical data also may include information obtained from outside sources, including diagnostic tests performed at another facility before the patient's admission to the hospital, where reliance on the outside reports by hospital medical staff is reasonable medical practice and consistent with hospital policy.[4] (For a more detailed discussion on reports from outside facilities, see Chapter 3.)

The medical record may be written, typed, or computer generated. Regardless of its form, the medical record should be a complete, accurate, and current account of the history, condition, and treatment of the patient and the results of the individual's hospitalization or outpatient treatment. The computerized record can expand the information network on a patient, enhancing completeness and accuracy as well as immediate availability of the record to authorized personnel. However, computerized medical records present special concerns, which are addressed in Chapter 6.

The medical record is used not only to document chronologically the care rendered to the patient, but also to plan and evaluate the treatment and to enhance communication among the patient's physician and other health care professionals treating the individual. The record provides clinical data for medical, nursing, and scientific research. Individuals who conduct medical and nursing audits and peer review evaluations rely heavily on documentation in medical records.

Hospital medical records are important legal documents for the hospital and the patient. For example, where hospital bylaws direct individual departments to develop standards of care, examination of patient records can provide verification that the standards are being maintained. Administrative and clinical assess-

---

[2]See *Laubach v. Franklin Square Hosp.*, 556 A.2d 682 (1989), holding that fetal monitor tracings are part of the medical record.

[3]Joint Commission on Accreditation of Healthcare Organizations (JCAHO), *Accreditation Manual for Hospitals*, (Oakbrook Terrace, Ill.: 1994), IM Standard IM 7.2.

[4]See Susan N. Chernoff, Refusal to accept test reports from outside laboratories and diagnostic facilities, *Topics in Health Records Management* (1988) 9(2), 81-88.

ment programs may be targets of legal scrutiny, and patient records can aid in the evaluation and justification of such programs.[5]

The most important legal function of medical records is to provide essential evidence in the defense of professional negligence actions. Since such actions often are litigated two to five years after the plaintiff received the treatment in question, the hospital record frequently is the only detailed record of what actually occurred during the hospitalization. Persons who participated in the plaintiff's treatment may not be available to testify on behalf of the defendants or may not remember important details of the case. A properly created record enables the hospital to reconstruct the patient's course of treatment and to show whether the care provided was acceptable under the circumstances.[6] The contents of the hospital record usually are admissible in evidence for or against the hospital and physicians. It is essential, therefore, that everyone involved in medical record documentation and management understand the legal implications of the record so that they will create and maintain a record that will be useful to them in any future litigation. (For a discussion of admissibility of medical records, see Chapter 7.)

LEGAL REQUIREMENTS FOR CONTENT OF A MEDICAL RECORD

The requirements that hospitals maintain medical records is found in state and federal statutes and regulations, municipal codes, and hospital accreditation standards. In some state statutes, a general definition of "medical records" provides guidance on what the records should contain. In Colorado, for example, legislation defines "medical record" as a "record of services pertaining to medical and health care, which are performed at the direction of a physician or other licensed health care provider on behalf of a patient by . . . health care personnel" including "such diagnostic documentation as X-rays, electrocardiograms, electroencephalograms, and other test results."[7] The Nevada statute defines health care records as "any written reports, notes, orders, photographs, X-rays, or other recorded data or information whether maintained in written, electronic or other form which is received or produced by a provider of health care, or any person employed by him, and contains information relating to the medical history, examinations, diagnosis or treatment of the patient."[8] In a few

---

[5]See Waters and Murphy, *Medical Records*, 247, note 1.

[6]See, e.g., *Foley v. Flushing Hosp. and Medical Cent.*, 359 N.Y.S.2d 113 (1974), where an infant plaintiff's medical records provided evidence sufficient to prevent dismissal of a malpractice suit.

[7]See Colo. Rev. Stat. § 18-4-412 (1991).

[8]Nev. A.B. 459 (New Laws 1993).

states, hospital-licensing statutes set forth the minimum record requirements. The Florida statute is illustrative:

> Each hospital . . . shall require the use of a system of problem-oriented medical records for its patients, which system shall include the following elements: basic client data collection; a listing of the patient's problems; the initial plan with diagnostic and therapeutic orders as appropriate for each problem identified; and progress notes, including a discharge summary.[9]

The Tennessee statute simply refers to standards prescribed by the hospital licensing board.[10]

For the vast majority of states, however, the regulatory agencies for hospitals as well as for other health care providers have jurisdiction to establish detailed requirements on medical record content. In most instances, the regulatory agency for hospitals has the power to promulgate rules and regulations governing the licensure of health care facilities,[11] including a list of the specific information that must be kept in the medical records of licensed hospitals.[12] The rules and regulations have the effect of law.

The regulations issued by these agencies cover a variety of different health care providers, as well as types of medical information. In Alabama, for instance, the State Board of Health enunciates minimum content requirements for different hospital records, including for admissions, medical and surgical, obstetrical, and newborns.[13] The state also has content requirements for nursing home medical records. California regulations on record content requirements for acute care hospitals distinguish between inpatient and outpatient medical records, as well as between records generated by other facilities, including intermediate care facilities, home health agencies, and adult day care centers.[14] Oregon regulations provide general requirements for the contents of medical records and add specific requirements for surgical, obstetrical, emergency department, outpatient, and clinic records.[15]

---

[9]Fla. Stat. § 395.016 (1992).

[10]Tenn. Code Ann. § 68-11-303 (1993).

[11]See, e.g., Ala. Code § 22-21-25(a) (1993); Iowa Code Ann. § 135B.7 (1992); La. Rev. Stat. § 40:2109(1992).

[12]See, e.g., Admin. R. of the Idaho Dept. of Health & Welfare, 16, tit. 03, Ch. 14, § 360.12 (1993); Mich. Admin. Code, r. 325.1028 (1987); S.D. Admin. R. § 44:04:09:05 (Jan. 7, 1993).

[13]Ala. Admin. Code, r. 420-5-7.07 (1992).

[14]Cal. Code Regs., tit. 22,m §§ 70749(o), 70527, 73423, 73439, 74211(a), 78431 (1993).

[15]Or. Admin. R. § 333-505.050 (1992).

The Illinois regulation illustrates the detailed record content requirements found in many states:[16]

> For each patient there shall be an adequate, accurate, timely, and complete medical record. Minimum requirements for medical record content are as follows: patient identification and admission information; history of patient as to chief complaints, present illness and pertinent past history, family history, and social history, physical examination report; provisional diagnosis; diagnostic and therapeutic reports on laboratory test results, X-ray findings, any surgical procedure performed, any pathological examination, any consultation, and any other diagnostic or therapeutic procedure performed; orders and progress notes made by the attending physician and when applicable by other members of the medical staff and allied health personnel; observation notes and vital sign charting made by nursing personnel; and conclusions as to the primary and any associated diagnosis, brief clinical resume, disposition at discharge to include instructions and/or medications and any autopsy findings on a hospital death.[17]

A few states, however, have regulations that specify only broad areas of information required in a medical record.[18] The Hawaii regulations provide that the "medical records shall clearly and accurately document a patient's identity, the diagnosis of the patient's illness, treatment, orders by medical staff, observations, and conclusion concerning the patient."[19] Iowa has a very general requirement that medical records be "accurate and complete" and signed by the attending physician.[20] Other states simply adopt the accreditation requirements of the Joint Commission[21] or Medicare conditions of participation requirements as the minimum state standard for medical records.[22]

---

[16]The following states also have detailed regulations: Alabama, Alaska, Arizona, Arkansas, California, Colorado, Florida, Georgia, Idaho, Indiana, Kentucky, Louisiana, Maine, Michigan, Minnesota, Mississippi, Missouri, Montana, Nebraska, Nevada, New Jersey, New Mexico, New York, North Carolina, North Dakota, Oklahoma, Oregon, South Carolina, South Dakota, Tennessee, Texas, Utah, Vermont, Washington, West Virginia, Wisconsin, and Wyoming.

[17]Ill. Admin. Code, tit. 77, § 250.1510(b)(2) (1991).

[18]See, e.g., Conn. Agencies Regs. § 19-13-D3(d) (Oct. 25, 1989).

[19]Haw. Admin. Rules § 11-93-21 (1992).

[20]Iowa Admin. Code § 481-51.6 (1990).

[21]See, e.g., Md. Regulations Code, tit. 10, §§ 10.07.01.057 and 10.07.01.09 (1992); R.I. Rules and Regulations for Licensing of Hospitals R23-17-HOSP § 25.7 (1991); Rules and Regulations for the Licensure of Hospitals in Va. § 208.5 (1982).

[22]See, e.g., Mass. Regs. Code, tit. 105, § 130.200 (1993).

For all hospitals seeking to participate in federal reimbursement programs, the federal law and regulations setting forth conditions of participation also impose record retention requirements. The law and regulations setting forth the Medicare program provide that a hospital must maintain clinical records on all patients.[23] Regulations issued by the Health Care Financing Administration (HCFA) require each hospital to maintain a medical record for every inpatient and outpatient that is accurately written, promptly completed and properly filed and retained, and accessible.[24] Moreover, the HCFA regulations on the conditions of participation for hospitals provide that all records must contain the following information as appropriate:

1. evidence of a physician examination, including a health history, performed no more than 7 days prior to admission or within 48 hours after admission;
2. admitting diagnosis;
3. results of all consultative evaluations of the patient and appropriate findings by clinical and other staff involved in the care of the patient;
4. documentation of complications, hospital-acquired infections, and unfavorable reactions to drugs and anesthesia;
5. properly executed informed consent forms for procedures and treatments specified by the medical staff, or by federal or state law if applicable, to require written patient consent;
6. all practitioners' orders, nursing notes, reports of a treatment, medication records, radiology and laboratory reports, vital signs, and other information necessary to monitor the patient's condition;
7. discharge summary with outcome of hospitalization, disposition of case, and provisions for follow-up care;
8. final diagnosis with completion of medical records within 30 days following discharge.[25]

In some cities, local or municipal codes require hospitals to record certain information not otherwise required by state law or regulation.[26] Various state hospital associations also may have established guidelines for the contents of medical records.[27] Finally, the Joint Commission requires hospitals to maintain patient care records, mandating that a medical record be "initiated and main-

---

[23]42 U.S.C. § 1395x(e) (1993).

[24]42 C.F.R. § 482.24(b) (1992).

[25]42 C.F.R. § 482.24(c)(2) (1992).

[26]See, e.g, Municipal Code of Chicago, Ill. § 4-140-180 (1991).

[27]See, e.g., Illinois Hospital Association, *Record Retention Guidelines* (1988).

tained for every individual assessed or treated."[28] Its standards of accreditation also impose content requirements.[29]

Whether or not specific statutory or regulatory guidelines apply, hospitals should adopt institutional policies concerning the content of medical records. The policy may be a detailed list of data required, or may reference other guidelines, such as state statutes, regulations, or Joint Commission standards. Generally, detailed policies require closer periodic review to keep them current, while broad policies remain applicable as circumstance and practice change. Hospitals should balance the need for providing enough specificity to guide medical records practitioners and hospital staff against the desire to avoid continual policy revisions. Most accredited hospitals in states with no statutory or regulatory direction on patient record content rely on the Joint Commission accreditation standards as a guide to record content policy.

To maintain the currency of their medical record policies, hospitals should keep abreast of state, federal, and Joint Commission medical records requirements. State and local associations of medical record practitioners often publish changes in the applicable law and accreditation standards. Hospitals also receive notice of these changes from state and national hospital associations and from hospital legal counsel. All health care institutions should develop reliable ways of monitoring new laws and regulations, and communicating any changes to the individuals responsible for making policy recommendations concerning medical record content, particularly medical record practitioners and the medical staff.

These individuals should understand the various functions of the medical record and their interrelationships as well as how those functions are affected by the nature of the specific institution and current legislative, regulatory, and licensing requirements. Creating an effective record content policy requires the involvement of a variety of disciplines within the institution. Policy makers must be willing to find ways to make practical adjustments to medical record content. In doing so, they should strike a balance between the administrative, financial, and other demands placed upon the medical record and the record's basic patient care function.

RECORD RETENTION REQUIREMENTS

In determining how long to retain medical records, a hospital should consider federal or state laws and regulations, sound hospital administrative policy, and

---

[28]Joint Commission, *Accreditation Manual for Hospitals* (Oakbrook Terrace, Ill.: 1994), Standard IM 7.1.

[29]*Id.* at IM 7.2.

sound medical practice. The nature of the institution and the resources available to maintain documents for an extended period of time also will influence the hospital's retention policy. Achieving a practical and workable medical record retention policy becomes more difficult in an era of reduced financial resources.

The hospital should consider several factors in establishing a retention policy: statutory and regulatory requirements, statutes of limitations and potential future litigation, requirements of the hospital's malpractice insurer, the need for records information in medical research and teaching, storage capabilities, cost of microfilming, computerization and other long-term storage methods, and recommendations of hospital associations. Clearly, the hospital first must comply with all applicable statutory and regulatory retention requirements. Where it considers it prudent to have a retention period longer than statutory or regulatory requirements, however, it may establish one.

Statutory and Regulatory Concerns

Medicare conditions of participation require hospitals to retain the original record or a legally reproduced form for a period of at least five years.[30] A few states also impose record retention requirements on general hospital medical records by statute.[31] In most jurisdictions, record retention requirements, like content requirements, appear in regulations issued by the state hospital licensing agency. While laws vary, there generally are four categories: (1) those requiring hospitals to preserve the entire patient record for very long periods, (2) those requiring the records to be maintained for ten years, (3) those requiring less than 10 years, and (4) references to other sources of law and guidance constituting the retention requirement of the state. Many jurisdictions also have special retention provisions for certain portions of a patient's record (such as X-rays, graphic data, and discharge summaries), special procedures for records of patients who are minors, and other provisions for records pertaining to deceased persons.

A few states impose extended retention requirements on hospitals. In Connecticut and North Dakota, for example, patient records must be preserved for a minimum of 25 years[32] and in Alabama for at least 22 years.[33] New Jersey requires a discharge summary to be kept for each patient for 20 years including a recapitulation of the significant findings and events that occurred during

---

[30]42 C.F.R. § 482.24 (1992).

[31]See, e.g., Alaska Stat. §18.20.085 (1993); Ind. Code § 16-4-8-12 (1992); La. Rev. Stat. § 40:2144 (1992); Miss. Code Ann. § 41-9-69 (1991); Tenn. Code Ann. § 68-11-305 (1993).

[32]Conn. Agencies Regs. § 19-13-D3(d)(6) (1989); N.D. Admin. Code § 33-07-01-16.3 (1990).

[33]Ala. Admin. Code, r. 420-5-7.07(1)(c), § 420-5-7.07(1)(c) (1992).

hospitalization and a statement concerning the patient's condition at discharge.[34] The original medical record must be kept for at least 10 years.

Most of the remaining states establish a shorter minimum time for preserving the entire patient record. About half of them require at least a ten-year preservation period,[35] while the rest prescribe some number less than ten. Arizona requires patient medical records to be readily retrievable for at least three years[36] and many other states prescribe a minimum of five or seven years.[37]

In some cases, licensing regulations identify no particular number of years for hospitals to maintain patient records. Instead, the rules refer to other sources of law to define the minimum requirements of record retention for state licensure purposes.[38] Many of these regulations simply incorporate the state statute of limitations for malpractice claims as the minimum retention period.[39] Other jurisdictions refer to the conditions of participation for federal reimbursement programs[40] or guidelines set by the American Hospital Association.[41]

A few states provide that records may be kept for a minimum number of years plus an additional period determined by the hospital.[42] This additional time could serve the hospital's needs for "clinical, educational, statistical, or administrative purposes,"[43] or extend for as long as the record has "research, legal, or medical value."[44] Of course, hospitals in any state may retain records beyond the period prescribed by statute or regulation if clinical, legal, or patient care policies indicate such a need. At least one state's regulations specify that nothing in the law should be construed to prohibit retention beyond the period prescribed.[45]

---

[34]N.J. Stat. § 26:8-5 (1993) and N.J. Admin. Code, tit. 8, § 43G-15.2(g)(1993). See also Ark. Rules and Regulations for Hospitals and Related Institutions, § 0601Y (1988); Kan. Admin. Regulations, § 28-34-9a(d)(1992).

[35]These states are among those that require patient records to be kept for a minimum of 10 years: Arkansas, Colorado, Kansas, Montana, Nebraska, New Mexico, Oregon, South Carolina, Tennessee, Texas, Utah, Vermont, and Washington.

[36]Ariz. Comp. R. & Regs., R9-10-221F (1982).

[37]The following states are among those that prescribe five-year retention periods: Kentucky, Oklahoma, Rhode Island, Virginia, and Wisconsin. The following states are among those that require seven-year minimum retention periods: Alaska, California, Indiana, New Hampshire, and Pennsylvania.

[38]See, e.g., Idaho, Illinois, Iowa, Maine, Massachusetts, Michigan, and North Carolina.

[39]See, e.g., Iowa Admin. Code, r. 641-51.6(1) (1990); Regulations for the Licensure of General and Specialty Hospitals in Maine, Ch. XII B (1972); Mo. Code Regs., tit. 19, § 3-20-021(3)D15 (1992), 19 CSR 3-20.020(3)D15 (1990); N.C. Admin. Code tit. 10r 03C.1405 (1991).

[40]See Mich. Admin. Code, r. 325.1021(4) (1987).

[41]See, e.g., Ill. Admin. Code, tit. 77, § 250.1510(d) (1991); N.C. Admin. Code tit. 10r 03C.1405 (1991).

[42]See, e.g., Missouri, North Carolina, North Dakota, and Wisconsin.

[43]Mo. Code Regs., tit. 19, § 3-20-021(3)D15 (1992); see also Wis. Admin. Code § HHS124.14(2)(c)(1988).

[44]N.D. Admin. Code § 33-07-01-16.3 (1990).

[45]Mont. Admin. R. § 16.32.328(5) (1989).

In addition to the general retention requirements described above, Medicare conditions of participation and several states have special statutory or regulatory provisions governing how long a hospital should maintain specific portions of a patient's record, such as X-rays, scans, and clinical laboratory reports.[46] Hospitals also must comply with retention laws on vital statistics, including records of births and deaths.[47]

Many states prescribe special retention requirements for records of patients who were minors at the time of treatment. These requirements usually indicate that hospitals must keep records until the patient reaches majority plus some additional time, or until the expiration of the general retention requirement, whichever is longer.[48] The prescribed extension ranges from one to ten years beyond the age of majority.

A few states also address the issue of deceased patients' records.[49] These regulations allow the facility to destroy records of a deceased patient before the expiration of the general retention requirement. Oklahoma, for instance, requires a hospital to maintain a patient's records for a minimum of five years after the patient was last seen, or at least three years beyond the patient's death.[50]

In states that have adopted the Uniform Preservation of Private Business Records Act,[51] the three-year records preservation requirement may apply to the medical records of private hospitals, if there is no statutory retention specifically governing medical records. So far only four states have adopted the Act,[52] and three of those[53] legislatively have established longer retention periods for medical records. However, in Illinois, where there is no statutory retention period for medical records, the Act may govern, even though it does not refer specifically to patient records.

Statutes of Limitations

Another key factor in establishing a record retention policy is the statute of limitations on contract and tort actions. A statute of limitations is a period of time

---

[46]See, e.g., 42 C.F.R. § 482.26(d)(2) (1992); Alaska Stat. § 18.20.085 (1993); Cal. Code Regs., tit. 22, § 70751(c) (1993); Idaho Code §§ 39-1394(b) and (c) (1993); 210 Ill. Comp. Stat. Ann. 90/1 (1993).

[47]See, e.g., Rules and Regulations for the Licensure of Hospitals in Virginia § 208.8.2 (1982).

[48]The following states are among those that have special provisions for records of minors: Arkansas, California, Colorado, Georgia, Kansas, Kentucky, Mississippi, Montana, Nebraska, New Hampshire, New Mexico, Pennsylvania, Rhode Island, South Carolina, Texas, Virginia, and Washington.

[49]See, e.g., Miss. Code Ann. § 41-9-69(1) (1991); Mont. Admin. R. § 16.32.328(1) (1989); N.D. Admin. Code § 33-07-01-16.3 (1990); Okla. Hospital Standards § 310:665-25-14 (1993).

[50]Okla. Hospital Standards § 310:665-25-14 (1993).

[51]U.L.A. vol. 14, p. 201 (1990).

[52]Md. Code Ann., [Bus. Reg.] §§ 1-303 to 1-307 (1993); N.H. Rev. Stat. Ann. §§ 337-A1 to 337-A6 (1992); Okla. Stat. tit. 67, §§ 251 to 256 (1992); 805 Ill. Comp. Stat. Ann. 410/1 to 410/6 (1993).

[53]Maryland, Oklahoma, and New Hampshire.

established by statute, measured in years, within which a party may bring a lawsuit. The time periods vary with the cause of action, e.g., contract, tort, or real estate.

Except in the case of minors' records, retaining the record for the limitations period would not impose a burden on the hospital medical records department, since limitation periods generally are shorter than the period the record would be retained for medical reasons. If the statute of limitations were used as a guide, the medical record of a minor would be kept until the patient reaches the age of majority plus the period of the statute. For example, in a state where the age of majority is 21 and the statute of limitations for torts is two years, the retention period for a newborn's record would be 23 years; in states in which the age of majority is 18, and the statute of limitations for torts is two years, the retention period for a newborn's record would be 20 years. While the possibility of an infant's waiting until majority to bring suit is slight, it can happen.[54] Although most suits by minors are brought soon after the accident causing the injury, a hospital is protected best if it retains records until the minor reaches majority and for an additional time equal to the applicable state statute of limitations on tort actions.

Medical Research and Storage Space Considerations

If the hospital's staffs engage in extensive medical research, especially retrospective investigations that require detailed medical record data, the institution may wish to establish a long retention period. Moreover, if the medical research conducted in the hospital involves experimental or innovative patient care procedures, the facility is well advised to retain its medical records for at least 75 years.

Hospitals that routinely provided head and neck radiation in the 1930s were fortunate if they had their medical records when lawsuits were filed in the 1970s alleging that the institutions negligently increased the plaintiffs' susceptibility to thyroid cancer. In one case arising from the experimental administration of diethylstilbestrol (DES) between 1950 and 1952, the plaintiffs alleged that the hospital and the drug company were negligent in failing to warn them of the danger to their children until more than 20 years after administering the DES and four years after becoming aware of the drug's dangers.[55] Although the court dismissed the complaint because no physical injury to the former patient was alleged, it did recognize a duty on the part of the hospital to notify patients of the ". . . risks inherent in DES treatment when they became aware, or should have become aware, of the relationship between DES and cancer."[56] To discharge

---

[54]See, e.g., *Bettigole v. Deiner*, 124 A.2d 265 (Md. Ct. App. 1956).

[55]*Mink v. University of Chicago*, 460 F. Supp. 713 (N.D. Ill. 1978).

[56]*Id.* at 720.

such a duty, hospitals must be able to identify patients who have received experimental drugs or treatment. The patients' medical records enable hospitals to identify such patients and, if necessary, assist hospitals in defending suits arising from experimental treatments. Even where there is no duty to notify the patient, hospitals are advised to maintain records longer than indicated by statutes of limitation because in most jurisdictions, the statute does not commence until the patient has discovered or reasonably should have discovered the causal relation between the injury and the treatment or drug administered.[57]

Another major consideration for a hospital in establishing a retention policy is its capability to store a large number of records. Available space, expansion rates, the endurance of the paper and folders used, the cost of microfilming, and storage safety requirements all affect the institution's ability to retain records. Some space savings may be achieved by microfilming records or storing them on optical disks or in computer media. The statutes and regulations of several states authorize microfilming or other photographic reproduction of records.[58] Therefore, where possible, the hospital might alleviate its retention problem by microfilming the records and destroying the original copies. Microfilming reduces the need for storage space but can raise other administrative problems. For example, members of the medical staff might object to the restrictions on the availability of particular records for purposes of research and review. The hospital would incur additional costs for reading and printing equipment. Where state law and regulations do not specifically authorize microfilming, hospitals nonetheless may microfilm their medical records and destroy the original records in accordance with law or regulations governing record destruction.

The hospital may microfilm its records itself, provided it has the proper staff and equipment, or it may send its records to an outside contract service to be filmed. If the hospital elects to use a contract service, it should do so pursuant to a written agreement that specifies, among other things, the method of record transfer, the method of reproduction, the quality and cost of the service, the time within which the service will be performed, safeguards against breach of confidentiality, indemnification to the hospital for loss resulting from the contractor's improper release of information or loss of records, and procedures for destroying the original records.

A hospital also might consider storing its records in computers. Before deciding on this method of recordkeeping, however, it should consult applicable

---

[57]*Fritz v. McGrath*, 431 N.W.2d 751 (Wis. Ct. App. 1988); *Dawson v. Eli Lilly & Co.*, 543 F. Supp. 1330 (D.D.C. 1982); *Girard v. U.S.*, 455 F. Supp. 502 (D.N.H. 1978); *Raymond v. Eli Lilly & Co.*, 371 A.2d 170 (N.H. 1977).

[58]See, e.g., Ga. Rules & Regulations for Hospitals, ch. 290-5-6.11(h) (1987); Idaho Code § 39-1394(a) (1985); La. Rev. Stat. § 40:2144(F) (1992); Mass. Ann. Laws, ch. 111, § 70 (1983); N.J. Stat. § 26:8-5 (1992).

laws governing hospital licensure, accreditation, federal conditions of participation, and all rules of evidence on the admissibility of copies of business records and hospital patient records at trial. (For a detailed discussion of computerized patient records, see Chapter 6.)

Association Guidelines

The American Hospital Association (AHA) and the American Health Information Management Association (AHIMA), formerly the American Medical Record Association (AMRA), have adopted a policy that recommends retaining complete records in original or reproduced form for a period of ten years after the most recent patient care entry and retaining certain parts of the record permanently. The guidelines recommend that after ten years, the complete record may be destroyed, unless destruction is prohibited by statute, ordinance, regulation, or law, provided that the institution:

1. retains basic information such as dates of admission and discharge, names of responsible physicians, records of diagnoses and operations, operative reports, pathology reports, and discharge resumés for all records so destroyed.
2. retains complete medical records of minors for the period of minority plus the applicable period of statute of limitations in the state in which the health care institution is located.
3. retains complete medical records of patients under mental disability in like manner as those of patients under disability o[r] minority.
4. retains complete patient medical records for longer periods when requested in writing by one of the following:
   a. an attending or consultant physician of the patient,
   b. the patient or someone acting legally in his behalf,
   c. legal counsel for a party having interest affected by the patient medical records.[59]

In addition, some state hospital associations have issued record retention guidelines that may be useful in developing a hospital record retention policy.[60]

Developing a Record Retention Policy

In the final analysis, no blanket record retention rule can be devised. The length of time medical records should be retained after they no longer are needed

---

[59]American Hospital Association, Statement on Preservation of Patient Medical Records in Health Care Institutions (1990).

[60]See, e.g., Ill. Hospital Association, *Record Retention Guidelines* (1988).

for medical and administrative purposes should be determined by the hospital administration with the advice of legal counsel, taking into account all factors, including the feasibility and cost of microfilming, the availability and cost of storage space, and the possible future need for such records, as well as the legal considerations arising from lawsuits by patients against the hospital or a third party.

In most professional negligence actions against a hospital, the institution must show that the care it provided was consistent with accepted medical practice at the time and reasonable under the circumstances. The hospital's medical records usually are essential to its defense of such action. Although courts generally reject the existence of a responsibility by one party to preserve evidence or records for another party's potential suit, in the absence of some special relationship or contractual duty between the parties,[61] several courts have recognized a hospital's duty to maintain patient records as a matter of statute or regulation.[62]

Specifically, in cases where the plaintiff had insufficient evidence to pursue a malpractice suit against a hospital because the hospital was unable to produce the patient's record, courts have found the facility liable for this independent act of negligence or have ruled that the plaintiff states a cause of action in negligence.

In one case,[63] a Florida court ruled that a hospital may be sued for its failure to make and maintain patient medical records because state law imposes a duty to make, maintain, and furnish such records to a patient or personal representative upon request. A woman whose husband died during the administration of anesthesia before surgery sued the hospital for negligence. She could not present expert testimony necessary to establish medical malpractice, however, because the anesthesiology records of her husband's treatment could not be located. The appeals court found that a hospital's duty to make and maintain medical records is imposed by state administrative regulations, and that state law further requires that copies of records be provided to patients at their request. The woman was entitled to sue the hospital for negligently breaching these duties, the court concluded, because the hospital otherwise "stands to benefit that the prospect of successful litigation against it has disappeared along with the crucial evidence."

An Illinois appeals court also ruled that state legislation governing the retention of X-rays creates the right to sue a hospital for its failure to keep X-

---

[61]See *Panich v. Iron Wood Products Corp.*, 445 N.W.2d 795 (Mich. Ct. App. 1989); *Koplin v. Rosel Well Perforators, Inc.*, 734 P.2d 1177 (D. Kan. 1987).

[62]See, e.g., *Fox v. Cohen*, 406 N.E.2d 178 (1980).

[63]See *Bondu v. Gurvich*, 473 So. 2d 1307 (Fla. Dist. Ct. App. 1984). See also *Thomas v. U.S.*, 660 F. Supp. 216 (D.D.C. 1987).

rays.[64] The court noted that state law requires hospitals to retain X-rays as part of their regularly maintained records for a period of five years. The statute clearly seeks to protect the property rights of persons involved in litigation, the court declared. According to the court, violating a statute that is designed to protect either property or human life is evidence of negligence.

A patient may not be entitled to sue a hospital for its failure to comply with records retention legislation, however, unless the individual also proves damages and a causal connection with the injuries sustained. In one case,[65] a court dismissed a negligence action against a hospital for failing to preserve all the X-rays taken of a patient. A Medical Malpractice Review Panel had rejected a malpractice complaint after considering only the X-rays still available. The court stated that the patient had failed to show any damages resulting from the alleged negligence of the hospital and dismissed the suit. Similarly, in the Illinois case discussed above,[66] the court ruled that the plaintiff was entitled to sue the hospital for violating the retention statute, but that to succeed, he would have to prove that the violation resulted in the dismissal of his suit against other health care providers.

DESTRUCTION OF THE RECORD

Upon expiration of the medical records retention period or after the record has been copied onto microfilm or computer, or converted to other machine-readable form, the record usually may be destroyed. In some states, the method of medical record destruction is controlled by statute and regulation. The Tennessee statute states:

> Upon retirement of the record as provided in . . . this section, the record or any part thereof retired shall be destroyed by burning, shredding, or other effective method in keeping with the confidential nature of its contents. Destruction of such records must be made in the ordinary course of business and no record shall be destroyed on an individual basis.[67]

Other states require hospitals to create, in accordance with applicable regulations, an abstract of any pertinent data in the medical record before destroying the record.[68] Although the states that have specified the method of record

---

[64]*Rodgers v. St. Mary's Hosp.*, 556 N.E.2d 913 (Ill. App. Ct. 1990).

[65]See *Hryniak v. Nathan Littauer Hosp. Assoc.*, 446 N.Y.S.2d 558 (App. Div. 1982).

[66]*Supra*, note 64.

[67]Tenn. Code Ann. § 68-11-305(c) (1993). See also Idaho Code § 39-1394(d) (1993).

[68]Miss. Code Ann. § 41-9-75 (1972). See also note 34, *supra*.

destruction generally permit destruction by shredding or burning, the Environmental Protection Agency recommends shredding and recycling.[69] Hospitals that deliver their medical records to a commercial enterprise for destruction should do so pursuant to a written agreement that sets forth safeguards similar to those discussed for microfilming agreements, including the method of destruction, safeguards against breach of confidentiality, indemnification provisions, and certification that the records have been destroyed properly.

Hospitals that destroy their own records also must establish procedures to protect the confidentiality of record information and ensure that records are destroyed completely. The hospital employee responsible for record destruction should certify that the records have been destroyed properly. Whether its records are destroyed commercially or by the hospital, the hospital should retain certificates of destruction permanently as evidence of its record disposal.

The hospital's medical records policies should include provisions governing destruction of records, and these provisions should be applied uniformly. Where it can be shown that a hospital failed to apply such a policy uniformly or where destruction was contrary to hospital policy, courts may allow the jury in a negligence suit to infer that if the records were available, they would show the hospital had acted improperly in treating the plaintiff.[70]

---

[69]See 40 C.F.R. § 246 et seq. (1992).

[70]*Carr v. St. Paul Fire Ins. Co.*, 384 F. Supp. 821 (W.D. Ark. 1974).

2

Medical Record Entries

INTRODUCTION

The quality of medical records created in hospitals depends largely on the individuals making record entries. Hospital medical, nursing, and other professional personnel, as well as students and others who write in patient records, must understand the importance of creating legible, complete, and accurate records and the legal and medical implications of failing to do so. A hospital that fails to comply with federal and state records laws risks loss of licensure, accreditation, and eligibility to participate in federal reimbursement programs. Moreover, court decisions have shown that a hospital's exposure to negligence liability increases if it condones improper entries by its staff.

Corrections to records, while perfectly permissible, can create serious problems for hospitals, especially those involved in negligence litigation, if appropriate changes are made in an improper manner. Significant alterations made simply to improve the defense of a lawsuit to defraud reimbursement agencies can have serious adverse consequences for the hospital, including the imposition of criminal sanctions. For all these reasons, therefore, a hospital's medical records policy should address the timeliness and manner for both creating and updating patient records.

IMPORTANCE OF A LEGIBLE, COMPLETE MEDICAL RECORD

The medical record often is the single most important document available to a hospital in the defense of a negligence action and ordinarily is admissible as evidence of what occurred in the care of the patient. (For a discussion of the admissibility of medical records, see Chapter 7.) Without a legible and complete medical record, the hospital may be unable to defend itself successfully against allegations of improper care. In addition, some courts will allow the jury to resolve any ambiguities in a patient's record in favor of the patient. Hospitals must ensure, therefore, that entries made in their medical records are thorough and proper.

Medical record entries should be made in clear and concise language that can be understood by all professional staff members attending the patient. An ambiguous or illegible record often is worse than no record, since it documents a failure of the hospital and professional staff involved to communicate clearly, and thus may impair the ability of the staff to provide proper treatment to the patient.[1]

Where a patient is treated by several physicians, for example, it is important that the individual's record be kept accurately so that the different providers understand the patient's progress and course of treatment. In one case in which inadequate records forced physicians who subsequently treated the patient essentially to guess what progress the patient had made, the court ruled that the hospital had failed to satisfy its duty toward the patient as established by Joint Commission standards.[2]

An illegible or unintelligible record entry introduced into evidence in a court action against the hospital may create suspicion in the minds of the jury that the entry was improper and thereby may weaken the hospital's defense. Persons making entries should place their signatures and positions or titles after each entry. For a discussion of digital or other computer signatures, see Chapter 6. Anyone who reads the medical record must be able to evaluate its contents and determine who participated in the patient's care, should the need arise to consult on a treatment question, or to reconstruct the hospitalization in defense of a professional negligence action.

The medical record should contain a complete account of the treatment given the patient. A record is complete if it contains information sufficient to show clearly what treatment the patient received, why it was given, and, if some routine procedure was not given, the reason it was not. The statutes and regulations of several states, Medicare conditions of participation, and Joint Commission standards require hospitals to maintain a complete record of the care rendered to a patient during hospitalization.[3]

---

[1]See *Larrimore v. Homeopathic Hosp. Ass'n of Del.*, 181 A.2d 573 (Del. 1962).

[2]*Thomas v. U.S.*, 660 F. Supp. 216 (D.D.C. 1987).

[3]See, e.g., Ill. Admin. Code, tit. 77, § 250.1510 (b)(2) (1991); N.J. Stat. § 26:8-5 (1992). See also Joint Commission, *Accreditation Manual for Hospitals* (1994), Standards IM 3.2 and 7.2 to FN. Under Joint Commission standards, all medical records must include at least the following: the patient's name and address, date of birth, and the name of any legally authorized representative; the patient's legal status, for patient receiving mental health services; emergency care provided to the patient prior to arrival, if any; the record and findings of the patient's assessment; a statement of the conclusions or impressions drawn from the medical history and physical examination; the diagnosis or diagnostic impression; the reason(s) for admission or treatment; the goals of treatment and the treatment plan; evidence of known

Maintaining a complete record is important not only to comply with licensing and accreditation requirements but also to enable the hospital to establish that adequate care was provided. If a hospital can demonstrate by testimony that, in accordance with its policy and procedures, it regularly keeps complete and accurate records, the absence of certain notations may be used in the hospital's defense. In *Smith v. Rogers Memorial Hosp.*,[4] the hospital's records did not show that the patient had complained of certain symptoms, and testimony that the hospital's records were generally reliable, was important evidence in rebutting the patient's claim that she had complained of the symptoms and had not received proper care.

Similarly, in *Hurlock v. Park Lane Medical Ctr.*,[5] the treating physician had ordered the patient turned in bed every two hours, but a notation of each turning did not appear in the patient's medical chart. The patient argued that the absence of notes was evidence that the hospital nurses negligently had failed to follow the physician's order, causing the patient to develop serious bedsores and necessitating amputation of her leg. Expert testimony established that, while proper nursing practice required notations to be placed in the patient's record, nurses sometimes get very busy and fail to document each action taken for patients such as the plaintiff who require special attention. In such cases, accepted nursing practice places patient care in priority over proper documentation. Without any direct evidence that the hospital nurses had failed to turn the patient as directed, equally plausible inferences about the hospital's actions arose from the medical record, the court ruled, and dismissed the suit.

In another case, *Krapivka v. Maimonides Hosp. Ctr.*,[6] a court held that the absence of any notation in a deceased patient's medical record indicating that the defendants had questioned him about his previous suicide attempts and family history of suicide did not mean that such questioning did not occur. Testimony indicated that the patient's psychiatric history had been taken as a part of routine

---

advance directives; evidence of informed consent for procedures and treatments for which informed consent is required by organizational policy; diagnostic and therapeutic orders; all diagnostic and therapeutic procedures and tests performed and the results; all operative and other invasive procedures performed, using acceptable disease and operative terminology that includes etiology, as appropriate; progress notes made by the medical staff and other authorized individuals; all reassessments, when necessary; clinical observations; the response to the care provided; consultation reports; every medication ordered or prescribed for an inpatient; every dose of medication administered and any adverse drug reaction; each medication dispensed to or prescribed for an ambulatory patient or an inpatient on discharge; all relevant diagnoses established during the course of care; and any referrals/communications made to external or internal care providers and to community agencies.

[4]382 A.2d 1025 (D.C. Ct. App. 1978), *cert. denied*, 439 U.S. 847 (1978).

[5]709 S.W.2d 872 (Mo. Ct. App. 1985). See also *Topel v. Long Island Jewish Medical Ctr.*, 431 N.E.2d 293 (Ct. App. 1981).

[6]501 N.Y.S.2d 429 (App. Div. 1986).

procedure, and that the patient had denied any previous suicide attempts. A positive response would have been recorded, the court stated.[7]

Conversely, the failure to maintain a complete record may lead to a finding that the hospital was negligent in its treatment of the patient. In *Collins v. Westlake Community Hosp.,*[8] the plaintiff alleged that the hospital's nursing staff negligently had failed to observe the condition and circulation of his leg during the time it was in a cast and that such failure caused the patient to lose the leg. The court examined the patient's medical record and concluded that the absence of nursing notes documenting observations of the leg during seven critical hours, particularly in view of the physician's order to "watch condition of toes," reasonably could have led the jury to infer that no observations were made during that time. The hospital's nurses testified in *Collins* that nurses do not always record observations on the chart when patients are checked, that usually they record only abnormal findings, and that this procedure is consistent with the principles of problem-oriented medical records, which many hospitals have adopted. Nonetheless, the court allowed the jury to infer from the absence of documentation that no observations had been made.[9]

Other courts also have allowed an inference of negligence where hospital records fail to include certain data, or fail to comport with adequate medical recordkeeping in general. In a California case,[10] an appeals court ruled that a physician's inability to produce his original records relating to a patient's treatment for a malpractice suit created an inference of the physician's consciousness of guilt. In another case,[11] a federal appeals court held that a jury was entitled to find, or at least to infer, negligence from an incomplete medical record where the plaintiff developed eye problems associated with an excessive use of oxygen at birth. Given the absence of documentation about the amount of oxygen actually ordered or administered, the court accepted testimony from the child's father regarding oxygen administration he remembered observing at the hospital. Based on this evidence, the court upheld the jury's finding of negligence.

A hospital's failure to insert proper notations of care on a patient's chart may lead not only to a finding of hospital negligence with respect to the patient's medical care, but also to difficulties in recovering the financial cost of the care

---

[7]*Id.* at 431.

[8]312 N.E.2d 614 (Ill. 1974). See also *Fatuck v. Hillside Hosp.*, 356 N.Y.S.2d 105 (App. Div. 1974), *aff'd* 368 N.Y.S.2d 161 (1975) (The absence of nursing notes documenting observation after an order that a psychiatric patient be checked every 15 minutes constituted a prima facie case of negligence when the patient escaped and committed suicide.)

[9]See also *Jarvis v. St. Charles Medical Ctr.*, 713 P.2d 62 (Utah 1986).

[10]113 Cal. Rptr. 296 (Ct. App. 1974).

[11]806 F.2d 1128 (1st Cir. 1986).

that was provided. This was illustrated in an Arkansas appeals court ruling on the accuracy of a computerized bill containing charges for services and medication that were not reflected in the patient's chart.[12] Because the evidence revealed the strong possibility that the bill contained charges for medication not given, services not rendered, procedures not performed, and supplies not delivered, the court ruled that the bill was insufficient to sustain the hospital's claim for the cost of the patient's medical care.

These cases illustrate the twofold problem facing hospitals that fail to create proper records: (1) the possibility for a plaintiff to rely on an inference or presumption of negligence concerning the actions omitted from the record and (2) the risk for the hospital of being unable to rebut the plaintiff's recreation of what occurred based on the memory of lay persons present at the hospital during the time in question.

While some courts have allowed juries to *infer* negligence based on reasonable conclusions drawn from incomplete patient records, other courts have gone further, allowing juries to *presume* negligence when records contain significant omissions. A presumption of negligence affects the hospital's burden in litigation to a much greater extent than a mere inference of negligence.

In general, a malpractice plaintiff must show each act of negligence by the hospital with a preponderance of the evidence. If a plaintiff fails to meet this burden, the court will dismiss the suit, even if the facility presents no evidence in its defense. A presumption of negligence shifts the responsibility to the hospital defendant to prove that it acted properly. This shift in the hospital's burden of proof makes defending against a malpractice suit more difficult, especially when medical records documenting its actions are incomplete.

In *Public Health Trust v. Valcin*,[13] for example, a patient alleged negligent performance of surgery, but the surgical notes were missing from the patient's record. The court applied a rebuttable presumption of negligence against the hospital, but only after the patient had proved that the absence of records hindered his ability to make his case.[14]

Failure to record a patient's condition completely and properly also can generate hospital liability if a patient is able to prove that the absence of information in the record resulted in injury. In Texas, a government hospital was found liable for negligent use of personal property for failing to record a patient's condition properly.[15] A patient who had suffered severe brain damage broke his hip sometime in the 24 hours following his admission to a hospital's rehabilita-

[12]*Tracor/MBA v. Baptist Medical Ctr.*, 780 S.W.2d 26 (Ark. Ct. App. 1989).

[13]507 So. 2d 596 (Fla. 1987).

[14]*Id.* at 599.

[15]*University of Tex. Medical Branch at Galveston v. York*, 808 S.W.2d 106 (Tex. Ct. App. 1991).

tion unit, but there was no indication in his medical record that such an injury had occurred. A trial court found that the hospital's failure to record accurately the patient's condition resulted in the failure to diagnose the injury until approximately nine days after it had occurred. The hospital appealed, arguing that the failure to record an essential entry in a medical chart is not negligent use of personal property and that the incomplete record was not the cause of the patient's injuries. However, an appeals court upheld the award, finding that there was sufficient evidence that the hospital's misuse of the record had caused damages.

Conversely, other courts have dismissed negligence suits against hospitals involving incomplete medical records, ruling that a facility cannot be liable for a patient's injuries where the inadequacy of the records does not proximately cause the patient's harm. One case involved a patient under the constant, direct care of an emergency room physician who did not request information about the individual's vital signs before making a diagnosis. The hospital's failure to take and record the patient's vital signs did not proximately cause an exacerbation of the patient's injuries stemming from the physician's misdiagnosis, the court ruled.[16] In a Washington appeals court opinion, a patient failed to show that the hospital knew that the physician had not placed certain information in the patient's chart as required by hospital rules, and that this failure contributed to the patient's injury. Accordingly, the court dismissed the suit against the hospital.[17]

To avoid liability, therefore, hospitals must be certain that all staff members clearly document the care provided to patients. In particularly sensitive cases, and when careful observations are essential, all staff members should document their contacts with patients more precisely. The hospital's efforts to increase efficiency never should prevent its staff from keeping records sufficiently detailed to enable it to show the type and quality of care rendered.

REQUIREMENTS FOR ACCURACY AND TIMELY COMPLETION

State law,[18] Joint Commission standards of accreditation,[19] and conditions of participation in federal reimbursement programs[20] require hospitals to keep accurate medical records. Not only are inaccurate records potentially detrimental to patient care, they also may constitute violations of licensing statutes and

---

[16]*Yaney v. McCray Memorial Hosp.*, 469 N.E.2d 135 (Ind. Ct. App. 1986).

[17]*Andrews v. Burke*, 779 P.2d 740 (Wash. Ct. App. 1989).

[18]See, e.g., Haw. Dept. of Health Regulations, § 11-93-21 (1992); Miss Code Ann. § 41-9-63 (1993); Licensing Standards for Hospital Facilities, N.J. Admin. Code, tit. 8, § 43G-15 (1990); 28 Pa. Code 135.12 (1993).

[19]Joint Commission, *Accreditation Manual for Hospitals* (Oakbrook Terrace, Ill.: 1994), Standard IM 3.2.

[20] 42 C.F.R. § 482.24(b) (1992).

accreditation standards. In addition, a hospital with inadequate patient records faces possible disqualification from federal reimbursement programs.

An improper record may allow a plaintiff in a professional negligence action to destroy the credibility of the entire record. In *Hiatt v. Groce,*[21] a Kansas court found that the clear discrepancy between what the medical record stated and what actually happened to the patient could justify the jury's finding that, if the medical record were erroneous in one respect, it could be erroneous in other respects as well and could be considered generally invalid.

Medical records not only must be accurate but also must be completed in a timely manner. Entries to the record should be made when the treatment they describe is given or the observations to be documented are made.[22] Specific requirements that entries be made within a certain time following a patient's discharge also exist. Regulations on participation in federal reimbursement programs require that hospital records be complete within 30 days following the patient's discharge.[23] Joint Commission standards require the hospital's medical staff regulations to state the time limit for completion of the record, which in no event should exceed 30 days.[24] In determining a time period for completing records, hospitals also should consult their state licensing regulations, which may prescribe a shorter length of time.[25]

Hospital medical staff bylaws and regulations also should require staff members to complete their patient records within the specified time and should provide an automatic suspension of clinical privileges for those who fail to comply. The hospital has well-established power to suspend privileges of any physician who fails to comply with its rules, including those pertaining to medical records.[26]

Incomplete records can be disastrous to a hospital's or physician's defense in a professional negligence action. Entries made in a record weeks after the patient's discharge have less credibility than those made during or immediately after the hospitalization. If an entry is made after a lawsuit is threatened or filed, it may appear to have been made self-servingly for purposes of establishing a defense rather than for documenting the actual treatment rendered.

---

[21]523 P.2d 320, 326 (1974).

[22]Joint Commission Standard IM 7.7.1 requires that all significant clinical information pertaining to a patient be entered into the medical record as soon as possible after its occurrence.

[23]42 C.F.R. § 482.24(c)(2)(viii) (1992).

[24]Joint Commission, *Accreditation Manual for Hospitals* (Oakbrook Terrace, Ill.: 1994), Standard IM 7.7.2.

[25]See, e.g., Kan. Admin. Regs. § 28-34-9a(f) (1992); Regulations for the Licensure of General and Specialty Hospitals in Maine, Ch. XII-J (1972), requiring records of patients discharged to be completed within 15 days after release.

[26]See, e.g., *Board of Trustees of Memorial Hosp. v. Pratt,* 262 P.2d 682 (Wyo. 1953).

In *Foley v. Flushing Hosp. & Medical Ctr.*,[27] the physician amended the patient's medical record to show that medication was given orally after the patient's father complained of injuries caused by injection of medication. The change in the record was dated to show when it was made, and there was no attempt to conceal the change. Nonetheless, the change, along with proof of the injury, ultimately was found to constitute sufficient evidence to go to the jury on the question whether the medication was administered orally or by injection.

Generally, individual practitioners and the hospital's medical staff organization are responsible for ensuring that patient records are completed within a reasonable time after the patient's discharge from the hospital. Usually, the medical records department is delegated the responsibility for making sure records are completed within the time specified by the hospital and for collating them into the permanent medical records. That department therefore should establish procedures for notifying attending physicians when records are incomplete and should follow up when a physician fails to respond.

The final responsibility for completeness of the record rests with the patient's attending physician and the medical staff through enforcement of its bylaws and regulations. A hospital that fails to have and enforce proper medical record completion policies subjects itself and its medical staff to liability for breach of its duty to monitor a patient's treatment and for any ensuing injuries. For example, in *Bost v. Riley,*[28] the court found that the hospital had breached its duty to the patient in failing to act when his physicians neglected to record progress notes on the individual's medical record. The court denied recovery, however, because the evidence did not indicate a causal link between the hospital's failure to act and the patient's injuries.

PERSON MAKING ENTRIES

As the number and types of people making entries in patient medical records increases, so does the potential for increased liability. Unnecessary or improper entries can give rise to negligence liability exposure, problems involving unlicensed persons practicing nursing or medicine, and poor patient relations. To diminish this exposure, hospitals should have policies governing who may enter information in a record. These policies should be developed carefully so that hospitals do not compromise patient care as they attempt to reduce liability exposure.

---

[27]341 N.Y.S.2d 917 (1973), *rev'd* 359 N.Y.S.2d 113 (1974). See also *Libbee v. Permanente Clinic*, 520 P.2d 361 (1974).

[28]262 S.E.2d 621 (Ga. Ct. App. 1979).

Most states do not restrict the type of professionals who may write entries in the chart—who may do so is a matter of individual hospital policy. Similarly, Joint Commission standards of accreditation simply provide that entries to medical records be made by individuals specified in hospital and medical staff policies.[29]

Joint Commission standards also require the practitioner responsible for certain parts of the medical record to authenticate those parts.[30] For example, when a nonphysician is appointed for a duty such as taking and recording a patient's medical history, the information must be authenticated appropriately by the physician responsible for the patient. Federal Medicare regulations require authentification by the author of the entry and the person responsible for ordering, providing, or evaluating the service furnished.[31] None of these sources specifically governs the type of person who properly may write entries in a patient's chart.

Given these broad legal and accrediting requirements, any person providing care to a patient should be permitted to document that care in the individual's medical record, regardless of the person's position in the hospital. It is the hospital's responsibility to establish policies that require individual practitioners to function within the scope of practice as authorized by state licensing or certification statutes or, in the absence of such statutes, as defined by their professional competence. Hospitals also should define the level of record documentation expected of practitioners working in the institution based on the practitioner's licensure, certification, and professional competence. To the extent the hospital permits nurse midwives, podiatrists, dentists, clinical psychologists, physicians' assistants, and other nonphysician practitioners to provide treatment, it should require them to document their treatment in accordance with hospital medical records policy.

The entries of certain individuals require a physician's countersignature. The purpose of countersignatures is to require a professional to review and, if appropriate, indicate approval of action taken by another practitioner. Usually, the person countersigning a record entry is more experienced or has received a higher level of training than the person who made the original entry. In any case, the person required to countersign should be the individual who has the authority to evaluate the entry. Countersignatures should be viewed as a means for carrying out delegated responsibility, rather than as additional paperwork.

In most hospitals, licensed house staff members may make entries in patient charts, but attending physicians are required to countersign some or all such

---

[29]Joint Commission, *Accreditation Manual for Hospitals* (Oakbrook Terrace, Ill.: 1994), Standard IM 7.1.1.

[30]*Id.*, Standard IM 7.9.3.

[31]42 C.F.R. § 482.24(c)(1) (1992).

entries.[32] Hospitals must determine the extent to which countersignatures are required beyond these minimum regulatory requirements. What is important is that the medical record show clear evidence of the attending physician's supervision of house staff members and others engaged in patient care.

When undergraduate medical students and unlicensed house staff members make record entries that show the application of medical judgment, medical diagnosis, the prescription of treatment, or any other act defined by applicable state law to be the practice of medicine, these entries should be countersigned by a licensed physician, who may be an attending or a resident physician. In most states, it is a violation of the medical licensure act for anyone to practice medicine without a license unless the individual is practicing under the direct, proximate supervision of a physician licensed to practice in the state. Therefore, without evidence of such supervision, the student or unlicensed resident might be held to have violated state law. The rules governing a physician's countersignature of medical record entries made by other authorized personnel should be set forth in the hospital's medical staff rules and regulations.

Similarly, the entries of undergraduate nursing students should be countersigned by a licensed professional nurse, if such entries document the practice of professional nursing as defined by the state's nursing licensure act. Without evidence of proper supervision, a nursing student practicing professional nursing could be held in violation of the state's nursing licensure act unless the act specifically authorizes nursing students to practice nursing in the course of their studies toward a registered nurse (R.N.) degree.[33] The nursing licensure acts of some states also authorize graduate nurses who have applied for a license to practice professional nursing for a limited time without a license.[34] Graduate, unlicensed nurses in those states may make entries in medical records without countersignature by a licensed nurse. In states that have no specific allowances for practice by such graduates, however, their entries should be countersigned. Moreover, hospitals may establish rules governing nursing student record entries that are more stringent than state law.

While state and federal law generally is silent on the entries of other students in the hospital, hospitals should require licensed professionals to countersign the students' record entries. The patient's medical record should show careful monitoring of students' scope of practice and competence.

In many hospitals, social workers participate in the care of patients and request that they be allowed to make entries in their patients' charts. Generally, there is

---

[32]See, e.g., Regulations for the Licensure of General and Specialty Hospitals in Maine, Ch. XII-I.3 (1972); Minimum Standards of Operation for Mississippi Hospitals, § 1709.4

[33]See, e.g., 225 Ill. Comp. Stat. Ann. 65/4 (b) (1993).

[34]See, e.g., 225 Ill. Comp. Stat. Ann. 65/4 (g) (1993).

no prohibition against such entries as long as the information placed in the record is relevant to the patient's treatment. Entries by social service staff members should be limited to relevant factual observations or to data and judgments that such staff members are competent to make; highly subjective remarks, if essential to the record, must be worded carefully and must be clearly relevant to the patient's care. Social workers should be discouraged from keeping other records of their observations and judgments that are not included in the medical record. Such additional records may not be subject to the same quality review procedures and confidentiality protections as are applicable to medical records.

AUTHENTICATION OF RECORDS

The requirement that the physician or other medical practitioner sign the records or a portion thereof exists to ensure authenticity. Most state regulations require that the signature or other authentication for each patient's record be made by the physician or medical practitioner qualified by the hospital staff rules to make such an entry.[35] Authentication is the key element in system reliability and security.

Traditionally, authentication was made by handwritten signature. However, numerous regulatory and accrediting organizations also contemplate authentication by a rubber stamp or computer key as well. The Joint Commission addresses the issue of authentication in its new Information Management standard. The standard requires that all entries in medical records be dated and authenticated, and a method be established to identify the authors of entries. Authentication may be by written signatures or initials, rubber stamp signatures, or computer key. When the two latter methods of authentication are used, however, the Joint Commission requires that the individual whose signature the stamp represents or whose computer key is authorized sign a statement that the individual alone will use the stamp or the code for the computer key. Such a statement must be filed in the facility's administrative offices.[36]

Medicare Conditions of Participation require that all entries to a patient's record be authenticated and dated promptly by the person responsible for ordering, providing, or evaluating the service furnished.[37] The author of each entry must be identified and authenticate the entry. Under those regulations, authentication may include signatures, written initials, or computer entry.

---

[35]See, e.g., Cal. Code Regs., tit. 22, § 70751(g) (1993); S.C. Code Regs. R. 61-16 § 601.1 (Dept. Health & Env. Control, 1992); Wis. Admin. Code § HSS 124.14(3)(b) (1988).

[36]Joint Commission, *Accreditation Manual for Hospitals* (Oakbrook Terrace, Ill.: 1994), Standards IM 7.7, 7.9.1, 7.9.2.1, 7.9.3).

[37]42 C.F.R. § 482.24(c)(1) (1992).

States also permit authentification by rubber stamp or computer key, in addition to the traditional handwritten signature. To safeguard against abuses in the utilization of stamps or computer codes, however, many states have adopted controls identical or very similar to those set forth in the Joint Commission's Information Management standard. For example, in California, the State Department of Health Services has regulations providing the following:

> Medical records shall be completed promptly and authenticated or signed by a physician, dentist or podiatrist within two weeks following the patient's discharge. Medical records may be authenticated by a signature stamp or computer key, in lieu of a physician's signature, only when that physician has placed a signed statement in the hospital administrative offices to the effect that he is the only person who:
>
> (1)   has possession of the stamp or key.
> (2)   will use the stamp or key.[38]

Arkansas permits physicians to use rubber stamp signatures if the method is approved in writing by the hospital administrator and the medical records committee.[39] In addition to Joint Commission restrictions on the use of such stamps, Arkansas requires that the stamp be locked in the medical records department when the physician is not using it.[40] Indiana requires that all physicians' orders for medication and treatment be in writing or acceptable computerized form and be signed by hand or computer key by the attending physician within 24 hours.[41] All of the states that permit this type of authentication impose controls to safeguard against abuse by limiting access to and use of the authenticating devices to the properly authorized individuals. With regard to rubber stamp signatures, most have adopted controls identical or very similar to those set forth in the Joint Commission's standard governing authentication.

Some states, however, do not specifically address the substitution of rubber stamps or computers for the physician's handwritten signature, or impose authentication requirements that appear to preclude the use of stamps or computer codes. For example, Alabama requires that entries in the medical record be made in ink or be typewritten and that they be authenticated and signed or initialed by the attending physician.[42] In Arizona, the person responsible for each

---

[38]Cal. Code Regs., tit. 22, § 70751(g) (1993).

[39]Rules and Regulations for Hospitals and Related Institutions in Arkansas, § 0601I (1988).

[40]*Id.*

[41]Ind. Admin. Code, tit. 410, § 9(1)(d) (1993).

[42]Ala. Admin. Code, r. § 420-5-7.07(1)(g) (1992).

entry "shall be identified by initials or signature."[43] In Kansas, each clinical entry must be signed or initialed by the attending physician, who must be identified properly in the record.[44] Kentucky requires that all orders for diet, diagnostic tests, therapeutic procedures, and medications be written, signed, and dated by the medical staff member.[45] Nebraska provides that "facsimiles" of physicians' signatures and initials are permitted "where appropriate safeguards have been taken to limit access and use of the facsimile or code to the individual physician."[46] New Jersey requires that all entries be written in ink, dated, and either signed by the recording person or authenticated through the use of a computerized medical records system.[47]

Because applicable law in these states may be ambiguous or conflicting, hospitals seeking to use alternatives to handwritten signatures should consult with their legal counsel. For example, in Massachusetts, while regulations require every maternal record to be "signed by a qualified obstetric or other consultant,"[48] they also incorporate the Medicare Conditions of Participation into the hospital licensing regulations.[49] The term "signed" with regard to maternal records, therefore, probably incorporates the broad Medicare definition of "authentication," which includes signature, written initials, or computer entry.[50] Massachusetts legislation defines "written" and "in writing" as "printing, engraving, lithographing and any other mode of representing words and letters; but if the written signature of a person is required by law, it shall always be his own handwriting or, if he is unable to write, his mark."[51]

Because the language of this statute is clear, several courts have construed it to mean a direct personal act of the person whose name is to be signed.[52] In a Massachusetts suit for personal injuries against a product manufacturer, the court ruled that the term "in writing" did not include tape-recorded statements.[53] The holding in that case suggests that maternity records in Massachusetts may be authenticated by alternative means because the regulations require them to be "signed" but not specifically "in writing."

---

[43]Arizona Hospital Licensing Regulations § R9-10-221 L (1982).

[44]Kan. Admin. Regs. § 28-34-9a(f) (1992).

[45]902 Ky. Admin. Regs. 20:3(11)(d)(7) (1983).

[46]Neb. Admin. R. & Regs., tit. 175, ch. 9 § 003.04A3 (1979).

[47]N.J. Admin. Code, tit. 8, § 43G.-15.2(b) (1993).

[48]Mass. Regs. Code, tit. 105, § 130.627(A) (1993).

[49]*Id.* at § 130.200.

[50]42 C.F.R. § 482.24(c)(1) (1992).

[51]Mass. Ann. Laws, ch. 4 § 7 (1993).

[52]See, e.g., *Irving v. Goodimate Co.*, 70 N.E.2d 414 (1946); *Finnegan v. Lucy*, 32 N.E. 656 (1892).

[53]*Fahey v. Rockwell Graphics Systems, Inc.*, 482 N.E. 2d 519, 528-529 (Mass. App. Ct. 1985).

In the absence of legislative guidance, courts nonetheless may interpret hospital regulations to include modern techniques of communication based on current business practices. For example, *Joseph Denunzio Fruit Co. v. Crane*[54] was a complicated contracts case involving, in part, the proper interpretation to be placed on written communications via teletype messages exchanged between certain parties. The court cited with approval several cases indicating that a signature may take a variety of forms, including handwritten, printed, stamped, typewritten, engraved, photographed, or cut from one instrument and attached to another. In *Denunzio,* the court accepted the teletype machine as a modern device satisfying a California law that requires written signatures for certain types of transactions, declaring that it is necessary to take a realistic view of modern business practices.[55]

Although some courts may be willing to accept an expansive definition of the terms "writing" and "signature," no general rule exists that authentication of medical records may be accomplished by any method other than a written signature. Any health care institution that intends to use rubber stamp signatures or to automate its medical record information should confer with legal counsel about proper authentication of records. If state law requires a handwritten signature for authentication, the institution must provide for such authentication, even if it maintains its records in computers. The only alternative for the institution or state hospital association is to embark on the often long and difficult task of obtaining an amendment of the applicable, restrictive state law.

Auto-Authentication

The introduction of computer technology to medical record management has provided opportunities to improve the speed and accuracy of the authentication process. Computerizing medical records, however, has introduced a new risk that the technology will replace rather than supplement the input of practitioners and hospital personnel into this process of verifying the accuracy and complete-ness of medical records. This is particularly apparent in the use of electronic signatures on medical record documents. While both federal and state authorities allow electronic signatures to replace handwritten ones, they also require that authentication, regardless of the format, attest to the accuracy of the record.[56]

For this reason, many of these agencies have become concerned about the process of auto-authentication, in which a physician authenticates a report by

---

[54]188 F.2d 569 (9th Cir. 1951), *cert. denied*, 342 U.S. 820 (1951), *aff'g* 79 F. Supp. 117 (S.D. Cal. 1948).

[55]79 F. Supp. at 128.

[56]See M. Kadzielski and M. Reynolds, Legal Review: Auto-authentication of Medical Records Raises Verification Concerns, *Topics in Health Information Management,* 14, no. 1, (1993): 77-82.

computer code before the report is transcribed. Physicians enter an electronic signature, and agree to review and correct transcripts of electronic medical records within a certain time frame. If no corrections are made by the deadline, the record is deemed complete. Authentication requirements imposed by the Joint Commission and state regulations assume, however, that the physician authenticating the record verifies its accuracy and completeness before signing. To the degree that an auto-authentication system does not allow a physician to make this verification, many regulatory agencies have adopted the position that the authentication requirement is not fulfilled.

For example, the Health Care Financing Administration's (HCFA) Medicare Conditions of Participation require authentication of each entry in a medical record and allow authentication by computer.[57] However, HCFA has indicated that any failure to obtain a physician's signature with respect to the record in its final form constitutes a deficiency in the authentication requirement.[58] One regional HCFA office has formally adopted the position that auto-authentication is not consistent with Medicare Conditions of Participation, stating in its *Operations Manual* that there must be a method of determining that a physician in fact authenticated the report after it was transcribed.[59] The California State Department of Health Services also has taken the position that an auto-authentication system that does not require a physician to verify the information in a record after it is transcribed is unacceptable. Electronic signatures are acceptable, according to this agency, only if they are entered after transcription and not "by default."[60] The American Health Information Management Association has proposed documenting medical records at the point of care, instead of retrospectively, criticizing authentication systems that obtain signatures from physicians well after the record has been used for patient care.

In addition to exposing hospitals to possible sanctions by administrative agencies, including the loss of eligibility for Medicare participation, the use of auto-authentication can generate difficulties in offering evidence in litigation, particularly malpractice suits. The outcome of such litigation frequently depends on establishing what actually took place. A physician's signature on the medical record gives evidence that the practitioner actually reviewed the record and acknowledged that it represented a complete and accurate record of the patient's course of treatment. Although a signature does not prove conclusively that the physician reviewed the record, it is stronger evidence of such verification than a signature on a separate form authorizing authentication of the record.

---

[57]42 C.F.R. § 482.24(c)(1) (1992).

[58]Vladeck Warns Auto-authentication Will Violate Medicare Conditions, *BNA Health Law Reporter*, (Oct. 21, 1993): 1423.

[59]*Supra*, note 56 p. 79.

[60]*Id.*, p. 80.

Auto-authentication systems frequently contain safeguards that protect some of the essential functions of the authentication process. For example, some facilities require physicians to sign an attestation that they will review all records, and unless they request corrections, the medical records department may enter the physician's signature. These attestations may include a provision in which the physician agrees not to dispute the accuracy of any record based on the absence of the doctor's signature on any document. Such an agreement provides no supporting evidence that a physician actually reviewed the record, however, and therefore does not resolve any concerns regarding the accuracy of the record's contents.

Other facilities allow physicians to authenticate unsigned progress notes in a medical record by signing a statement on a cover page that they are authenticating all progress reports for a particular hospitalization. A separate authentication is required for other types of reports in the file, including operative reports, physical reports, discharge summaries, etc. Because progress reports are authenticated by the physician when they are created, they are more likely to be accurate and complete.

Under another system of auto-authentication of dictated and transcribed reports, a physician receives a copy of all transcribed reports and a periodic list of unsigned and dictated reports. The physician then indicates next to each report on the list whether he or she wants to sign it or authorize auto-authentication of the report. The level of accountability increases in this type of system because the physician receives a copy of each report and individually selects each report for either signature or auto-authentication.

Although the introduction of computer technology has enabled hospitals to introduce new methods for facilitating a physician's role in the authentication process, health care institutions should not lose sight of their responsibility in creating accurate and complete medical records. Any computer system that does not require physicians to review reports after they are transcribed is likely to fall short of both federal and state authentication standards, as well as to create serious liability risks for the facility implementing such a system. (For a discussion of computerized medical records, see Chapter 6.)

VERBAL ORDERS

Hospitals should require physicians to deliver their orders in writing , except in situations in which verbal orders are unavoidable. Written orders are preferable to verbal ones because written orders create fewer chances for error.

However, written orders often are impossible—for example, where the physician is on unit but is unable to write the order before it is carried out or when the physician is off the unit and must give directions over the telephone. Hospital licensing regulations in most states require all physician orders to be written in the patient's medical record and authenticated.[61] Joint Commission standards require that all diagnostic, therapeutic, and medication orders be included in the medical record.[62] At least one state requires that verbal orders be transcribed and authenticated by the physician within 24 hours,[63] although other state licensure laws extend the time period for signing verbal orders to 48 hours.[64] Joint Commission standards provide that medical staff regulations must stipulate a time frame for authenticating verbal medication orders.[65] The medical staff also must identify any category of diagnostic or therapeutic verbal orders that represent a potential hazard to the patient, and specify a time frame within which such orders must be authenticated.[66] Regardless of licensing laws or accreditation standards, hospital policy should require all verbal orders to be transcribed within a specified time.

A physician's signature on a transcribed verbal order authenticates the order and indicates that it was written correctly. Who may receive and transcribe a physician's verbal order is a matter of hospital policy and should be set forth clearly in hospital policies or in the medical staff rules and regulations. Under Joint Commission standards, medical staff rules and regulations must identify by title and category the personnel who are qualified to accept and transcribe verbal orders.[67] Hospital policies, therefore, should be predicated on the concept that only personnel who are qualified to understand physicians' orders should be authorized to receive and transcribe verbal orders.

In view of the increased potential for error in the transcription of verbal orders, hospitals should discourage all verbal orders except those that must be issued by telephone. Physicians should be responsible for writing their orders in the medical record unless they are not present when the order must be given. If they cannot write their orders in the record, they should authenticate them before leaving the unit. In most hospitals, nursing or house staff members receive and transcribe telephone orders from attending physicians. Although not practicable

---

[61]See, e.g., S.C. Code Regs. R. 61-16 § 601.6 (Dept. Health & Env. Control, 1992); Standards, Rules and Regs. for Hospitals and Related Facilities, ch. 3, § 7(i) (Wyo. Dept. of Health, 1979).

[62]Joint Commission, *Accreditation Manual for Hospitals* (Oakbrook Terrace, Ill.: 1994), IM Standards 7.2.11 and 7.2.19.

[63]Ind. Admin. Code, tit. 410, r. 15-1-9(d) (1993).

[64]See, e.g., Neb. Admin. R. & Regs., tit. 175, ch. 9 § 003.04A5 (1979); S.C. Code Regs. R. 61-16 § 601.6 (Dept. Health & Env. Control, 1992); Rules and Regulations for Hospitals and Related Institutions in Arkansas § 0602 B.2 (1988).

[65]Joint Commission, *Accreditation Manual for Hospitals* (Oakbrook Terrace, Ill.: 1994), IM Standard 7.8.1.

[66]*Id.*, IM Standard 7.8.2.1.

[67]*Id.*, IM Standard 7.8.

in all cases, having a second person at the hospital on the telephone to witness the conversation reduces error and controversy concerning the order given. For especially sensitive orders, such as "do-not-resuscitate" orders, hospitals should require a witness to the order.

CORRECTIONS AND ALTERATIONS

Some medical record entry errors are inevitable. Hospitals therefore should establish clear procedures for making necessary corrections. Generally, two kinds of errors occur: (1) minor errors in transcription, spelling, etc., and (2) more significant errors involving test results, physician orders, inadvertently omitted information, and similar substantive entries. As a general rule, the person who made the incorrect record entry should correct the entry.

While the majority of states have no specific statutory or regulatory rules concerning altering medical records, some state regulations specify how corrections should be handled. For example, in Arkansas errors in medical records must be corrected by drawing a single line through the incorrect entry, labeling the entry as an error, and initialing and dating it.[68] In Massachusetts, health care facilities may not erase mistakes, use ink eradicators, or remove pages from the record.[69]

In the absence of such regulations, however, hospitals should make clear their own rules governing corrections. If the correction is a significant one, a senior person designated by hospital policy should review the correction to determine whether it complies with the institution's guidelines for record amendments. Hospital personnel should make only changes that are within their scope of practice as defined by state licensing and certification laws. A registered nurse, for example, should not amend a physician's medication order unless directed to do so by the physician or by a senior hospital official pursuant to established hospital policy. Obvious minor errors, such as spelling, do not require intervention by senior personnel. The person who made the error should correct it, if possible, but any practitioner working with the record may correct such a minor error.

The person correcting a charting error in the record should cross out the incorrect entry with a single line, enter the correction, initial the correction, and enter the time and date the correction was made. Mistakes in the record should not be erased or obliterated, because erasures and obliterations could arouse

---

[68]Rules and Regulations for Hospitals and Related Institutions in Arkansas, § 601 G (1988). See also N.J. Admin. Code, tit. 8, § 8:43G-15.2(K) (1993). (Corrections shall be made by drawing a single line through the error and initialing and dating the correction.)

[69]Mass. Regs. Code, tit. 105, § 150.013(B) (1990).

suspicions in the mind of a jury as to the contents of the original entry. A single line drawn through incorrect entries leaves no doubt as to the original information being corrected. Where a correction requires more space than is available near the original entry, the person correcting the record should enter a reference to an addendum to the record and enter the more lengthy correction in the addendum.

If the patient requests that the record be amended, hospital personnel should advise the patient's attending physician of the changes requested. A physician who considers the amendment inappropriate should discuss the matter with the patient. Any amendments made at the patient's request should be included in an addendum to the record. The physician also should add an entry to document that the change was made at the request of the patient, who thereafter will bear the burden of explaining the change. The hospital should establish a policy governing such amendments.

A few states have regulations that address changes or amendments to medical records at the request of parties. In Maryland, legislation requires health care providers to establish a procedure by which an interested person may request an addition or correction to a medical record.[70] If the facility does not make the requested change, it must permit the individual to insert a statement of disagreement in the record, as well as provide a notice of the change or statement of disagreement to every person to whom it previously disclosed inaccurate, incomplete, or disputed information.[71] New York law also allows a qualified person to challenge the accuracy of information in a medical record. In the event that a facility refuses to amend a record in accordance with the person's request, it must allow the individual to write a statement challenging the accuracy of the record and include the statement as part of the permanent record.[72]

In the event of a threatened or actual suit against the hospital or a member of its staff, hospital personnel and medical staff should make no changes in the complainant's medical record without first consulting defense counsel. Attempts to alter medical record entries to favor the providers always are inappropriate and do not necessarily help their defense, particularly if the patient has obtained a copy of the record before the changes were made.

If the plaintiff can show that the record was altered without justification by a defendant, the plaintiff may be able to destroy the credibility of the entire record. In a Connecticut case in which the hospital's nurses rewrote an entire section of the patient's medical record following the patient's injury in the hospital, the court held in the subsequent negligence action that:

---

[70]Md. Code Ann. [Health-Gen.] § 4-304 (1993).

[71]*Id.*

[72]N.Y. Comp. Codes R. & Regs, tit. 405, § 11(6) (1989).

[i]n addition to all the other evidence in the case, the significance of the revised hospital record should not be overlooked. Although the defendant understandably attempts to minimize what was done by characterizing the action as merely one of ordering expanded notes and by attributing it to poor judgment, the trier [of fact] was not required to be so charitable. An allowable inference from the bungled attempt to cover up the staff inadequacies . . . was that *the revision indicated a consciousness of negligence.* [Emphasis added.] The court so charged and the jury could so find.[73]

If a hospital that is being sued or threatened with a suit discovers that an original record entry is inaccurate or incomplete, it should request that clarifications or additions to the record be placed in a properly signed and dated addendum to the record.

In addition, deliberately altering a medical record or writing an incorrect record may subject the individual and the hospital to statutory sanctions. In some states, a practitioner who makes a false entry on a medical record is subject to license revocation for unprofessional conduct.[74] Under federal statutes and regulations, altering or falsifying a chart for purposes of wrongfully obtaining Medicare or state health care funds is a crime and subjects the violator to a substantial fine or imprisonment.[75]

---

[73]*Pisel v. Stamford Hosp.*, 430 A.2d 1 (Conn. 1980). See also *Libbe v. Permanente Clinic*, 520 P.2d 361 (Or. 1974) where the jury could infer that the nurse who falsified the patient's chart to show that she had checked the fetal heartbeat every half-hour made that entry because in retrospect she knew such procedure was good nursing practice. Her knowledge, along with other evidence, could be used to establish the appropriate standard of care.

[74]See, e.g., Ky. Rev. Stat. § 311.595(9) (1992).

[75]42 U.S.C. § 1320a-7b(a) (1993).

3

Special Medical
Records Problems

INTRODUCTION

This chapter discusses selected special medical records problems that arise frequently in hospital settings. The issues raised apply to a broad range of medical records problems; other special problems involving access are discussed in Chapter 5. In some instances, the hospital must deal with special types of patients, such as child abuse victims, celebrities, and hostile patients. Hospitals also deal with particularly difficult issues involving dying patients. Some of the documentation problems discussed here, such as the treatment of a child abuse victim or differences of opinion among professional staff members, require documentation of potentially competing interests.

Although these situations require physicians and other hospital personnel to adhere to the general legal standards discussed throughout this book, they also demand additional attention to careful documentation. Individuals making medical records entries relating to these special problems must be extraordinarily precise and objective in their notations. These situations also suggest that the hospital, with the assistance of legal counsel, should develop a workable and appropriate policy to provide its personnel and medical records practitioners with a consistent protocol.

RECORDS OF CHILD ABUSE

Every state has mandatory reporting laws obligating hospital personnel who have reason to believe that a child has been abused to report their findings to a designated state agency. These reporting requirements, discussed in more detail in Chapter 5, specify the nature and content of the information provided to the state agency. Most state laws require that a hospital staff member covered by the statute who suspects child abuse notify the person in charge of the institution, who in turn makes the necessary report.

When the physician assesses a child to determine whether reasonable cause exists to believe the youngster is abused or neglected, careful notations must be made in the medical record. Specifically, a detailed and objective documentation and description of all pertinent physical findings should be noted clearly in the record. In addition, any tests performed or photographs taken to document the suspected abuse should be noted carefully. This detailed information will be the basis upon which a determination of abuse is made. Therefore, it is essential that it be accurate, specific, and thorough.

The record should include a history of the injury, including details reported by the parent or guardian of how the injury allegedly happened, the date and time of the injury, sequence of events, names of witnesses, time interval between the injury and the time medical attention was sought, and the identities of the interviewers. If the parents, guardians, and child are interviewed separately, the date, time, and place of the sessions also should be documented.

Conflict between Child Abuse Reporting and Patient Confidentiality

Courts have struggled with the conflict between state mandatory child abuse reporting statutes and state and federal statutes prohibiting disclosure of certain medical records.[1] More recently, state legislatures have incorporated waivers of the physician-patient privilege into child abuse statutes and the courts increasingly favor disclosure in cases involving possible child abuse; the extent of disclosure remains ambiguous, however, in many jurisdictions.

Patient Confidentiality Statutes

As a general rule, information in a patient's medical record may not be disclosed without the individual's consent.[2] State and federal statutes support this rule. For example, the evidentiary statutes of many states establish a privilege that protects statements made in the course of treatment by a physician where a physician-patient relationship exists. This physician-patient privilege enables a patient (and, in some states, a physician or hospital) to object to any attempt to introduce such statements in a court proceeding.[3]

---

[1]For a discussion of the requirements for a court order for disclosure in child abuse cases, see, Cosgrove, Substance Abuse Record Confidentiality and Child Abuse Reporting Requirements, 2 *Topics in Health Record Management* 81 (Sept. 1981).

[2]See Medical Records *Hospital Law Manual*, (1991).

[3]*Id.*

Some states also have enacted statutes that prohibit or restrict disclosure of certain types of patient information in court or elsewhere. The Illinois Mental Health and Developmental Disabilities Confidentiality Act,[4] for example, prohibits the disclosure of information concerning a person undergoing treatment for mental illness or developmental disabilities (as defined by the act) except under certain circumstances. The statute states that all records kept by a therapist or agency in the course of providing mental health or developmental disabilities services to a patient concerning the patient and the service are confidential and may not be disclosed, except as provided in the act.[5]

Federal law also protects certain patient information. Persons receiving treatment for alcoholism or drug abuse are protected by federal legislation that establishes strict confidentiality requirements for patient records maintained by federally assisted substance abuse treatment centers.[6] A health care facility may not disclose record information on patients protected by these acts except under circumstances specifically described in the statutes[7] or unless a court has found "good cause" for authorizing disclosure and has entered an appropriate order to that effect.[8] The statutes do not define the term "good cause," and courts therefore must decide on proper definitions.[9]

The public policy underlying these special confidentiality rules is to encourage people to seek medical or psychiatric treatment when they need it. The rules rely upon the assumption that, if statements made to physicians and other health care providers will not be disclosed, people will be more willing to discuss highly personal and confidential matters relating to their illnesses.

Child Abuse Reporting Laws

Most states have enacted child abuse reporting statutes. Common to many of them are mandatory reporting of suspected or actual abuse and a grant of immunity to persons who make reports in good faith.[10] Increasingly, child abuse laws have broadened the definition of "abuse" to include emotional injury as well as physical and sexual factors.[11] Abuse for the purpose of child abuse

---

[4]See 740 Ill. Comp. Stat. Ann. §§ 110/1-110/17 (1993).

[5]*Id.* § 110/3.

[6]42 U.S.C. § 290 dd-2 (1993). For a detailed discussion of these statutes and regulations, see Chapter 5.

[7]42 U.S.C. § 290dd-2(a) (1993).

[8]42 C.F.R. § 2.64 (1991).

[9]See Note 1, *supra*, Cosgrove, at 82.

[10]See e.g., 325 Ill. Comp. Stat. Ann. § 5/9 (1993).

[11]*Id.* § 5/3.

reporting legislation also has been held to include a mother's ingestion of amphetamines and opiates while the child was in vitro.[12]

A typical child abuse statute authorizes a designated state agency to intervene for the child's protection and to assist the person committing abuse in finding appropriate counseling or treatment. As the known incidence of child abuse has increased with better reporting, the public's interest in its prevention has grown. As a result, some laws now declare that any evidence of a child's injuries may be admitted in any legal proceeding arising from the alleged abuse.[13] The public policies supporting child abuse reporting statutes are for the protection of children and the reduction of abuse through appropriate counseling.

Conflicting Policies

The public policies underlying mandatory child abuse reporting and protection of patient confidentiality appear to conflict. If the patient discloses information in the course of treatment for mental illness or alcoholism that suggests or confirms that the person abused a child, the question arises as to how the state agency may obtain such information as evidence in a legal proceeding instituted either to protect the child from further abuse or to prosecute the perpetrator for criminal wrongdoing.

In *State of Minn. v. Andring*,[14] the Supreme Court of Minnesota grappled with this apparent conflict. In that case, the defendant was charged with three counts of criminal sexual conduct involving his 10-year-old stepdaughter and his 11-year-old niece. State authorities had learned of the abuse from sources other than the defendant's medical records. Released on bail, the defendant described his sexual contact with young girls while undergoing treatment for depression and alcoholism at a crisis unit. In its criminal case against the defendant, the state sought to discover his medical records and statements made to crisis unit personnel. The defendant argued that the federal Comprehensive Alcohol Abuse and Alcoholism Prevention, Treatment, and Rehabilitation Act protected his records from disclosure and that the state's physician-patient privilege similarly protects the statements he made at the unit.

The Minnesota Supreme Court held that the federal alcoholism treatment act and regulations do not preempt the state's child abuse reporting law. Examining the legislative history of the two statutes, the court found that the state law had been enacted in response to the federal Child Abuse Prevention and Treatment Act, which requires a state to enact a child abuse reporting law in order to qualify

---

[12]*In re Troy D. v. Kelly D.* 263 Cal. Rptr. 869 (Ct. App. 1989).

[13]See, e.g., 325 Ill. Comp. Stat. Ann. § 5/10 (1993).

[14]342 N.W.2d 128 (Minn. 1984).

for federal funds for child abuse programs. It also found that Congress had enacted the federal child abuse statute and the federal alcoholism treatment statute in the same year. The court concluded that Congress could not have intended one statute to preempt the very state law it had itself mandated in another statute, and ruled that: "the confidentiality of the patient records provision of the alcohol treatment act does not preclude the use of patient records in child abuse proceedings to the extent required by [the state child abuse reporting statute]."[15]

Pointing to the public policy of encouraging persons who abuse children to seek treatment voluntarily, the court held that the child abuse reporting statute abrogates the physician-patient privilege. The court ruled, however, that the privilege is abrogated:

> only to the extent that it would permit evidentiary use of the information required to be contained in the maltreatment report—the identity of the child, the identity of the parent, guardian, or other person responsible for the child's care, the nature and extent of the child's injuries, and the name and address of the reporter.[16]

Thus, the court permitted some erosion of the physician-patient privilege, but only to the extent necessary to give force and effect to the abuse reporting statute.

A key fact in the *Andring* case was that the state already had obtained through other sources the information required to be reported by the law. In Indiana, the same issue arose but with a different result, in a case involving a patient who was charged with criminal child molestation.[17] The state attempted to acquire access to communications between the patient and a hospital psychiatrist during family therapy sessions that had been recommended by the Department of Public Welfare. Although the Indiana reporting law states that the physician-patient privilege is not a reason to exclude evidence in any judicial proceeding resulting from a child abuse report, the court noted that the reporting was not at issue in this case because the abuse already had been reported. The central purpose of the child abuse reporting statute is the protection of children, not the punishment of those who mistreat. The statute's purpose already had been served, the court concluded, and it was unnecessary to abrogate the physician-patient privilege any further.

However, other courts have held that the statutory waiver of the physician-patient privilege extends to criminal proceedings involving the prosecution of the child abuser. For example, a father who was accused of raping his two children attempted to exclude conversations that he had had with a nurse while

---

[15]*Id*. at 132.

[16]*Id*. at 133.

[17]*Daymude v. State*, 540 N.E. 2d 1263 (Ind. Ct. App. 1989).

seeking treatment for the symptoms of a sexually transmitted disease.[18] During the consultation, the patient had admittted to having sex with both his son and daughter. The court declared that in accordance with child abuse reporting legislation, the physician-patient privilege did not apply to exclude the conversation from evidence. In adopting the statute, the legislature balanced the need for confidential medical treatment against the need to protect child victims, and opted to provide the broadest possible exceptions to the physician-patient privilege, the court concluded.

In another case, the Louisiana Supreme Court also endorsed the view that waiver of the physician-patient privilege in the state's child abuse reporting statute applies to criminal proceedings against the child abuser.[19] An individual who was charged with raping his 5-year-old niece objected to the state's attempt to introduce evidence indicating that he had tested positive for gonorrhea. The incident of abuse had been discovered because the child herself had contracted gonorrhea. The court admitted the evidence, noting that other states have similar waivers of privilege in their child abuse reporting laws and had applied them in criminal proceedings.

Because of the importance of the public policy issues in child abuse reporting legislation, courts appear unwilling to exclude medical record evidence on the basis of physician-patient privilege. Statutory waivers of the privilege, which frequently apply to any proceedings involving the abuse of a child, have been interpreted broadly. In addition and as was illustrated in *Andring*, the public policy of protecting children under state legislation can be seen as more important than offering absolute protection to the records of drug and alcohol abuse patients under federal law. The cases indicate that states will be permitted to pierce the shield provided by both the federal alcoholism treatment act and state physician-patient privilege, at least to the extent necessary to protect the children involved.

EMERGENCY DEPARTMENT RECORDS

Various state and federal regulations[20] and laws discussed throughout this book govern hospital records, including emergency department records. Some state laws and regulations specify the information to be recorded; other states specify which broad areas of information concerning the patient's treatment

---

[18]*State v. Etheridge*, 352 S.E.2d 673 (N.C. 1987).

[19]*State v. Bellard*, 533 So. 2d 961 (La. 1988).

[20]Medicare regulations on the conditions of participation formerly specifically addressed emergency service or emergency department records, but now no longer differentiate between the two. 42 CFR §§ 482-24 (1993).

must be included; some states simply declare that the medical record shall be adequate, accurate, or complete. State hospital licensure rules and regulations also may provide requirements and standards for the general maintenance, handling, signing, filing, and retention of hospital records.

In addition, some states specifically regulate the contents of emergency department records. Alaska requires that the emergency services record contain patient identification, the time and means of transportation to the facility, current condition, diagnosis, record of treatment provided, condition on discharge or transfer, and disposition, including instructions given for follow-up care, and the name of the physician who saw the patient.[21] Arkansas specifies content requirements for emergency department records, and mandates that they must be completed immediately or, if the physician treats the patient by telephone orders, within 24 hours.[22] Indiana imposes the same content requirements for emergency and outpatient records,[23] while Ohio has the same content requirements for both alcoholism inpatient and emergency care records.[24] Oklahoma requires that an emergency medical record contain documentation if a patient leaves against medical advice.[25]

The Joint Commission on Accreditation of Healthcare Organizations (Joint Commission) also has set up standards for emergency care records. The standards for accreditation of hospitals provide that in addition to the information required for all medical records,[26] emergency care records should contain:

- the time and means of arrival
- the patient's leaving against medical advice
- conclusions at the termination of treatment, including final disposition, patient's condition at the time of discharge, and any instructions for follow-up care[27]

The Joint Commission also states that a copy of an emergency care record should be available to the practitioner or medical organization responsible for follow-up care.[28] Finally, in accordance with the Emergency Medical Treatment

---

[21]Alaska Admin. Code, tit. 7, § 12.870 (f) (Jan. 1984).

[22]Ark. Reg. § 0604.2 (1993).

[23]Ind. Admin. Code, tit. 410, r. 15-1-9 (1993).

[24]Ohio Admin. Code § 3701-55-15 (1993).

[25]Okla. Hospital Standards, § 310:665-25-11 (1993).

[26]Joint Commission on Accreditation of Healthcare Organizations, *Accreditation Manual for Hospitals* (Oakbrook, Ill.: 1994) Standard IM 7.2.

[27]*Id.*, Standard IM 7.6.

[28]*Id.*, Standard IM 7.6.2.

and Active Labor Act,[29] discussed below, Joint Commission standards state that unless extenuating circumstances are documented in the patient's record, a hospital may not arbitrarily transfer a patient to another facility if it has the means for providing adequate care.[30]

EMERGENCY MEDICAL TREATMENT AND ACTIVE LABOR ACT

The importance of establishing complete and accurate emergency care records increased significantly with the enactment of federal legislation designed to prevent the transfer of hospital patients for economic reasons. In 1985, Congress passed Section 9121 of the Consolidated Omnibus Reconciliation Act (CO-BRA)[31] to prevent the transfer of patients for economic reasons. These antidumping statutes, codified at Sections 1866 and 1867 of the Social Security Act,[32] apply to every hospital that participates in the Medicare program and that has an emergency room. In 1989, Congress amended its patient antidumping legislation by adopting new patient transfer provisions[33] that took effect on July 1, 1990. The amendments contain a number of new recordkeeping and documentation requirements, and mandate that hospitals assume additonal responsibility concerning on-call physicians and emergency department coverage.

COBRA's enforcement provisions impose a civil monetary penalty of up to $50,000 for hospitals that negligently violate the law (or up to $25,000 for those with fewer than 100 beds) for each violation. Hospitals that fail to substantially meet the COBRA requirements are subject to suspension or termination of their Medicare provider agreements. A physician who is responsible for the examination, treatment, or transfer of an individual, including a physician on call who negligently violates the law, is subject to a civil money penalty of up to $50,000 per violation. If the violation is gross and flagrant or is repeated, the physician is subject to exclusion from Medicare and Medicaid. An individual who suffers personal harm as a direct result of a hospital's violation of the law can sue the hospital for personal injury damages and equitable relief. A medical facility that suffers a financial loss as a direct result of a hospital's violation of the law can sue the hospital for damages and equitable relief.

Under COBRA, any hospital with an emergency department must provide for an appropriate medical screening examination to any individual, or someone acting on that person's behalf, who comes to the department and requests treatment for a medical condition. A hospital must use ancillary services

---

[29]42 U.S.C. § 1395dd (1993).

[30]*Accreditation Manual* (1994): Standard ES 1.4.2.

[31]42 U.S.C. § 1395dd (1993).

[32]42 U.S.C. §§ 1395cc and 1395dd (1993).

[33]P.L. 101-239 (1989).

routinely available to the emergency department when providing medical screening. A hospital cannot delay a medical screening examination, further medical examination, or treatment to inquire about the individual's method of payment or insurance status.

Although the new law contains no specific requirements for documentation of a medical screening, a hospital should carefully document this type of patient care to defend against charges that it violated the law. The emergency department should create and retain a record of each medical screening it conducts. If the medical screening indicates that the individual does not have an emergency condition, the hospital will have satisfied its obligations under the law. For evidence purposes, however, its records should demonstrate that the screening was conducted and that such a conclusion was reached.

Proper documentation is particularly important if the individual refuses to consent to the screening or refuses to undergo recommended further treatment. If a hospital offers an individual further medical treatment, and informs the person of the risks and benefits of the examination or treatment but the individual refuses to consent, the institution will have fulfilled its obligations under the law. The hospital must take all reasonable steps to obtain the individual's written informed consent to refuse treatment. Similarly, if a hospital offers to transfer the individual and informs the person of the risks and benefits of the transfer, but the individual refuses to consent, the hospital will have fulfilled its obligations under the law. A hospital must take all reasonable steps to obtain written informed consent when an individual has refused an examination, treatment, or transfer.

If the hospital determines that an individual has an emergency medical condition, the institution must either stabilize the condition or transfer the person to another medical facility. An individual who has not been stabilized can be transferred only if:

- the individual (or a legally responsible person acting on the individual's behalf), after being informed of the hospital's obligations and of the risk of transfer, requests transfer to another facility, or
- a physician, or other qualified person in consultation with a physician when a physician is not physically present, has signed a certification that, based on the information available at the time of transfer, the medical benefits reasonably expected from the provision of medical treatment at another medical facility outweigh the increased risks to the individual and, in the case of labor, to the unborn child, from effecting the transfer.

Documentation on the stabilization of a patient's condition or a transfer, therefore, should be accurate and complete in order to prove that the hospital complied with its duties under the law. The documentation should indicate the status of the individual's condition and the treatment provided to achieve stabilization. In the event of a transfer, the record also should include a statement by medical personnel that within reasonable medical probability, no material deterioration of the patient's emergency medical condition will result from the transfer or will occcur during the transfer process.

In the event of a transfer, specific records must accompany the patient to the receiving facility. The transferring hospital must send a copy of all medical records related to the emergency conditions that are available at the time of transfer, including observations of signs or symptoms, preliminary diagnosis, treatment provided, results of any tests, the informed consent to transfer, the physician's certification, and the name and address of any on-call physician who refused or failed to appear within a reasonable time to provide necessary stabilizing treatment.

COBRA also requires that hospitals with emergency departments adopt a policy to ensure compliance with the antidumping law and maintain records of all patient transfers for at least five years. It requires that hospitals post signs in their emergency departments specifying the rights of individuals and women in labor with respect to examination and treatment for emergency medical conditions, and indicating whether the hospital participates in the Medicaid program. The signs must be posted in places most likely to be visible to individuals entering the emergency department as well as to persons waiting for examination and treatment. The signs should contain clear and simple wording that can be understood and that is clearly readable at a distance of 20 feet.

COBRA has generated a number of court cases on a variety of issues. One involves the question whether COBRA only applies to emergency department activities. One court has ruled that when an emergency department finds that a patient is suffering from an emergency condition, the individual cannot be discharged until the condition is stabilized, regardless of whether the person remains in the emergency department or is moved to another unit.[34] Documenting stabilization therefore can be an important function of other hospital departments.

Extending this reasoning, the Virginia Supreme Court held that COBRA applied although the patient never was seen in the emergency department and was in stable condition when she was admitted to the hospital.[35] The case involved a woman who was 33 weeks pregnant and had experienced premature rupture of the uterine membranes. She was admitted to the hospital, but her condition deteriorated over the ensuing five days. While she was in active labor and showing signs of fetal distress, a physician ordered her to be transferred to another facility. Approximately two hours after the transfer, the patient was taken "emergently" to the delivery room where she delivered a child by

[34]*Thornton v. Southwest Detroit Hosp.*, 895 F.2d 1131 (6th Cir. 1990).

[35]*Smith v. Richmond Memorial Hosp.*, 416 S.E.2d 689 (Va. 1992).

Caesarean section. Both mother and child sustained substantial injuries. The court ruled that the woman could sue the hospital under COBRA for an inappropriate transfer because the language of the law does not restrict it to the emergency room.

States also have become increasingly involved in the problems of patient transfers. In Texas, hospitals now are required to adopt a policy providing that patient transfers will not be based on race, religion, national origin, age, sex, physical condition, or economic status.[36] Hospital policy must provide that each patient arriving at the facility will be evaluated by a physician there or by an on-call staff physician who physically can reach the patient within 20 minutes or be in direct telephone communication with authorized personnel. Hospitals also must ensure that patients in need of emergency care are transferred only for medical reasons. In some jurisdictions, therefore, appropriate documentation is necessary to prove compliance with state antidumping laws.

Conclusion

COBRA and similar state law requirements are quite technical, and courts will hold providers to the letter of the law. Institutions should review all applicable emergency department record provisions of these statutes and regulations with legal counsel and be certain that hospital policy and procedures are in full compliance. Although federal or state statutes impose special recordkeeping requirements, complete documentation is important in emergency department records just as it is in all medical records. Hospitals must be able to rely on the information in the records to defend against claims of medical malpractice. Without accurate and complete records, it may be difficult, if not impossible, to offer evidence that contradicts a patient's contention that the person received negligent medical care.

An example of the type of evidentiary difficulties a hospital might encounter as a result of incomplete emergency care records arose in *Louisville Gen. Hosp. v. Hellmann*.[37] A patient who was hospitalized for two and a half weeks before dying of a head injury had been treated in the hospital emergency department for ten hours on the day of admission. The physician testified that he had monitored the decedent's vital signs every 30 minutes during that time, and the fact that the emergency department record did not contain notes on each examination was customary procedure at the hospital. To prove the veracity of the physician's statement, the court ordered the hospital to produce all the emergency department records it had compiled during the 30 days immediately preceding the date the patient was admitted. Although an appeals court subsequently ruled that this

---

[36]Tex. Health & Safety Code § 241.027(b) (1993).
[37]50 S.W.2d 790 (Ky. 1973).

would place an undue burden on the hospital, and reduced the order to the production of 100 records selected at random, the decision demonstrates the willingness of the court to look for a pattern of recording treatment in the emergency department of a defendant hospital and emphasizes the importance of maintaining complete emergency department records.

RECORDING DISAGREEMENTS AMONG PROFESSIONAL STAFF

All members of the medical team have a duty to take reasonable actions to safeguard the lives of their patients. Nurses as well as medical professionals other than physicians often are given the responsibility of monitoring and coordinating patient care. As a result, in the exercise of reasonable professional judgment and in order to minimize the possible liability for negligence, nonphysician medical professionals may be expected to intervene to clarify or object to physicians' orders they believe are improper. For example, in *Carlsen v. Javurek,*[38] a nurse anesthetist refused to follow a physician's orders prescribing an anesthetic that the nurse knew was contraindicated. Although nurses usually are obligated to follow physicians' orders, the court recognized that if, for example, the two professionals fail to agree on proper anesthetic, the surgery should be cancelled. If a nurse and physician are unable to agree, the nurse should obtain the intervention of a responsible medical or administrative officer, according to the hospital policy.

It is essential for nurses and other medical professionals to document their efforts to fulfill their duty to object to improper orders and to obtain responsible intervention to settle a professional disagreement. At the same time, it is important to create a medical record that is sufficiently objective and factual that it could not be used as evidence against the physician or the institution in a negligence action.

Although there are no clear answers to the medical records issues presented, in instances of disagreements among physicians and other medical professionals several suggested approaches may be helpful. If hospital policy requires that resolution of disagreements be documented in the medical record, the basic guideline for making these entries is that they be objective, concise, and completely factual rather than judgmental. The medical record is no place for vindictiveness or groundless opinion. All persons making entries into the records should be taught how to document these problems. For example, consider the following hypothetical case:

At 10 A.M. Ms. Jones, a staff nurse, finds on the order sheet an order from Dr. Smith to give 0.5 mg. of Digoxin intravenously to an infant patient. Recognizing that 0.5 mg. is a lethal dose, Ms. Jones telephones Dr. Smith at 10:10 A.M.. and advises him that in her opinion the order is incorrect. Dr. Smith immediately

---

[38]526 F.2d 202 (8th Cir. 1975).

acknowledges an error in the placement of a decimal and tells Ms. Jones the order should read "0.05 mg." Ms. Jones amends the order in accordance with the hospital's telephone order policy and administers the correct dosage, 0.05 mg.

Ms. Jones might document this incident in the nurses' notes as follows:

10:10 A.M..Called Dr. Smith concerning his order of 0.5 mg. of Digoxin IV. Dr. Smith directed that the order be changed to 0.05 mg. of Digoxin IV and be administered this A.M.. Physician order sheet amended accordingly.

/s/ M. Jones, R.N.

Now, assume that Dr. Smith disagreed with Ms. Jones that the order was incorrect and told her to follow the order as written. Ms. Jones informed Dr. Smith that she could not follow the order without seeking further advice through the institution's responsible intervention procedure. Following the intervention procedure, Ms. Jones contacted Dr. Brown, chairman of the department of pediatrics, at 10:15 A.M. and described the situation. At 10:30 A.M. Dr. Smith telephoned Ms. Jones and directed her to change the order to "0.05 mg. Digoxin IV." We can assume that Dr. Brown had a brief, but effective, conversation with Dr. Smith between 10:15 and 10:30 A.M.

Ms. Jones might properly document the incident in the nurses' notes as follows:

10:10 A.M. Called Dr. Smith concerning his order of 0.5 mg. of Digoxin IV. Dr. Smith confirmed the order.

10:15 A.M. Called Dr. Brown concerning Dr. Smith's order of 0.5 mg. of Digoxin IV.

10:30 A.M. Received telephone order from Dr. Smith to change order to read 0.05 mg. Digoxin IV. Physician order sheet amended accordingly.

/s/ M. Jones, R.N.

In another hypothetical case, Ms. Jones finds a written order in the chart of a 55-year-old patient for 125 mg. of Propranolol orally every six hours. In her experience, this is an unusually large dose. At 10 A.M. she calls the prescribing physician, Dr. Smith, to discuss the order. Although Dr. Smith tells Ms. Jones that this is a proper dosage for this patient, Ms. Jones still is uneasy about the order. In accordance with her hospital's intervention procedure, she contacts the chairman of the department of medicine, Dr. Black, at 10:10 A.M. Dr. Black calls Ms. Jones at 10:45 A.M. and advises her that he has discussed the case with Dr. Smith and that he, Dr. Black, believes the order is proper. Ms. Jones administers the Propranolol and might document her actions in the nurses' notes as follows:

10 A.M. Called Dr. Smith concerning his order of 125 mg. of Propranolol q6hrs. Dr. Smith confirmed his order.

10:15 A.M. Called Dr. Black concerning Dr. Smith's order of 125 mg. of Propranolol q6hrs.

10:45 A.M. Dr. Black telephoned and stated that he had discussed the order of 125 mg. of Propranolol q6hrs. with Dr. Smith and confirmed Dr. Smith's order.[39]

Although these hypothetical cases obviously are simplified, they provide an example of how medical records entries documenting intervention procedures should appear: concise, objective, and above all factual. The more complex the intervention, the more care the nurse or other professionals must take in documenting the facts. Statements such as "Dr. Smith is negligent again" or "Dr. Smith's order is incorrect" are unnecessary, inappropriate, and, should any legal action arise from the case, possibly harmful not only to the physician and the institution but also to the nurse involved.[40]

There are varying opinions among health care professionals concerning whether these kinds of professional discussions and disagreements should be documented in a medical record, and, if so, in what manner. Regardless of the position one takes on the issue, it is clear that a health care institution must have a policy on the question.[41] Otherwise practitioners are left to work out their differences on their own. That inevitably leads to inconsistent patient care and record documentation practices and can result in dangerous medical records entries made by professionals in the heat of anger.

MEDICAL RECORDS AND THE 'RIGHT TO DIE'

Do-Not-Resuscitate Orders

The term "cardiopulmonary resuscitation" (CPR) describes a procedure developed over the last two decades to reestablish breathing and heartbeat after cardiac or respiratory arrest. The most basic form of CPR, which is being taught to the public, involves recognizing the indications for intervention, opening an airway, initiating mouth-to-mouth breathing, and compressing the chest externally to establish artificial circulation. In hospitals, and in some emergency transport vehicles, CPR also can include the administration of oxygen under pressure to the lungs, the use of intravenous medications, the injection of stimulants into the heart through intravenous medications, the injection of

---

[39]William Roach, Responsible Intervention: A Legal Duty To Act, *Journal of Nursing Administration* 7 (July 1980): 23–24.

[40]*Id.*

[41]Disagreements among health care professionals have not generated cases on documentation issues, but have resulted in cases involving employment issues. See *Kirk v. Mercy Hosp. Tri-County*, 851 S.W.2d 617 (Mo. Ct. App. 1993) in which the court ruled that a hospital wrongfully discharged a nurse for complaining to other hospital employees about the level of care given by a physician to a hospital patient.

stimulants into the heart through catheters or long needles, electric shocks to the heart, insertion of a pacemaker, and open heart massage. Some of these procedures are highly intrusive and even violent in nature.

These interventions all are justified medically and are indicated for patients whose conditions are not yet diagnosed or for those who have a hopeful prognosis. However, as the National Conference on Cardiopulmonary Resuscitation and Emergency Cardiac Care, sponsored by the American Health Association and the National Academy of Sciences National Research Council, concluded: "The major objective of performing CPR is to provide oxygen to the brain, heart, and other vital organs until appropriate, definitive medical treatment (advanced cardiac life support) can restore normal and ventilatory action."[42]

To ensure that CPR is not initiated where it is not indicated, it is common practice to write "Do not resuscitate" (DNR) or "No CPR" on the orders for treatment of the patient. Many institutions call the CPR team by announcing "Code Blue," so the order might read "No Code Blue." DNR orders provide an exception to the universal standing order to provide CPR. The order is directed to on-call staff members who, because of the urgency of cardiac arrest, are unable to consult with the patient or primary care physician as to the desired course of treatment.

In 1987, the Joint Commission approved a standard that required all hospitals to have a resuscitation policy in place by January 1, 1988.[43] Joint Commission standards require that the policy describe the mechanisms for reaching the DNR decisions and for resolving conflicts in decision making.[44] The policy also must require that the order be written by the physician who is primarily responsible for the patient's care and inscribed in the patient's medical record.[45] The fear of legal liability for physicians who write DNR orders has virtually disappeared in light of numerous court decisions that endorse such practices, provided that the principles of informed consent are respected[46] and in light of the Joint Commission's recognition of this practice.

In *In re Dinnerstein*,[47] the earliest reported case (1978) in which a court ruled directly on the appropriateness of DNR orders without prior court authorization,

---

[42]Standards and Guidelines for Cardiopulmonary Resuscitation (CPR) and Emergency Cardiac Care, 255 *J.A.M.A.* 2905 (1986): 2915.

[43]See Joint Commission, *Perspectives* 7(5/6)(1987):5, and *Accreditation Manual* (1994): Standard MA 1.3.7.

[44]*Accreditation Manual* (1994): Standard RI 2.2.1.

[45]*Id.*, Standard RI 2.4.

[46]Briefly, a physician must obtain the informed consent of a competent patient or the consent of an incompetent patient's family before entering a DNR order. Hospital policies often require daily review of DNR orders to determine if they remain consistent with the patient's condition and desires.

[47]380 N.E.2d 134 (Mass. App. Ct. 1978). This result was approved *In re Spring*, 405 N.E.2d 115 (Mass. 1980).

the practice was upheld. The court in *In re Severns*[48] authorized a DNR order but did not state whether court authorization always is required. The District of Columbia Court of Appeals has stated its approval of the practice without court authorization.[49] Numerous other courts have recognized the practice.[50]

Clearly, the risk of legal liability from a failure to resuscitate is greater if the record does not contain a written DNR order or explanation. The importance of proper documentation is illustrated in one case in which a DNR order was legally challenged. In *Hoyt v. St. Mary's Rehabilitation Center*,[51] a Minnesota court ordered a hospital to remove a patient's name from the DNR list. Because of irreversible brain damage following neurological surgery, the 41-year-old patient functioned at approximately the level of a 2-year-old. Her parents, who had received court appointment as her guardians, had agreed with the physicians that resuscitation was not appropriate. Hoyt, who met the patient after the brain damage and visited her daily, challenged the DNR order.

In a unique departure from the principles regarding who may bring cases to court, the court created a new basis for standing to sue. It said that "third parties with a sincere interest in the ward and an ability to present the matter to the court" have standing and found that Hoyt had the requisite interest and ability. The court held that resuscitation decisions are within the authority of the guardian and that the only role of the court is to ensure that the decisions be made "only after appropriate consideration." The role of the third party was limited to suggesting the need for court review of the guardians' consideration. In this case, the court found that the guardians were unaware of the nature of the treatment to be denied and did not demonstrate sufficient consideration of what the patient would have wanted. The court focused on whether the patient would have wanted to continue indefinitely at her present level in four areas: (1) pain, (2) intellectual activity, (3) happiness, and (4) personal relationships. The court also mentioned that consideration should be given to whether payment would be of concern to the patient. The court ordered the patient's name to be taken off the DNR list until "knowledgeable approval" by the guardian to put her name back on the list.

The *Hoyt* case is important for at least two other reasons. First, it illustrates that there is an acceptable range of opinion on when DNR orders are appropriate. It demonstrates judicial acceptance of such orders when patients are neither comatose nor near death if there is knowledgeable concurrence by the physician and the patient's guardian. Second, it demonstrates that such decisions must be

---

[48]425 A.2d 156 (Del. 1980).

[49]*In re J.N.*, 406 A.2d 1275 (D.C. Ct. App. 1979).

[50]*In re Quinlan*, 355 A.2d 647 (N.J. 1976); *Severns v. Wilmington Medical Ctr., Inc.*, 421 A.2d 1334 (Del .1980).

[51]No. 774555 (Dist. Ct. Hennepin County, Minn. Feb. 13, 1981).

made carefully after due consideration because it may be necessary to justify them in a subsequent court action. It is doubtful that many other courts will grant standing to third parties with a "sincere interest" because of the traditional deference to family and physician decision making in these matters and the desire of courts to control their dockets. However, there are other channels, such as professional licensing boards, through which questions could be raised.

Decisions on Life-Sustaining Treatment

It is well established that competent adults have the right to refuse treatment unless state interests outweigh that right. Courts long have recognized that a patient's right to make decisions concerning medical care necessarily includes the right to decline medical care.[52] The Georgia Supreme Court allowed a competent 33-year-old patient to turn off the ventilator upon which he was dependent because the state had conceded that its interest in preserving life did not outweigh the patient's right to refuse medical treatment.[53] In Nevada, the state did not vigourously contest an application from a 31-year-old mentally competent quadraplegic to disconnect his respirator.[54] These cases illustrate a growing acknowledgement that a competent patient's right to terminate medical treatment outweighs a state's interest in preserving life.

A patient's ability personally to exercise the right to determine medical treatment does not exist if the individual is incompetent. Some patients who never have expressed their wishes regarding treatment become irreversibly incompetent and unable to communicate. Others never have had an opportunity to express their wishes because of youth or mental retardation. With increasing frequency courts are confronting these issues, and many have concluded that because competent adults have the right to refuse treatment, there must be a means for the same right to be exercised on behalf of incompetent patients.

The U.S. Supreme Court addressed this issue in the well-publicized *Cruzan* case.[55] In that case, the parents of a young woman in a persistent vegetative state since her injury in an automobile accident in 1983 requested court authorization to remove the gastrostomy tube through which their daughter received life-sustaining nutrition and hydration. The court recognized that a competent person has the right to refuse medical treament, but that an incompetent patient is unable to exercise such a right. A state has the right to set standards governing how this

---

[52]*White v. Chicago & N.W. Ry Co.,* 124 N.W. 309 (1910).

[53]*Georgia v. McAfee,* 385 S.E. 2d 651 (Ga. 1989) .

[54]*McKay v. Bergstedt,* 801 P.2d 617 (Nev. 1990).

[55]*Cruzan v. Director, Mo. Dep't. of Health,* 110 S.Ct. 2841 (1990).

right may be exercised on behalf of the incompetent patient and how to ensure that the decision respects as much as possible the wishes expressed by the patient while competent, the Court ruled.

Both the federal and state legislatures have responded to the need to formalize the decision-making process for competent and incompetent patients who are faced with life-sustaining treatment decisions. Every state now has some type of statute that regulates patients' right to stipulate, in advance of incompetency, what medical measures should be used to sustain their lives. Legislation at the federal level also imposes duties on health care providers to inform patients of their right to accept or refuse medical treatment.

Patient Self-Determination Act

Legislation requiring that all federally funded facilities inform patients of their rights under state law to accept or refuse medical treatment was enacted as part of the Omnibus Budget Reconciliation Act of 1990, more commonly referred to as the Patient Self-Determination Act (PSDA).[56] Since December 1, 1991, when the PSDA took effect, health care providers and institutions that receive Medicare or Medicaid funding have been required to inform patients of their legal rights to accept or refuse medical or surgical treatment and the right to formulate advance directives. "Advance directive" is defined as a written instruction, such as a living will or durable power of attorney for health care, recognized under state law and relating to the provision of medical care when the individual is incapacitated. The PSDA applies to hospitals, long-term care facilities, home health care agencies, hospice programs, and health maintenance organizations. Under the PSDA, each state must prepare a written description of the law in that state on advance directives and distribute this information to any individual admitted as an inpatient at a hospital, as a resident in a skilled nursing facility, or as an enrollee of a health maintenance organization and to recipients of home health care, personal care services, or hospice program services.

In accordance with the law, health care facilities must develop written policies requiring that patients receive legal information on the exercise of their rights as well as information about the policy itself. Written information distributed by the health care provider must have two components: (1) a summary of individual rights under state law and (2) the written policies of the provider itself as to implementation of those rights. The summary of state law ultimately should be furnished by the appropriate state agency to facilitate uniformity among institutions. The provider itself is required to draft a written policy and provide a copy of it to patients at the time of admission.

---

[56]P.L. 101-508, 104 Stat. 291 (1990), codified at 42 U.S.C. § 1395cc(f) (1993).

The PSDA requires that a patient's medical record indicates whether or not the individual has an advance directive, but does not specifically require that a copy of the directive be obtained and made part of the medical record. However, state law may otherwise impose this duty on attending physicians or hospitals, and Joint Commission standards state that an "advance directive is in the patient's medical record"[57] Hospitals therefore would be well-advised to require that the advance directive be made a part of the medical record, with provisions for confirming its continued validity upon any readmission or renewal of services.

The PSDA also requires that a facility include in its policy a means for ensuring compliance with the requirements of state law (either statutory or case law) on advance directives. As discussed in a subsequent section, state statutes frequently include model forms for both living wills and durable powers of attorney, but allow patients to use any written model that essentially contains the same information as the statutory one. This means that hospital policy specifically should delegate the responsibility to ensure that the forms in the medical record, to the extent that they are different from the relevant statutory model, comply with the requirements of state law with respect to wording, signatures, and other required information.

As mentioned earlier, the Joint Commission also has incorporated in its accreditation standards many of the duties imposed on hospitals by the Patient Self-Determination Act. A specific standard addresses the issues of patients' rights and requires that hospitals' policies describe the means by which those rights are protected and exercised.[58] A patient's rights as defined in the standard include the opportunity to create advance directives, access to information necessary to make informed decisions about medical treatment, and the right to participate in discussions of the ethical issues that may arise during the individual's care.[59] Advance directives must appear in the patient's medical record and be reviewed periodically with the patient or the surrogate decision maker.[60]

Living Will Legislation

The most widely available instrument for recording future health care-related decisions is the living will. The vast majority of states have enacted legislation recognizing the right of a competent adult to prepare a document providing direction as to medical care if the adult becomes incapacitated or otherwise unable to make decisions personally. Historically, living will legislation was

---

[57]*Accreditation Manual* (1994): Standard RI 1.1.3.2.3.

[58]*Id.*, Standard RI 1.1.

[59]*Id.*, Standard RI 1.1.3.

[60]*Id.*, Standard RI 1.1.3.2.3.

limited to directives for the treatment of terminal illness. There was some doubt as to whether a patient could use a living will as an instrument to request withholding or withdrawing of artificial nutrition. However, several states since have amended their living will laws so that this form of advance directive can be specifically applied if the patient is suffering from a terminal condition or is irreversibly unconscious.[61]

Living will legislation covers a variety of topics, including how to execute such a document, physician certification of terminal illness or irreversible coma, immunity from civil and criminal liability for providers who implement the decisions, and the right to transfer a patient to another facility if a provider cannot follow the directive for reasons of conscience. Although some state laws used to contain statutorily dictated wording for written directives, the trend has been away from mandating the contents of living wills toward requiring that they contain "substantially" or "essentially" the same information as the statutory model. North Carolina law states that the statutory form "is specifically determined to meet the [legislative] requirements," implying that other forms would be acceptable if they rigidly meet the same requirements.[62] West Virginia law states that a directive can be in "essentially" the same form as the one in the statute but may include other specific directions.[63] Arkansas provides that in the absence of knowledge to the contrary, a health care provider may presume that a declaration complies with the law and is valid.[64]

State legislation also specifies the formality with which the directive must be executed. All the acts require witnesses, and some disqualify certain people from being witnesses—such as, relatives, those who will inherit the estate, those who have claims against the estate, the attending physician, and employees of the physician or hospital. Normally, the qualifications of the witnesses are not of concern to the hospital or physician because the directive usually includes a certification by the witness that they are not disqualified.

State laws also specify the means to revoke a directive. Written revocations generally must meet minimal requirements; i.e., they must be signed, dated, and communicated to the attending physician. In most states, any verbal revocation is

---

[61]The terminology varies from state to state, with some statutes referring to "permanent unconscious condition" (Cal. Health & Safety Code § 7189 (1993)), "permanently unconscious" (Ark. Rev. Stat. § 20-17-201(11)(1993)), "irreversible coma" (N.M. Stat. Ann. § 24-7-2(B)(1993)), or "persistent vegetative state" (N.C. Gen. Stat. § 90-321(a)(4)(1993)). See also the Illinois Health Care Surrogate Act, which applies not only when a patient is terminally ill but also when a patient is permanently unconscious or suffering from an incurable or irreversible illness for which the application of life-sustaining treatment would impose an inhumane burden on the patient and provide only minimal medical benefits. 755 Ill. Comp. Stat. Ann. § § 40/1-40/55 (1993).

[62]N.C. Gen. Stat. § 90-321(1993).

[63]W.Va. Code § 16-30-3(e) (1993).

[64]Ark. Code Ann. § 20-17-211 (1993).

effective upon communication to the attending physician.[65] If a copy of the directive is in the medical record, and the hospital receives notice of revocation, a note should be entered on the declaration stating that the patient has revoked it. If the original directive is in the record, a patient cannot revoke it by physical destruction.

The effect of the directive also is defined in state law. The majority of statutes specify that any physician may decline to follow the directive but must make an effort to transfer the patient to a physician who will follow it.[66] Some states provide that a directive shall not apply while the patient is pregnant;[67] Texas includes a provision in its model form relating to the nonapplicability of a declaration if the patient is pregnant.[68]

In states that do not specify whether a directive is effective if the patient is pregnant at the time of implementation, the legal ramifications of withholding or terminating life-sustaining treatment for a pregnant patient are by no means clear. The right of a pregnant patient to refuse care for herself and consequently for her unborn child is a much-debated issue and hinges to a large extent on the evolving legal status of abortion. Institutions should seek direction from the courts before implementing a pregnant patient's directive to withhold or withdraw life-sustaining treatment if the fetus she is carrying is viable. In one case, the court allowed a hospital to perform a Caesarean section on a dying, mentally incompetent woman to save the life of a viable 26-week-old fetus.[69] How courts would respond to a similar situation if the fetus is not viable, however, is difficult to predict.

State legislation generally makes it a crime to interfere with the proper use of directive forms. Unauthorized cancellation or concealment of a directive in order to interfere with a patient's wish not to be treated generally is a misdemeanor. Falsification or forgery of a directive or withholding knowledge of revocation in order to cause actions contrary to the patient's wishes when those actions hasten death is a felony under state law.

Durable Power of Attorney

A power of attorney is a written document that authorizes an individual, as an agent, to perform certain acts on behalf of and according to the written directives of another—the person executing the document—from whom the agent obtains authority. The agent is called the attorney-in-fact and the person executing the

---

[65]See, e.g., Cal. Health & Safety Code § 7189(a) (1993), and W. Va. Code § 70.122.040 (1993).

[66]See, e.g., Tex. Health & Safety Code § 672.016 (1993); W.Va. Code § 16-30-71 (1993); Or. Rev. Stat. § 127.625 (1993) (physician must notify health care representative, who must make a reasonable effort to transfer the patient).

[67]See, e.g., Cal. Health & Safety Code § 7189.5 (1993); and Kan. Rev. Stat. § 65-28,103 (1992).

[68]See Tex. Health & Safety Code Ann., § 672.004 (1993).

[69]*In re A.C.* 533 A.2d 611 (D.C. 1987) .

document is called the principal. If a state law provides for a durable power of attorney, such as the Uniform Durable Power of Attorney Act, adopted by the vast majority of states,[70] the subsequent disability or incompetence of the principal does not affect the attorney-in-fact's authority.

Most durable power of attorney legislation is general in nature, however, and is not tailored to health care decision making. For this reason, the vast majority of states have gone further to provide for durable powers of attorney specifically for health care decisions. Under that type of legislation, the state authorizes the appointment of an individual who is specifically empowered to make personal health care-related decisions for another person in the event that the individual becomes incapacitated. Many state legislatures have provided model forms in their laws that include specific choices for the conditions under which life-sustaining treatment may be withdrawn.

For the power of attorney to have any legal effect, the principal must be mentally competent when executing it. The requirements governing witnesses and notarization of the instrument vary with state law. The validity of the power of attorney is governed by the law of the state in which the power is executed.

The exact wording of durable powers of attorney varies from state to state and like living wills is dictated largely by models contained in the statutes. In general, these documents grant agents full power and authority to make health care decisions for principals to the same extent as principals would themselves if they were competent. In exercising this authority, the agent must, to the extent possible, make decisions that are consistent with the principal's desires using the substituted judgment doctrine[71] or that are based on what the agent believes to be the principal's best interests.[72] The power of attorney can enumerate specifically the principal's desires as to different types of life-sustaining measures, admission or discharge from facilities, pain relief medication, and anatomical gifts. It also should allow the agent to gain access to the principal's medical records to be able to make informed decisions.

The principal should anticipate the possible resignation or inability of the attorney-in-fact to carry out these duties. The principal can provide for this circumstance by giving the attorney-in-fact power to appoint a substitute. Because of the personal nature of the attorney-in-fact's role, however, the principal may prefer to name an alternate with the durable power of attorney.

Of paramount importance is the actual determination of the principal's disability or incompetence. The durable power of attorney should state who will determine the principal's incompetence and set the standards to be used in

---

[70] 8 U.L.A. 74 (1982). All states have adopted this act except Georgia, Illinois, and Louisiana.

[71] See, e.g., Idaho Code § 39-4505 (1993).

[72] The American Bar Association, Commission on Legal Problems of the Elderly, has adopted a model Health Care Powers of Attorney containing this broad grant of authority.

making that determination. It is best for one or more physicians, named in the document or chosen according to a procedure established in the writing, to determine incompetence.[73] Disability and incompetence should be defined in the durable power of attorney and should be mutually acceptable to the principal and physicians involved. Copies of the durable power of attorney should be given to the attorney-in-fact, the principal's physician, and close family members. In accordance with Joint Commission standards, the document also should be included in the hospital medical record.

A competent principal can revoke the durable power of attorney at any time. The instrument also may be terminated if it contains an expiration clause. Some state legislatures stipulate a maximum duration for durable powers of attorney, providing that unless a shorter period is defined in the document, it will expire automatically at the end of a given number of years.[74] An expiration clause allows the principal periodically to reconsider the directives in the writing. Under the Uniform Durable Power of Attorney Act, a revocation is not effective until the attorney-in-fact has received notice of the revocation. In fact, if the attorney-in-fact states in an affidavit that he or she did not know the document had been revoked at the time of acting, the affidavit serves as conclusive proof of the nontermination of the power of attorney.

Health care providers view the durable power of attorney for health care as a more flexible instrument than a living will. The scope of a living will generally is limited to situations where the patient is either terminally ill or permanently unconscious. The power of attorney, on the other hand, can apply to a wider range of situations in which the patient is unable to communicate a choice regarding a health care decisison. In addition, the power of attorney allows the agent to make any decision regarding an incapacitated patient's health care and is not limited to specific life-sustaining measures.

Because of the lack of uniformity in state laws, it is possible that a valid power of attorney in one state may not be enforceable in other jurisdictions. Three elements must be present for the power of attorney to be enforced in another state: (1) The laws in the new jurisdiction must recognize the authority of a principal to grant an agent the power to make health care decisions. (2) The document must meet the procedural formalities imposed by the jurisdiction in which it is to be enforced. (3) It must be legally possible to exercise the agent's powers in the new jurisdiction. Problems can arise, for example, because state legislation sometimes prohibits specific categories of individuals from acting as agents, mandates the use of specific language in durable powers of attorney, or prohibits a surrogate decision maker from authorizing specific types of medical

---

[73]The ABA model suggests that incapacity should be determined by the agent and the attending physician.

[74]See, e.g., Cal. Civ. Code § 2436.5 (1993).

treatment. Health care providers specifically should seek legal counsel to determine the validity of an out-of-state power of attorney, and include such a requirement in their policies.

Autopsy Authorizations

Autopsies are the most frequent cause of litigation involving dead bodies and hospitals. Autopsies are performed primarily to determine the cause of a patient's death. This finding can be crucial in detecting crime or ruling out transmittable diseases that may be a threat to the public health. More frequently, the cause of death can determine whether death benefits are payable under insurance policies, Workers' Compensation laws, and other programs.

Community mores and religious beliefs long dictated respectful handling of dead bodies. Societal views have evolved now to the point that a substantial portion of the population recognizes the benefit of autopsies. Out of respect for those who continue to find them unacceptable, the law requires appropriate consent before an autopsy can be performed, except when one is needed to determine the cause of death for public policy purposes.

The consent to the autopsy, whether given by the decedent, by family members, or by other persons authorized to do so in the particular state, must be documented in the patient's medical record. A few states require that an autopsy be authorized in writing. Many states include telegrams and recorded telephone permissions as acceptable forms of authorization. Common law does not require that the authorization be documented in a particular way, so evidentiary considerations are the primary basis for deciding the appropriate form of consent. A written authorization or recorded telephone authorization obviously is the easiest to prove.

In *Lashbrook v. Barnes*,[75] the mother of the deceased claimed that, although she had signed an autopsy authorization, the body had been mutilated. The court quoted the authorization in its entirety and dismissed the suit against the physician. Because the authorization was in writing, the mother's consent was not an issue, and the court focused only on whether the autopsy had been performed in the usual manner. That case demonstrates the benefits of obtaining and including in the medical record written authorization for an autopsy.

HOSTILE PATIENTS

Hostile patients present problems for everyone in a health care facility. Whether the hostility arises from the patient's condition, general nature, or the

---

[75]437 S.W.2d 502 (Ky. 1969).

treatment received at the institution, an individual often is more inclined to take legal action if a problem in treatment actually occurs. Moreover, hostile patients may be less inclined to remember all the facts of a treatment situation or to view them in a light favorable to the hospital. Therefore, hospital staff members should take greater care in documenting hostile patients' treatment.

Practitioners should take a common-sense approach to such documentation. No special rules of law apply to records of hostile patients. If the patient is hostile, the hospital simply should take care to create a detailed medical record that leaves little ambiguity about the person's care. Practitioners should avoid making derogatory remarks about a hostile patient in the medical record. They add nothing to the ability of other practitioners to care for the patient, and the individual is likely to interpret them as further proof of the practitioners' bad faith. If hostility is clinically significant, it should be described in clinical terms in the medical record.

CELEBRITY PATIENTS

When patients who are subject to close scrutiny by news media are hospitalized for conditions that might be embarrassing for them, special care often must be taken to protect their confidentiality. While news media take an interest in patients who may have become newsworthy temporarily, they often use more aggressive tactics in obtaining information concerning celebrities. As a result, some hospitals have established special procedures for handling celebrity patient records.

As an extra precaution against unauthorized disclosure, some hospitals omit the patient's name from the record or use a code name that corresponds to a master code maintained by the medical records director and hospital chief executive officer. While this device may give added protection to the patient, it may conflict with state statutes and regulations and should be employed only with the advice of the institution's counsel. Some hospitals place the medical records of celebrity patients in a special secure file accessible only to the medical records director and other designated persons. This approach may not provide the same degree of protection as the former method, but it is not likely to violate record content requirements of state law. (For a more extensive discussion of media access to medical records, see Chapter 8, Invasion of Privacy.)

ADOPTION RECORDS

Medical records practitioners in health care institutions may not frequently encounter requests from individuals seeking to inspect a medical record where the request is either primarily or incidentally premised on a desire to obtain information about the natural parents of an individual who has been adopted (the "adoptee"). Parties to an adoption address such requests more frequently to either the agency that handled the adoption or the court that entered the adoption order. As infrequent as such requests may be, hospitals nonetheless may find it difficult to formulate an appropriate response because of the policy conflict between laws that permit patient access to medical records and adoption laws that typically require the sealing of court records to protect the privacy of the natural parents of the adoptee.

Most states have statutes or administrative regulations that permit patients to inspect their medical records. (See Chapter 5 for a more detailed discussion of the rules governing patients' access to medical records.) Some of this legislation is quite detailed,[76] while other states simply provide that patients may have access to their records upon request. In jurisdictions where statutes do not specifically grant patients the right to access their records, hospitals generally adopt guidelines and procedures that allow for access while respecting confidentiality. For the most part, however, general rules on patient access to medical records do not resolve the competing policy interests that arise when one of the parties to an adoption attempts to access either the original birth records or the medical records of the natural parents. As a result, courts frequently have intervened to resolve the problem, and many state legislatures have amended their adoption statutes to establish mutual consent adoption registries.

The problem presents several dimensions, the most significant of which are the following three:

1. Do the natural parents of the adoptee have and retain a right to inspect part or all of the adoptee's medical records?
2. Do the adopting parents of the adoptee require a right to inspect part or all of the adoptee's medical records?
3. Do adoptees ever acquire a right to inspect part or all of their medical records?

Adoption Laws and Confidentiality

Adoption laws and the rights of parties involved in such proceedings frequently have collided with laws governing the confidentiality of medical records. The history and fundamentals of adoption legislation explain the reasons for this conflict.

All fifty states have adoption laws that generally cover the adoption procedures, the rights of all parties, and the process by which an adoption is

---

[76]See, e.g., Cal. Health and Safety Code § 1795.12(b)(c) (1993).

accomplished. In almost all instances, some form of court action is involved. For years, the majority of states provided that the court records on adoption and the adoptee's original birth certificate could be sealed and made confidential by court order. Until the 1980s, moreover, most statutes prohibited access to adoption records unless a party, generally the adoptee, could demonstrate "good cause" to access the record based on medical or psychological needs.

Many individuals and adoptee advocacy organizations challenged the consitutional validity of those statutes. A principal claim of these organizations and individuals is that adequate medical and social history are so vital to the psychological well-being and health of adoptees and their offspring that their entitlement to this information constitutes a fundamental right.

In *In re Roger B.*,[77] for example, the plaintiff challenged the Illinois adoption statute, asserting that his status as an adult adoptee "who had feelings of inadequacy and uncertainty as to his background be permitted access to his adoption records, and that the statute was unconstitutional." The court upheld the statute and ruled that adoptees have no "fundamental right to examine [their] adoption records."[78] The court determined that confidentiality was required to protect the privacy of both the natural and the adopting parents, and that the need to do so does not disappear when the adoptee reaches adulthood.

In another case,[79] the plaintiffs challenged the constitutionality of a New Jersey statute that requires the state registrar to place under seal the original birth certificate of any child who is adopted, thereby concealing the identity of the natural parents. The statute provides that the seal of secrecy may be broken only upon the order of a court for good cause shown. The plaintiffs argued that the statute abridged their right to privacy and their right to receive information and denied them equal protection of the law.

The court rejected all of the plaintiffs' constitutional challenges, and in doing so discussed the purpose of the New Jersey Adoption Act—the promotion of "policies and procedures socially necessary and desirable for the protection not only of the child placed for adoption but also for the natural and adopting parents."[80] If this information is kept confidential, all three parties are helped, the court said: (1) The natural parents will place the child with a reputable agency because they know their actions and motivations will not become public. (2) The adoptive parents may raise the child without fear of interference from the natural parents and without fear that the birth status of an illegitimate child will be revealed. (3) The child is protected from the stigma of illegitimacy, which, although fading in modern society, still may exist.

---

[77]418 N.E.2d 751 (Ill. 1981).

[78]*Id.* at 757.

[79]*Mills v. Camden Dept. of Vital Statistics*, 372 A.2d 646 (N.J. 1977).

[80]*Id.* at 649.

More recently, the Fifth Circuit dismissed constitutional challenges to the Texas adoption statute, that alleged that adoptive parents had been denied access to many of the facts essential "to the care and treatment of children with special needs, including facts about the existence or extent of physical, sexual, and emotional abuse, mental and physical handicaps, and medical needs of the children; and other vital information, such as the social, genetic, and medical history of the biological parents and the children's siblings."[81] The parents argued that the practice of providing incomplete information about the children's backgrounds amounted to government interference in their decision to adopt and violated their right to "informed" decision making on behalf of their family. The court concluded that the parents had failed to demonstrate that the state had violated any constitutional right in proceeding the way it did.

Access to Adoption Records under State Statutes

Significant reform of adoption legislation occurred in most states during the 1980s in response to a growing recognition of the need to give adoptees and their adoptive parents greater access to background information. These reform initiatives have focused on providing adoptive and prospective adoptive parents access to health-related information at the time of the placement for adoption. Mandatory disclosure not only has answered the need for such information before an adoption is finalized, in particular for adoptive parents; it also has eliminated the necessity of attempting to locate and access such information many years after it was compiled. The majority of state laws now require that certain background information be provided to adoptive parents when the child is placed for adoption.[82]

In some states, however, the decision as to whether to disclose information is left to the discretion of the state or private adoption agency.[83] In South Carolina, for example, the release of nonidentifying health information to adoptive parents, biological parents, or adoptees is left to the sole discretion of the chief executive officer of the agency if that individual perceives that the release would serve the best interests of the persons concerned.[84] Some states have chosen to leave the decision to the judiciary, requiring a court order before information can be released.[85]

Frequently, however, mandatory disclosure provisions do not apply in the same manner to all adoptions within a state. Oklahoma's disclosure statute

---

[81]*Griffith v. Johnston*, 899 F.2d 1427 (5th Cir. 1990), at 1433.

[82]See, e.g., Ala. Code § 26-10A-31 (1993); Colo. Rev. Stat. § 19-5-207 (1993); Ga. Code Ann. § 19-8-23 (1993); Haw. Rev. Stat. § 578-14.5 (1993).

[83]See Del. Code Ann., tit. 13, § 924 (1993); N.M. Stat. Ann. § 32A-5-40 (1993); Okla. Stat. Ann., tit. 10, § 57 (1992).

[84]S.C. Code Ann. § 20-7-1780 (1991).

[85]D.C. Code Ann. § 16-311 (1993).

allows state or private adoption agencies to release the medical history of the child, the biological parents, and the grandparents to prospective adoptive parents, but does not grant the same permission to attorneys who handle private placement adoptions, although such adoptions are authorized under state law.[86] Other states impose similar disclosure restrictions on private placement adoptions.[87] In several states, adoptions by stepparents or relatives are not covered by the mandatory disclosure of medical and genetic background information.[88]

For adoptions that occurred before mandatory disclosure rules came into effect, the majority of state statutes specifically authorize the direct disclosure of health-related information to adult adoptees, although some laws do not impose any age restriction on an adoptee's right of access.[89] For example, the Wisconsin statute reads:

> The department shall release the medical information under sub. (2) to any of the following persons upon request:
> 1. An individual or adoptee 18 years of age or older.
> 2. An adoptive parent of an adoptee.
> 3. The guardian or legal custodian of an individual or adoptee.
> 4. The offspring of an individual or adoptee if the requester is 18 years of age or older.[90]

In some jurisdictions, adoption legislation contains no provision for disclosure of medical or social background information to the adoptee.[91] Other states allow the release of nonidentifying medical or social information to adoptees at agency discretion or upon court order.[92]

Access to Adoption Records by Court Order

For many years, most state laws permitted adoptees, or other parties, to access court adoption records, including any medical record information they contain, if the individual could demonstrate "good cause." Although most states no longer require court authorization, several still do. Courts have intervened on numerous occasions to determine whether "good cause" for the release of

---

[86]Okla. Stat. Ann., tit. 10, § 57 (1992).

[87]See Ga. Code Ann. § 19-8-23 (1993); 750 Ill. Comp. Stat. Ann. § 50/18.4 (1993).

[88]Tex. Fam. Code Ann. § 16.032 (1993).

[89]See Conn. Gen. Stat. § 45a-746(1993) (adult); 750 Ill. Comp. Stat. Ann. § 50/18.4 (1993) (18 or older); N.D. Cent. Code § 14-15-16 (1993) (adult); Or. Rev. Stat. § 109.342 (1991) (age of majority); Wis. Stat. § 48.432(3)(a)(1) (1991-1992)(18 or older). But see Neb. Rev. Stat. § 43-146.02 (1992) (no age provision) and Vt. Stat. Ann., tit. 15, § 461(a)(1991) (no age restriction).

[90]See Wis. Stat. § 48.432(3) (1991-1992).

[91]For example, Idaho, New Jersey, Rhode Island, Virginia.

[92]See, e.g., Tenn. Code Ann. § 36-1-131(a) (1993).

adoption records exists, focusing primarily on either the medical or psychological need for such information.[93]

Medical Needs

A medical necessity generally satisfies the "good cause" requirement of many statutes. In *Chattman v. Bennett*,[94] for example, the court held that a female adoptee who was considering having children could have access to any medical reports or related matter in the court records of her adoption. Her concern that some genetic or hereditary factor in her background might foretell a medical problem for any children constituted "good cause." Although the court provided the plaintiff with medical information relating to possible genetic or hereditary conditions, it ordered the deletion of any nonpertinent information, including the names of the natural parents.

To satisfy the "good cause" requirement of most statutes, the need to obtain information on hereditary or genetic diseases had to be supported with detailed descriptions. In a New York case,[95] an adoptee sought the medical histories of his natural parents and their ancestors to assist his physician in diagnosing and preventing degenerative diseases. The plaintiff's physician's evidence that "the urgency of some ailments (e.g., cardiac) do not permit for court petitions upon attack's unexpected occurrence, and any time delay might well prove fatal or seriously disabling to the patient" did not satisfy the "good cause" requirement, the court found. In another New York case,[96] an adoptee who was suffering from a heart condition sought genetic information that would assist in evaluating and treating his condition. In addition, he needed some medical history about his biological parents to be recertified as a pilot. The court ruled that the adoptee's need for information did not automatically entitle him to access to the adoption record, and that a more detailed inquiry was needed.

Psychological Needs

Although there exists a wide disparity in how courts have exercised the judicial discretion they possess in this area, they generally have been less sympathetic to adoptees' psychological needs for such information than to their medical needs. Courts frequently are suspicious that psychological need is mere

---

[93]In Louisiana, adopted children retain the right to inherit from their natural parents and other blood relatives. Louisiana courts therefore may consider the right of an adoptee to inherit as a good cause, or "compelling necessity," for disclosure of adoption records.

[94]93 N.Y.S.2d 768 (App. Div. 1977).

[95]444 F. Supp. 170 (E.D.N.Y. 1978).

[96]*Golan v. Louis Wise Serv.*, 514 N.Y.S.2d 682 (Ct. App. 1987).

curiosity, rejecting a psychological need to know without proof of some serious psychological disorder. In one case,[97] the adoptee sought the records of both her adoption and the sealed Board of Health records on her birth. She asserted that because she did not know who her natural parents were, she was experiencing psychological problems that impaired her musical skills, was fearful of entering into an incestuous marriage, and was unable to establish her religious faith. The court held that the plaintiff had only demonstrated curiosity about the identity of her natural parents, and curiosity would not satisfy the good cause requirement.

Similarly, the Rhode Island Supreme Court rejected an adoptee's attempt to access her adoption records, finding that her curiosity and desire to discover her natural identity were insufficient to establish good cause for disclosure of adoption records.[98] The adoptee's need to obtain information did not arise from any mental or physical ailments she suffered as a result of not knowing her true identity, the court concluded. In another case, a court denied access to an adoptee with a severe depressive illness in spite of the fact that her psychiatrist recommended that it would benefit her treatment.[99] In New Jersey, however, a court ruled that a psychological need to know may suffice to prove good cause, and that a request for medical or other types of background information should be granted unless there are compelling reasons to withhold the information.[100]

Guidelines for Medical Record Practitioners

State legislation, for the most part, will dictate the approach for medical records practitioners in responding to requests to inspect the birth records of adoptees. Obviously such requests will be rare, primarily because adoptees and their adopting parents seldom possess the information that would be necessary to locate the adoptee's birth record. Circumstances will arise, however, in which the adoptee or the adoptive parent possesses sufficient information to permit medical records practitioners to locate the adoptee's birth records. When confronted with such a request, the medical records practitioner should consider the following guidelines:

- Natural parents of a child placed for adoption relinquish their right to inspect their child's medical record after the person has been adopted because all parental rights with respect to that child have been terminated.

- Adoptive parents acquire all parental rights with respect to the adoptee following formal adoption, including, in most states, the right to inspect the

---

[97]*In re Linda M.*, 409 N.Y.S.2d 638 (N.Y. Surr. Ct. 1978).

[98]*In re Assalone*, 512 A.2d 1383 (R.I. 1986).

[99]See *In re Dixon*, 323 N.W.2d 549 (Mich. Ct. App. 1982).

[100]See *Mills v. Atlantic City Dep't. of Vital Statistics*, 372 A.2d 646 (N.J. 1977).

adoptee's medical records until the adoptee attains the age of majority. However, adoptive parents should not be permitted to inspect any information in the adoptee's birth record that, for example, contains information identifying the adoptee's natural parents, in deference to the natural parents' legitimate privacy interests. Medical records practitioners should exclude all such identifying information pertaining to the natural parents before making the adoptee's medical record available to the adoptive parents for inspection.

- Adoptees have the right to inspect their medical records on reaching the age of majority, subject to the same limitations with respect to identifying information relating to the adoptee's natural parents set forth in the preceding paragraph addressing the inspection rights of adoptive parents.

REFUSAL TO ACCEPT OUTSIDE TEST REPORTS

At numerous hospitals, physician medical staff members are requesting that they be permitted to use test reports from outside clinical laboratories and diagnostic centers to satisfy preadmission or preoperative test requirements and that their institutions permit them to enter these reports in the hospitals' medical records. In some instances, the physicians own the outside facility that would conduct the test and produce the report.[101] Some physicians have established small laboratories or diagnostic facilities in their professional offices and want to conduct preadmission and preoperative tests there as part of the patients' routine office visits. Note, however, that the number of physicians' office laboratories have decreased since the Clinical Laboratory Improvement Amendments of 1984 (CLIA 188)[102] imposed a federal regulatory scheme on such laboratories. The issue these requests present to a hospital is whether it may exclude from its medical records the reports of laboratory and diagnostic testing performed by outside facilities. This section discusses the serious legal questions that arise in the consideration of this issue.

Antitrust Issues

Potential antitrust problems arise when a hospital proposes to exclude all outside test results from its medical records. Two antitrust theories, the tying

---

[101]Note, however, that federal legislation prohibits physicians or their immediate families from referring their Medicare or Medicaid patients to a clinical laboratory in which the physician or his immediate family has an investment interest or compensation arrangement with the provider. More recently, Congress expanded that prohibition to other categories, including radiology. See Omnibus Reconciliation Act of 1993, §§ 13562 and 13624.

[102]P.L. No. 101-578 (1988).

theory and the monopolization theory, can create substantial risk for the hospital if it adopts such a policy. As with most antitrust problems, the facts are critical to the analysis. Factual issues that are important to a consideration of a restrictive policy include the following:

- Does the hospital have market power over the provision of hospital services in the relevant geographic area?
- What quality standards will the outside diagnostic facility be required to meet, and will they be substantially similar to the hospital's standards for quality of test results?
- What share of the market does the hospital have now for testing its patients?
- What evidence of anticompetitive intent on the part of the hospital or the physicians would be found if an antitrust case were to be filed?

Although the actual facts of hospitals' efforts to establish restrictive policies involving outside test reports will vary in each case, the facts will determine the outcome of the antitrust analysis.

Tying Analysis, Sherman Act, Section I

Under Section 1 of the Sherman Act,[103] the tying of two products traditionally has been considered a per se antitrust offense. The tying offense can occur when competition in the tied product market is foreclosed by exercising power in the market for the tying product. The prohibition against tying has been applied to hospitals.[104] The first element of a tying offense requires two separate products—a tying product and a tied product. Separate market demand for each product must exist. When a hospital wishes to restrict outside diagnostic test reports from its medical records, two separate products are involved: hospital services (the tying product) and diagnostic testing (the tied products).[105] For most hospitals, diagnostic tests probably would be found to be a separate product market from hospital care. The "tying" product, hospital services, is considered for this purpose to be all hospital services except diagnostic tests performed by the hospital for its patients. The "tied" product market would include all diagnostic testing, including preadmission testing later repeated by the hospital, diagnostic tests performed on hospital outpatients, and tests sent by the hospital to outside facilities.

The second element of the test for unlawful tying is the conditioning of one service on the purchase of another. That is what a hospital is trying to do in

---

[103] 15 U.S.C § 1.

[104] See, e.g., *Jefferson Parish Hosp. Dist. No. 2 v. Hyde*, 466 U.S. 2 (1984).

[105] In this section, the term "diagnostic tests" refers to laboratory testing, radiology testing, and EKG interpretations.

establishing a prohibition against outside diagnostic test reports: to make other hospital services available only if diagnostic services also are purchased from the hospital.

The third element of a tying offense requires that the amount of commerce affected in the tied product is "not insubstantial." Courts have treated dollar volumes as low as $50,000 as "not insubstantial."[106] If the threat of the outside diagnostic testing facility is significant enough for a hospital to be concerned about the competition, the dollar amount for a finding of substantial commerce in the tied product is likely to be met.

The final element in the tying test is economic power in the tying product market, or "market power." Market power is defined as the ability to force a purchaser to do something it would not do in a competitive market.[107] That power could be derived from having a large market share or a unique product that competitors cannot offer. Definitions of geographic markets in the hospital industry in recent court cases are critical to findings with respect to market power. The courts define the relevant geographic market according to the facts of each case. Depending on the facts, therefore, a hospital's power in a particular market will vary according to how large or small the court finds the market to be.

If a hospital has no market power in the relevant geographic market (as that market may be determined by a court), a possible tying claim would be asserted under the rule of reason standard, rather than under a per se rule. The rule of reason standard is a less stringent test under antitrust law. Under that approach, the hospital would have the opportunity to present evidence as to the justifications for its prohibition of outside test results, including a quality-of-care rationale. Any anticompetitive intent on its part would become more significant. The usefulness of the quality-of-care defense will depend in large measure on whether a hospital can show that its restrictive policy is related to the inability of outside facilities to provide tests of quality the same as or better than those the hospital provides.

If the outside laboratory meets licensure requirements under state law, CLIA requirements under federal law, and meets applicable laboratory accreditation standards, or meets the same standards as other laboratories such as the large commercial clinical laboratories whose test results the hospital will accept, the hospital may be unable to justify the prohibition against inclusion of outside laboratory test results in its medical records based on a quality-of-care defense. That certainly will be true if no factual record exists of reduced quality in test reports prepared by the outside laboratory.

---

[106]See *United States v. Loew's Inc.,* 371 U.S. 38 (1962).

[107]Note 104, *supra,* at 13-14.

While radiology and EKG analyses are not subject to separate licensing standards in most states, a hospital may be able to demonstrate that it historically has required physicians with specific qualifications to analyze these diagnostic tests, particularly if the rule is based on applicable hospital accreditation and state licensing requirements. The hospital may continue to require these quality controls for radiology and EKG tests performed by outside facilities. If it documents poor quality results from a specific outside source, exclusion of outside test results based on a quality-of-care argument may be possible.

If the hospital adopts a policy containing a blanket exclusion of outside test results, it must be certain that its motivation is not anticompetitive and that no evidence exists that would reflect a concern about the competitive effect of the outside diagnostic center on the institution's financial performance. For example, if a hospital accepted the reports of other outside laboratories but excluded reports from a laboratory owned by physicians, the court might find that the hospital had an anticompetitive motive. A plaintiff could use any unprivileged conversations between hospital management and others concerning the hospital's anticompetitive thinking as proof of anticompetitive motive in the exclusionary policy.

Given the complexity of the possible facts in each case, therefore, it remains uncertain whether a blanket prohibition against the inclusion of outside test results in hospital medical records could be supported under the rule of reason analysis.

Monopolization Theory, Sherman Act, Section 2

The monopolization theory requires a showing of willful monopolization or willful maintenance of an existing monopoly and antitrust injury suffered as a result.[108] Monopoly power consists of "power to control prices or exclude competition" in the relevant market.[109] The "relevant market" under the monopolization theory might not be the same as the "relevant market" used under the tying theory. Under a monopolization theory, the focal point would be the market for diagnostic services performed for hospital patients.

Most hospitals actually perform most of the tests included in their patients' medical records. It is likely, therefore, that those hospitals would be found to have market power in the diagnostic services market. A competitor could show that a blanket prohibition on inclusion of outside reports in medical records is intended to allow the hospital to use its existing market power to create barriers to the entry of additional competitors for diagnostic service.

Where a physician-owned diagnostic center may adversely affect a hospital's financial performance significantly, it is likely that proof of the hospital's

---

[108] 15 U.S.C. § 2; *United States v. Grinnell*, 384 U.S. 563 (1966).

[109] *Id.* at 571; *Bhan v. NME Hospitals Inc.*, 669 F. Supp. 998 (E.D. Cal. 1987).

anticompetitive intent (or intentional monopolization) would be revealed during litigation. Anticompetitive intent could be inferred based on when the hospital adopts its restrictive policy. Unprivileged conversations between the hospital and third parties or documents also may suggest anticompetitive intent. The lack of any specific history of poor quality test results from the outside diagnostic facility also would suggest anticompetitive intent.

Antitrust injury could be shown if a hospital competitor could demonstrate that it was injured by the hospital's exclusionary conduct, and that the conduct was motivated by anticompetitive intent. If the competitor's ability to enter the market were reduced due to the hospital's refusal to include the diagnostic facility test reports in hospital medical records, it is likely that the competitor could show economic harm resulting from the hospital's conduct. Substantial antitrust risks thus may arise if a hospital adopts a blanket policy prohibiting the inclusion of outside test results in its medical records. This is so whether the question is approached as a tying question under Sherman Act Section 1 or under a monopolization theory pursuant to Sherman Act Section 2. However, careful factual research, particularly of the relevant geographic market for the provision of hospital services and possibly of the market for diagnostic services, could provide a more optimistic prognosis in some cases. A conservative approach suggests that a blanket prohibition on outside test results can create the risk that potential competitors may have sufficient basis for at least a prima facie claim of antitrust violation.

Other less restrictive alternatives such as the imposition of strict guidelines for acceptable outside testing may be appropriate and may help avoid exposure to antitrust liability or the expense of antitrust litigation. Those guidelines should be uniform for all outside facilities whose test reports are included in the medical records. For example, outside laboratories could be required to meet the standards for a particular class of licensed laboratories under applicable state licensing laws, assuming that this requirement also is met by any other laboratories whose results would be included in medical records. The guidelines should be clearly related to quality control.

Licensure and Accreditation Issues

The Joint Commission standards require that a hospital provide for the prompt performance of adequate testing, either on site or in a reference/contract laboratory.[110] When outside laboratories are used for testing hospital patients, the

---

[110]See *Accreditation Manual for Hospitals*, (1994): Standards PA, 1.1, 1.1.1 and *Accreditation Manual for Pathology and Clinical Laboratory Services*, (1993): Standard PA 1. Standard PA 1.1.1 states that "all laboratory testing done while the patient is under the care of the organization and of a member of the medical staff is done in the organization's laboratories (including the central laboratory and any ancillary, near-patient-testing, and point-of-care-testing laboratories) or in approved reference laboratories."

Joint Commission requires that the director of pathology and clinical laboratory services recommend reference laboratory services to the medical staff for acceptance.[111] If the hospital does not have centralized pathology and clinical laboratory services, the medical staff must establish a mechanism to identify acceptable reference and/or contract laboratory services.[112] Reference and contract laboratories must meet applicable federal standards for clinical laboratories.[113] The name of the laboratory performing the test must be included in the report in the patient's clinical record.[114]

The Joint Commission also imposes standards on the use of outside radiology sources. The facility must establish a means for providing radiation oncology services when they are not provided directly by the hospital.[115] When those services are provided outside the hospital, the off-site source must meet Joint Commission standards for radiation oncology services.[116] Authenticated reports of services are entered in the patient's medical record.[117]

Some licensing acts also impose controls on the use of outside laboratories for testing of hospital patients. In Illinois, a hospital may use outside laboratories only if the following conditions are met:

- The outside laboratory is either part of a hospital licensed under the Illinois Hospital Licensing Act or approved to provide these services as a laboratory under the Illinois Clinical Laboratory Act.
- The original report from the outside laboratory is contained in the medical record.
- The conditions, procedures, and availability of examinations performed in the outside laboratory are in writing and available in the hospital.[118]

Quality assurance concerns appear to be the primary motivation for the regulations imposed by hospital licensing acts and the Joint Commission on the use of outside sources for laboratory and radiology testing of hospital patients. Inaccurate test reports from any outside sources that are incorporated into the patient's medical record and that could form the basis of treatment decisions create quality assurance and risk management concerns for the hospital. The same concerns as to the use of outside laboratory and radiology testing for hospital patients could justify a hospital's decision to regulate the use of such

---

[111]*Accreditation Manual for Hospitals* (1994): Standard PA 1.1.2.

[112]*Id.*, Standard PA 1.1.2.1.

[113]*Id.*, Standard PA 1.1.2.2.

[114]*Accreditation Manual for Pathology and Clinical Laboratory Services* (1993): Standard PA 4.1.1.

[115]*Accreditation Manual for Hospitals* (1994): Standard RA 1.4.

[116]*Id.*, Standard RA 1.5.

[117]*Id.*, Standard RA 3.3.

[118] Ill. Admin. Code, tit. 77. § 250.510(b).

tests for persons who were not hospital patients at the time they were tested (e.g., to satisfy preadmission and preoperative testing requirements).

In formulating a policy on outside testing sources, therefore, a hospital should assess the risk and likelihood of poor quality performance by outside testing sources as well as the ease of monitoring those sources' compliance with quality assurance standards of the hospital. If the hospital can demonstrate that quality assurance is a real concern, it may exclude outside test reports from its medical records and prohibit their use to meet preadmission or preoperative testing requirements unless the outside source is recommended by the relevant department head, approved by the medical staff, and complies with the state's hospital licensing act, Joint Commission standards, and other reasonable quality assurance standards of the hospital. If the hospital determines that quality assurance presents no basis on which to exclude outside test reports, it should require that the original report from the outside facility be placed in the hospital's medical records, the name of the outside source be placed in the report, and the outside source meet the other relevant licensing and accreditation requirements.

Medicare/Medicaid Issues

The Medicare program does not require or prohibit the inclusion of outside laboratory or diagnostic test reports in hospital patient records. Medicare conditions of participation specify that hospital medical records must contain information to justify admission and continued hospitalization, support the diagnosis, and describe the patient's progress.[119] They also require entries to be authenticated promptly by the person responsible for ordering, providing, or evaluating the service furnished.[120] Medicare requires hospitals to ensure that all laboratory services provided to their patients are performed in Medicare-approved facilities.[121] A hospital, therefore, could exclude laboratory test results from sources that do not meet Medicare requirements but probably could not exclude authenticated laboratory test results from Medicare-approved laboratories. Medicare provides no basis for excluding authenticated radiology and EKG test results from outside laboratories. A hospital can require, however, that any diagnostic services provided to its patients meet applicable Medicare conditions of participation.

Medicaid reimbursement is a creature of state law, and the rules on the reimbursement of diagnostic tests performed outside of a hospital will vary with each state's Medicaid program. As a general rule, however, the principles discussed in connection with Medicare reimbursement also apply in most

---

[119]42 CFR § 482.24 (1993).

[120]*Id.*

[121]42 CFR § 482.27 (1993).

Medicaid reimbursement situations. Hospitals considering establishing a restrictive policy on outside laboratory and diagnostic test reports should analyze the applicable Medicaid law and regulations of their respective states as part of their evaluation of the policy.

Common Law Issues

General principles of hospital and physician liability offer no specific guidance concerning whether a hospital may adopt a medical records policy that excludes outside test reports. Therefore, a hospital must determine whether it is reasonable for a physician to rely on the results of outside tests and whether it is reasonable for a hospital to permit such reliance by allowing outside test results to be included in its medical records. Hospitals and physicians must observe the applicable standards of care required of them.

A physician or hospital may be required by applicable standards of care to repeat tests that were done outside the hospital when the patient's condition has altered since the prior tests were performed, when the diagnosis conflicts with another physician's diagnosis, or when it may be beneficial to have the test repeated or interpreted by a physician with greater specialized knowledge. A hospital probably would not violate applicable standards of care by permitting inclusion of test results from outside sources that meet appropriate quality assurance standards so long as the physician retains the ability to repeat tests, if necessary. Case law offers no guidance as to whether excluding outside test reports and requiring that all tests performed outside the hospital be repeated in the hospital violate applicable standards of care.

DISPOSITION OF RECORDS IN A CHANGE OF OWNER OR CLOSURE

When a hospital undergoes a change in ownership or closes, its obligation to maintain the safety and confidentiality of its patient records continues. The procedures for handling patient records in such situations is governed primarily by state law and regulations, which vary across the country. There are no guidelines addressing the issue published by any national professional organization such as the American Hospital Association; however, some overall recommendations can be drawn from the various state laws. Under many state laws, a hospital planning to change ownership or to close must notify the state department of health or other licensing agency of its intentions.[122] It also should make

---

[122]See Ill. Admin. Code, tit. 77, § 250.120(f) (1993).

arrangements for safekeeping its records and should inform the licensing agency of its plans. There are several ways for a hospital to handle the disposition of its records, depending on whether a change of ownership or closure is involved.

When ownership changes and the facility remains open to patients, custody of the records should be transferred to the new governing body and the files should remain stored at the hospital. In some states, this arrangement is required by law.[123] In California, for example, before the change in ownership occurs, both parties must submit written documentation informing the Department of Health Services that the newly licensed facility will take custody of the prior licensed facility's patient records, or that some other arrangement has been made whereby the records remain available to both parties and other authorized persons.[124] Similarly, Washington requires that patient records, registers, indexes, and analyses of hospital services be kept in the hospital building and maintained by the new owner in accordance with the law.[125] A similar procedure should be followed in jurisdictions that do not have such laws.

When a hospital closes, the records usually must be transferred to another location. Most state laws do not specify where the records should be kept; however, they require the hospital to notify the licensing agency in writing about the arrangements made for safekeeping the records.[126] This notification should include the location of the storage facility and the name of the person acting as custodian.[127] In many states the licensing agency will accept custody of the records after a hospital closes; in fact, a few states require the hospital to index the records and deliver them to the agency for safekeeping.[128] Other states encourage the hospital to transfer its records to another hospital in the area.[129] Nebraska requires the closing hospital to transfer records to the licensed facility to which the patient is transferred; otherwise the disposing hospital should dispose of all remaining records by shredding, mutilation, burning, or other equally effective protective measure.[130] Utah regulations suggest returning the records to the attending physician if that person still is in the community.[131] Where no other facility is located nearby (for example, in very rural areas) and no physician wants to keep the records, the files might be stored at the closest government office of any kind or at a law firm.

---

[123]See, e.g., Or. Admin. R. § 333-505-50(14) (1990); S.C.Code Regs. r. 61-16 § 601.7(c)(1992).

[124]Cal. Code Regs., tit. 22 § 22-70751(e)(1993).

[125]Wash. Admin. Code § 246-318-440-(11)(d) (1990).

[126]See, e.g., Kan. Admin. Regs. § 28-34-9a(d)(2)(1992); N.J. Admin. Code, tit. 8, § 43G-15.1(c)(1993).

[127]See, e.g., Texas Admin. Code § 1-22.1.6 (1989).

[128]See, e.g., Tenn. Code Ann. § 68-11-308 (Supp. 1993).

[129]See, e.g., Indiana Admin. Code, tit. 410, § 15-1-9(2)(b)(2)I(1992); Miss. Code Ann. § 41-9-79 (1993).

[130]Neb. R. & Regs., tit. 175, ch. 9 § 003.04A6 (1983).

[131]Utah Admin. R. 432-100-7.406(D) (1993).

In general, the closing hospital must notify the licensing agency of its arrangements for recordkeeping before the closing is completed. Illinois requires at least 90 days' notice.[132] California requires only 48 hours.[133] In Washington, the Department of Health must approve the planned arrangements ahead of time.[134] In addition, the closing hospital should notify former patients as to how to obtain access to their records should the need arise.[135]

Once the records of a closed hospital are moved, they must be preserved safely for some time. In Pennsylvania, a special law requires that records be stored at least five years after the hospital discontinues its operations. After that time, a hospital wishing to destroy any remaining records may do so after notifying the public and providing opportunity for patients to claim their files.[136] In Tennessee, records may be destroyed ten years after the hospital closes.[137] Most state laws, however, do not address the issue of record retention when a hospital closes. In the absence of legal guidance or contractual obligations on record retention, a hospital should make arrangements to retain the records for at least as long as required by its record retention policy.

Special issues arise for facilities covered by the Confidentiality of Alcohol and Drug Abuse Patient Records regulations.[138] If a program covering these federal regulations is "taken over or acquired" by another program, it must notify its patients of the change in ownership and obtain written consent to transfer custody of the records to the new owner or another program designated by the patient.[139] In the absence of such consent, the program must delete all patient identifying information from the records or destroy them.[140] This provision applies regardless of whether the physical site of the program changes or remains the same after the ownership change. Patients who refuse consent to transfer their records to the acquiring program or some other facility must withdraw from treatment. The original program then may edit or destroy the records pursuant to the regulations unless another legal requirement directs the facilities to preserve the records for some additional period of time.[141]

---

[132]77 Ill. Admin. Code, tit. 77, ch. I § 250.120(k) (1993).

[133] Cal. Code Regs., tit. 22, § 70751(d) (1993). See also, Utah Admin. R 432-100-7.406(D)(1)(1993) (requiring notice within three business days of closure).

[134]Wash. Admin. Code § 246-138-440(11)(e) (1990).

[135]See, e.g., Colo. Dept. of Health Standards for General Hospitals, ch. IV § 4.2.2 (1993); Utah Admin. R 432-100-7.406(D)(2) (1993).

[136]Pa. Admin. Code § 115.23(c) (1993).

[137]Tenn. Hospitals Rules & Regs. § 1200-8-4-.03-(1)(F)2 (1986).

[138]42 C.F.R. §§ 2.1 et. seq. (1992).

[139]42 C.F.R. § 2.19(a)(1) (1992).

[140]*Id.*

[141]42 C.F.R. §§ 2.19(a)(1) and (2) (1992).

The obligation to obtain consent from every patient may be burdensome for the facility; however, the Department of Health and Human Services (HHS) has determined that the burden is outweighed by the public policy to protect the confidentiality of substance abuse patients' records. When a substance abuse treatment program completely discontinues operations, it must destroy all medical records unless any patients consent to transferring their records to another program, or a different law requires the records to be maintained.[142] Records kept pursuant to another legal requirement must be sealed and labeled.[143] According to HHS, this other legal requirement may be a state law governing the disposition of medical records during a closure or change in ownership, or the applicable statute of limitations for malpractice claims.

When the retention period expires, the federal regulations authorize destruction of the records.[144] The federal rules do not require the program to notify patients before destroying their records; however, other laws may do so. Hospitals should work closely with the state licensing agency when arranging for the preservation of medical records upon change in ownership or closure. Although the state laws governing this area are not specific, the licensing agency is likely to provide guidance for handling records in a manner that preserves confidentiality and ensures the availability of the records for access by patients. Facilities subject to the federal Confidentiality of Alcohol and Drug Abuse Patient Records regulations must be sure to follow the applicable requirements of that law as well.

---

[142] 42 C.F.R § 2.19(a)(2) (1992).
[143] 42 C.F.R § 2.19(b)(1) (1992).
[144] 42 C.F.R § 2.19(b)(2) (1992).

4

AIDS Patients' Records

INTRODUCTION

One of the more significant special problems in medical record management is acquired immunodeficiency syndrome (AIDS) or human immunodeficiency virus (HIV) positive patient records. The issues presented by these records continue to complicate the operation of health institutions' medical record departments, particularly with respect to special confidentiality and reporting provisions. The complexity and variety of the laws governing these records can interfere with the ability of record managers to cope with the demands of government agencies, researchers, hospital administrators, and the patients themselves. It is important, therefore, for medical records administrators to understand the laws applicable to such records and to keep abreast of legal developments as they occur.

Most states impose a duty on physicians and/or hospitals to report all cases of "contagious," "infectious," or "sexually transmitted" diseases to the department of health. The statutory or regulatory definitions of reportable diseases typically include AIDS, as all states must report AIDS cases to the federal Centers for Disease Control (CDC). Some jurisdictions also require reporting of AIDS-Related Complex (ARC) and HIV diagnoses to the state department of health. Several states have special reporting laws for AIDS and related conditions in addition to their general reporting laws.

In conjunction with a reporting requirement, most statutes or regulations also contain a confidentiality provision prohibiting the attending physician and hospital from releasing medical information to persons other than the patient and the department of health. However, many exceptions to this rule allow disclosure of AIDS-related information to one or more of the following persons: medical professionals, emergency assistance personnel, spouses, persons with whom the patient has shared needles, peer review organizations, blood banks, medical facilities handling body parts of the deceased, funeral directors, directors of correctional facilities, third-party reimbursers, employers, and schools. Courts also can order disclosure of AIDS patients' records in circumstances not addressed directly by legislation. These laws are important because they authorize the release of information in a patient's records without the individual's consent—and, in some cases, despite the person's protests.

The question of when AIDS-related information may be disclosed without consent is a particularly sensitive issue because of the strong interests involved. The patient wants to prevent any disclosure of information because of the personal nature of the disease and the stigma attached to it. The public has an interest in fostering medical treatment and encouraging blood and organ donations by protecting confidentiality. Health care providers need to know the patient's condition in order to protect themselves from the virus while providing proper care to the person. The government seeks access to AIDS-related information in order to conduct scientific research and monitor the spread of the disease. Finally, third parties, such as spouses, need to know whether their partners are carriers of the deadly virus.

These conflicting interests have prompted many state legislatures to enact special confidentiality statutes governing the disclosure of AIDS-related information in patients' medical records. These laws typically state that no person may disclose or be compelled to disclose the identity of any person on whom a test for HIV is performed, or the results of such a test, except as provided. The statutes often list a set of circumstances under which information may be released.

It is important to note that these laws prohibit disclosure of the identity of a person who has undergone an HIV test regardless of the results of the test. In addition, disclosure of the test results is prohibited. But while the confidentiality statutes create special civil and criminal liability for unauthorized disclosures, they are not intended to discourage health care practitioners from indicating the results of an HIV test in a patient's file.[1]

DUTY TO REPORT

Some jurisdictions have statutes requiring health care providers to report cases of AIDS and/or HIV-related illnesses to the state or local department of health.[2] The remaining states have general disease reporting laws. Those laws give the

---

[1]See, e.g., N.Y. Pub. Health Law § 2782(8) (1993).

[2]These states include Colorado, Florida, Idaho, Illinois, Indiana, Iowa, Kansas, Maine, Maryland, Michigan, Mississippi, Texas, Washington, and Wisconsin.

department of health in each state the authority to issue rules that have the effect of law.

AIDS is reportable under rules in each of the 50 states. Many states also require HIV and/or ARC reporting. The reporting laws and regulations vary widely. Some place the duty of reporting on the attending physician,[3] while others require the hospital, laboratory, or other facility to file the report.[4]

Physicians in the majority of states are responsible for reporting positive test results. Institutions subject to reporting include hospitals, blood banks, plasma centers, and laboratories. Health maintenance organizations also have reporting responsibility in a significant number of states.[5] Minnesota has a self-reporting law that requires health care workers diagnosed with HIV to report that information to the commissioner of health no more than 30 days after learning of the diagnosis or 30 days after becoming licensed or registered by the state.[6] The Minnesota law also requires health care workers who personally know of another health care worker's failure to comply with infection control procedures to report that to the appropriate licensing board or a designated hospital official within 10 days.[7]

The laws also vary with respect to what information must be reported. Many jurisdictions require the patient's name and address to be disclosed in the report, along with age, race, and sex.[8] Other states prohibit the release of any identifying information.[9] Some states require reporting by demographics with names required only in specific situations.[10]

All of the laws distinguish between the forms of the disease for purposes of reporting. In many states, the identity of patients with full-blown AIDS cases is reportable while the identity of HIV-positive patients is exempt.[11] These jurisdictions sometimes permit the names of AIDS patients to be released while prohibiting the identification of persons who test positive only for HIV infec-

---

[3]See, e.g., Colo. Rev. Stat. § 25-4-1402(1) (1993); Fla. Stat. ch. 384.25(2) (1992); Iowa Code Ann. § 141.8 (1992); Kan. Stat. Ann. § 65-6002(a) (1992).

[4]See, e.g., 410 Ill. Comp. Stat. Ann. 310/4 (1993); Iowa Code § 141.8 (1992); Wis. Stat. § 146.025(7) (1991-1992); see also Wis. A.B. No. 585 (New Laws 1993).

[5]See AIDS Policy Center, *Intergovernmental Health Policy Project* (October 1992).

[6]Minn. Stat. § 214.19 (1993).

[7]*Id.*

[8]See, e.g., Colo. Rev. Stat. § 25-4-1402(4) (1993); Idaho Code § 39-606 (1993); Mich. Comp. Laws § 333.5114 (1992).

[9]See, e.g., 410 Ill. Comp. Stat. Ann. 310/4 (1993).

[10]AIDS Policy Center, *Intergovernmental Project* (October 1992).

[11]See, e.g., Fla. Stat. ch. 384.25(2) (1992) (except where patient consents to partner notification); Kan. Stat. Ann. § 65-6002(a) (1992).

tion.[12] A growing number of states require the identity of persons with either AIDS or HIV to be reported.[13]

In Iowa, for example, the physician who orders an HIV test must report positive results to the department of health, but may not include the patient's name and address in the report without the person's written consent. The same rules apply to directors of blood banks, plasma centers, and clinical laboratories.[14] On the other hand, physicians must release patients' names and addresses to the health department, along with other information, when they diagnose AIDS or an AIDS-related condition or attend to patients who die from an AIDS-related condition.[15] Many laws require the attending physician to submit a written report on a patient within seven days after a reportable diagnosis is confirmed.[16]

In Maryland, the director of a medical laboratory in which serum samples are tested for HIV must submit a report within 48 hours of an HIV-positive test result. The report must contain statistical data but no identifying information may be revealed.[17] Other institutions that obtain or process semen, blood, or tissue must obtain a blood sample from all potential donors in order to test for HIV. All positive test results must be reported to the department of health.[18]

Michigan law requires all persons who obtain a positive HIV result for a test subject to report the name, address, age, race, and sex of the subject within seven days. Reports must be filed with both state and local health departments. Only licensed clinical laboratories are exempt from those requirements. Patients who submit to HIV testing in a physician's private practice office or the office of a physician engaged by an HMO may request their doctor not to reveal their name, address, or telephone number.[19]

DISCLOSURE OF MEDICAL RECORDS INFORMATION

Access by the Patient

All patients have a limited right to access their own medical records.[20] The HIV confidentiality statutes protect this right by including the test subject and authorized representative in the list of persons with lawful access to the subject's

---

[12]See, e.g., Fla. Stat. Ann. ch. 384.25(2) (1992); Iowa Code § 141.8 (1992).

[13]See, e.g., Ark. Code Ann. § 20-15-904 (1993); Colo. Rev. Stat. § 25-4-1402 (1993).

[14]Iowa Code Ann. § 141.8 (1992).

[15]*Id.*

[16]See, e,g, Iowa Code § 141.8 (1992); Mich. Comp. Laws Ann. § 333.5114 (1989).

[17]Md. Code Ann., Health-Gen. § 18-205,207 (1993).

[18]Md. Code Ann., Health-Gen. § 18-334(b) (1993).

[19]Mich. Comp. Laws § 333.5114 (1992).

[20]See Chapter 5, Access to Medical Records Information.

test results.[21] A provider who orders an HIV test for a patient may inform the patient or representative of the results without liability.[22]

Access by Third Parties with Patient Authorization

Many of the HIV confidentiality laws allow the patient to authorize release of test results to third parties.[23] This provision permits a health care practitioner to release confidential information to persons who otherwise are precluded from access to the patient's records. A patient might authorize release to any insurance company, employer, or school. The practitioner should require that such release be in writing and signed by the patient or the patient's representative. A copy of the release should be attached to the patient's records.

Disclosure to Health Care Workers

Most AIDS disclosure laws allow information to be released to medical personnel involved in the patient's care and without the patient's consent. The California law, for example, states that: "The information may be disclosed to providers of health care or other health care professionals or facilities for purposes of diagnosis or treatment of the patient."[24]

Authorizing disclosure under these circumstances can serve several purposes. To facilitate proper medical treatment for AIDS victims, many statutes authorize release of AIDS information to the patient's medical provider. The provider then may place the results of an HIV test directly into the patient's record.[25] Physicians often are authorized to reveal information directly to other health care providers for purposes of treating the patient.[26] In addition, the laws reflect a concern for the safety of medical workers who are at risk for HIV infection during performance of their duties. Several statutes authorize the attending physician to reveal an HIV patient's identity to other health care workers who come into contact with body fluids or body parts of the patient, or who work directly with HIV patients.[27]

---

[21]See, e.g., Del. Code Ann., tit. 16 § 1203 (1993); 410 Ill. Comp. Stat. Ann. 305/9 (1993).

[22]However, a patient may sue a health care provider for negligently advising the patient that he or she has tested HIV positive. See *Johnson v. United States*, 735 F. Supp. 1 (D.D.C. 1990).

[23]See, e.g., 410 Ill. Comp. Stat. Ann. 305/9 (1993).

[24]Cal. Civ. Code § 56.10 as amended by Cal. A.B. No. 525 (New Laws 1993); see also N.C. Gen. Stat. § 130A-143 (1993).

[25]See, e.g., W.Va. Code § 16-3c-3(5) (1993).

[26]See, e.g., Cal. Health & Safety Code § 199.215(a) (1993); Haw. Rev. Stat. § 325-101(a)(10) (1993); Iowa Code § 141.23(1) (1992); Me. Rev. Stat., tit. 22 § 19203 (1992); Mich. Comp. Laws § 333.5131(5)(a) (1992).

[27]See, e.g., Kan. Stat. Ann. § 65-6004 (1992); 410 Ill. Comp. Stat. Ann. 305/9(h) (1993).

Some statutes permit disclosure upon finding that the medical worker has a "reasonable" or "medical" need to know the information to provide proper care. Other laws allow disclosure whenever generally relevant to the patient's treatment. Many of the laws are unclear, however, as to whether the authorized disclosures are permissive or mandatory. This question bears on the ability of a concerned worker to demand that a physician confirm the test results of an AIDS patient whom the worker suspects is positive for the virus.

Many statutes also are unclear as to whose interests must be analyzed for purposes of disclosure—the worker's or the patient's. For example, a "need to know" for purposes of providing patient care may refer to the worker's need to take precautions to prevent becoming infected while rendering treatment to the patient; on the other hand, the "need to know" might relate to special treatments available only for AIDS patients. Not every medical worker involved with the patient has a legitimate need to know that the person has been tested for HIV. Only a limited class of medical practitioners have access to such information under the confidentiality statutes.

In California, for example, the results of an HIV test may be recorded in the subject's record and otherwise revealed without the patient's consent to providers of care for purposes of "diagnosis, care, or treatment of the patient."[28] The results of an HIV test may be disclosed to an agent or employee of the health care provider who provides "direct patient care and treatment."[29] These provisions foster discussion among experts needed to provide proper patient care; they also reveal a concern for the safety of health care workers who come into contact with the deadly disease. Delaware law provides that no person may disclose the identity of any subject of an HIV test, or the results thereof, in a manner that permits identification of the test subject except, among other circumstances, to:

> (3) An authorized agent or employee of a health facility or health care provider if the health facility or health care provider itself is authorized to obtain the test results, the agent or employee provides patient care or handles or processes specimens of body fluids or tissues, and the agent or employee has a medical need to know such information to provide health care to the patient.[30]

The Delaware statute seems to reflect concern for the patient, rather than for the safety of health care workers, because the third prong of the test—the employee's "medical need to know"—must be tied into the purpose "to provide

---

[28]Cal. Health & Safety Code § 199.215(a) (1993).

[29]*Id.*, § 199.24(c) (1993).

[30]Del. Code Ann., tit. 16 § 1203 (1993).

health care to the patient." Thus, the "medical" aspect of the need to know refers to the patient's medical interests, not the employee's own health concerns.[31]

Illinois has adopted a similar three-part test for disclosing AIDS information to other health care providers; however, the third prong of that test requires only that the employees have a need to know the information.[32] In comparison, Hawaii allows disclosure of AIDS, ARC, and HIV records by the patient's health care provider to another health care provider "for the purpose of continued care of [or] treatment of the patient."[33] This broadly written provision defers to the judgment of the physician on the question of disclosure, but allows release of the information in an emergency to the extent necessary to protect the life or health of the patient.

Kentucky law curiously authorizes release of medical information only to the physician retained by the person infected with AIDS or another sexually transmitted disease. The statute is silent on the extent to which the physician may release such information to co-workers involved in the patient's care, except in the case of an emergency when information may be released to protect the life or health of the patient.[34] Maine authorizes disclosure of HIV test results to the health care provider designated by the patient. The patient's physician then may make results available only to other providers working directly with that person, and only for the purpose of providing direct patient care.[35] This provision appears to be permissive, and it is unclear whether a provider of direct care could demand successfully that the physician confirm that a suspected AIDS patient had indeed tested positive for the HIV infection. Missouri similarly allows the release of HIV test results to "health care personnel working directly with the infected individual who have a reasonable need to know the results for the purpose of providing direct patient health care."[36] Again, it is unclear whether the "reasonable need to know" relates to the worker's safety or the patient's proper care. In either case, the Missouri law is fairly typical in limiting the circle of disclosure to persons directly involved with the patient.

New Hampshire law is permissive and concerned for the patient's treatment. The relevant statute provides that:

> a physician licensed to practice in this state or other health care provider may disclose information pertaining to the identity and test results of a person tested for a human immunodeficiency virus to other physicians

---

[31] See also Iowa Code § 141.23(1)(c) (1992).

[32] 410 Ill. Comp. Ann. Stat. 305/9(1) (1993).

[33] Haw. Rev. Stat. § 325-101(a)(10)(1993).

[34] Ky. Rev. Stat. Ann. § 214.420(3) (1993).

[35] Me. Rev. Stat. Ann., tit. 22 § 19203 (1992).

[36] Mo. Rev. Stat. § 191.656(2)(b) (1992), *as amended by* S.B. No. 233 (New Laws 1993).

and health care providers directly involved in the health care of the person when the disclosure of such information is necessary in order to protect the health of the person tested.[37]

The Texas statute also is permissive but includes concern for the safety of health care workers. It provides that results of an HIV test may be released to a physician, nurse, or other health care personnel who have a "legitimate" need to know the result to provide for their protection and the patient's health and welfare.[38] The New York confidentiality provision authorizes release of confidential HIV-related information only to an agent or employee of a health facility or health provider if that agent is permitted to access medical records, the facility is authorized to obtain HIV information, and the agent either provides health care to the protected individual or maintains medical records for billing or reimbursement.[39] The statute then provides that a provider or facility is authorized to receive HIV-related information when knowledge of such material is "necessary to provide appropriate care or treatment to the protected individual or a child of the individual."[40]

Like the New York law, Utah's confidentiality provision demonstrates a concern for persons other than the patient and health care workers. The statute provides for disclosure to a health care provider, health care personnel, and public health personnel with a "legitimate need to have access to the information in order to assist the patient, or to protect the health of others closely associated with the patient." The statute expressly notes that the above language does not create a duty to warn third parties, but is designed to assist providers in treating and containing AIDS, HIV, and other infectious diseases.[41] This provision clearly authorizes disclosure to certain medical personnel working closely with the patient, but also extends to family members, sexual partners, and needle partners.[42]

---

[37]N.H. Rev. Stat. Ann. § 141-F:8(IV) (1992).

[38]Tex. Health & Safety Code art. 81.103(b)(5) (1993).

[39]N.Y. Pub. Health Law § 2782-1(c) (1993).

[40]*Id.,* § 2782-1(d) (1993).

[41]Utah Code Ann. §§ 26-6-20.5 (1993) and 26-25a-101(2)(h) (1993).

[42]While state legislation authorizes disclosure to health care workers treating the patient, it is possible that courts will impose a duty on patients to reveal whether they have AIDS. In a case that appears to be the first of its kind, a surgical technician successfully sued a patient for fraudulently concealing the fact that she had AIDS when filling out forms before undergoing surgery. After the technician was cut with a scalpel while removing sutures, the patient revealed her true health status. The technician had not been wearing gloves at the time of the exposure. Although the technician consistently has tested negative for HIV since the incident, the court awarded her damages for fraud but refused to award her damages for negligent infliction of emotional distress. *Boulais v. Lustig,* BC038105 (Cal. Super. Ct. 1993).

Many laws also permit disclosure of a patient's identity to facilities that procure, process, distribute, or use blood, other body fluids, body parts, tissues, or organs.[43]

The statutes discussed above govern the release of all HIV-related information. Others focus directly on disclosure of the reports submitted to the department of health. Colorado, as described above, has a mandatory AIDS and HIV reporting law applicable to physicians and health care institutions.[44] It also provides that such reports held by a health care provider or facility, physician, clinic, blood bank, or other agency shall be strictly confidential and shall not be released, shared, or made public except as provided.[45] Louisiana has a special law requiring a hospital to notify a nursing home of an HIV patient's condition when the hospital transfers the patient to the home. A similar duty is placed upon a nursing home transferring an HIV patient to a hospital.[46]

The unauthorized disclosure of information relating to a patient's HIV status can lead to liability on various grounds, based on either state statutes or the common law. A California court allowed a patient to sue a health care provider for disclosing his HIV status to an insurance carrier based on the statute's constitutional right to privacy.[47] After receiving treatment for injuries sustained at work, a patient told the physician's nurse to be careful because he was HIV positive, but made it clear that he was disclosing the information solely for the purpose of protecting health care professionals. The physician's report mentioning AIDS as a possible source of the patient's symptoms was sent to the insurance company, the insurance carrier, and the Workers' Compensation Appeals Board. The court found that the circumstances surrounding the patient's disclosure clearly demonstrated his anticipation that the information would remain private. Enforcing such reasonable expectations of privacy fosters disclosures of HIV-positive status only when necessary and protects against misuse of information, the court held, concluding that the disclosure was protected under the constitutional right to privacy.

In another case, a New Jersey hospital was found liable for failing to protect the confidentiality of a diagnosis of AIDS in a staff physician who had been treated at the facility.[48] The test results were placed in the physician's medical chart, which was kept at the nurses' station on the floor where the physician was

---

[43]See, e.g., N.Y. Pub. Health Law § 2782-(1)(e) (1993); Va. Code Ann. § 32.1-36.1(A)(8) (1993); Wis. Stat. § 146.025(5)(a)(3)-(5)(a)(5) (1991-1992), renumbered as 252.15(5)(a)(4)-(5)(a)(5) in Wis. A.B. No. 585 (New Laws 1993).

[44]Colo. Rev. Stat. § 25-4-1402 (1993).

[45]*Id.,* § 25-4-1404 (Supp. 1993); see also Idaho Code § 39-610 (1993).

[46]La. Rev. Stat. Ann. § 40:1099(B) (1992); see also Miss. Code Ann. § 41-23-1(5)(1993).

[47]*Estate of Urbaniak v. Newton,* 277 Cal. Rptr. 354 (Ct. App. 1991).

[48]*Behringer v. Medical Ctr. at Princeton,* 592 A.2d 1251 (N.J. Super. Ct. 1991).

an inpatient. There were no restrictions on access to the record. Within hours of the diagnosis, the physician's condition was widely known within the hospital. The court found the hospital negligent for failing to take reasonable precautions regarding access to the physician's record.[49]

Disclosure without Consent to Emergency Medical Personnel

Many confidentiality statutes allow the release of HIV-related information without the patient's consent to medical technicians who provide emergency care to an HIV-positive patient. The statutes vary, however, in the purpose for such disclosure. Some link disclosure to the health of the patient; others indicate a concern for the safety of the emergency workers, and many reflect an ambiguous balance between the two concerns.

In some states, for example, confidential HIV-related information may be released to medical personnel in a "medical emergency" to the "extent necessary to protect the health or life of the patient."[50] The Hawaii law defines "medical emergency" as any disease-related situation that threatens life or limb.[51] Other states authorize disclosure to health care providers rendering medical care when knowledge of HIV test results is "necessary" to provide "appropriate emergency care or treatment" to the patient.[52] Both types of laws demonstrate concern for the patient's treatment.

Other laws reflect a concern for the safety of rescue workers. Illinois allows release of the identity of the subject of an HIV test to "[a]ny health care provider or employee of a health facility, and any firefighter or any EMT-A or EMT-I, involved in an accidental direct skin or mucous membrane contact with the blood or bodily fluids of an individual which is of a nature that may transmit HIV, as determined by a physician in his medical judgment."[53]

A few states impose an affirmative duty on an attending physician or health care facility to respond to inquiries by emergency rescuers as to contact with a patient later diagnosed with a contagious disease or virus including HIV. The rescuers entitled to receive such information include paid or volunteer firefighters, emergency medical technicians, rescue squad personnel, and law enforcement officers. The notification must occur within 48 hours after confirmation of the

---

[49]For a more detailed discussion of liability for improper disclosure of medical record information, see Chapter 8.

[50]See, e.g., Colo. Rev. Stat. § 25-4-1404(1)(c) (1993); Fla. Stat. Ann. ch. 384.29(1) (1992); Iowa Code § 141.10-(1)(c) (1992); Kan. Stat. Ann. § 65-6002(1992); Ky. Rev. Stat. Ann. § 214.420(3)(e) (1993).

[51]Haw. Rev. Stat. § 325-101 (1993).

[52]Del. Code Ann., tit. 16 § 1203(a)(4) (1988).

[53]410 Ill. Comp. Stat. Ann. 305/9 (1993). See also Wis. Stat. § 146.025(5)(a) (11) (1991).

patient's diagnosis. The information must be communicated in a manner that protects the confidentiality of both the patient and rescuer.[54]

In Maryland, each medical care facility must develop and disseminate written procedures for exposure notification. A facility or provider acting in good faith under this section is not liable for failure to give notice of exposure where the rescuer does not properly initiate the process as developed.[55] Washington law authorizes certain emergency rescuers and other health care workers who come into contact with the body fluids of another person to request that an HIV test be performed on that person. The person making such request is then entitled to know the results.[56]

Disclosure without Consent to Spouse or Needle Sharer

Several of the confidentiality statutes provide for notification of an HIV patient's spouse, needle-partner, or other "contact" at risk for the infection.[57] These provisions usually are permissive and do not create a duty on the part of the physician to warn all third parties. Thus, a contact who develops the virus but who was not informed of risk by the partner's physician cannot bring a lawsuit against the physician under the statute. On the other hand, a physician who reveals the risk to a contact as authorized is not liable to the patient for breach of confidentiality.

These laws usually require that the physician protect the identity of the patient when making such disclosures, however. Further, before any disclosure, the physician must discuss the importance of notification with the patient and inform the patient of the physician's intent to notify the patient's contact.

For example, California provides that:

> no physician and surgeon who has the results of a confirmed positive test to detect infection by the probable causative agent of acquired immune deficiency syndrome of a patient under his or her care shall be held criminally or civilly liable for disclosing to a person reasonably believed to be the spouse, or to a person reasonably believed to be a sexual partner or a person with whom the patient has shared the use of hypodermic needles, or to the county health officer, that the patient has

---

[54]La. Rev. Stat. Ann. § 40: 1099A, *as amended by* La. H.B. 1580 (New Laws 1993); see also Md. Code Ann., Health-Gen. § 18-213(b), (c), and (d)(1992); Mich. Comp. Laws § 333.20191 (1992).

[55]Md. Code Ann., Health-Gen. § 18-213(f) and (i)(1993).

[56]Wash. Rev. Code § 70.24.105(2)(h) (1991).

[57]See 410 Ill. Comp. Stat. Ann. ch. 325/5.5 (1993).

tested positive on a test to detect infection by the probable causative agent of acquired immune deficiency syndrome, except that no physician and surgeon shall disclose any identifying information about the individual believed to be infected.[58]

Before notifying the above individuals, however, the physician and surgeon must confer with the patient. Moreover, the provision is only permissive, and imposes no duty on any provider.[59]

South Carolina law simply states that:

A physician or state agency identifying and notifying a spouse or known contact of a person having Human Immunodeficiency Virus (HIV) infection or Acquired Immunodeficiency Syndrome (AIDS) is not liable for damages resulting from the disclosure.[60]

The statute also provides that "contact" means the exchanges of body products or body fluids by sexual acts or percutaneous transmission. Virginia and Texas authorize the release of HIV test results to the spouse of the test subject, but not to other sexual partners.[61]

A physician who wishes to notify a contact under one of these laws should discuss such plans in depth with the patient. The physician should remind the patient of the moral obligation to disclose the condition to third parties at risk. In addition, patients should be aware that some states impose criminal liability on an HIV carrier who knowingly engages in activities likely to spread the virus.[62] The physician should fully document the discussion in the patient's room. If the patient still refuses to reveal the condition to sexual partners or others at risk after this consultation, the physician then may contact the third parties directly; however, the physician should not proceed in a manner that identifies the patient. The physician also should be sensitive to the effect of the message on the third party who may be completely unaware of the situation. While the statutes do not create a duty to warn third parties, other state laws may impose such an obligation.

Disclosure without Consent to Other Persons

In addition to authorizing disclosure to providers, contacts, and health departments, some confidentiality statutes also permit release of information to health

---

[58]Cal. Health & Safety Code §199.25(a) (1993).

[59]See also N.Y. Pub. Health Law § 2782(4)(a) (1993).

[60]S.C. Code Ann. § 44-29-146 (1991); see also W.Va. Code § 16-3C-3(d) (1993).

[61]Va. Code § 32.1-36.1(A)(II)(Supp. 1989); Tex. Health & Safety Code § 801.103(b)(7) (1993).

[62]See, e.g., Fla. Stat. ch. 384.24 (1992).

facility staff committees, accreditation committees, and oversight review organizations.[63] In addition, New York allows disclosure to an authorized agency in connection with foster care or adoption of a child, to third-party reimbursers or their agents to the extent necessary to reimburse health care providers for health services, and to the medical directors of correctional facilities.[64] Wisconsin authorizes release to a funeral director or person who performs an autopsy on an HIV patient, a coroner, and a sheriff or keeper of a prison.[65]

Texas law permits a blood bank to report positive test results of an infectious disease to other blood banks that indicate the donor's name; however, the name of the disease may not be revealed. The blood bank also may report results to the hospital where the blood was transferred, to the physician performing the transfusion, and to the recipient. Reports made under this provision may not identify the donor.[66]

Disclosure of Health Care Provider's Status to Patients

Health care facilities also must confront the difficult issue of whether to reveal a health care worker's HIV status to patients. In this regard, it is important to distinguish between disclosure before treatment and disclosure after treatment.

The CDC Guidelines recommend that HIV-positive workers notify prospective patients of the HIV status of the workers before the patients undergo exposure-prone invasive procedures. Some states[67] also require health care workers who perform exposure-prone procedures to notify prospective patients of their seropositive status and obtain written consent from patients before patients undergo exposure-prone procedures.

A New Jersey court has upheld a hospital's requirement that an HIV-positive surgeon disclose his HIV status to prospective patients as part of the informed consent procedure.[68] In Maryland, an appeals court has allowed two patients of a surgeon who died of AIDS to sue his estate based on the claim that he had failed to inform them before surgery that he was infected with HIV.[69] A physician's duty of care must include disclosure that an operating surgeon's HIV-positive status poses a risk, however minimal, of transmission of the AIDS virus during surgery, the court concluded.

---

[63]See, e.g., Del. Code Ann., tit. 16 § 1203(a)(7) (1993); 410 Ill. Comp. Stat. Ann. 305/9(f) (1993).

[64]N.Y. Pub. Health Law § 2782-l(1) (i) and (n)(1993).

[65]Wis. Stat. § 146.025 (1991-1992, renumbered as 252.15 (5)(a)(7) in Wis. A.B. No. 585 (New Laws 1993).

[66]Tex. Health & Safety Code § 81.103 (f) and (h)(1993).

[67]See, e.g., Tex. Health & Safety Code Ann. § 85.204 (1993).

[68]See *Behringer v. Medical Ctr. at Princeton*, 592 A.2d 1251 (N.J. Super. Ct. April 25, 1991).

[69]*Faya v. Almaraz; Rossi v. Almaraz*, Nos. 143 &144 (Md. Ct. App. Mar. 9, 1993).

With respect to disclosure after exposure, a hospital may make the decision to inform patients that a provider who treated them is HIV positive. Some states allow notification of an individual who may have been exposed to HIV through contact with an HIV-infected provider.[70] In states that have HIV confidentiality statutes that forbid such disclosure, however, the hospital would need to obtain court authorization before disclosing such information.

In a Pennsylvania case, for example, the high court allowed a hospital to disclose the identity of an AIDS-infected obstetrics-gynecology resident to patients who had been treated by the resident.[71] Two hospitals where the physician had worked requested court permission to disclose the physician's name and medical information to more than 200 patients who had been associated to some degree with the physician in the course of their treatment. Under Pennsylvania law, information derived from HIV testing must remain confidential, but courts may authorize disclosure of such information if there is a compelling need to do so. The court emphasized in this case that the physician was involved in invasive surgical procedures where the risk of sustaining cuts and exposing patients to tainted blood was high. His medical problem became a matter of public concern the moment he picked up a surgical instrument and became involved in surgical procedures, the court declared. After weighing the physician's privacy interests against the interests of public health, the court concluded that the latter should prevail, in spite of the small potential for transmission of the disease.

The CDC Guidelines recommend a case-by-case approach to deciding whether patients should be notfied of possible exposure.[72] The Guidelines state:

> The public health benefit of notification of patients who have had exposure-prone procedures performed by health care workers infected with HIV . . . should be considered on a case-by-case basis, taking into consideration an assessment of specific risks, confidentiality issues, and available resources. Decisions regarding notification and follow-up studies should be made in consultation with state and local public health officials.

Disclosure by Court Order

Several of the confidentiality statutes include standards by which a court may authorize disclosure of the results of a patient's HIV test. Some statutes allow

---

[70]410 Ill. Comp. Stat. Ann. 325/5.5 (1993).

[71]*In re Application of Milton S. Hershey Medical Ctr. of Pa. State Univ.*, Nos. 70, 71 M.D. (Appeals Docket 1992) (Pa. Nov. 4, 1993).

[72]Centers for Disease Control, *Morbidity and Mortality Weekly Report* (July 12, 1991).

disclosure under a "lawful court order."[73] Others require the person seeking access to show a "compelling need," with no other means of acquiring the information. In determining whether a compelling need exists, the court must balance the petitioner's interest against the patient's privacy interest and the public interest. The public interest will not be served if disclosure deters future testing, fosters discrimination, or discourages donations of blood, organs, or semen.[74] The petitioner may be required to show that other ways of obtaining the information are not available or would not be effective.[75]

Many statutes provide that the patient's true name may not be included in any documents filed with the court—a pseudonym must be substituted. The test subjects must be given notice and opportunity to participate in the proceedings if not already a party. All proceedings are conducted in camera unless the test subject agrees to a hearing in open court, or the court determines that a public hearing is necessary to the public interest and proper administration of justice.[76] Even in the absence of such statutory directives, courts have struggled to balance the interests involved when one person requests disclosure of medical information relating to another person.

Most of the cases have involved claims by patients who contracted AIDS through blood transfusions and who request the facility that provided blood to produce a list of donors' names and addresses. The patient frequently alleges that access to the blood donor's identity is necessary to establish whether the hospital or supplier used proper screening and testing procedures when they accepted the blood.[77]

Liability for Failure To Comply with Confidentiality Provisions

The confidentiality statutes create special civil and criminal liability for persons who make unauthorized disclosures of HIV test results. Civil liability gives the test subject a private cause of action for damages against the person who disclosed the information. Criminal liability, on the other hand, allows the state attorney to prosecute the offender and impose fines and/or a jail sentence. In most states, a person who consciously disregards the statute is subject to harsher penalties than one who is negligent.

---

[73]Wis. Stat. § 146.025(5)(a)(9)(1991-1992), *renumbered as* 252.15(5)(a)(9) in Wis. A.B. 585 (New Laws 1993).

[74]See, e.g., Del. Code Ann., tit. 16 § 1203(a)(10) (1993); 410 Ill. Comp. Stat. Ann. 305/9 (1993); see also *In re Application of Milton S. Hershey Medical Ctr. of Pa. State Univ., supra.*

[75]Mich. Comp. Laws Ann. § 333.5131(3) (1992).

[76]See, e.g., Del. Code Ann., tit. 16 § 1203(a)(10) (1993); W.Va. Code § 16-3C-3(a)(9) (1993).

[77]For a more extensive discussion of these cases, see Chapter 8, Liability for Improper Disclosure of Medical Records.

In Virginia, for example, any person who willfully or through gross negligence makes any unauthorized disclosure is liable for a civil penalty of up to $5,000 per violation payable to a special state fund.[78] The person who is the subject of an unauthorized disclosure also may recover actual damages or $100, whichever is greater, plus reasonable attorneys' fees and court costs. Wisconsin provides for actual damages and costs, plus exemplary damages up to $1,000 for a negligent violation and $5,000 for an intentional violation. Where an intentional disclosure causes bodily or psychological harm to the test subject, the offender may be fined up to $10,000 and imprisoned up to nine months.[79]

In addition to receiving damages and attorneys' fees, an aggrieved party in Illinois may request other appropriate relief, including an injunction.[80] Colorado provides for a criminal penalty only, imposing misdemeanor fines up to $5,000 and imprisonment up to two years.[81]

---

[78]Va. Code § 32.1-36.1(B) and (C) (1993).

[79]Wis. Stat. § 146.024(4) (1991-1992), renumbered as § 252.14(4) in Wis. A.B. No. 585 (New Laws 1993).

[80]410 Ill. Comp. Stat. Ann. § 305/13 (1993).

[81]Colo. Rev. Stat. § 25-4-1409(2) (1993).

5

Access to Medical Records Information

INTRODUCTION

The hospital owns the physical medical record, subject to the patient's interest in the information contained therein. The medical record is a confidential document and access to it generally should be limited to the patient or an authorized representative, the attending physician, and other hospital staff members possessing legitimate interests in the record relating to the patient's care.

Several exceptions to this general rule permit other individuals to review the patient's medical record. These exceptions include disclosures made pursuant to the federal Freedom of Information Act (FOIA); disclosures required by federal and state reimbursement regulations, including Medicare and Medicaid; disclosures necessary to meet peer review organization (PRO) requirements and other review requirements; state statutory reporting requirements; and reports made to law enforcement and other governmental agencies for appropriate purposes. Each of these exceptions to the general rule of confidentiality is discussed in this chapter.

In addition, access to certain types of patient records is more restricted than to records under the general rule. For example, alcohol and drug abuse records may not be disclosed except as specifically authorized by the applicable federal regulations, and access to records of mental health patients is limited severely in some states.

To comply with all of these laws, each hospital must devise an effective record security procedure that protects and preserves both the physical medical record and the patient's general interest in confidentiality. Hospitals converting all or part of their medical records to computer media should be especially careful to establish adequate record security measures. (For a detailed discussion of the confidentiality and other potential risks associated with computerized medical records, see Chapter 6.)

Hospitals often receive numerous forms of legal process, such as subpoenas or court orders, requiring them to provide patient record information. Facilities must be prepared to respond appropriately to such requests. Their responses should be based on a careful review of the relevant state and federal laws governing medical record confidentiality and access.

Hospitals can be liable to their patients for the improper or unauthorized disclosure of medical record information. In addition to federal and state statutory penalties, hospitals and practitioners may be liable in common law for defamation, invasion of privacy, betrayal of professional secrets, and breach of contract. (Liability for improper disclosure of records is discussed in detail in Chapter 8.)

OWNERSHIP OF THE MEDICAL RECORD

It is generally accepted that the medical record is owned by the hospital, subject to the patient's interest in the information it contains.[1] The basic rule of record ownership is established by statute in many states. The Tennessee statute, for example, states that:

> [h]ospital records are and shall remain the property of the various hospitals, subject however to court order to produce the same. Unless restricted by state or federal law or regulation, a hospital shall furnish to a patient, or a patient's authorized representative such part or parts of such patient's hospital records without unreasonable delay upon request in writing by the patient or such representative.[2]

Most states with specific rules on record ownership include these provisions in their state hospital-licensing regulations. A typical regulation provides that medical records are the property of the hospital and shall not be removed from its premises except for court purposes.[3]

The issue of ownership of medical records generally arises when a hospital opposes access to the record by or on behalf of the patient. State legislation frequently subjects the hospital's right of ownership to the patient's right of access to the information contained in the medical record. In the absence of

---

[1] See Confidentiality of Patient Health Information position statement, American Health Information Management Association (1985).

[2] Tenn. Code Ann. § 68-11-304 (1993); see also Miss. Code Ann. § 41-9-65 (Supp. 1993).

[3] See, e.g., 902 Ky. Admin. Regs. 20:016(11)(c) (1990); Or. Admin. R. § 33-505-050(12) (1990); 28 Pa. Code § 115.28 (1993); Tenn. Code Ann. § 68-11-304 (1993).

statutory or regulatory authority, a few courts have held that a medical record is hospital property in which the patient has a limited property interest. In *Pyramid Life Ins. Co. v. Masonic Hosp. Ass'n. of Payne County,*[4] for instance, a patient's health insurer sought access to the hospital records for purposes of settling an insurance claim where the patient had authorized disclosure. The court recognized that the "records maintained by [the hospital] pertaining to care and treatment of patients and to expenses incurred by patients . . . [were] the property of the hospital." However, the court did grant access to the insurer because the patient in this case had authorized disclosure.[5]

While a patient may have a statutory interest in information contained in the medical record, there is no independent constitutional right to such information. In *Gotkin v. Miller,*[6] a former mental patient writing a book about her experiences was denied access to her medical records by her treating hospitals. At trial, the patient argued that the hospitals had violated her federal constitutional rights. The district court ruled that the hospitals' withholding of information did not violate any of the patient's rights, including her right to information as a corollary to her right of free speech, her right of privacy, her freedom from unreasonable searches and seizures of property, or deprivation of her property without due process of law. In affirming the district court opinion, the court of appeals refused to recognize that psychiatric patients have a constitutionally protected property interest in the direct and unrestricted access to their records.

When questions of medical records ownership arise, the hospital attorney should be aware that, although the institution owns every medical record, patients generally have a right to review their records. When a patient seeks access to records, the hospital through its legal counsel should consult state and federal statutes governing hospital licensure, mental health patients, and specific programs such as alcoholism and drug abuse treatment centers, along with any licensing regulations applicable to hospitals and their special programs. In addition, all relevant court decisions must be reviewed before questions regarding a specific case can be answered.

ACCESS BY OR ON BEHALF OF THE PATIENT

In the past, hospitals in many states would deny access to the medical record by patients who usually did not challenge such refusal. Most jurisdictions now

---

[4]191 F. Supp. 51 (W.D. Okla. 1961).

[5]See also, *Wallace v. Univ. Hosps. of Cleveland,* 164 N.E.2d 917, 918 (Ohio Ct. Comn. Pleas 1959), *modified and aff'd,* 170 N.E.2d 261 (Ohio Ct. App. 1960), *appeal dismissed,* 172 N.E.2d 459 (Ohio 1961).

[6]379 F. Supp. 859 (E.D.N.Y. 1974), *aff'd,* 514 F.2d 125 (2d Cir. 1975). The rules governing access to the medical records of mental health patients are more restrictive than those for other types of medical treatment in many jurisdictions.

expressly grant the patient or the patient's representative the right to examine and copy the individual's hospital record. While the general rule remains that the medical record is a confidential document, well-established exceptions exist for access by the patient, the patient's authorized representative, and the attending physician and hospital staff members who possess a legitimate need to review the chart.

The basic rules of confidentiality and access to medical records are established in many states by statute or regulation. A few states simply specify that the medical record is confidential and impose a general obligation on hospitals to develop an appropriate policy for record confidentiality without further statutory or regulatory guidance.[7] Enactments in other states similarly embody the principle of confidentiality and the patient's right of access. In Connecticut, for example, a statutory Patient's Bill of Rights[8] provides that patients are entitled to confidential treatment of personal and medical records. Patients may approve or refuse their release to any individual outside the facility, except in the case of the patient's transfer to another health care institution or as required by law or a third party payment contract. Numerous other statutes, including those of Maryland and Michigan, provide that medical records are confidential and may be disclosed only with the patient's consent[9] or as provided in the statutes.[10]

Most state laws expressly allow a patient or authorized representative to inspect the records. The person seeking access typically must make a written request to the hospital and pay reasonable clerical costs before the records become available. The hospital usually is responsible only for making the records available at reasonable times and place. Connecticut law states that upon written request, a provider must furnish patients with copies of their health records at a cost of no more than 25 cents per page plus postage and the cost of X-ray materials.[11] In California, facilities must provide for patient inspection within five working days of the request and provide copies within 15 working days and upon payment of fees.[12] Georgia also requires hospitals to provide access to patients upon receipt of a written request, but allows the institutions to require payment of the copying and mailing costs before releasing the records.[13]

Many statutes allow patients to review their records upon request during the course of hospitalization. The Minnesota statute is an example. It includes definitions of "patient" and "provider," and states that:

---

[7]See, e.g., Ala. Admin. Code, r. § 420-5-7.07(h) (1992); S.D. Admin. R. § 44:04:09:04 (1993).

[8]Conn. Gen. Stat. § 19a-550(b)(9)(1993) *as amended by* Conn. H.B. No. 7270 (New Laws 1993).

[9]Mich. Comp. Laws § 333.6112 (1991).

[10]Md. Code Ann. [Health Gen.] § 4-302(a)(2) (1993).

[11]Conn. Gen. Stat. § 20-7c(b) (1992) *as amended by* Conn. H.B. No. 6960 (New Laws 1993).

[12]Cal. Health & Safety Code § 1795.12 (1993).

[13]Ga. Code Ann. §§ 31-33-2 and 31-33-3 (1993).

(a) Upon request, a provider shall supply to a patient complete and accurate information possessed by that provider concerning any diagnosis, treatment and prognosis of the patient in terms and language the patient can reasonably be expected to understand.

(b) Upon a patient's written request, a provider, at a reasonable cost to the patient, shall promptly furnish to the patient (1) copies of the patient's health record, including but not limited to laboratory reports, X-rays, prescriptions, and other technical information used in assessing the patient's health condition, or (2) the pertinent portion of the record relating to a condition specified by the patient. With the consent of the patient, the provider may instead furnish only a summary of the record. The provider may exclude from the health record written speculation about the patient's health condition, except that all information necessary for the patient's informed consent must be provided.

(c) If a provider . . . reasonably determines that the information is detrimental to the physical or mental health of the patient, or is likely to cause the patient to inflict self-harm, or to harm another, the provider may withhold the information from the patient and may supply the information to an appropriate third party or to another provider . . . The other provider or third party may release the information to the patient.

(d) A provider . . . shall release information upon written request unless, prior to the request, a provider . . . has designated and described a specific basis for withholding the information as authorized by paragraph (c).[14]

Other statutes grant patients an unrestricted right of access to their medical records only after discharge from the hospital. The Illinois law is typical:

Every private and public hospital shall, upon the request of any patient who has been treated in such hospital and after his or her discharge there from, permit the patient, his or her physician or authorized attorney to examine the hospital records, including but not limited to the history, bedside notes, charts, pictures and plates, kept in connection with the treatment of such patient, and permit copies of such records to be made by him or her or his or her physician or authorized attorney. A request for examination of the records shall be in writing and shall be delivered to the administrator of such hospital.[15]

---

[14]Minn. Stat. § 144.335(2) (Supp. 1993).
[15]735 Ill. Comp. Stat. Ann. § 5/8-2001 (1993).

Florida has similar legislation, providing that a licensed facility, upon receiving a request but only after discharge of the patient, must furnish a patient or representative a true and correct copy of the record.[16]

Many statutes allow the hospital to refuse to grant the patient's request for disclosure where the individual seeks access to psychiatric information, where release of psychiatric information would be detrimental to the patient's mental health,[17] or where release of any medical information would adversely affect the general health of the person.[18] In some instances, the psychiatric patient can obtain at least a summary of the records following termination of the treatment program.[19] In New York, the provider may deny access to a patient's records where the requested information can reasonably be expected to cause substantial and identifiable harm to the subject or others that outweighs the right to access.[20] In most states where a patient lawfully can be denied access to records, however, the hospital may be required to deliver copies of the record to the patient's representative or attorney.[21]

Several states' statutes contain special provisions concerning a patient's access to particular portions of the record, such as X-rays;[22] others have separate rules governing access by a minor patient;[23] and still others allow a provider to prepare a summary of the record for inspection and copying rather than allowing the patient access to the entire record.[24]

Some statutes and regulations providing access to records by patients prescribe a time limit for the hospital's response. For example, New York requires the provider to respond to a request to review records within ten days after receiving the request.[25] California law requires the hospital to provide for inspection of records within five working days after receiving a request and to provide copies of the record within 15 days.[26] Illinois allows 60 days to respond.[27] Minnesota law states that a provider must furnish copies of a medical record to

---

[16]Fla. Stat. § 395.017 (1992).

[17]See, e.g., Cal. Health & Safety Code § 1795.14(b) (1993); Colo Rev. Stat. § 25-1-801 (1993).

[18]See, e.g., Haw. Rev. Stat. § 622-57 (1993); Me. Rev. Stat., tit. 22 § 1711 (1992); Minn. Stat. Ann. § 144.335(2)(c) (1993).

[19]Colo. Rev. Stat. § 25-1-801(1) (1993).

[20]N.Y. Pub. Health Law § 18(3) (1993).

[21]See, e.g., Haw. Rev. Stat. § 622-57 (1993); Me. Rev. Stat. Ann., tit. 22 § 1711 (1992); Minn. Stat. § 144.335(2)(c) (1993) (provider may withhold information from patient and may supply the information to appropriate third party); Okla. Stat. Ann., tit. 76 § 19 (1992).

[22]See, e.g., Cal. Health & Safety Code §§ 1795.12(c) and (e) (1993).

[23]See, e.g., Cal. Health & Safety Code § 1795.14 (1993); N.Y. Pub. Health Law § 18(2)(c) (1993).

[24]See, e.g., Cal. Health & Safety Code § 1795.20(a) (1993); Minn. Stat. § 144.335(2)(b) (1993).

[25]N.Y. Pub. Health Law § 18 (1993).

[26]Cal. Health & Safety Code § 1795.12 (1993).

[27]735 Ill. Comp. Stat. Ann. 5/8-2001 (1993).

a patient "promptly" after receiving the request.[28] As the laws in each state vary with respect to the time allowed for hospitals to respond, every hospital must check requirements in its own area. Where the laws are silent on the matter, a hospital should develop a policy for providing copies of patient records as soon as possible after the institution reasonably can locate the record and prepare a copy for the patient.

In the absence of statute or regulation, courts in some jurisdictions have recognized a hospital's common law duty to allow a patient limited access to records.[29] In *Cannell v. Medical and Surgical Clinic*, for instance, the court found that the fiduciary qualities of the physician-patient relationship require the provider to disclose medical data to the patient or agent upon request, and that the patient need not engage in legal proceedings to attain higher status in order to receive such information.[30] Other courts have held that, although a hospital may have a common law duty to disclose all or part of a patient's record, there is no obligation to do so free of charge.[31] However, because the vast majority of states now grant statutory recognition to a patient's right of access, courts are less likely to become involved in enunciating legal precedent on this issue.

Before the hospital provides access to a third party with the patient's authorization, it may take reasonable precautions to verify the authority of the person seeking the information. Some state statutes specifically authorize hospitals to take these measures.[32] Courts also have recognized a hospital's right to verify the validity of a patient's authorization. In one case, a state appeals court held that a hospital records clerk properly refused to release certain files on the basis of a signed authorization form containing alterations that were unacceptable under hospital records policy.[33] On the other hand, a hospital will be liable for unreasonably restricting access to medical records as tantamount to refusal to release the records.[34]

Determining who is the patient's representative for purposes of accessing records also can generate difficulties for hospitals. In *Emmett v. Eastern Dispensary and Casualty Hosp.*,[35] for instance, the son of a deceased patient requested to see his father's medical record in order to bring a wrongful death action against the hospital. However, the hospital refused to release the records because the son was not the father's administrator and, therefore, not the father's

---

[28]Minn. Stat. § 144.335(2)(b) (1993).

[29]See, e.g., *Hutchins v. Texas Rehabilitation Comm'n.*, 544 S.W.2d 802 (Tex. Ct. App. 1976); *In re Weiss*, 147 N.Y.S.2d 455 (N.Y. Sup. Ct. 1955).

[30]315 N.E.2d 278 (Ill. App. Ct. 1974); see also *Emmett v. Eastern Dispensary and Casualty Hosp.*, 396 F.2d 931 (D.C. Cir. 1967); *Parkson v. Central DuPage Hosp.*, 435 N.E.2d 140 (Ill. Ct. App. 1982).

[31]*Rabens v. Jackson Park Hosp. Found.*, 351 N.E.2d 276, 279 (Ill. Ct. App. 1976).

[32]See Cal. Health & Safety Code § 1795.12(d) (1993).

[33]*Thurman v. Crawford*, 652 S.W.2d 240, 242 (Mo. Ct. App. 1983).

[34]*Id.*

[35]396 F.2d 93 (D.C. Cir. 1967).

legal representative. The court ruled that, while the decedent's proper legal representative is the only person authorized to bring a suit for wrongful death, the purpose of a suit is to benefit the spouse and next of kin. Therefore, the court concluded, the hospital's duty of disclosure to the patient extended to the patient's son, his only surviving relative and next of kin.

In addition to meeting its legal obligations, a hospital may have some practical reasons for allowing a patient to examine the records during hospitalization. Hospitals should consider whether refusal to permit such an inspection will create unnecessary problems for the institution and its staff. An inpatient who is denied access to a chart may become hostile and more difficult to treat. Moreover, the patient may be more likely to file a claim against the hospital if treatment ends in a poor result.

Therefore, unless the attending physician has a reasonable basis for believing that disclosure of the medical record will harm the patient, the hospital should allow the individual to review the record. In some instances, a record review coordinated by the patient's attending physician will enhance the patient's understanding of actions taken by the physician, thereby promoting better hospital-patient relations and decreasing the likelihood of any claims being filed against the facility. If inpatients are allowed to examine their records, however, the hospital should employ its customary record security procedures. (Record security is discussed later in this chapter.)

Psychiatric Records

In some states, the rules on access to the medical records of mental health patients differ from those applicable to medical records generally. In past years, mental health patients were denied access to their medical records even where nonmental health patients in the same jurisdiction had such a right. It was widely believed that authorizing psychiatric patients to review their records would be injurious to their health.

Today, however, mental health patients in some states have the same right to inspect their records as do other patients, althouth only a few laws expressly grant such individuals a right to access their records.[36] In other states, the laws provide that records of psychiatric patients or institutionalized persons are confidential and shall be disclosed only as provided by the statute. In New Jersey, for example, the statute governing psychiatric patients makes confidential all records that directly or indirectly identify an individual who is receiving or has received mental health services, except if the person or legal guardian

---

[36]See, e.g., Haw. Rev. Stat. § 334E-2(a)(15) (1993); 740 Ill. Comp Stat. Ann. 110/4(a) (1993).

consents.[37] Such a provision, granting the patient a statutory right to records confidentiality, can be construed to create a corresponding implied right of access for the patient. A federal trial court has ruled that this provision allows patients confined in mental institutions to obtain access to all of their records maintained by the state, even if their guardians do not consent to disclosure, unless the state can challenge the patients' capacity to give informed consent.[38]

Even where a patient has a clear right to review the records, state legislation frequently imposes limits on the exercise of that right. For example, the New York mental hygiene law establishes the confidentiality of clinical records and authorizes the patient to make a written request to review the files.[39] The facility maintaining the records must inform the patient's treating physician upon receipt of the request. The facility must permit the patient to inspect the records or provide copies unless the treating practitioner determines that the requested review could "reasonably be expected to cause substantial and identifiable harm to the patient."[40] If review is denied, the patient has a right to obtain review of that decision without cost by the appropriate records committee.[41] The patient also has a right to judicial review of an adverse determination by the committee.[42]

State legislation in some jurisdictions allows mental health patients to petition a court to seal the records of treatment. Under New York legislation, for example, patients must demonstrate by competent medical evidence that they are not currently suffering from mental illness, that they have not received inpatient services for treatment of mental illness for a period of three years, and that the interests of both the petitioners and society would be served best by sealing the records.[43] One court has ruled that society has an interest in sealing mental health records to remove the barriers that would prevent a former psychiatric patient from participating fully in society without fear of stigma or discrimination.[44] In the absence of a statutory right to expunge mental health records, some courts have authorized such action for records that result from an

---

[37]N.J. Rev. Stat. § 30:4-24.3 (1993).

[38]*Bonnie S. v. Altman*, 683 F. Supp. 100 (D.N.J. 1988).

[39]N.Y. Mental Hyg. Law § 33.16(b)1 (1993).

[40]*Id.* § 33.16(c).

[41]*Id.* § 33.16(c)(4).

[42]*Id.* § 33.16(c)(5); see also *Davis v. Henderson*, 549 N.Y.S.2d 241 (N.Y. App. Div. 1989) where the court remitted the petitioner's claim for judicial review that a psychiatric facility had denied his request to review his records but had failed to inform him of his right to committee review. The court ordered the case returned to the facility for further proceedings under the New York Mental Hygiene Law.

[43]See, e.g., N.Y. Mental Hyg. Law § 33.14(a)(1) (1993).

[44]*Smith v. Butler*, 544 N.Y.S.2d 711 (N.Y. Sup. Ct. 1989).

illegal commitment or illegal involuntary examination proceeding involving falsehood or perjury.[45]

If a state does not have specific legislation governing access to psychiatric records, access falls under the general rules of confidentiality effective in the jurisdiction. Typically, only a person authorized by a competent patient can obtain access to that patient's records, including those relating to psychiatric treatment. If a patient is incompetent, the duly authorized legal guardian may access the records in the same manner that the patient would.[46] However, the hospital should request to see the appropriate authorization before permitting access to a person who claims to be acting on behalf of an incompetent patient. A guardian who has been appointed for a specific purpose does not necessarily have the authority to review an incompetent patient's records.[47]

Similarly, where an incompetent patient has a guardian assigned by a court to act in the person's best interests, the hospital should be careful not to release the records to other persons associated with the patient. In one case, for example,[48] the mother of an involuntarily committed minor requested access to records pertaining to her daughter's treatment, but the child's court-appointed guardian objected. The mother alleged but could not prove that decisions made by the hospital were not in the best interests of her daughter. The court denied the mother's request, emphasizing that one purpose of appointing a guardian is to protect the minor from parental efforts to terminate treatment for reasons unrelated to the best interests of the child.[49]

Records of Minors

Generally, a hospital may disclose the medical record of a minor patient only with the authorization of one of that individual's parents. Parents typically are

[45]*Johnston v. State*, 466 So. 2d 413 (Fla. Dist. Ct. App. 1985) *citing Wolfe v. Beal*, 384 A.2d 1187 (Pa. 1978).

[46]See, e.g., *Gaertner v. State*, 187 N.W.2d 429 (Mich. 1971).

[47]See, e.g., *Application of Patarino*, 142 N.Y.S.2d 891 (N.Y. Ct. Cl. 1955).

[48]*In re Application for the Commitment of J.C.G. to Trenton Psychiatric Hosp.*, 366 A.2d 733 (Hudson County Ct. 1976).

[49]Cases involving a guardian purportedly acting on behalf of a mental health patient should be distinguished, however, from those involving an "interested person" who may have independent rights under state law to participate in mental health proceedings affecting a patient. See, e.g., *In re Wollan*, 390 N.W.2d 839 (Minn. Ct. App. 1986), where the court granted records access to the sister of a mentally ill and dangerous patient as an "interested person" entitled to notification of any change in the patient's status and the right to request review of the change of status under Minnesota law. See also *In re New York News*, 503 N.Y.S.2d 714 (N.Y. 1986), where the court granted a newspaper access to sealed mental health records as a party "properly interested" in such records under applicable New York law.

allowed access to such records on behalf of a minor patient. If a guardian has been appointed to act in the child's behalf, only the guardian may access the patient's records and authorize release of information to others.

A number of state statutes governing access to medical records include specific directions about disclosing the records of a minor. For example, Minnesota defines the term "patient" to include a parent or guardian of a minor and then directs each hospital to provide copies of the record to the "patient" upon request.[50] The California statute has separate provisions dealing with access to a minor's records and disclosure of such records to third parties.[51] The provision on access provides that any adult patient, any minor patient authorized by law to consent to treatment, and any patient representative shall be entitled to inspect patient records upon written notice to the hospital and payment of reasonable fees. However, a minor patient shall be entitled to inspect only records pertaining to health care of the type for which the minor may lawfully consent.

Notwithstanding the general right of access granted to a minor's representative under California law, a representative may not access the minor's records if the individual has a right of inspection under the general rule of patient access by virtue of the minor's authority to consent to the type of medical treatment described in the record.[52] In addition, a health care provider may deny access to a minor's representative if it determines that access would have a detrimental effect on the provider's professional relationship with the minor.[53] The California statute defines "representative" as a parent or guardian of a minor who is a patient or former patient.[54]

A minor patient may authorize release of medical information to third parties if the information was obtained during the course of providing health care services to which the minor lawfully could consent under other provisions of the law.[55] In all other cases, the minor's legal representative must consent.[56]

---

[50]Minn. Stat. § 144.335(1)(a) (1993).

[51]Cal. Health & Safety Code § 1795.12(a) (1993); see also N.Y. Pub. Health Law § 17 (1993) (release of medical records), and N.Y. Pub. Health Law § 18 (1993) (access to patient information).

[52]Cal. Health & Safety Code § 1795.12(a) (1993).

[53]*Id.* § 1795.14(a)(2). See *In re Daniel C.H.*, 269 Cal. Rptr. 624 (Ct. App. 1990), in which the court applied this provision to deny a parent access to a minor child's psychotherapy records. The parent contended that he was entitled to access the child's confidential communications because as a parent, he has the right to receive information concerning the medical condition of his child. The court ruled, however, that access would cause substantial harm to the child, who might refuse to be open with the therapist out of fear of disclosure to the parent.

[54]*Id.* §§ 1795.10(c) and (e).

[55]Cal. Civil Code § 56.11(c)(1) (1993).

[56]*Id.* § 56.11(c)(2) (1993).

The New York law on access to a minor's record is similar to California's; however, New York allows the provider to deny access where release of information would have a detrimental effect on an infant's relationship with parents or guardian.[57] Further, a minor patient's records involving abortion or venereal disease never can be released to the parent or guardian.[58] In all other cases, the parent or guardian can authorize release to third parties.

The statutes of many states simply are not clear on the question of parental or guardian access to a minor's records. Most statutes permit access with the consent of "the patient,"[59] or "the patient or his authorized representative."[60] In those states, hospitals should follow the general rule and obtain the authorization of the minor's parent before disclosing the patient's records to third parties.

In this regard, a hospital must examine carefully the definitions of terms such as "patient" and "representative" in the statute because not all states define those terms in the same way. Moreover, the same state may provide one definition under the provisions on direct access and another definition for disclosure to third parties.

Most importantly, a hospital treating or planning to treat a young person must double-check the legal age for giving consent to the particular treatment involved. While a "minor" in most states is a person under 18 years of age,[61] many jurisdictions create exceptions for certain types of medical treatment. For example, in California, a 12-year-old may consent to mental health treatment if the child presents a serious danger to self or others, or has been the victim of alleged incest or child abuse.[62] A married minor of any age lawfully can consent to any hospital, medical, or surgical care.[63] In Illinois, a 17-year-old can consent to a blood donation.[64]

RECORD DUPLICATION AND FEES

Although hospitals have a duty to permit patients and their representatives to inspect and copy their medical records, hospitals are not obligated to do so free. The authority to charge duplication fees and the amounts of those fees result from either specific statutory provisions or from case law.

---

[57]N.Y. Pub. Health Law § 18(2)(c) (1993).

[58]Id. § 17 (1993).

[59]See, e.g., Colo. Rev. Stat. § 25-1-801(1)(a) (1993); Fla. Stat. Ann. ch. 395.017(1) (1993); Haw. Rev. Stat. § 622-57 (1993).

[60]See, e.g., Me. Rev. Stat., tit. 22 § 1711 (1992); Tenn. Code Ann. § 68-11-304(a) (1993).

[61]See Cal. Fam. Code § 6500 (1993).

[62]Id. § 6924 (1993).

[63]Id. § 7002 and 7050 (1993).

[64]210 Ill. Comp. Stat. Ann. 15/1 (1993).

In some states, a hospital may impose a reasonable charge for copying records as a matter of statute. Hospitals in Montana are not required to permit examination or photocopying of a medical record until a reasonable fee is paid.[65] While many of the statutory or regulatory provisions on fees enunciate a "reasonable" standard to determine the amount, other states have stipulated specific maximum amounts that hospitals may charge for these services. For example, in Louisiana, a hospital may require payment of a reasonable copying charge before releasing a patient's medical record. The amount may not exceed $1 per page for the first 25 pages, 50¢ per page thereafter, and a maximum handling charge of $10.[66]

In the absence of a statute, courts have applied similar rules on a hospital's right to charge fees for accessing a medical record. For example, in *Rabens v. Jackson Park Hosp. Foundation*,[67] a court in Mississippi held that a hospital obligated to disclose record information to the patient could charge a fee for reproducing that information. In an Illinois case,[68] a court held that the hospital properly refused to reproduce and release voluminous patient records when it received only a form request and offer to pay for "reasonable access." The court ruled that the hospital properly could allow the person making the request to review the full record and indicate what parts he was willing to pay to have copied.

Whether the authority to charge an access fee derives from legislation or case law, the price a hospital charges for reproducing any portion of a patient's medical record should be based on the facility's actual or reasonable cost to remove the record from the record library and duplicate the portions requested. Courts consistently have applied this definition of "reasonable" charge. In a New York trial court ruling,[69] for example, the statute allowed the hospital to impose a "reasonable charge" for copying a patient's record. The court held that the charge per page must be based on actual costs and not a "mere estimate." The court said that the hospital ordinarily is responsible for keeping patient records and could not charge the patient for maintaining them; however, it could recover for the use of its photocopying equipment, wages paid to the equipment operator, and administrative overhead incurred in responding to the patient's request for a copy of the records.

Another court clearly stated that the hospital was not permitted to make a profit from the patient's request.[70] The court also declared that the charge billed

---

[65]Mont. Code. Ann. § 50-16-541 (1993).

[66]La. Rev. Stat. § 40:12.99.961(A)(2)(b) (1993).

[67]337 So. 2d 931 (Miss. 1976).

[68]*Young v. Madison Gen. Hosp.*, 351 N.E.2d 276 (Ill. App. Ct. 1976).

[69]*Mauer v. Mount Sinai Hosp.*, 193 N.Y.L.J., No. 22, (N.Y. Sup. Ct., N.Y. County, Feb. 1, 1985).

[70]*Graham v. Thompson*, 421 N.W.2d 694 (Mich. Ct. App. 1988).

to paying requesters could not include any amount subsidizing the expense of photocopying for nonpaying parties who received free copies of records under hospital policy.

In responding to patient requests for photocopying records, a hospital may contract with a third party to perform the work.[71] Whenever the hospital makes such an arrangement, it must ensure confidentiality of the records in its contract with the party providing the copying services. (For more about liability for improper disclosures of medical records information, see Chapter 8.)

Alternatively, patients might choose to rent a portable photocopy machine and copy the records themselves. Patients choosing that option must reimburse the hospital for retrieving the file and for time spent by a hospital employee supervising the copying.[72] A patient does not have the right to unsupervised inspection and copying of records off hospital premises.[73] When responding to the patient's request to access and copy records, the hospital has the obligation to make the records available at a reasonable time and place.[74] Those arrangements must be made within the time prescribed by law or within a reasonable time after the hospital receives the request for information.

RECORD SECURITY

It is essential that each hospital establish an effective procedure for safeguarding medical records. Record security is critical to protecting patient confidentiality and preventing intentional alteration or falsification of records by hospital staff or others. Unfortunately, some hospitals have learned through experience that, given the opportunity, patients occasionally will remove important sections or alter significant information in their records simply to improve their chances of bringing a successful negligence action against the facility.

Other organizations or individuals also have strong interests in the information in certain medical records, and these people may go to great lengths to discover that information. In one case,[75] for example, agents of an insurance company obtained confidential information about two hospitalized insurance claimants by hiring an investigator to telephone an unnamed source at the hospital. Although the court dismissed criminal charges of theft filed against the agents because confidentiality of medical records information was not a "thing

---

[71]*Terry v. HCM Inc.*, No. 87-CH-3250 (Ill. Circuit Ct., Cook County, Aug. 26, 1987).

[72]*McDonald v. State Univ. of N.Y.*, 514 N.Y.S.2d 789 (N.Y. App. Div. 1987); *Paterna v. Zandieh*, 515 N.Y.S.2d 54 (N.Y App. Div. 1987); *Hayes v. County of Nassau*, 512 N.Y.S.2d 134 (N.Y. App. Div. 1987).

[73]*Paterna, supra*, n.72 at 55.

[74]See, e.g., N.Y. Pub. Health Law § 18.2(f) (1993).

[75]*People v. Home Ins. Co.* 591 P.2d 1036 (Colo. 1979).

of value" under that state's theft statutes, the case indicated the extent to which some people would go to obtain medical records information.

To protect medical records from abuse, hospitals should adopt the following security measures as a minimum:

- It should require that competent medical records or risk management personnel review every record before it is examined by the patient or representative. The reviewer should notify the appropriate hospital executive if the record is incomplete or otherwise defective, or if it reveals a problem that could give rise to negligence liability by the hospital or its staff.
- It should never allow an original medical record to be removed from the hospital's premises unless required by legal process (appropriate response to legal process is discussed later in this chapter), or pursuant to a defined hospital procedure that permits inpatients going to another facility for testing to take their medical records with them. This procedure for allowing patients to take their records should be permitted only if the individual is returning to the hospital the same day, and provided that the patient is accompanied by a responsible hospital employee.
- It should never allow anyone who is not an authorized hospital employee or staff member to examine a medical record without supervision. That includes a patient and/or a representative. Where a patient or other person is properly authorized to review a record under the principles of law discussed above, the hospital should provide accommodations for record inspection in its medical records department or in another location under proper surveillance.

Security for computerized medical records raises special concerns, which are discussed in Chapter 6.

ACCESS BY OTHERS

Access to a patient's medical record by third parties is governed by state and federal law. In most states, the statute encompassing patient records confidentiality contains exceptions for access by persons other than the patient. Usually, hospital personnel may review the records without consent for purposes related to the patient's care.[76] Medical records information also may be released to hospital personnel as necessary for billing the patient.[77] Some states also

---

[76]See, e.g., Cal. Civ. Code § 56.10(c)(1) (1992); Fla. Stat. ch. 395.017(3)(a) (1992); Wis. Stat. § 146.82(2) (1991-1992).

[77]See, e.g., Wis. Stat. § 146.82(3) (1991-1992).

authorize release to the patient's insurer, employer, or health services plan for billing purposes.[78] A few states have simple confidentiality provisions but allow the hospital to release patient information upon lawful court order.[79] Finally, many states grant access to professional licensing bodies and peer review committees.[80] The availability of patient records to these groups is discussed in detail later in this chapter.

Special laws govern access to certain kinds of medical records, and usually impose more strict requirements for confidentiality. Such laws also may expand the list of third parties who lawfully may obtain access to record information without the patient's consent. Hospital personnel involved with the release of medical information must understand all of these rules and exceptions.

Alcohol and Drug Abuse Patient Records

Provisions in the Public Health Service Act[81] address access to the records of drug or alcohol abuse patients. Under these provisions, records of the "identity, diagnosis, prognosis, or treatment" of any patient maintained in connection with either program are confidential, and may not be disclosed except for certain purposes and under certain circumstances.[82] Any person or program that releases information in violation of the act is subject to criminal fines.[83]

The Secretary of HHS has promulgated regulations on access to records of alcohol and drug abuse patients covered by the federal acts.[84] The regulations, like the statutes, generally prohibit disclosure of certain types of information about an alcohol or drug abuse patient except as specifically authorized.[85]

Virtually every alcohol and/or drug abuse treatment center is subject to the statute and regulations. Under the regulations, any facility operating a "program" that is "federally assisted" falls within the scope of this legislation.[86] "Federal assistance" is defined broadly to include any program that receives a

---

[78]See, e.g., Cal. Civ. Code §§ 56.10(c)(2) and (3) (1992).

[79]See, e.g., Wis. Stat. § 146-82(4) (1991-1992).

[80]See, e.g., Cal. Civ. Code § 56.10(c)(5) (1992) (identifying information that may not be removed from the premises).

[81]Originally enacted as Drug Abuse Prevention, Treatment, and Rehabilitation Act. See generally 21 U.S.C. §§ 1101–1800(1992) and the Comprehensive Alcohol Abuse and Alcoholism Prevention, Treatment, and Rehabilitation Act. See generally 42 U.S.C. §§ 4541–4594 (1992).

[82]42 U.S.C. § 290dd-2 (1992).

[83]*Id.* § 290dd-2(f) (1992).

[84]The regulations are codified at 42 C.F.R. 2.1–2.67 (1992).

[85]*Id.* §§ 2.12(a) and 2.13(a) (1992).

[86]*Id.* § 2.12(a)(1)(ii) (1992).

state or municipal grant if the state or local government in turn has received any unrestricted grants or funds from the federal government.[87] If contributions to a program are deductible under federal income tax law, the program is regarded as a recipient of federal financial assistance. Few programs are totally privately funded, receive no tax deductions for contributions, and/or are neither licensed nor regulated by the federal government. Accordingly, almost every drug or alcohol abuse progam is governed by this legislation.[88]

"Program" refers to an individual, partnership, corporation, governmental agency, or other legal entity holding itself out, in whole or part, as providing, and does provide, alcohol or drug abuse diagnosis, treatment, or referral for treatment. For a general medical care facility or any part of it to qualify as a "program," it must have an identified unit that provides such services, or medical personnel whose primary function is to provide such services and who are identified as providers of such services.[89] The terms "diagnosis," "treatment," "alcohol abuse," and "drug abuse" are defined specifically in the regulations.[90]

The provisions for the release of information apply only if an individual is a "patient" under the law. The regulations define "patient" as any individual who has requested or received a diagnosis or treatment for alcohol or drug abuse at a federally assisted program.[91] One court ruled that a person who enters a hospital emergency room for immediate treatment of conditions arising from a drug overdose is a "patient" under the regulations because that individual clearly "applied for treatment or diagnosis of drug abuse."[92] Further, the court ruled, the emergency room qualified as a "program" because it provides diagnoses, treatment, and referrals and because many drug users enter the hospital through the emergency room as the first step to further drug treatment.

An alcohol or drug abuse treatment program under this legislation may not disclose any information, recorded or not, that would identify a patient as an

---

[87]However, if a state receives federal money earmarked for certain purposes not including an alcohol or drug abuse treatment program, a facility receiving state funds is not subject to the federal laws governing alcohol and drug abuse patient records. See *Listion v. Shelby County*, slip op. No. 93007-3 R.D., Tenn. Ct. App. (Oct. 23, 1987).

[88]Whenever a person or program seeks to invoke the protection of the federal statute and regulations in order to assure the confidentiality of patient records, that person or program bears the burden of demonstrating the applicability of the federal laws. See *Samaritan Health Serv. v. Glendale*, 714 P.2d 827 (Ariz. Ct. App. 1986) where the facility claiming protection under 42 U.S.C. § 290ee-3 failed to show that it operated a program subject to the law; see also *State v. Gulletson*, 383 N.W.2d 338 (Minn. Ct. App. 1986).

[89]42 C.F.R. § 2.11 (1992).

[90]*Id.* (1992).

[91]*Id.* (1992).

[92]*U.S. v. Eide*, 875 F.2d 1429, 1435 (9th Cir. 1989).

alcohol or drug abuser either directly, by reference to other publicly available information, or through verification by another person.[93] This blanket prohibition clearly covers a broad range of information about a patient, including nonwritten information and indirect indications of a patient's identity.[94]

Hospitals subject to these rules must be wary of implicit disclosure of confidential information. If a general care hospital fails to disclose information about a drug or alcohol abuse patient that it routinely discloses about other patients, it could be liable for implicitly admitting that the patient was being treated for drug or alcohol abuse. Hospitals therefore should delete such patients from their registers unless the individuals consent to having their presence acknowledged. Although that practice will protect the patients' identity as required by the alcohol and drug abuse regulations, it creates other problems for hospitals that maintain patient registers at their switchboards and information desks. Hospitals must devise methods for identifying drug or alcohol abuse patients that do not allow its personnel to release information inadvertently.

The medical records of alcohol and drug abuse patients may be disclosed with their consent under certain circumstances. The regulations provide a list of elements required for lawful consent, along with a sample consent form.[95] In general, the consent must be in writing, signed by the patient or authorized signatory, and must describe the kind of information to be disclosed and the purpose for disclosure. The person releasing the medical records must notify the recipient of the fact that the latter in turn will be bound by the regulations and prohibited from further disclosure.[96] A facility releasing information in accordance with this provision should document its notice to the recipient in writing; a routine form letter sent to each recipient of alcohol and drug abuse patient records would facilitate meeting this requirement.

Under the regulations, minors may consent to the release of their drug and alcohol abuse records if, under state law, they may consent to the treatment.[97] The regulations do not address directly the circumstances under which a minor may consent to such treatment, but instead expressly defer to state law on the issue. Consequently, a minor's ability to consent to the release of treatment records covered by the federal law will vary from state to state. Where state law

---

[93]42 C.F.R. § 2.12(a)(1)(i) (1992).

[94]But see *State v. Braun*, 376 N.W.2d 451 (Minn. Ct. App. 1985), where the court suggested that personal observations made to police officers by a counselor at a drug treatment center relating to a patient's parole for drug-related offenses were not "records" under the regulations, even if reduced to writing by the counselor.

[95]42 C.F.R. §§ 2.31(a) and (b) (1992).

[96]*Id.* § 2.32 (1992).

[97]*Id.* § 2.14(b) (1992).

mandates parental consent to alcohol and drug abuse treatment for a minor, the federal regulations require parental consent to any disclosure of information relating to such treatment.[98] Federal regulations also specifically authorize disclosure to parents or guardian of facts relevant to reducing a substantial threat to the minor's life or physical well-being where the individual lacks capacity to make a rational decision about whether to release the records.[99] The regulations also contain a special provision on release of information by incompetent patients.[100]

Disclosure without consent is permitted under limited circumstances. For example, disclosure to medical personnel may be made in a medical emergency posing an immediate threat to health.[101] A program proceeding under this provision must enter the following information directly into the patient's record:

- the name of the medical personnel to whom disclosure was made and their affiliation with any health care facility;
- the name of the individual making the disclosure;
- the date and time of the disclosure; and
- the nature of the emergency.[102]

Another important exception to the general ban on disclosure without the patient's consent applies to communications between persons who need the information to perform duties arising out of diagnosis, treatment, or referral for treatment of alcohol or drug abuse. However, such exchanges of information are permitted only if they occur within a program or between a program and an entity that has direct administrative control over the program.[103] The ban on disclosure does not apply to communications between a program and a "qualified service organization," defined as including companies providing data processing, bill collecting, lab work, legal services, and other services to the program.[104] On the other hand, the ban on disclosure expressly is extended to third party payers, entities with direct administrative control over programs receiving information

---

[98]*Id.* § 2.14(c) (1992).
[99]*Id.* § 2.14(d) (1992).
[100]*Id.* § 2.15 (1992).
[101]*Id.* § 2.51(a) (1992).
[102]*Id.* § 2.51(c) (1992).
[103]*Id.* § 2.12(c)(3) (1992).
[104]*Id.* §§ 2.12(c) (4) and 2.11 (1992).

from the program related to diagnosis, treatment, or referral, and persons receiving information from a covered program with the patient's consent as provided under the regulations.[105]

Disclosure without consent may be made for audit and evaluation[106] or for research purposes.[107] The regulations provide for additional measures in these situations to protect patient information and identification. The regulations allow certain disclosures of information to the Food and Drug Administration where a tainted drug may threaten the health of an individual at the facility.[108] Other exceptions are made for disclosures to law enforcement officials relating to a patient's commission or threat to commit a crime on program premises or against program personnel[109] and to reporting suspected child abuse and neglect under state law.[110] The current federal regulations expressly defer to state law and allow the release of medical records on alcohol and drug abuse treatment to satisfy the reporting requirements under this type of legislation. A program subject to both state and federal law in this regard must be careful to release only the particular information required by state law as part of a child abuse report. Any release of information beyond that required by state law constitutes a breach of the federal regulations.

Disclosure without consent also may be made in response to a court order issued for good cause.[111] In general, the statute provides that an order for disclosure may issue only for good cause. In assessing good cause, the court shall weigh "the public interest and the need for disclosure against the injury to the patient, to the physician-patient relationship, and to the treatment services." [112]

The regulations issued by the Secretary of HHS add further requirements. They permit a person with a legally recognized interest in disclosure of records covered by the federal provisions to apply for a court order to use the records for noncriminal purposes.[113] A court may issue an order to disclose records for noncriminal purposes only for "good cause." For "good cause" to exist, the evidence must demonstrate that the information is not available through other means, and that the public interest and need for disclosure outweigh the potential injury to the patient, the physician-patient relationship, and the treatment services.[114]

---

[105]*Id.* § 2.12(d) (2) (1992).

[106]*Id.* § 2.53 (1992).

[107]*Id.* § 2.52 (1992).

[108]*Id.* § 2.51(b) (1992).

[109]*Id.* § 2.12(c)(5) (1992).

[110]*Id.* § 2.12(c)(6) (1992).

[111]42 U.S.C. § 290dd-2(b)(2)(C) (1992); see also 42 C.F.R. §§ 2.61–2.67 (1992).

[112]42 U.S.C. § 290dd-2 (1992).

[113]42 C.F.R. § 2.64 (1992).

[114]*Id.* § 2.61(d) (1992).

If the records are to be used in criminal investigation or prosecution of patients, different criteria govern their release. These criteria relate to the seriousness of the underlying crime; the value of information in the records to the investigation or prosecution; the unavailability or ineffectiveness of other ways to obtain the information; the public interest and need for disclosure versus the potential injury to the patient, physician-patient relationship, and the ability of the program to provide services to others; and the availability of independent counsel for the person holding the records.[115]

Many of the programs subject to the federal laws on alcohol and drug abuse patient records also are governed by state law, including state rules on confidentiality and state mandatory reporting laws. The operation of both sets of rules may create conflicts for the program.

The federal regulations provide that the statutes authorizing them do not preempt state law.[116] They state that if disclosure permitted by the federal regulations is prohibited under state law, federal law should not be interpreted to authorize a violation of the state law. On the other hand, the regulations provide that state law may not authorize or compel any disclosure prohibited by the federal regulations. In other words, if the federal law permits disclosure prohibited by state law, the disclosure is not to be made; and if federal law prohibits disclosure, disclosure should not be made, regardless of the state law governing the issue. Nevertheless, a program subject to both sets of rules must be careful to release only the particular information required by state law as part of a child abuse report. Any release of information beyond that required by state law constitutes a breach of the federal regulations.

Several states have enacted their own provisions for access and disclosure of alcohol and drug abuse patient records.[117] These statutes typically impose a general ban on disclosure of records by covered programs except as provided in the law. Exceptions to confidentiality generally are created for disclosures relating to financial and compliance audits, program evaluation, between qualified personnel involved in the patient's treatment, and to qualified persons responding to a medical emergency. Alcohol and drug abuse treatment programs in each state must be aware of the particular state laws applicable to them in addition to the federal laws governing their patient records.

Privacy Act Records

The Privacy Act of 1974,[118] designed to give private citizens some control over information collected by the federal government, restricts the type of informa-

---

[115]*Id.* § 2.65(d) (1992).

[116]*Id.* § 2.20 (1992).

[117]See, e.g., Cal. Health & Safety Code § 11977 (1993); Md. Code Ann. [Health Gen.] § 8-601(c) (1993); Wis. Stat. § 51.30(4) (1991-1992).

[118]5 U.S.C. § 552a (1993).

tion that a federal agency lawfully may collect concerning an individual citizen or legal alien and limits the uses of such information. Under the Privacy Act, an agency may maintain only information that is relevant and necessary to its authorized purpose.[119] An agency may not disclose any information about a private individual through any means of communication to any person or other agency except as authorized in writing by the person or under certain conditions described in the Act.[120]

The Privacy Act also requires each federal agency to allow individuals to gain access to their records or any information pertaining to them and copy any or all of the information.[121] Individuals also may make requests to amend or modify their records, and the agency must either make the changes or provide an explanation for declining to do so.[122] In certain cases, the head of the agency must review the decision to deny a requested change.[123]

The Privacy Act allows an agency to disclose information about an individual without that person's consent only in certain circumstances. Disclosures may be made to officers and employees of the agency who need the information to perform their duties; for the purposes for which the information was collected; for certain statistical and law enforcement purposes; to Congress, the Comptroller General, or the National Archives and Records Administration; pursuant to a valid court order; or where a person shows compelling circumstances affecting the health or safety of the individual to whom the information relates.[124]

The Privacy Act provides civil remedies for individuals aggrieved by an agency's failure to comply with the law.[125] An injured individual may bring suit against the agency in federal court and, possibly, enjoin the agency from continuing its action and recover reasonable attorney fees and court costs. The Act provides for criminal fines against an officer or employee of an agency for certain willful violations of the statute.[126]

It is important to emphasize that the Privacy Act applies only to federal agencies. Hospitals operated by the federal government, therefore, are bound by the Act's requirements with respect to the disclosure of the medical records of their patients. In addition, medical records maintained in a records system operated under a contract with a federal government agency are subject to the

---

[119]*Id.* § 552a(e) (1993).

[120]*Id.* § 552a(b) (1993).

[121]*Id.* § 552a(d) (1993).

[122]*Id.* §§ 552a(d)(1) and (2) (1993).

[123]*Id.* § 552a(d)(3) (1993).

[124]*Id.* § 552a(b) (1993).

[125]*Id.* § 552a(g)(1) (1993).

[126]*Id.* § 552a(i)(1) (1993).

Privacy Act.[127] Private or state-owned hospitals generally are not subject to civil or criminal liability under the Act for their unlawful disclosure of patient information, or for any unlawful disclosure by a federal agency to which the hospital properly reports. The fact that a hospital or other health care facility receives federal funding or is subject to federal regulation does not automatically subject it to the Act.[128]

Freedom of Information Act

The Freedom of Information Act (FOIA),[129] enacted in 1966, provides public access to information on the operations and decisions of federal administrative agencies. The law provides that specific categories of information are available to the public unless one of the nine specific exceptions to the general rule of disclosure applies. Medical records may be exempt from FOIA under specific circumstances.

The FOIA requires each federal agency to make certain information available for public inspection and copying, including final opinions, concurring and dissenting opinions, and orders made in the adjudication of cases,[130] statements of policy and interpretations adopted by the agency and not published in the *Federal Register*;[131] and administrative staff manuals and instructions to staff that affect a member of the public.[132] Each agency must make the information available unless the materials are published promptly and copies offered for sale.[133]

All other records, except those specifically excluded under the FOIA, must be made available promptly to any person upon request who reasonably describes such records and complies with the agency's published rules covering the time, place, and fee for inspecting and copying.[134] Each agency also is required to maintain and make available a current index for public inspection and copying. The index must provide identifying information as to matters covered by the FOIA.[135] However, an agency may delete identifying details when it makes

---

[127] *Id.* § 552a(m)(1) (1993).

[128] *St. Michael's Convalescent Hosp. v. Cal.*, 643 F.2d 1369 (9th Cir. 1981).

[129] 5 U.S.C. § 552 (1993).

[130] *Id.* § 552(a)(2)(A) (1993).

[131] *Id.* § 552(a)(2)(B) (1993).

[132] *Id.* § 552(a)(2)(C) (1993).

[133] *Id.* § 552(a)(2) (1993).

[134] *Id.* § 552(a)(3) (1993).

[135] *Id.* § 552(a)(2) (1993).

available an opinion, statement of policy, interpretation, or staff manual or instruction to prevent a clearly unwarranted invasion of an individual's personal privacy. In each case, justification for the deletion must be explained fully in writing.[136]

Nine specific exceptions to the general FOIA disclosure are provided.[137] One of these exceptions, known as "Exception Six," covers "personnel and medical files and similar files, the disclosure of which would constitute a clearly unwarranted invasion of personal privacy.[138]

To qualify for protection from FOIA disclosure, medical records information must satisfy the three elements described in Exception Six:

1. the information must be contained in a personnel, medical, or similar file
2. disclosure of the information must constitute an invasion of privacy
3. the invasion clearly is unwarranted.[139]

An agency seeking to withhold information has the burden of showing that the requested material satisfies each and every element of Exception Six.[140]

In determining whether the information sought falls within this exception, the relevant consideration is whether the privacy interests associated with the information are similar to interests that generally arise from personnel or medical information, and not whether the data are recorded in a manner similar to a personnel or medical file.[141] A file is considered similar to personnel and medical files if it contains intimate details of an individual's life, family relations, personal health, religious and philosophical beliefs, and other matters that, if revealed, would prove personally embarrassing to a person of normal sensibilities. Whether file materials are similar turns on whether the facts that would be revealed would infringe on some privacy interest as highly personal or as intimate in nature as that at stake in personnel and medical records.

Once a court determines that requested information is the type of material covered by Exception Six, it must address whether disclosure of such informa-

---

[136]*Id.* § 552(a)(2) (1993).

[137]*Id.* § 552(b) (1993).

[138]*Id.* § 552(b)(6) (1993).

[139]*Sims v. C.I.A.*, 642 F.2d 562 (D.C. Ct. App. 1980), *rev'd and aff'd on other grounds*, 471 U.S. 159 (1985); see also *Citizens for Envtl. Quality Inc. v. U.S. Dep't. of Agric.*, 602 F. Supp. 532, 537 (D.D.C. 1984) where the court characterized its analysis under Exception Six as a two-step inquiry to determine, first, whether information sought is found in personnel, medical, or similar files and, second, whether release would constitute a clearly unwarranted invasion of privacy.

[140]*Sims, supra,* n. 138 at 566.

[141]*Harbolt v. Department of State*, 616 F.2d 772, 774 (5th Cir. 1980), *cert. denied*, 449 U.S. 856 (1980).

tion would constitute an invasion of privacy. Several courts have emphasized that Exception Six was intended to prevent public disclosure of intimate details about an individual's life, such as marital status, legitimacy of children, identity of fathers of children, medical condition, welfare payments, alcohol consumption, family fights, and reputation.[142] On the other hand, information connected with commercial matters, business judgments, or professional relationships is not covered by the exception.[143]

If a court concludes that the release of information would constitute an invasion of personal privacy as contemplated by Exception Six, it must balance the personal interest in preventing disclosure against the public interest in obtaining access to the information.[144] In this regard, courts have interpreted the language "clearly unwarranted invasion of personal privacy" as an expression of a congressional policy that favors disclosure and an instruction to tilt the balance in favor of disclosure.[145] An agency seeking to prevent the release of information under Exception Six, therefore, must make a detailed and factual showing of the likely consequences of disclosure in individual cases.[146] The possibility of embarrassment, identification, or speculation about the identity of an individual that would result from disclosure will outweigh the public interest.[147]

An agency is required to provide reasonably segregable nonexempt portions of an otherwise exempt record to any person requesting such record.[148] Federal agencies that maintain medical records or have obtained medical records legitimately from a hospital are required, both by the Privacy Act and by this exception to the FOIA, to withhold disclosure of such records unless a court, in balancing individual and public interests in the information, orders disclosure or unless such records are requested by Congress.

Although original medical records maintained by a federal agency are exempt from disclosure under Exception Six, disclosure may be required under the FOIA of any information taken from these records in connection with government-funded medical research and incorporated into research reports to a sponsoring agency. Determining whether the data belong to the researchers or to the agency is crucial in resolving a request for access under these circumstances because only the agency is subject to FOIA.

---

[142]*Sims, supra*, n.139 at 574, quoting *Rural Hous. Alliance v. U.S. Dep't. of Agric.*, 498 F.2d 73, 77 (D.C. Cir. 1974).

[143]*Sims, supra*, n.139 at 574-575, citing *Board of Trade of Chicago v. Commodity Futures Trading Comm'n.*, 627 F.2d 392, 399-400 (D.C. Cir. 1980).

[144]*Sims, supra*, n.139 at 573.

[145]*Id.* 575; *Citizens for Envtl. Quality, supra*, n.139 at 538.

[146]*Sims, supra*, n.139 at 575.

[147]*Id.*, and *Citizens for Envtl. Quality, supra*, n.139 at 538.

[148]5 U.S.C. § 552(b) (1993).

The U.S. Supreme Court has ruled[149] that "written data generated, owned, and possessed by a private controlled organization receiving federal study grants are not 'agency records' within the meaning of the [Freedom of Information] Act when copies of those data have not been obtained by a federal agency subject to the FOIA. Federal participation in the generation of the data by means of a grant from the Department of Health, Education, and Welfare (HEW) does not make the private organization a federal 'agency' within the terms of the Act."[150] The Court held that the grantee's data would become agency records if it could be shown that the agency directly controlled the day-to-day activities of the grantee.[151]

Hospitals receiving federal funds for medical research can minimize the risk of disclosure of research data under FOIA, therefore, by limiting the agency's supervision of studies conducted by hospital staff. The hospital also should obtain the agency's acknowledgment that the data are confidential and will not be disclosed except as required by law.

State Open Records Laws

Many states have their own freedom of information laws granting public access to records maintained by state agencies.[152] In some states, the statute is called the "public records" or "open records" law. Like the federal Freedom of Information Act, these typically contain exceptions for medical records where disclosure would constitute an unwarranted invasion of personal privacy.[153] A few states simply exempt all hospital or medical records from the public records law[154] or include them in a list of public records available only upon court order and in other limited circumstances.[155] Most case law arising under the state acts deals with determining whether a private interest in confidentiality outweighs the public interest in disclosure.

In *Child Protection Group v. Cline*,[156] for example, a West Virginia court outlined five factors for determining whether release of personal information

---

[149]*Forsham v. Harris*, 445 U.S. 169 (1980).

[150]*Id.* 171.

[151]*Id.* 180.

[152]See, e.g., Ala. Code § 36-12-40 (1993); Fla. Stat. ch. 119.01 (1993); Md. Code Ann. State Gov't. § 10-611 (1993).

[153]See, e.g., Ill. Comp. Stat. Ann. 140/7 (1993).

[154]See, e.g., La. Rev. Stat. § 44:7 (1992); Miss. Code Ann. § 41-9-68 (1993).

[155]See, e.g., Iowa Code Ann. § 22.7 (1993).

[156]350 S.E.2d 541 (W.Va. 1986).

under the state freedom of information act would constitute an "unreasonable" invasion of privacy: (1) whether disclosure would result in a substantial invasion of privacy and, if so, how serious; (2) the extent or value of the public interest involved and the purpose or object of individuals seeking disclosure; (3) whether the information was available from other sources; (4) whether the information was given with an expectation of confidentiality; and (5) whether it is possible to mold relief to limit the invasion of privacy. After examining these issues, the court in this case authorized release of a bus driver's psychiatric records to parents of schoolchildren after the driver acted in a manner raising serious questions about his ability to operate the bus safely.

Whether specific documents are the kind covered by an exception to a state public records law sometimes is unclear. In *Head v. Colloton*,[157] for instance, a state hospital objected to an attempt to access its bone marrow transplant registry under the Iowa Public Records Act, arguing that the registry was protected from disclosure under the statutory exemption to the Act for "hospital and medical records of the condition, diagnosis, care, or treatment of a patient or former patient, including outpatient." Although the court concluded that only hospital records relating to patient care and treatment are exempt from disclosure under the law, it concluded that the bone marrow records related to a patient and therefore were not accessible.

PRO RECORDKEEPING

The Tax Equity and Fiscal Responsibility Act of 1982[158] repealed the Professional Standards Review Organization (PSRO) program and replaced it with the Peer Review Organization (PRO) program as a component of Medicare law. Under the revised statute, a PRO, or "utilization and quality control peer review organization," means an entity composed of a substantial number of licensed doctors of medicine and osteopathy in the area representative of practicing physicians in the area, or an entity with a sufficient number of such doctors available under arrangement to assure adequate peer review of services provided in a hospital by the various specialties and subspecialties.[159]

At least one member of the PRO's governing body must be an individual representing consumers.[160] A PRO must be able to perform the required review functions efficiently and effectively, and must measure the pattern of quality of

---

[157]331 N.W.2d 870 (Iowa 1983).

[158]42 U.S.C. §§ 1320c–13 (1993).

[159]*Id.* §§ 1320c-1(1)(A) and (B) (1993).

[160]*Id.* § 1320c-1(3) (1993).

care provided in the area against objective criteria that define acceptable and adequate practice.[161]

PROs are charged with a number of functions. Most importantly, they must review some or all of the professional activities conducted by physicians and providers who receive federal reimbursement under Medicare. In conducting these reviews, PROs must determine (1) whether services and items were reasonable and necessary; (2) whether the quality of services met professionally recognized standards; and (3) whether inpatient services could have been provided more economically on an outpatient basis consistent with the provision of appropriate medical care.[162] The statute also requires PROs to conduct certain other reviews, including readmissions occurring within 31 days of discharge[163] and some or all ambulatory surgical procedures.[164]

In carrying out its functions, a PRO must collect and maintain records of relevant information, and permit access to such records and use of information as required by the Secretary of HHS subject to the statutory provisions prohibiting disclosure of certain PRO information.[165] Under the PRO regulations,[166] HCFA or any person, organization, or agency authorized by HHS or federal statute to monitor a PRO will have access to, and may obtain copies of, medical records of Medicare patients maintained by institutions or health care practitioners.[167] The statute and regulations address access and disclosure of medical records and PRO information in other contexts considered below.

PRO Access to Individual Patient Records

The statute grants PROs broad authority to access patient records and other information. First, it provides that each PRO shall examine the pertinent records of any practitioner or provider of health care services subject to its review[168] and may require the institutions or practitioners to provide copies of records or information to the PRO.[169] Second, a PRO has authority to access and require copies of Medicare records or information held by intermediaries or carriers if the PRO determines that such material is necessary to carry out its review

---

[161]*Id.* § 1320c-1(2) (1993).

[162]*Id.* §§ 1320c-3(a)(1)(A)–(C) (1993).

[163]*Id.* § 1320c-3(a)(13) (1993).

[164]*Id.* § 1320c-3(d) (1993).

[165]*Id.* § 1320c-3(a)(9) (1993).

[166]42 C.F.R. §§ 462.1–476.143 (1992).

[167]*Id.* § 476.131 (1992).

[168]42 U.S.C. § 1320c-3(a)(7)(C) (1993).

[169]42 C.F.R. § 476.111(a)(1992).

functions.[170] Third, a PRO has the right to all information collected by institutions or other entities for PRO purposes.[171] Finally, all information collected or generated by institutions or practitioners to carry out quality review studies must be disclosed to the PRO.[172] The regulations add that a PRO may have access to records of non-Medicare patients in accordance with its quality review responsibilities under the Act if authorized by the institution or practitioner.[173] Clearly, PROs have authority to review and copy confidential patient medical records and related information collected by physicians, facilities, intermediaries, and carriers.

Third Party Access to Information Collected by a PRO

The statute provides that, in general, any data or information acquired by a PRO in the exercise of its duties and functions shall be held in confidence and not disclosed except as specifically authorized under the law.[174] First, a PRO may disclose information to the extent necessary to carry out the purposes of the statute.[175] It also may release information for purposes specifically authorized by statute, including to assist investigations into program fraud and abuse, where a risk to the public health is presented, and for purposes of state licensing, accreditation, and health planning.[176] A PRO may disclose information as authorized by the Secretary of HHS to assure adequate protection of rights and interests of patients, practitioners, or providers of health care.[177]

The Secretary of HHS has the authority to issue additional regulations on disclosure of PRO information requiring PROs to provide reasonable physical security measures to prevent unauthorized access to the information and to ensure the integrity of the data.[178] The PRO must instruct its officers and employees and employees of health care institutions participating in its activities of their responsibility to maintain confidentiality. No individual participating in the PRO review process on a regular basis shall have authorized access to confidential PRO information unless that person has been properly trained and has signed a statement indicating an awareness of the legal penalties for

---

[170]*Id.* § 476.112 (1992).

[171]*Id.* § 476.113(a) (1992).

[172]*Id.* § 476.113(b) (1992).

[173]*Id.* § 476.111(c) (1992).

[174]42 U.S.C. § 1320c-9(a) (1993).

[175]*Id.* § 1320c-9(a)(1) (1993).

[176]*Id.* §§ 1320c-9(a)(3) and 1320-9(b) (1993).

[177]*Id.* § 1320c-9(a)(2) (1993).

[178]42 C.F.R. § 476.115(a) (1992).

unauthorized disclosure.[179] PRO information may be stored in a shared health data system unless such storage would prevent the PRO from complying with the regulations.[180] PRO information may not be disclosed by the shared health data system unless the source of the information consents or the PRO requests disclosure as permitted by the regulations.[181]

The regulatory provisions governing disclosure of PRO information distinguish "confidential" from "nonconfidential." "Confidential information" is defined as:

- information that explicitly or implicitly identifies an individual patient, practitioner, or reviewer,[182]
- sanction reports and recommendations,
- quality review studies that identify patients, practitioners, or institution,
- PRO deliberations.[183]

The phrase "implicitly identifies" is defined to mean "data so unique or numbers so small that identification of an individual patient, practitioners, or reviewer would be obvious." Nonconfidential information is not defined by the regulations, but the term presumably refers to information falling outside the definition of "confidential information."

A PRO is required to disclose nonconfidential information to any person upon request. Such information may relate to the norms, criteria, and standards used for initial screening of cases and other review activities; routine reports submitted by the PRO to HCFA to the extent they do not contain confidential information; and quality review studies from which the identification of patients, practitioners, and institutions has been deleted.[184] A PRO also must

---

[179]*Id.* § 476.115(d) (1992).

[180]*Id.* §§ 476.143(a) and (b) (1992).

[181]*Id.* § 476.143(c) (1992).

[182]A federal district court in Tennessee, interpreting this provision, granted a hospital a permanent injunction to prevent a PRO from disclosing information relating to its investigation of care rendered to a patient at a hospital. The provision states that PRO information is confidential if it reveals the identity of an individual patient or provider but does not specifically protect information that identifies a hospital. The hospital contended that the exclusion of hospital-specific information from the definition of confidential information was intended to be narrow and not to apply to an investigation of a specific patient's complaint. What is nonconfidential under the regulations is aggregate, statistical information about hospitals in general, the hospital said, but not the type of information involved in this case. Examining the regulatory history of the confidentiality provisions, the court found that they only contemplated disclosure of facility-specific information on a statistical nature. Although HHS has interpreted the regulations as allowing disclosure of all hospital-specific information, the court concluded that this interpretation does not comply with the history or purpose of the regulations.

[183]42 C.F.R. § 476.101(b) (1992).

[184]*Id.* § 476.120(a) (1992).

disclose to state or federal health planning agencies all aggregate statistical information that does not implicitly or explicitly identify individual patients, practitioners, or reviewers.[185] In addition to these mandatory disclosures, a PRO may disclose any of the above nonconfidential information to any person, agency, or organization on its own initiative.[186]

The regulations generally require a PRO that intends to disclose nonconfidential information to give 30-day advance notice to any institution identified in the material and provide a copy to the facility. The institution may submit written comments to the PRO that must be included with the information disclosed or forwarded separately.[187] Where the PRO plans to disclose "confidential information," it also must give advance notice. If the request for information comes from a patient or representative, the PRO must provide the notice to the practitioner who treated the patient.[188] On the other hand, if the request comes from an investigative or licensing agency, the PRO must: (1) notify the practitioner or institution, (2) provide the practitioner or institution with a copy of the requested information, and (3) include comments submitted by the practitioner or institution in the disclosure to the agency.[189]

There are three exceptions to the general requirement that a PRO give advance notice to a practitioner or institution before confidential information is disclosed:

1. If a PRO determines that the requested information is necessary to protect against an imminent danger to individuals or the public health, notice of the disclosure may be sent to the practitioner or institution at the same time the disclosure is made, rather than 30 days in advance.[190]
2. If the disclosure is made during a fraud and abuse investigation conducted by the Office of the Inspector General (OIG) or the General Accounting Office (GAO), no notice is required.[191]
3. If the disclosure is made during a fraud and abuse investigation conducted by any other state or federal agency, no notice is required if the agency specifies in writing that the information is related to a potentially prosecutable criminal offense.[192]

---

[185]*Id.* § 476.120(b) (1992).
[186]*Id.* § 476.121 (1992).
[187]*Id.* § 476.105(a) (1992).
[188]*Id.* § 476.105(b)(1) (1992).
[189]*Id.* § 476.105(b)(2) (1992).
[190]*Id.* § 476.106(a) (1992).
[191]*Id.* § 476.106(b)(1) (1992).
[192]*Id.* § 476.106(b)(2) (1992).

All disclosures of confidential information by a PRO must be accompanied by a written statement informing the recipient that the information may not be further disclosed except as provided by the regulations.[193]

Records held by a PRO that identify patients are not subject to subpoena or discovery in a civil action, including an administrative, judicial, or arbitration proceeding.[194] However, this last restriction does not apply to HHS, OIG, GAO, or to administrative subpoenas issued during the course of HHS program audits and investigations, or during administrative hearings held under the Social Security Act.[195]

There is no access or disclosure of PRO information beyond that described in the statute and regulations.[196] That provision is designed to avoid the litigation experienced under the former PSRO law where attempts to characterize PSROs as federal agencies under FOIA led to conflicting court decisions.[197]

Patient Access to PRO Information

Generally, a PRO must disclose patient-identified information in its possession to that individual or representative upon written request, provided that all other patient and practitioner identifiers have been removed.[198] First, however, the PRO must discuss the appropriateness of disclosure with the patient's attending practitioner.

If the practitioner states that the released information could harm the patient, the PRO must disclose the material to the patient's representative rather than directly to the patient.[199] If the patient is mentally, physically, or legally unable to designate a representative, the PRO must disclose the information to a person responsible for the patient as determined by the PRO in accordance with the regulations.[200] The PRO must disclose patient information directly to the patient unless knowledge could be harmful.[201]

---

[193]*Id.* § 476.104(a)(2) (1992).

[194]*Id.* § 476.138(b) (1992).

[195]*Id.* § 476.138(a)(3) (1992).

[196]*Id.* § 476.138(b)(2)(1992).

[197]See, e.g., *Public Citizen Health Research Group v. Department of Health, Educ. and Welfare*, 668 F.2d 537 (D.C. Cir. 1981).

[198]42 C.F.R. § 476.132(a)(1) (1992).

[199]*Id.* §§ 476.131(a)(2) and (c)(2) (1992).

[200]*Id.* § 476.131(c)(3) (1992).

[201]*Id.* § 476.131(c)(1) (1992).

REPORTING AND OTHER DISCLOSURE REQUIREMENTS

Many state laws and some federal laws allow hospitals to disclose confidential medical record information without the patient's consent. Certain disclosures, such as child abuse reports, are mandatory; others are permissive.

Disclosure of medical record information under statutory or regulatory requirements does not subject a hospital or practitioner to civil liability, even if the disclosure is made against the patient's express wishes. Hospitals must be aware of the special disclosure rules applicable in their jurisdictions because the rules often vary among states.

Hospitals choosing to participate in cancer or other registries should seek the creation of statutory or regulatory authority for release of medical record information to such registries. If legislative action is impractical, participating hospitals should exercise care in drafting agreements with registries. Such contracts should contain safeguards against improper disclosure of confidential information by the registry and should include indemnification of the hospitals for claims that may result from release of data to the registry or from improper disclosure by the registry.

Child Abuse

Laws in most jurisdictions require hospitals and practitioners to report cases of actual or suspected child abuse. The exact list of persons and facilities subject to the reporting requirement varies among the states, and persons working in various health care institutions should check their state's particular child abuse law. It is important that hospitals understand who in their facility must report, when reports are due, and what information must be presented in a child abuse report. While most statutes protect persons required to report from civil liability, voluntary reports or release of extra information not required or permitted by law do not have similar protections.

To comply with child abuse reporting requirements, hospitals must first determine whether a patient is a "child" under the relevant statute. A "child" for abuse reporting purposes is not necessarily synonymous with "minor" under state law. Definitions of these terms vary in different state laws. In Massachusetts, for example, child abuse reports must be filed for all persons under 18 years of age who satisfy other criteria for reporting.[202] In New York, an "abused child" may be older than 18 in some cases.[203] Determining what individuals have a duty

---

[202]Mass. Ann. Laws ch. 119 § 51A (1993).

[203]N.Y. Soc. Serv. Law § 412 (1993).

to report under child abuse legislation is another issue hospitals must address. Some states have broad mandatory requirements that all "persons" with certain knowledge of child abuse make a report.[204] In a hospital setting, this type of statute imposes obligations on all personnel, not only on practitioners who treat victims of child abuse. Most statutes require reporting by practitioners and others who know or have "reason" to suspect or believe that a child they know or observe in their official or professional capacity is abused or neglected.[205]

Other states impose mandatory reporting obligations on specific categories of people, including designated health care professionals. Practitioners and other health care workers subject to mandatory reporting may be listed directly in the child abuse reporting provisions[206] and/or may be cross-referenced to the state health care professional licensing statute. Most child abuse reporting requirements are mandatory for health practitioners; only a few laws are permissive.[207]

In some states, the list creates a fixed group of professionals subject to reporting;[208] in other states, the list is merely illustrative, stating that all individuals who provide health care services, including those listed, must report.[209] In a few states, persons involved with hospital admissions have an explicit duty to report, along with practitioners.[210]

Only certain conditions diagnosed in children are reportable, and the child abuse statute in each state includes definitions of conditions that trigger the duty to report. Some statutes define an "abused and neglected" child as a single term.[211] Others distinguish "abuse" from "neglect."[212] Still others provide definitions of other related terms such as "sexual abuse."[213] Some states refer to abuse by the child's parent or other person responsible for the child's welfare.[214] A few statutes apply to child abuse or neglect of a child caused by "any" person.[215]

---

[204]See, e.g., 23 Pa. Cons. Stat. § 6311 (1993); N.J. Stat. § 9:6-8.10 (1993); Tex. Fam. Code Ann. § 34.01 (1993).

[205]See, e.g., Fla. Stat. ch. 415.504(1) (1992); Md. Code Ann. [Fam. Law] § 5-704 (1993); N.Y. Soc. Serv. Law § 413 (1993).

[206]See, e.g., Haw. Rev. Stat. § 350-1.1(a) (1993); Md. Code Ann. [Fam. Law] §§ 5-701(h) and 5-704(a) (1993); Wash. Rev. Code § 26.44.020(3) (1991).

[207]See, e.g., Miss. Code Ann. § 93-21-25 (1993).

[208]See, e.g., N.Y. Soc. Serv. Law § 413 (1993).

[209]See, e.g., Fla. Stat. Ann. ch. 415.504(1)(a) and (b) (1992); Haw. Rev. Stat. § 350-1.1(a) (1993); Tenn. Code Ann. § 37-1-403(a) (1993).

[210]See, e.g., Fla. Stat. Ann. ch. 415.504(1) (1992).

[211]Fla. Stat. Ann. ch. 415.503(1) (1992); Haw. Rev. Stat. § 350-1 (1993).

[212]La. Children's Code art. 603 (1992); Tex. Fam. Code § 34.012 (1993); see also New York law, which defines "abused child" and "maltreated child" separately. N.Y. Soc. Serv. Law § 412 (1993).

[213]Cal. Penal Code § 11165.1 (1992).

[214]See, e.g., Fla. Stat. Ann. ch. 415.503(1) (1992); Haw. Rev. Stat. § 350-1 (1993); La. Children's Code, art. 603 (1992).

[215]See, e.g., Tex. Fam. Code § 34.01 (1993).

The definitions in every state generally include both physical and mental harm or threats of harm caused by the acts or omissions of certain persons. Sexual abuse, unusual punishment, or other unexplained physical injuries constitute signs of abuse under most laws.[216] Impairment of the child's ability to perform or function and other signs of emotional or psychological distress indicate potential abuse in many states.[217] Exploitation and abandonment are typical elements of child abuse, along with failure to provide adequate supervision, food, clothing, shelter, or health care.[218]

Most statutes require certain information to be included in a child abuse report. Typically, the name of the person making the report, the name and address of the child, the extent of the child's injuries, and the child's present whereabouts must be disclosed, along with other pertinent information relating to the cause of abuse and the identity of the individual(s) responsible.[219] Massachusetts requires the child's age and sex to be disclosed in addition to the child's parents' names and addresses.[220] In New York, persons making the reports must reveal their identities and any actions they have taken, including photographs or X-rays and removal or keeping the child.[221]

Persons who comply with the reporting provisions generally are immune under the statute from any resulting civil or criminal liability.[222] Several courts have extended civil immunity to reports made in good faith but based on a negligent diagnosis.[223] California legislation that grants immunity to health care providers when they make mandated reports of child abuse also protects providers from liability when they make reports that are not required but merely are authorized under the law.[224] On the other hand, persons who fail to make required reports or who knowingly make false reports may be criminally liable.[225]

Most child abuse statutes stipulate that both the report and the identity of the individual who makes it are confidential.[226] Moreover, in most states, disclosures

---

[216]See, e.g., Fla. Stat. Ann. ch. 415.503 (1992); Haw. Rev. Stat. § 350-1(1993); Tex. Fam. Code § 34.012 (1993).

[217]See, e.g., Haw. Rev. Stat. § 350-1(1993); Tex. Fam. Code § 34.012 (1993).

[218]See, e.g., Fla. Stat. ch. 415.503 (1992); Haw. Rev. Stat. § 350-1(1993); Tex. Fam. Code Ann. § 34.012 (1993).

[219]See, e.g., N.Y. Soc. Serv. Law § 415 (1993); Tenn. Code Ann. § 37-1-403 (1993); Wash. Rev. Code Ann. § 26.44.040 (1991).

[220]Mass. Ann. Laws., ch. 119 § 51A (1993).

[221]N.Y. Soc. Serv. Law § 415 (1993).

[222]See, e.g., Fla. Stat. Ann. ch. 415.511 (1992); Haw. Rev. Stat. § 350-3 (1993).

[223]See, e.g., *Maples v. Siddiqui*, 450 N.W.2d 529 (Iowa 1990).

[224]See *Ferraro v. Chadwick*, 270 Cal. Rptr. 379 (Ct. App. 1990); *rev. denied*, No. 501657 (Cal. Aug. 15, 1990).

[225]See, e.g., Haw. Rev. Stat. § 350-1.2 (1993); Mass. Ann. Laws, ch. 119 § 51A (1993); Tex. Fam. Code § 34.031 (1993).

[226]See, e.g., Fla. Stat. Ann. ch. 415.51(7) (1992); Haw. Rev. Stat. § 350-1.4(b)(1993); Tenn. Code Ann. § 37-1-612 (1993).

authorized by such laws do not violate the physician-patient privilege that otherwise would prevent the use of confidential medical information at trial or in other legal proceedings. (For a more extensive discussion of how physician-patient privilege operates in conjunction with child abuse reporting laws, see Chapter 3.)

Abuse of Adults and Injuries to Disabled Persons

Several states have enacted reporting requirements for cases of known or suspected abuse of senior citizens, institutionalized persons, nursing home residents, and persons suffering from physical or mental impairments.[227] Like the child abuse statutes discussed above, the laws on abuse of adults typically define terms such as "abuse" and "neglect" and require various health practitioners to report instances where they have a reasonable basis for believing such abuse or neglect has occurred. The statutes usually list the kinds of information to be included in a report, such as the identity of the person reporting, the name and address of the victim, the time and place of the incident of abuse, the name of the suspected wrongdoer, and other information concerning the victim's statements and persons with knowledge of the incident. A practitioner usually may make an initial incident report by telephone, then follow up with a written report within a certain time period.

Most jurisdictions have general reporting requirements. Some states also require reports based on particular diagnoses of institutionalized or disabled adults—for example, Maryland mandates general reports of abuse suffered by developmentally disabled[228] or mentally impaired persons.[229]

The Minnesota Vulnerable Adult Act defines the terms "vulnerable adult," "abuse," and "neglect," and requires "a professional . . . engaged in the care of vulnerable adults" to report known abuse or neglect, instances where the professional has reasonable cause to believe abuse or neglect is occurring or has occurred, and known cases of a vulnerable adult who has sustained physical injury not reasonably explained by the history of injuries provided by caretakers.[230] The Minnesota Act extends immunity for reports made in good faith under the law and imposes criminal liability on mandated reporters who intentionally fail to report and liability for damages on those who negligently fail to report.[231]

---

[227]See, e.g., Cal. Welf. & Inst. Code §§ 15600–15657.3 (1993); Fla. Stat. Ann. ch. 415.101–415.114 (1992); Iowa Code §§ 235B.1–235B.16 (1993).

[228]Md. Code Ann. [Health-Gen.] § 7-1005 (1993).

[229]Md. Code Ann. [Health-Gen.] § 10-705 (1993).

[230]Minn. Stat. Ann. §§ 626.557(2) and (3) (1993).

[231]*Id.* §§ 626.557(5) and (7) (1993).

Controlled Drug Prescriptions and Abuse

Some states require physicians and others to identify patients obtaining prescriptions for certain controlled drugs and to report their names to the appropriate state or federal agency.[232] Other states require the provider to maintain records of such prescriptions for government inspection.[233]

Other states require physicians to report diagnoses of drug abuse. New Jersey requires health care practitioners to report the names of drug-dependent persons within 24 hours after determining that the person uses a controlled dangerous substance for purposes other than treatment of sickness or injury as prescribed and administered under the law.[234]

Occupational Diseases

A few states require physicians to report diseases or abnormal health conditions caused by or related to conditions in the workplace.[235] The reports are made to the state's department of public health and usually include the name, address, occupation, illness of the patient, and the name and address of the patient's employer. The reports are confidential except for statistical purposes and in extreme medical emergencies.[236] The purpose of these statutes is to enable public health officials to investigate occupational diseases and to recommend methods for eliminating or preventing them.

Abortion

Several states require hospitals and practitioners to report abortions they perform, along with a variety of information about the patient, the procedure, and any resulting complications.[237] Some states impose independent reporting

---

[232]See, e.g., Cal. Health & Safety Code § 11164 (1993); Mass. Ann. Laws ch. 94C § 24(a) (1993); N.Y. Pub. Health Law § 3333 (1993).

[233]See, e.g., Mass. Ann. Laws ch. 94C § 9(d) (1993).

[234]N.J. Stat. § 24:21-39 (1993); but see *Commonwealth v. Donaghue*, 358 N.E.2d 465 (Mass. Ct. App. 1976), where a Massachusetts state court struck down its drug abuse reporting statute as unconstitutionally vague because practitioners could not define the term "chronic use" triggering such reports under the existing version of the law.

[235]See, e.g., Tex. Health & Safety Code § 84.004 (1993).

[236]*Id.* § 84.006.

[237]See, e.g., Cal. Health & Safety Code § 25955.5 (1993); Fla. Stat. Ann. ch. 390.002 (1992); Tex. Health & Safety Code. § 245.011 (1993).

requirements on physicians who diagnose a woman as having complications from an abortion.[238] A few states require reports only for abortions performed on minors.[239] At least one court has upheld the requirement that physicians disclose the names and addresses of women receiving abortions as rationally related to a compelling state interest in maternal health and not an infringement upon the physician-patient relationship, the right to an abortion, or any personal right of privacy.[240]

Birth Defects and Other Conditions in Children

Many states require, or at least permit, health practitioners and others to report diagnoses of various birth defects and children's conditions to the state department of health.[241] Reportable conditions include congenital and acquired malformations and disabilities,[242] Sudden Infant Death Syndrome,[243] sentinel birth defects,[244] Reye's syndrome,[245] diseases of the eyes of infants,[246] and abnormal spinal curvature.[247]

Cancer

Many states require disclosure of information from the medical records of cancer patients to central state or regional tumor registries.[248] These registries usually contain demographic, diagnostic, and treatment information about patients who suffer from the same or similar diseases and are designed to provide raw data for studies concerning the incidence of a disease in the population; long-term prognosis of the disease; type, duration, and frequency of treatment rendered to patients with the disease; and other indicators of the health care

---

[238]See, e.g., 720 Ill. Comp. Stat. Ann. 510/10.1 (1993).

[239]See, e.g., Ala. Code § 26-21-8(c) (1993).

[240]See, e.g., *Schulman v. New York City Health and Hosp. Corp.* 342 N.E. 2d 501 (1975).

[241]See, e.g, N.J. Rev. Stat. § 26:8-40.21 (1993); Wis. Stat. § 14.028 (1991-1992), renumbered as 253.12 Wis. A.B. 585 (New Laws 1993).

[242]See, e.g., Ala. Code § 21-3-8 (1993); Fla. Stat. Ann. ch. 383.14 (1992).

[243]See, e.g., Cal. Health & Safety Code § 10253 (1993).

[244]See, e.g., Md. Code Ann. [Health-Gen.] § 18-206 (1993).

[245]See, e.g., Mass. Ann. Laws ch. 111 § 110B (1993).

[246]See, e.g., Mass. Ann. Laws ch. 111 § 110 (1993).

[247]See, e.g., Tex. Health & Safety Code § 37.003 (1993).

[248]See, e.g., Cal. Health & Safety Code § 211.3 (1993); Fla. Stat. Ann. ch. 385.202 (1992); Haw. Rev. Stat. § 324-21 (1993).

industry's ability to manage the disease. Usually operated by statewide, tax-exempt organizations funded by federal grants, the registries rely to a large extent on the cooperation of individual hospital registries and obtain patient information directly from participating hospitals pursuant to agreements between the hospitals and the registry.

Death or Injury from Use of a Medical Device

The Safe Medical Devices Act,[249] a federal statute enacted in 1990, requires hospitals to report any death resulting from the use of a medical device to HHS within ten days of discovery. The hospital must identify in the report the device's manufacturer, if known, and must notify the manufacturer when a device caused or contributed to a patient's serious illness or injury. If the hospital cannot determine the manufacturer, the report of the illness or injury must be sent to the Secretary of HHS. The Joint Commission also requires compliance with the Safe Medical Devices Act as one of its accreditation standards.[250]

Other Health-Related Reporting Requirements

Hospitals and practitioners in the various states may be required or permitted to report other instances of health-related conditions and injuries to the appropriate state board of health. Examples of miscellaneous reporting laws include instances of veterans' exposure to Agent Orange or other causative agents,[251] diagnosis of brain injuries in patients,[252] burn injuries and wounds in cases of suspected arson,[253] cases of cerebral palsy,[254] identities of women who took diethylstilbistrol during pregnancy,[255] adverse reactions from investigational drug products,[256] environmentally related illnesses and injury,[257] and lead poisoning.[258]

---

[249]P.L. 101-629, 104 Stat. 4511 (1990), codified at 21 U.S.C. § 360i (1993).

[250]Joint Commission on Accreditation of Healthcare Organizations, *Accreditation Manual for Hospitals* (Oakbrook Terrace, Ill., 1994): P.L. 3.4.

[251]Iowa Code Ann. §§ 36.1–36.10 (1993); Tex. Health & Safety Code §§ 83.001–83.010 (1993).

[252]Iowa Code § 135.22 (1993).

[253]La. Rev. Stat. Ann. § 403.4 (1992).

[254]Mass. Ann. Laws ch. 111 § 111A (1993).

[255]N.J. Stat. Ann. § 26:2-116 (1993).

[256]Fla. Stat. Ann. ch. 499.019 (1992).

[257]Haw. Rev. Stat. §§ 321-311–321-317 (1993).

[258]Cal. Health & Safety Code §§ 309.7–309.77 (1993).

Wisconsin requires reports by coroners and medical examiners concerning the results of mandatory blood tests performed on victims of snowmobile[259] and boating[260] accidents. That state allows a physician to report a patient's name and other information to the state department of transportation without the patient's consent when the physician believes the patient's physical or mental condition affects the person's ability to reasonably control a motor vehicle.[261]

Some states provide reimbursement for certain health services provided to qualified persons. Facilities wishing to participate in these programs typically are subject to reporting requirements as to the care provided. Programs may involve primary health care services,[262] maternal and infant care,[263] or other services funded by the state.

Communicable Diseases

Communicable disease reporting laws require hospitals and practitioners to inform public health authorities of cases of infectious, venereal, or sexually transmitted diseases. These are among the oldest compulsory reporting statutes in many states. The statutes or regulations usually list the particular diseases that must be reported and direct practitioners to give local public health officials the patient's name, age, sex, address, and identifying information, as well as the details of the illness.[264] The health department may have authority to request patient records for purposes of conducting epidemiological investigations.[265] Hospitals should disclose only the information required by the statute.

An increasing number of states have enacted special laws governing reports of Acquired Immune Deficiency Syndrome (AIDS) and Human Immunodeficiency Virus (HIV) cases. Many of the statutes require both AIDS and HIV to be reported; the information required in these reports varies from state to state. Providers should know what information should be released in their jurisdictions. (For a detailed discussion of access and disclosure issues involving AIDS and HIV patients' records, see Chapter 4.)

A few states have laws authorizing hospitals to disclose confidential information when emergency medical personnel come into contact with a patient

[259]Wis. Stat. §§ 350.15 and 350.155 (1991-1992).

[260]Wis. Stat. § 30.67 (1991-1992).

[261]Wis. Stat. § 146.82(3)(a) (1991-1992).

[262]See, e.g., Tex Health & Safety Code §§ 31.001–31.017 (1993).

[263]Tex. Health & Safety Code §§ 32.001–32.020 (1993).

[264]See, e.g., Ala. Code §§ 21-11A-1-21-11A-73 (1993); Fla. Stat. Ann. ch. 384.21–384.34 (1992); Haw. Rev. Stat. §§ 325-1–325-3 (1993).

[265]See, e.g., Fla. Stat. Ann. ch. 395.017(4) (1992).

suffering from a reportable condition.[266] The procedures for notifying the emergency personnel vary among the states, and hospitals should know the proper routine before releasing any information. Some states allow the hospital to directly notify the person at risk, others require the hospital to notify authorities at the state board of health, who then contact the emergency personnel. In either case, the hospital usually is precluded from revealing the name of the afflicted patient.

Misadministration of Radioactive Materials

Federal regulations require hospitals or practitioners using radioactive materials in the practice of nuclear medicine to obtain a federal license[267] and report any misadministration of radioactive materials to the Nuclear Regulatory Commission (NRC).[268] "Misadministration" is defined as the administration of a radiopharmaceutical or radiation other than the one intended, or to the wrong patient, or by route of administration other than that intended by the prescribing physician, or a diagnostic or therapy dosage of radiopharmaceutical that differs from the prescribed dosage by certain amounts, or a therapy radiation dose with certain errors causing a total treatment dose differing by more than 10 percent from the final prescribed total treatment dose.[269]

ACCESS BY HOSPITAL STAFF

Hospitals' policies generally allow members of their medical and nursing staffs to access patient records without patient consent for certain authorized purposes. At the same time, hospitals are responsible for safeguarding each record and its content against loss, defacement, tampering, or use by unauthorized individuals.[270] Guidelines addressing this generally are found in hospital or medical staff bylaws and, less frequently, in state statutes or regulations.

Several state statutes permit the release of confidential patient information to qualified personnel for the purpose of conducting scientific research, audits, program evaluations, official surveys, education, and quality control activities,

---

[266]See, e.g., Cal. Health & Safety Code § 1797.188 (1993); Fla. Stat. Ann. ch. 395.0147 (1992).

[267]10 C.F.R. §§ 35.11 and 35.12 (1993).

[268]*Id.* § 35.33 (1993).

[269]*Id.* § 35.2 (1993).

[270]See also Joint Commission on Accreditation of Healthcare Organizations, *Accreditation Manual for Hospitals* (Oakbrook Terrace, Ill., 1994), IM. 2.3.

without patient authorization.[271] In addition, the Joint Commission says that clinical and administrative data can be aggregated and analyzed for supporting decisions, tracking trends over time, making comparisons within the organization and among organizations, and improving performance.[272]

The confidentiality statutes in many states expressly permit access to patient records by health care providers and others for purposes of providing diagnosis or treatment, and during medical emergencies.[273]

In most states, hospital licensing regulations permit access to patient records by "authorized" personnel or persons granted access by hospital policy. The hospital then is made responsible for ensuring that only authorized persons review the records.[274] A few states list certain persons authorized to review records as a matter of regulation.

Access to certain patients' records by medical staff is expressly governed by some state and federal laws. For example, there are special federal statutes and regulations on access to certain alcohol or drug abuse treatment records (discussed earlier). These provide for the general confidentiality of drug and alcohol patients' records with an exception for disclosure to persons in connection with their duties to provide diagnosis, treatment, or referral for treatment of abuse.[275] There also is a statutory exception to confidentiality for release of patient record information during a bona fide medical emergency.[276]

Some states also address alcohol and drug abuse patient records. These laws typically provide an exception to the general ban on disclosure of such records for the exchange of information relating to the patient's treatment among qualified personnel involved in the treatment.[277] Other states incorporate the federal alcohol and drug abuse regulations directly into their own laws.[278]

Some states have special laws on staff access to records of mental health patients[279] and AIDS patients.[280] Not all staff members have access to those types of records. Again, the laws vary from state to state, and hospitals should consult the particular rules applicable to them.

---

[271]See, e.g., R.I. Gen. Laws § 5-37.3-4 (1992); Cal. Civ. Code § 56.10 (1992).

[272]Joint Commission on Accreditation of Healthcare Organizations, *Accreditation Manual for Hospitals,* Scoring Guidelines (Oakbrook Terrace, Ill., 1994), IM.8–IM8.1.12.

[273]See, e.g., Cal. Civ. Code § 56.10(c)(1) (1992); Fla. Stat. ch. 395.017(3)(a) (1992).

[274]See, e.g., 90 Ky. Admin. Regs. 20:016 (11)(C) (1990); Mo. Code Regs., tit. 19 § 30-20(D)(7)(1992).

[275]42 C.F.R. § 2.12(c)(3)(1992).

[276]42 U.S.C. § 290dd-2(b)(2)(1993); 38 U.S.C. § 7332(b)(2)(1993).

[277]See, e.g., Wis. Stat. § 51.30(4) (1991-1992); 20 Ill. Comp. Stat. Ann. 305/8-102 (1993).

[278]See, e.g., Md. Health-Gen. Code § 8-601(c)(1993).

[279]See, e.g., Fla. Stat. ch. § 394.459(9)(c)(1992); Wash. Rev. Code § 71.05.390(1)(1991).

[280]See, e.g., Haw. Rev. Stat. § 325-101 (1993); Wis. Stat. § 252.15(5) (1991-1992), renumbered as Wis. A.B. 585 (New Laws 1993).

As for limited access to special records, the Joint Commission standards state that:

> When certain portions of the medical records are so confidential that extraordinary means are necessary to preserve their privacy, (such as in the treatment of some psychiatric disorders), these portions may be stored separately, provided the complete record is readily available when required for current medical care or follow-up, for review functions, or use in performance improvement activities.[281]

When a portion of a patient's record is stored separately under this standard, the medical record or computer system must so indicate to alert personnel that part of the record is stored elsewhere.[282]

In the absence of state statutory law, the majority of hospitals allow access to a patient's medical record to persons directly involved in the care of the patient. Records also may be examined for mandatory clinical and financial audits, for utilization review, and for other quality assurance activities. Records may be available for research as described later in this chapter. Nontreating physicians generally should not have automatic access to patients' medical records unless the information is related to one of the purposes discussed previously.

Hospital policy should include procedures for medical and hospital staff members to follow to obtain access to medical records. These procedures may be incorporated in hospital or medical staff bylaws and regulations, as well as in appropriate hospital policy manuals.

DISCLOSURES FOR MEDICAL RESEARCH

Many medical research projects involve the use of patients' medical records. These records are important for determining responses to specific types of therapy, relationships involving population characteristics and incidence of illness, or for obtaining statistical information important for developing more efficient treatments. Several states have adopted specific provisions allowing disclosure of patient information for research purposes.[283]

The California research provision is found in its records confidentiality statute. Other states have independent medical research statutes allowing providers to release patient information for research purposes. When responding to requests for patient data for research, a health care provider must consult the

---

[281] Joint Commission, *Accreditation Manual for Hospitals*, Scoring Guidelines (Oakbrook Terrace, Ill., 1994), IM.2–IM.2.3.

[282] Joint Commission, *Accreditation Manual for Hospitals* (1994), IM 7.10.

[283] See, e.g., Cal. Civ. Code § 56.10(c)(7) (1993); Fla. Stat. ch. 405.01 (1992).

provision effective in its state, if one exists. The statutes vary in terms of who can release information, to whom, what can be released, and for what purposes.

Some states have special rules for access to certain types of records for research purposes. In addition to its general rule on research, for example, California has a special provision governing access to records of patients with developmental disabilities.[284] Florida and Iowa have special statutes addressing researcher access to mental health records.[285]

Federal regulations also cover research involving human subjects and the release of patient information for research purposes where HHS conducts or funds the study in whole or part or by grant, contract, cooperative agreement, or fellowship.[286] Hospitals that are federal grantees or contractors conducting experimental medical research on human subjects are required to establish an Institutional Review Board (IRB) to evaluate proposed research protocols.[287] The IRB is responsible for determining whether the research would be beneficial to society and whether adequate safeguards are available to protect the human subjects at risk.[288] The facility engaged in research must give assurances that the medical research projects will be subject to continuing review by the IRB.[289]

Hospitals permitting their staffs to conduct medical research studies must establish an IRB to evaluate the risks posed to the patient by disclosure of medical records information and the potential benefits of the research. The IRB must reconcile the hospital's duty to protect the confidentiality of patients' records with its interest in conducting medical research projects and the corresponding public interest in advancing medical science. Often, the best way to achieve both goals is for the hospital to impose controls and limitations on staff access to medical records for authorized continuing research. Some hospitals inform patients on admission that their records may be made available to approved investigators. This practice informs potential subjects that their records may be used in a research project undertaken by someone who is not a member of the hospital staff but whose project is approved by the IRB or medical committee of the hospital.

A hospital should try to obtain written authorization by the patient for access to medical records; however, it often is impractical to obtain patient consent for retrospective studies. Therefore, in the absence of such consent, the IRB must implement safeguards consistent with applicable federal regulations and state

---

[284]Cal. Welf. & Inst. Code § 4514(e) (1993).

[285]Fla. Stat. ch. 394.459(9)(c) (1992); Iowa Code § 229.25 (1993).

[286]45 C.F.R. §§ 46.101–46.124 (1992).

[287]Id. § 46.103 (1992).

[288]Id. § 46.111 (1992).

[289]Id. § 46.103 (1992).

law for medical investigators seeking access to the past medical records of discharged patients.

The federal regulations on medical research generally require informed consent when studies involve a human being. The regulations provide that certain information must be presented to prospective subjects under circumstances allowing them sufficient opportunity to consider whether to participate in the study. One of the items that must be disclosed is a statement describing the extent, if any, of confidentiality of records identifying the person.[290]

The federal regulations governing alcohol and drug abuse patient records also allow release of information from alcohol and drug treatment records without consent for certain research activities.[291] The director of an alcohol or drug treatment program covered by the rules must determine that the recipient of patient identifying information is qualified to conduct research and has research protocols protecting the information and preventing unauthorized redisclosure of the material. The researcher must provide a satisfactory written statement that three or more individuals independent of the research project have reviewed the protocol and determined that patients' rights and welfare are protected adequately and that the risks of disclosing patient identifying information are outweighed by the potential benefits of the research.[292]

The federal regulations governing research contain special rules for studies involving the fetus, pregnant women, or in vitro fertilization,[293] biomedical and behavioral research,[294] and studies involving children as the research subjects.[295] State laws may impose special requirements on certain types of research.[296]

Even after a hospital properly releases patient data to an authorized researcher whose final project omits any patient identifiers, problems still arise over access to identifying material by third parties. The general rule is that no academic privilege exists to protect research from discovery by third parties in litigation and the fact that researchers promise confidentiality to research participants does not confer absolute immunity.[297]

In one case, for example, a drug company sought production of research documents maintained by a university relating to certain cancer in women.[298]

---

[290]*Id.* § 46.116(a) (1992).

[291]42 C.F.R. § 2.52 (1992).

[292]*Id.* § 2.52(a) (1992).

[293]45 C.F.R. §§ 46.201–211 (1992).

[294]*Id.* §§ 46.301–306 (1992).

[295]*Id.* §§ 46.401–409 (1992).

[296]See, e.g., Cal. Welf. & Inst. Code § 4514(e) (1993) (persons with developmental disabilities).

[297]See, e.g., *In re Snyder*, 115 F.R.D. 211, 213 (D. Ariz. 1987).

[298]*Deitchman v. Squibb & Sons, Inc.* 740 F.2d 556 (7th Cir. 1984). See also *Anker v. G.D. Searle & Co.*, 126 F.R.D. 515 (D.N.C. 1989).

The company served a subpoena for the documents on the university as part of its defense against a products liability suit filed by several women who alleged that their cervical and uterine cancer had been caused by in vitro exposure to the manufacturer's drug diethylstilbestrol (DES). Researchers at the university had compiled the only centralized repository of data on genital tract cancer in the country. The data, which included the medical records and follow-up information on many women with the disease, had been delivered voluntarily to the researchers by medical practitioners across the country relying on the researchers' written promises of confidentiality. The court weighed the hardship to the university researchers and the registry that disclosure would cause compared with the hardship to the drug company if it were denied access to the information. The court held that, because the public holds a vital interest in promoting research, the registry enjoys a qualified privilege against unnecessary disclosure, but that the privilege was not absolute. The court ruled that in this case, access to the registry was "absolutely essential" for the company to analyze its accuracy and methodology in preparing a proper defense at trial.

It thus concluded that, while the company had no right to all materials in the registry as it originally had requested, not all of the data in the registry were protected from discovery. The court found it possible to fashion a discovery order to protect the registry against loss of confidential information and unreasonable financial and temporal costs while still giving the company discoverable information at its own expense. Even if the elimination of names and addresses from the patient files would not protect the patients' confidentiality in view of the vast amount of data amassed by the pharmaceutical company and the unlimited resources available to it, the court stated, the company nonetheless was entitled to some discovery.

In the absence of state regulations establishing standards for disclosing patients' medical records for biomedical or epidemiological research purposes without patient consent, the hospital IRB or research committee should require the medical researchers to satisfy the following safeguards before authorizing disclosure of confidential records to them:

- the information must be treated as confidential
- the information must be communicated only to qualified investigators pursuing an approved research program designed for the benefit of the health of the community
- adequate safeguards to protect the record or information from unauthorized disclosure must be established
- the results of the investigation must be presented in a way that prevents identification of individual subjects[299]

---

[299]Walters, The Use of Medical Records for Research at Georgetown University, IRB, *Review of Human Subjects Research* (March 1981): 1.

Absent statutory law, hospitals should prohibit access to medical records by investigators whose medical studies do not include these minimum safeguards as determined by the IRB or another appropriate committee.

UTILIZATION REVIEW AND QUALITY ASSURANCE

In addition to their uses in medical research, patients' records play a critical role in each hospital's effort to improve the quality of health care services and to increase the efficiency with which they are provided. Patients' records are a primary source of data for such utilization review and other quality assurance activities. Health care providers and health law practitioners must be aware of the statutes, regulations, and judicial opinions in their jurisdictions that affect the ability to use medical records for these purposes.

To address the laws covering access to patient records for quality review purposes, it is important to distinguish between the two types of review processes. The first type is the federal Peer Review Organization (PRO) system, part of the Medicare program governed by federal statute and regulation.[300] Hospitals seeking federal reimbursement for Medicare services must contract with a PRO as a condition of participation in the program.[301] PROs have authority to review patient records in carrying out their responsibilities to assess the reasonableness and adequacy of medical care.[302] PRO access and disclosure of patient records is discussed in detail earlier in this chapter.

The second type of review is hospital utilization review and quality assurance. These two review programs are conducted by hospital staff members and consist of in-house monitoring of both the quality and cost of providing services. The basic requirements for these review programs are set forth in the standards of accreditation adopted by the Joint Commission and the various state laws.

Before 1994, the Joint Commission had issued separate standards for quality assurance and utilization review. In 1994, it stated that the standards in those two chapters "had been recast to focus on improving individual and organizational performance," and had been moved to the chapters on "Leadership" and on "Improving Organizational Performance."[303] The standards in those chapters combine the former quality assurance and utilization review standards, reflecting the Joint Commission's process-oriented approach to those functions. The standards concentrate on the monitoring, evaluation, and comparison of various data in order to identify problems and correct them.

---

[300]See generally 42 C.F.R. §§ 476.101–476.143 (1992).

[301]*Medicare & Medicaid Guide* ¶ 12,330.

[302]42 C.F.R. §§ 476.111 and 476.112 (1992).

[303]Joint Commission, *Accreditation Manual for Hospitals*, QA (Oakbrook Terrace, Ill., 1994): 189.

Although this process relies on many data sources, the most valuable sources clearly are patients' medical records. Many states have enacted statutes authorizing hospitals to disclose patient records to staff quality control, peer review, and medical review committees. Some of these statutes provide that a health care practitioner *may* release confidential patient information to a peer review committee.[304] On the other hand, the Nebraska law states that a provider is *obligated* to give a review committee information it requests.[305] Other statutes indicate that physicians or other health care practitioners who provide information to a review committee are immune from liability if their actions were taken in good faith.[306] Each type of statute permits review committees access to confidential patient information as relevant and necessary to carry out their functions.

Some states without statutes specifically granting record access to quality control committees may have case law that permits disclosures. In a Missouri appeals case, for example, a staff physician sought to prevent the disclosure of his patients' records to a hospital committee that was investigating his qualifications and competency.[307] Missouri had a physician-patient privilege statute that decreed that a physician was incompetent to testify as to any information received during a professional consultation with a patient. The physician argued that the privilege should prevent the use of patient records in a competency determination because that would constitute a type of testimony at what basically was a hearing. The court reviewed the privilege's history and noted that no state ever had treated the privilege as an absolute prohibition against a physician's disclosure. After balancing the parties' opposing interests, the court concluded the privilege was inapplicable because "[t]he public's interest in the disclosure of the information to the internal staff of the hospital and in assuring proper medical and hospital care outweigh[ed] the patient's interest in concealment."[308]

The laws vary from state to state. Hospital administrators and health law practitioners therefore should consult the statutes, regulations, and case law in their jurisdictions before authorizing the use of patients' medical records for quality assurance and utilization review.

WARRANTS AND SEARCHES

Health care facilities have a strong interest in the privacy of their medical records, and as a general rule hospitals may refuse to release records to

---

[304]See, e.g., Alaska Stat. § 18.23.010(b) (1993); Cal. Civ. Code § 56.10(c)(4) (1993).

[305]Neb. Rev. Stat. § 71-2047 (1992).

[306]See, e.g., Conn. Gen. Stat. Ann. § 19a–17b (1992); Del. Code Ann., tit. 24 § 1768 (1993); Fla. Stat. ch. 766.101(3)(a) (1993).

[307]*Klinge v. Lutheran Medical Ctr. of St. Louis*, 518 S.W.2d 157 (1975).

[308]*Id.* 166.

government officials. However, such government officials are entitled to search and seize medical records if they first obtain a judicially issued search warrant. Because a search warrant requires the approval of a neutral magistrate and must state specifically the place to be searched, the objects to be seized, and the reason for the search, it effectively precludes general "fishing expeditions" by the government. Nevertheless, in some instances government officials are entitled to access to medical records even in the absence of a search warrant.

The Fourth Amendment to the United States Constitution is the source of the search warrant requirement, to protect persons and their houses, papers, and effects from unreasonable searches and seizures. The amendment is designed "to safeguard the privacy and security of individuals against arbitrary invasions by governmental officials."[309] Although the amendment was intended to apply primarily to private residences, its proscription of warrantless searches as presumptively unreasonable applies to commercial premises as well.[310] Generally, therefore, government access to medical records without a search warrant is presumptively unreasonable and violates the Fourth Amendment.

Although the search warrant requirement has been associated almost exclusively with criminal investigations, the U.S. Supreme Court has stated specifically that administrative or regulatory searches also come within the Fourth Amendment's scope.[311] Whether a court will impose a warrant requirement on an administrative search, however, depends on whether the search is designed to enforce a general regulatory scheme or is aimed at specific licensed industries. The Supreme Court has imposed a warrant requirement when an administrative search is conducted pursuant to general regulatory legislation that applies to all residences, structures, or employers within a given jurisdiction. For example, the Court has required a warrant in situations involving a residential search pursuant to a municipal housing code,[312] a commercial search of a locked warehouse to enforce a municipal fire code,[313] and routine commercial inspections of business premises not open to the public under the Occupational Safety and Health Act of 1970.[314]

Courts have treated searches of specific licensed industries differently, however. In *Colonnade Catering Corp. v. United States,*[315] the Supreme Court upheld a statute providing for warrantless inspection of the business records of licensed liquor dealers. The Court refused to adhere to cases such as *Camara* and others

---

[309]*Camara v. Municipal Court*, 387 U.S. 523, 528 (1967).

[310]See *Marshall v. Barlow's, Inc.*, 436 U.S. 307, 312 (1978).

[311]*See v. City of Seattle*, 387 U.S. 541, 545 (1967); see also *Camara, supra* n.310, at 535.

[312]*Camara, supra* n.310, at 540.

[313]*Id.* 545-546.

[314]*Marshall, supra*, n.310, at 315.

[315]397 U.S. 72 (1970).

that impose a warrant requirement on searches conducted under general regulatory laws. Instead, because the liquor industry is one long subject to stringent government regulation, the Court deferred to congressional standards of reasonableness for this warrantless regulatory search.

Similarly, in *United States v. Biswell*,[316] the Court upheld a statute authorizing warrantless inspections of the business premises of federally licensed firearms dealers. Although the firearms industry did not share the liquor industry's long history of regulation, the Court nonetheless deemed it essential to federal and state law enforcement efforts to closely scrutinize interstate firearms traffic. More importantly, the Court examined the privacy interests of a firearms dealer and concluded that:

> [i]nspections for compliance with the Gun Control Act pose only limited threats to the dealer's justifiable expectations of privacy. When a dealer chooses to engage in the pervasively regulated business and to accept a federal license, he does so with the knowledge that his business records, firearms, and ammunition will be subject to effective inspection.[317]

The Supreme Court has stated that a warrant may not be required for searches that protect very strong national interests, or of businesses that either are federally licensed or have a long history of supervision and pervasive regulation. State and lower federal court decisions also have recognized these two basic types of administrative searches, involving both general regulatory schemes and specific licensed industries, and have analyzed situations involving government access to health care facilities generally and medical records specifically. After making the inquiry into the thoroughness of regulation and determining that the medical facility is not a pervasively regulated business, a court balances the privacy interest of the institution against the government interest to determine whether a warrantless search nevertheless would be reasonable.

Nursing Homes and Pharmacies

Courts have authorized warrantless searches of medical facilities, but only in certain narrowly defined situations. A signifcant case in this regard is *People v. Firstenberg*,[318] a California appeals court decision that upheld a warrantless inspection of the business records of a skilled nursing facility. A county health

---

[316]406 U.S. 311 (1972).

[317]*Id.* 316.

[318]155 Cal. Rptr. 80 (Ct. App. 1979).

inspector routinely inspected the facility's records, without a search warrant, and discovered that the defendant, a licensee of the facility, had commingled patients' funds with his own. The court rejected the defendant's challenge to the warrantless search on the grounds that the health care industry in California had been pervasively regulated and that the state's interest in regulating the industry outweighed the facility's privacy interest.

Two factors may distinguish the *Firstenberg* decision from situations involving searches of a hospital's medical records. First, the California legislature has subjected not only the general health care industry, but also long-term health care facilities in particular, to a thorough regulatory scheme. Such intense regulation is similar to the regulation of alcohol and firearms on the federal level, which was the key in *Colonnade* and *Biswell*. Because many states now regulate not only general health care but also specific categories of facilities, the reasoning applied in this decision would apply in other jurisdictions.

The second distinguishable characteristic of *Firstenberg* lies in the nature of "skilled nursing facilities." In that regard the court stated:

> It is, of course, obvious that [frequent and unannounced] inspections are crucial to the effective oversight of the physical well-being of patients, to assure that they are not neglected or even abused. Frequent, unannounced inspections are also essential to effective protection of patients' financial welfare. Financial records can easily be concealed or even falsified. Patients are helpless to protect themselves. . . . [Most] nursing home patients are neither aware of, nor capable of protesting, misuse of their funds. The knowledge that records can be examined without prior notice is the surest guarantee that nursing home licensees will fulfill their fiduciary responsibilities toward their patients. Such inspections are also the most effective method of assuring that those who fail to fulfill these responsibilities are identified so that their conduct can be corrected or their licenses revoked. The necessity for unannounced warrantless inspections in the long-term health care industry is just as great as in the firearms industry and such inspections are, therefore, reasonable within the meaning of the Fourth Amendment.[319]

Similarly, a New York court upheld a state statute that authorized thorough warrantless inspections of "hospitals and home health agencies," a term that includes nursing homes.[320] The court emphasized the need to protect the interests of "elderly and infirm persons entrusted to nursing homes." Because of the

---

[319]*Id.* 85-86.

[320]Uzzilia v. *Commissioner of Health*, 367 N.Y.S.2d 795 (1975).

overriding interest of the state in protecting nursing home residents, and because of the thorough regulation of nursing homes in New York, the court concluded that such warrantless searches did not violate the Fourth Amendment.

Hospital patients may not be as vulnerable a population as those in nursing homes, however. Because it may be difficult to assert that the government has no interest whatsoever in medical records, a hospital should argue that the government's interest is sufficiently protected by limits established by the warrant-obtaining procedure. Whether a court will require a warrant depends somewhat on whether the burden of getting the warrant will negate the purpose of making the search. Medical facilities should assert that requiring the government to obtain a search warrant secretly will not in any way diminish the opportunity or effect of inspecting medical records. In sum, hospitals should argue that there are no exigent circumstances that compel warrantless inspection.

Courts also have authorized warrantless searches of pharmacy records. A New York case[321] involved the warrantless search of pharmacy records by state health inspectors, pursuant to statute. The court found that pharmacy records in New York are subject to inspection without warning because the pharmacist accepts a state license subject to the right of warrantless inspection, thereby consenting to warrantless searches. Accordingly, the court refused to impose a warrant requirement even though health inspectors had time and opportunity to procure a warrant.[322]

Day Care Centers and Abortion Clinics

Federal courts have invalidated statutes allowing warrantless searches of health care facilities that perform abortions. In an Ohio case, the court rejected the contention that those health care facilities are part of a pervasively regulated business or an industry long subject to close inspection.[323]

Similarly, a Louisiana district court also refused to recognize that the performance of abortions by hospitals and clinics is a pervasively regulated business.[324] Rather, the court ruled that the medical profession has "a history of respect towards the recognized need for privacy in the doctor-patient relationship. The strong privacy interest in this relationship far outweighs the minimal state interest in sanitary conditions and properly trained personnel."

---

[321] *People v. Curco Drugs, Inc.,* 350 N.Y.S.2d 74 (N.Y. Crim. Ct. 1973).

[322] See also *Vermont v. Welch,* 624 A.2d 1105 (Vt. 1992) upholding warrantless inspections of pharmacy records.

[323] See *Akron Ctr. for Reproductive Health Inc. v. City of Akron,* 479 F. Supp. 1172 (N.D. Ohio 1979).

[324] *Margaret S. v. Edwards,* 488 F. Supp. 181 (E.D. La. 1980).

State Statutes

That a state statute authorizes warrantless searches of medical records does not affect the foregoing two-step analysis. A court nevertheless must determine whether the statute violates the Fourth Amendment by analyzing the extent of medical facility regulation and by striking the privacy interest balance as discussed above. A statute that broadly allows inspections of all aspects of medical facilities, including medical records, would probably violate the Fourth Amendment because the statute's terms are too broad, thus failing to protect private interest adequately. For example, the Washington state Supreme Court rejected a statute that authorized any state or local law enforcement officer to "visit and inspect the premises of each massage business establishment."[325] The court emphasized that a statute empowering warrantless searches at least must state sufficiently the scope, time, and place of inspection, and that the authorized inspection must be relevant to the statute's purposes. Statutes authorizing broad warrantless inspections of medical facilities are subject to the same judicial rejection.

Searches Pursuant to Warrants

A medical facility should review search warrants to determine whether they are sufficiently detailed before responding. The warrant must state with particularity the scope and place to be searched. A court cannot properly issue a warrant based on a government assertion of valid public interest; rather, the government must state specifically why it requires a search of specific medical records. The object of the warrant procedure is to take away from the government the unfettered discretion to inspect and seize any medical records. Thus, a medical records practitioner who believes that a search warrant is indeed insufficiently particular should affirmatively withhold consent to the search, for consent to an administrative search can be implied easily. On the other hand, a search warrant that states in detail the time and place of the search, and the specific records to be searched, must be obeyed.

LAW ENFORCEMENT AGENCIES

As a general rule, hospitals should not release medical records or other patient information to law enforcement personnel without the patient's authorization. In

---

[325]*Washington Massage Found. v. Nelson*, 558 P.2d 231 (Wash. 1976).

the absence of statutory authority or legal process, a police agency has no authority to examine a medical record. If, however, a law enforcement official provides the facility with a valid court order or subpoena, the hospital, upon the advice of its attorney, should provide the information requested.

On the advice of its counsel, the hospital may determine that it would be in the community's best interest to release specific medical record information to law enforcement personnel. To do so, the hospital may rely on the doctrine of qualified privilege. (For an elaboration of this and other principles of the law of defamation, see Chapter 8.) This common law doctrine permits a party (i.e., the hospital) with a duty or a legitimate interest in conveying the information to engage in communications to a second party (i.e., the law enforcement agency) with a corresponding interest in receiving the particular information. The data transferred must be made in good faith, given without malice, and based on reasonable grounds.[326]

Thus, the doctrine of qualified privilege protects the hospital only if the law enforcement officer who receives the medical record information acts under the authority of law. Before releasing such information, hospital personnel should determine that there is a basis for the request and that the officer requesting it is performing official duties. The information released should be only what is appropriate to the purpose for which the particular request is made; a hospital should not release a patient's record in whole unless there are reasonable grounds for doing so. For example, if the law enforcement officer is requesting the results of a blood alcohol test, the hospital should not release information concerning the patient's unrelated prior hospitalization for a fractured leg.

In addition to the doctrine of qualified privilege and cases involving court subpoenas, there are statutory exceptions to the general rule requiring hospitals to refrain from releasing patient information to law enforcement agencies in the absence of patient consent. State law varies widely as to the release to government agencies of medical record information without patient authorization. In South Carolina, for example, the medical records confidentiality statute allows disclosure of medical record information without a patient's consent only in certain instances, including when "[d]isclosure is necessary in cooperating with law enforcement, health, welfare and other agencies, or when furthering the welfare of the patient or family."[327]

---

[326]See *Tarasoff v. Regents of the Univ. of Cal.,* 551 P.2d 334 (Cal. 1976), where the court held that the physician or the hospital had an affirmative duty to report a patient to law enforcement agencies because the patient's medical or psychological condition represented a foreseeable risk to third persons. The physician or hospital in this situation should have disclosed information that the patient had threatened to kill the eventual victim since the physician and hospital are protected by the doctrine of qualified privilege. See also *Hicks v. U.S.,* 357 F. Supp. 434 (D.D.C. 1973), *aff'd.,* 511 F.2d 407 (D.C. Cir. 1975).

[327]S.C. Code Ann. § 44-22-100 (1991).

Thus, some patient records, such as those involving victims of crime or carriers of contagious disease not specifically designated by statute, may be revealed to government officials without the patient's consent in the course of routine police investigations or public health inquiries. However, such disclosures should be made only pursuant to the state statute's confidentiality restrictions. In such situations, the hospital should demonstrate respect for the patient's privacy rights by seeking disclosure consent from the patient, preferably during the hospital admissions process.

State law also varies widely as to a hospital's duty to report certain kinds of information, such as cases involving gunshot or knife wounds,[328] child abuse (see discussion earlier in this chapter), and disorders affecting a motorist's ability to drive safely.[329] In states having these types of reporting statutes, a patient's consent is not required in order to release the record. In fact, under some statutes hospitals may be guilty of criminal misdemeanor if they fail to report certain cases. Statutory reporting requirements are discussed earlier in this chapter.

RESPONSE TO LEGAL PROCESS

Hospitals may be required to release medical record information pursuant to legal process that they receive. The term "legal process" generally refers to all of the writs that are issued by a court during a legal action, or by an attorney in the name of the court but without court review. Hospitals generally are concerned with two types of legal process—the subpoena and the court order.

Subpoenas

Hospitals customarily receive two types of subpoenas: (1) a subpoena *ad testificandum*, which is a written order commanding a person to appear and to give testimony at a trial or other judicial or investigative proceeding; and (2) a subpoena *duces tecum*, which is a written order commanding a person to appear, give testimony, and bring all documents, papers, books, and records described in the subpoena. These devices are used to obtain documents during pretrial discovery and to obtain testimony during trial.

Those authorized to issue subpoenas vary from state to state. In most states, judges, clerks of the court, justices of the peace, and other officials are so

---

[328]See, e.g., N.Y. Penal Law § 265.25 (1993); Cal. Penal Code § 11160 (1993).

[329]See, e.g., Cal. Health & Safety Code § 410 (1993).

authorized.[330] In federal courts, only the clerks of the courts are so authorized.[331] The form of the subpoena is prescribed by statute in certain states.[332] A valid subpoena usually contains the following information:

- name of the court (or other official body in which the proceeding is being held)
- names of the plaintiff and the defendant
- docket number of the case
- date, time, and place of the requested appearance
- specific documents sought (if a subpoena *duces tecum*)
- name and telephone number of the attorney who caused the subpoena to be issued
- signature or stamp and seal of the official empowered to issue the subpoena

For federal courts, subpoenas generally are served in person by United States marshals; for state courts, generally by sheriffs. However, many state statutes provide that any competent person not less than 18 years of age may serve subpoenas.[333] The manner of service varies from state to state: In some, the subpoena may be served by mail or delivery,[334] and in others it must be physically handed to the person by the server.[335] Usually, subpoenas must be served within a specified period of time in advance of the required appearance. In several states, statutes establish this period with specific reference to medical records. An example of such a statute is that of Connecticut:

> A subpoena directing production of such hospital record shall be served not less than twenty-four hours before the time for production, provided such subpoena shall be valid if served less than twenty-four hours before the time of production if written notice of intent to serve such subpoena has been delivered to the person in charge of the record room of such hospital not less than twenty-four hours nor more than two weeks before such time for production.[336]

Several cases have addressed the legitimacy of disclosing certain medical records in response to a grand jury subpoena. For example, the Illinois Supreme

---

[330]Ark. Stat. Ann. § 16-19-501 (1993); Ga. Code Ann. § 15-10-2 (1993).

[331]Fed. R. Civ. P. 45(a).

[332]See, e.g., Kan. Stat. Ann. § 60-245a (1992).

[333]See, e.g., Ga. Code Ann. § 24-10-23 (1993).

[334]*Id.*

[335]See, e.g., Alaska Stat. § 24.25.020 (1993).

[336]Conn. Gen. Stat. § 4-104 (1992); see also N.Y. Civ. Prac. L. & R. 2306 (1993).

Court has ruled that disclosure to a grand jury of the identities of abortion clinic patients does not violate the physician-patient privilege or the patients' constitutional right of privacy.[337] Similarly, a grand jury may gain access to information that psychiatric patients have consented to release from their medical records to insurers for reimbursement purposes, another court has ruled, because such consent constitutes a waiver of any physician or psychotherapist privilege that may exist, given the patients' "expectation that the confidential character of the records would necessarily be compromised pursuant to the reimbursement process."[338]

Court Orders

Occasionally, a state or federal court, or a state commission, orders a hospital to release medical records or other confidential patient information or to produce patient records in court. Written court orders usually are served upon hospitals in a manner similar to that of subpoenas, but also may be issued verbally in court to the hospital's attorney. Provided the court order does not violate a statute or regulation, the hospital should make every effort to comply with it. A hospital can contest a court order and present its case to the court before any sanctions for failure to comply are imposed. Failure to comply with a final, valid court order subjects either the person ordered to act or hospital corporate officers, if the corporation has been ordered to act, to a contempt-of-court citation. Hospital corporate officers are liable if the institution declines to follow the order even if a hospital department head is the person who actually does not act.

A court order requiring the disclosure of medical records will not violate the statutory physician-patient privilege if "sufficient steps" are taken to safeguard the identity of the patients involved, the Arizona Court of Appeals has ruled.[339] Although the state supreme court had ruled previously that a trial court's order requiring physicians to disclose the names, addresses, and the means of contacting patients they had treated undermined the purpose and intent of the physician-patient privilege, the question remained as to whether the removal of all information in medical records that tended to identify the patients would render the records discoverable. In this case, the appeals court, noting that the Arizona Supreme Court had objected only to identification of the patients, ruled that the disclosure of anonymous records is permissible.

---

[337]*People v. Florendo*, 447 N.E.2d 282 (Ill. 1983).

[338]*In re Pebsworth*, 705 F.2d 261, 262 (7th Cir. 1983); but see *People v. Smith,* 514 N.E.2d 211 (Ill. App. Ct. 1987) subpoena duces tecum seeking information identifying abortion clinic's clients quashed; see also *In Re Grand Jury Subpoena*, 710 F. Supp. 999 (D.N.J. 1989); but see *People v. Helfrich*, 570 N.E.2d 733 (Ill. App. Ct. 1991).

[339]*Ziegler v. Superior Court*, 656 P.2d 1251 (Ariz. Ct. App. 1982).

Compliance

A hospital should comply with valid legal process, properly served upon it, in the manner prescribed by its state's statutes. In recent years, many states have enacted statutes establishing compliance procedure with specific reference to subpoenas of medical records.[340] Other states have not enacted such statutes and thus treat subpoenas of medical records like any other subpoenas. Hospital administrators should be aware of current developments in their own states in this rapidly changing area of the law. Failure to comply correctly with a subpoena, without reasonable justification, is punishable as contempt of court.

The time permitted for compliance with subpoenas of medical records varies from state to state. For example, some states require that a hospital comply with the date specified on the subpoena.[341] Others specify a time period by statute.[342] Generally, the records must be sealed, then enclosed in an envelope, and may be opened only with the court's authorization. Most states expressly permit copies to be submitted in lieu of the original documents. A few states specify that the court may subpoena the originals if the copies are illegible or if their authenticity is in dispute.[343]

In several states, records furnished in compliance with legal process must be accompanied by an affidavit from the hospital's record custodian to certify the records' genuineness. Mississippi requires that the affidavit state:

- that the affiant is a duly authorized custodian of the records and has authority to certify said records,
- that the copy is a true copy of all the records described in the subpeona,
- that the records were prepared by personnel of the hospital, staff physicians, or persons acting under the control of either, in the ordinary course of hospital business at or near the time of the act, condition or event reported therein, and
- the amount of the reasonable charges of the hospital for furnishing such copies of the record[344]

Other states have substantially similar provisions.[345] These statutes provide, in addition, that if the hospital possesses none, or only part, of the records described

---

[340]Conn. Gen. Stat. § 4-104 (1992); Ky. Rev. Stat. Ann. § 422.305 (1993); N.Y. Civ. Prac. L. & R. § 2306 (1993).

[341]See, e.g., N.Y. Civ. Prac. L. & R. § 2306 (1993).

[342]See Va. Code Ann. § 8.01-413 (1993).

[343]See Ala. Code § 12-21-6 (1993); Nev. Rev. Stat. Ann. § 52.355 (1993).

[344]See Miss. Code Ann. § 41-9-109 (1993).

[345]See, e.g., Ark. Code Ann. §§ 16-46-302 and 16-46-305 (1993); Nev. Rev. Stat. Ann. § 52.325 (1993).

in the subpoena, the custodian must so certify in the affidavit. The custodian also may be required to attend the proceeding if the subpoena orders that individual to do so.

In most cases, the director of the medical records department is served with a subpoena because that staff member is deemed to have custody of the medical records. However, very few states define the term "custodian." Some states do specify that the custodian may be any person who prepares records, such as a physician, nurse, or therapist, or anyone entrusted with the care of the records.[346]

A hospital is not expected to respond to requirements that would be considered unreasonable. If it receives a subpoena after the date upon which it is required by statute to be served, the hospital has no obligation to respond. Certainly if the subpoena arrives the day after the designated response date that appears on the document, the hospital need not respond. The hospital cannot reasonably respond to a subpoena that commands presentation of records so voluminous or old that they cannot be reproduced by the return date given. Finally, a hospital is not expected to comply with a subpoena that commands production of records that are not in the hospital's possession.

For such cases, the administrator, with the advice of counsel, should develop responses for the hospital to subpoenas and court orders. If the attorney or official who initiated the subpoenas becomes unreasonable, the hospital should refer the matter to its legal counsel. If the subpoena was initiated by a plaintiff in an action against the hospital, the institution should not comply with the subpoena, but should require the plaintiff to file a motion to produce the records so that, if appropriate, the hospital will have an opportunity to argue against disclosure. If a subpoena is invalid or improper, the hospital may file a motion to quash it. The court or other issuing authority will determine after a hearing on the motion whether to enforce, modify, or quash the subpoena.

Hospital counsel can serve as important advisers to their clients in connection with the receipt of, and response to, legal process. The attorney not only should assist hospital administration and medical records practitioners in designing a procedure for processing subpoenas and court orders, but also should be available to advise the institution when it receives unusual subpoenas or those that demand records that may not be released in response to a subpoena. The hospital's counsel often is the best person to deal with other attorneys who have made unreasonable demands for records from the hospital.

The person assigned to process subpoenas of medical records should respond in accordance with a procedure established by the hospital and approved by its attorney. The procedure should include at least the following steps:

---

[346]See, e.g., Nev. Rev. Stat. § 52.325 (1993).

- examination of the record subject to subpoena to make certain that it is complete, that signatures and initials are legible, and that each page identifies the patient and the patient's hospital number
- examination of the record to determine whether the case forms the basis for a possible negligence action against the hospital and, if so, to notify the appropriate administrator (in some hospitals, the medical records department performs this function in coordination with the risk management or legal department)
- removal of any material that may not properly be obtained in the jurisdiction by subpoena, such as, in some states, notes referring to psychiatric care, or copies of records from other facilities, and correspondence
- enumeration of each page of the medical record, and writing the total number of pages on the record jacket
- preparation of a list of the medical record contents to be used as a receipt for the record if the record must be left with the court or an attorney (most medical records departments use a standard form for this purpose)
- use of a photocopy of the record, whenever possible, rather than the original, in responding to legal process

Rather than send original medical records to a court or an attorney through the mail, hospitals should designate a person to deliver them in person. Hospitals lose all control over their records once they are placed in the mail, and the loss of an original medical record may be a serious problem for a hospital defendant in a negligence action for a patient who may require future hospitalization.

6

Medical Records in the Electronic Era

INTRODUCTION

While hospitals and other health care providers rely on cutting-edge technology to provide medical treatment to patients, an increasing number also realize the benefits of technological advances in administration and record-keeping. In the recent past, most health care providers maintained patient records in paper files, eventually transferring the completed records to microfilm for safekeeping. Many providers now, however, use computers and computer networks, microwave technology, facsimile machines, and optical scanning and storage equipment in the creation, transmission, storage, and retrieval of medical records.

Automation of a provider's records can enhance quality of care by permitting quick capture of information in a patient's record and by improving access to a patient's records by the many health professionals who may be involved in a patient's care. In addition, quality improvement and quality assurance programs can be strengthened with the help of automated record systems. Automated record systems create the possibility of linking the patient record to expert diagnostic systems and other computer decision support tools to further enhance the quality of patient care. A fully integrated computer-based record system can also increase efficiency by reducing the volume of paperwork required for admissions, order entry, reporting of the results of radiological examinations and laboratory tests, and pharmacy dispensing. This, in turn, diminishes the overall time spent on updating and filing the records. In addition, a computerized record system can assist with patient scheduling, DRG and case-mix analysis and other management, staffing, and costing functions.[1]

---

[1]"Patient bedside system enters the computer age," Hospitals, July 1989, p. 76.

Although a computer-based patient record system can improve efficiency and the quality of care rendered by a provider, it may also increase a provider's exposure to liability for improper disclosure of personal health information and for computer sabotage committed by persons gaining unauthorized access to a computerized record system. Questions also arise as to whether providers with fully computerized record systems satisfy state licensure requirements, and the conditions of participation for Medicare reimbursement. It is also important to structure, install, and maintain automated patient record systems in a manner that supports admissibility of records on the system into evidence and the reliability of those records as evidence. Before considering these legal issues in more detail, it is important to understand the current environment and the trend toward automation of patient records.

CURRENT ENVIRONMENT AND EMERGING TRENDS

The trend toward computerization of all types of health care information has accelerated significantly in the past decade. Important strides have been made toward automating exchanges of information in the health care industry, although many of the efforts to date have focused on records containing financial, rather than medical, information. To date, there has been no widespread conversion from paper to computer format of all of the elements comprising a patient record. Increasingly, however, patient care data, such as medical laboratory reports, have become widely available in electronic form. Health care reform initiatives and the consolidation of providers into integrated delivery systems have further heightened the need for comprehensive automation and automated exchange of health care information. Hospitals and other providers must now develop strategies to deal with this new world of health information management.

Health information experts have noted two emerging trends in health information management. First, increased automation will permit management of health information based on the electronic patient record and the automatic transmission of information required for case and utilization management, claims processing, and other financial transactions. These information exchanges will increasingly be accomplished without the need for significant human intervention. In addition, access to health care information will become more widespread, with health care data networks permitting the exchange of health information concerning individuals by providers, payers, care managers, employers, vendors, support organizations, and others, with the information then stored in distributed or centralized databases.[2]

---

[2]See, B. Broccolo, D. Fulton, and A. Waller, The Electronic Future of Health Information: Strategies for Coping with the Brave New World, *Journal of AHIMA*, 64, no. 12 (1993): 38-51.

In 1991, a report by the General Accounting Office cited numerous advantages of computerizing medical records, including enhanced accuracy, accessibility, and comprehensiveness of records.[3] The same year, the Institute of Medicine (IOM) published the report of an extensive study on the computer-based patient record,[4] and recommended the development of computer-based patient records to improve health care and the management of health care data. According to the IOM report, health care professionals and organizations should adopt the computer-based patient record for use as the standard for medical and all other records related to patient care. During the Bush administration, in response to an invitation from Dr. Louis Sullivan, then Secretary of Health and Human Services, a forum of health care leaders created three health care industry work groups to look at issues related to the automation of health care information: The Work Group for Electronic Data Interchange, the Work Group on the Computerization of Medical Records, and the Work Group on Administrative Costs and Benefits. In its report, issued in 1993, the Work Group on Computerization of Medical Records recommended development of national standards for documenting and sharing patient information, including standard patient data definitions, codes, termination and universal patient, provider and payer identifiers.[5] This Work Group also recommended establishment of national standards for protecting the confidentiality of patient information through the enactment of federal legislation applicable to all health care information.

In a 1993 report commissioned by Senator John Glenn, the Office of Technology Assessment identified privacy issues arising from computerization of medical information, examined current law relating to privacy of medical information, and examined models and rules to protect privacy.[6]

Anticipating the emergence of community and regional health data networks, the IOM Committee on Regional Health Data Networks issued a report recommending preemptive federal legislation to establish a uniform requirement for the assurance of confidentiality and the protection of the privacy of person-identifiable health data and specifying a Code of Fair Health Information Practices that assures a proper balance among required disclosures, use of data and patient privacy and:

---

[3]General Accounting Office, *Medical ADP Systems: Automated Medical Records Hold Promise To Improve Patient Care* (Washington, D.C.: GAO, January 1991).

[4]Institute of Medicine, *The Computer-Based Patient Record: An Essential Technology for Health Care* (Washington, D.C.: National Academy Press, 1991).

[5]Report of the Work Group on Computerization of Medical Records, *Toward a National Health Information Infrastructure*, April 1993.

[6]U.S. Congress, Office of Technology Assessment, *Protecting Privacy in Computerized Medical Information*, OTA-TCT-576 (Washington, D.C.: Author, September 1993).

- imposes penalties for violation of this statute, including civil damages, equitable remedies, and attorneys' fees, where appropriate;
- calls enforcement by the government and permitting private aggrieved parties to sue;
- establishes that compliance with the statute's requirements would be a defense to charges based on improper disclosure.[7]

A fully computerized patient record system is one that captures, stores, retrieves, and transmits patient health data, including clinical, administrative, and payment data. A fully automated computer-based patient record is one in which all of the data and images collected over the course of a patient's health care are created, authenticated, modified, stored, and retrieved by computer. Computer-based records may be created using a variety of media, including magnetic media such as disks and tapes and digital media such as optical disks.

LEGAL ISSUES RAISED BY AUTOMATED MEDICAL RECORDS AND RECORD SYSTEMS

Use of automated patient records and record systems also presents new legal questions concerning providers' relationships with regulators and with patients. When a provider is contemplating installation or modification of a fully automated record system, it is important to ascertain whether the system will comply with applicable licensure laws and regulations, with Medicare requirements, and with applicable accreditation requirements. In addition, preserving the confidentiality and integrity, accessibility, accuracy, and durability of medical records on an automated system presents special problems. Computerized medical records present unique security concerns because of their vulnerability to computer viruses and other sabotage. Courts have not yet dealt with the liability and damages issues relating to patient injuries caused by computer viruses and other forms of sabotage committed against a computerized medical record system. Finally, it is vital that computerized patient record systems be designed, installed, and maintained in a manner that preserves the reliability of records created and stored on such systems so that such records will be admissible as evidence in court and will be credible as evidence.

---

[7]Institute of Medicine, *Health Data in the Information Age* (Washington, D.C.: National Academy Press, 1994).

Confidentiality and Integrity Issues

A computerized medical record system must be designed, installed, and maintained to preserve both the confidentiality and the integrity of patient health information. A report issued in 1993 by the Office of Technology Assessment defined confidentiality and integrity as follows:

- *Confidentiality* involves control over who has access to information.
- *Integrity* means that information and programs are changed only in a specified and authorized manner, that the computer resources operate correctly, and that the data in them are not subject to unauthorized changes.[8]

The Joint Commission on Accreditation of Healthcare Organizations (Joint Commission) has promulgated standards relating to information confidentiality and integrity, requiring that hospitals have a functioning mechanism to preserve confidentiality and to safeguard medical records against loss, destruction, and unauthorized access or use.[9] Significant legal risks directly associated with computer-based patient systems relate to the failure to preserve the confidentiality or integrity of data.

The legal obligation to protect the confidentiality of patient health information derives from various sources, but is primarily based on state statutes and the common law. Other sources of health care providers' duty to maintain the confidentiality of patient health care information include federal statutes and regulations, such as those concerning alcohol and drug abuse patient records, Medicare regulations, accreditation standards, and ethical standards promulgated by various health care trade and professional associations (see Chapter 5, Access to Medical Records Information, for a more complete discussion of these subjects). In addition, the function of medical records as evidence in trials and administrative hearings requires a provider to protect its records from unauthorized access.

Legal confidentiality obligations do not vary with the medium on which patient records are stored. The same confidentiality requirements apply to paper records and computer-based patient records, even though special safeguards may be legally mandated to preserve the confidentiality of computer-based patient records.[10] Confidentiality obligations do, however, vary from state to

---

[8]See, U.S. Congress, Office of Technology Assessment, *Protecting Privacy in Computerized Medical Information*, OTA-TCT-576 (Washington, D.C.: Author, September 1993): 89.

[9]Joint Commission on Accreditation of Healthcare Organizations, *Accreditation Manual for Hospitals* (Oakbrook Terrace, Ill.: 1994) Standards IM. 2.2.2 and 2.3.

[10]See, e.g., Illinois Hospital Licensing Requirements, 77 Ill. Admin. Reg. § 250.1510.

state. They may also vary depending on the nature of the recordkeeper and the type of information recorded. In some instances, medical record confidentiality requirements also vary according to the type of information transaction involved or the purpose of a particular disclosure of information. When individual health care data are transmitted across state lines, it may not always be clear which state's law applies or which courts will have jurisdiction if a dispute arises over disclosure of an individual's health information.

Computerization of patient information increases the risk of unauthorized disclosure of personal medical information, thereby necessitating special safeguards to keep the information confidential. The ease with which personal health information can be collected, stored, and accessed on a computer-based record system means that, generally, more information is included in a computer-based record than in a paper record. The detailed and sophisticated health information often found in computer-based records and the trend toward use of this information for nonhealth purposes makes computerized patient records attractive targets. A single breach of a computerized record system's security can lead to disclosure of hundreds or even thousands of records and to potentially catastrophic liability for such disclosure, because computers are capable of accessing, copying, and transmitting large numbers of records within a very short time span.

Because of the complexity of health care delivery and the increasing specialization of health care providers, many individuals will be involved in creating or using computerized patient records in institutions or group practice settings. This will often mean that a record can be accessed from numerous locations. Communications technology also makes possible off-site access to patient records. This stands in sharp contrast to paper records, which generally can only be accessed from a single location.

Automation of the information distribution process, and computer and communication linkages allow widespread access to patient records, not only by the parties involved in providing care, but also by secondary users of the information.[11] Secondary users of patient record information include life, health, and disability insurers, employee health benefit plans and support organizations, educational institutions, both the civil and criminal justice systems, rehabilitation and social welfare programs, credit agencies and banking centers, public health agencies, and researchers. Accordingly, confidentiality must be maintained and unauthorized access to patient records prevented both by inside and outside users of computerized patient record systems and by primary and secondary users of individual health information.

---

[11]U.S. Congress, Office of Technology Assessment, *Protecting Privacy in Computerized Medical Information*, OTA-TCT-576 (Washington, D.C.: Author, September 1993).

Unauthorized disclosure of patient record information can lead to various forms of liability, which are more thoroughly examined in Chapter 8. Briefly, state legislation imposes both criminal and civil penalties for breaches of the duty of confidentiality. Many jurisdictions also grant statutory private rights of action to patients who are injured by the unauthorized disclosure of confidential medical information. Licensure statutes and regulations frequently contain sanctions for improper disclosure of medical record information. Under the common law, several legal theories can also support a finding of liability for improper disclosure of personal health information. These theories include invasion of privacy, breach of confidentiality, breach of implied contract, defamation, and intentional infliction of emotional distress. In addition, federal statutes, such as those governing release of alcohol and drug abuse patient records, provide penalties for the improper release of information (see discussion in Chapter 5).

System Security Measures

Because of the potential for large-scale breaches of data security is much greater in a computerized medical record system, and because a provider bears the greatest risk of liability for unauthorized disclosure, a provider who implements such a system must be sure that it adequately protects confidentiality with respect to both internal and external users of the system. Computer system security must, therefore, balance the need for ready access to patient information by those involved in patient care with the need to protect against unauthorized access.[12] This may require some delicate balancing between conflicting objectives. A provider may be liable when its records are so highly guarded that medical information is not readily available to those caring for a patient; on the other hand, the provider can be liable for breaches of confidentiality that result from permitting easy access to medical records by unauthorized personnel.

The level of system security required by law for systems containing patient records is not clear. Under general principles of negligence liability, however, it is clear that security must be reasonable at a minimum. Because what is considered reasonable security changes over time, it is important that system security be periodically reviewed and updated.

To comply with legal requirements, a medical record system must provide for both system and data security. Data security exists when data are protected from improper disclosure or unauthorized or unintended alteration.[13] System security

---

[12]See, A. Waller and D. Fulton, The Electronic Chart: Keeping It Confidential and Secure, *Journal of Health and Hospital Law*, 26, no. 4, 104 at 107.

[13]Institute of Medicine, *The Computer-based Patient Record: An Essential Technology for Health Care* (Washington, D.C.: National Academy Press, 1991).

implies that a defined system functions in a defined operational environment, serves a defined set of users, contains prescribed data and operational programs, has defined network connections and interactions with other systems, and incorporates safeguards to protect the system against defined threats to the system and its resources and data.[14]

Appropriate computer security can generally be achieved through a combination of technical measures, system management, and administration and procedures. It is generally preferable to incorporate the technical safeguards into the system application or program (i.e., the medical record system) rather than relying on network infrastructure for security.[15] Technical safeguards include personal identification and user verification techniques, access control software and audit controls, computer architecture, communications linkage safeguards, and encryption.

Personal Identification and User Verification. Personal identification assists in ensuring that a user of a communication or computer system is authorized to do so and may be held accountable for his or her actions. The most common method of verifying the user's identity is through a secret password or code, which must be used to access a system or a particular part of a system. If password identification is used, the passwords should be at least five characters in length, and the system should require the users to change passwords frequently. Relying solely on passwords to identify users often fails to provide adequate security for computer systems. Users may share passwords, may leave passwords at their work stations or write them on desk blotters, or an unauthorized person attempting to gain access to the system may correctly guess one or more passwords if users use common words as passwords. User verification systems frequently involve a combination of identifiers, such as a key card in conjunction with a password or access code or some physical characteristic of the user, e.g., thumbprint.[16] Biometric identification involves verifying the identity of the user, based on a unique physical feature of the user, such as fingerprint, written signature, voice print, typing pattern, retinal scan, or hand geometry. Biometric identification generally provides a high level of security, but may be cost-prohibitive for many health care providers.

Access Control Software and Audit Trails. Once a system has identified a user, it is still necessary to limit the user's access to the resources and data that he or she is authorized to access. Data access control software prevents a user from

---

[14]Institute of Medicine, *Health Data in the Information Age* (Washington, D.C.: National Academy Press, 1994).

[15]See, U.S. Congress, Office of Technology Assessment, *Protecting Privacy in Computerized Medical Information*, OTA-TCT-576 (Washington, D.C.: Author, September 1993): 91.

[16]U.S. Congress, Office of Technology Assessment, *Protecting Privacy in Computerized Medical Information*, OTA-TCT-576 (Washington, D.C.: Author, September 1993): 94-95.

accessing or modifying a file unless the user has been given prior authorization. Through authorization checking, a system can determine whether a user's access request is valid, based on the permission assigned to the user, and then grant or deny the access request. Auditing access and attempted access by users helps to ensure user accountability. An examination of audit trails may also reveal suspicious patterns of access and lead to detection of improper conduct by both authorized and unauthorized users.

Computer Architecture. The computer itself may also be designed to enhance security by monitoring its own activities, preventing users from gaining access to data they are not authorized to see, and may also be designed to be secure from sophisticated tampering and sabotage.

Communications Linkage Safeguards. Since computer links to telecommunications lines may make the computers vulnerable to improper access or through the lines or through taps on the lines, a security system should also include security features designed to limit such improper use or access. One means of limiting access via dial-up lines has been dial-back protection devices. New security modems combine features of a modem with network security features, such as passwords, dial-back, and encryption.[17]

Encryption. Encryption is a method of protecting data vulnerable to unauthorized access or tampering. It is used to encode data for transmission or for storage in a computer. Encryption can provide an electronic signature to verify that a message has not been tampered with, and to protect against fraud or repudiation by a sender. Encryption can protect confidentiality by encoding a message so that its meaning is not obvious. An encrypted message is encoded in such a way as to permit interpretation of the message only with the appropriate key, to which only authorized parties have access. Encryption can also protect data integrity through message authentication. Message authentication allows a system to verify that a message arrived in exactly the same form that it was sent, without errors or alterations, that it came from the stated force, and that it was not falsified by an impostor or fraudulently altered by the recipient. Digital signatures can also be created through encryption. Like a handwritten signature, this digital signature can also be used to verify that information has not been altered after it is signed, thereby ensuring message integrity.

Implementing System Security

With respect to inside users of a system, the security system should permit only authorized users to have access to medical records. Access may be

---

[17]For a more detailed discussion of technical safeguards, see, U.S. Congress, Office of Technology Assessment, *Protecting Privacy in Computerized Medical Information*, OTA-TCT-576 (Washington, D.C.: Author, September 1993): 89-99.

controlled and users may be identified in one or more of the ways discussed above, including passwords, key cards, and access codes and biometric identification. In addition, a system should allow access to the system through only one work station at a time for each user identifier. It is wise to program a system to log off automatically when a work station has not been used for a predefined period of time. A user's access to the system should be limited to that portion of the system or record that relates to the user's position and duties. A system can be programmed to lock out an individual who attempts to retrieve files that he or she is not authorized to access or who repeatedly attempts to gain access to the system using an improper access code. In such cases, the system can be programmed to sound an alarm at the work station or at an operator's console. It is important to strictly limit access to sensitive records and portions of records containing highly sensitive health information for which the law provides a higher level of confidentiality protection. Such information includes HIV antibody test results, AIDS patient records (see Chapter 4), alcohol and drug abuse patient records (see Chapter 5), and records of celebrities (see Chapter 3). Because of the intense controversy over abortion, common sense dictates that abortion records be accorded the same level of protection as other highly sensitive health records, whether or not such protection is expressly required under applicable law.[18]

The scope of a user's access should be periodically reviewed and modified as appropriate. It is vital that a user's access to the system be promptly terminated when the person's employment, medical staff membership, or other relationship justifying access to patient records is terminated. When a user's relationship with the provider is to be terminated involuntarily, it may be wise to terminate the user's access to the system just prior to notifying the user of the termination. Access to records by each authorized user should be periodically reviewed to discourage casual browsing through records. Such casual browsing increases the risk that confidentiality will be breached.

Provider policy should specifically prohibit revealing or sharing passwords and other user identifiers and should also prohibit attempting to access records beyond the scope of one's authorization. Hospitals and other institutional providers should require medical staff members to sign confidentiality statements, in which they acknowledge that passwords, access codes, and the like are for personal use only and assume responsibility for any entries made using the medical staff member's identifier. Policies against sharing passwords or other identifiers or permitting another person access to the system should be strictly enforced.

---

[18]Some providers have chosen not to store highly sensitive health information on computers or to encrypt such information or use other techniques to provide a higher level of security for records or the portions of records containing such information.

Implementing External Security

Improper access to computerized medical records must also be prevented with respect to outside users of a medical record system. Controlling access from multiple and sometimes remote locations is more difficult than controlling access from one centralized location. Dial-up access makes it possible for external parties to try repeatedly to gain access to a system without being visible if a system is unmonitored. There are several possible methods to combat external parties' attempts to gain unauthorized access to a patient record system. Such methods include recording and monitoring such attempts to gain access to the system, having the computer system call back users requesting remote access, and requiring remote users to have physicians' "keys," such as encoded disks, in order to gain access.

Regardless of whether providers outsource their patient records to a computer outsource vendor or acquire their own systems, third party vendors and consultants will usually be involved in some way in developing, installing, operating, and maintaining the patient record system. These third parties may have access to live patient data, either on-site or from remote locations. Such third party access to patient data may be occasional or ongoing. When a provider outsources its patient records, the outsource vendor will have possession of the patient records. Such vendors and consultants are generally not subject to the same legal or ethical obligations with respect to confidentiality as are providers. If such a third party improperly discloses confidential patient information, the provider permitting the third party access to patient information can expect to be held responsible for any harm resulting from the improper disclosure, unless the provider can demonstrate that all reasonable precautions to prevent such disclosure have been taken.

In many cases, the contract between the provider and the vendor or consultant will disclaim any liability for damages such as those that would result from a disclosure in breach of a patient's confidentiality or will limit the amount of damages for which the vendor or consultant may be liable. It is, therefore, advisable to include in all contracts with such third parties obligations for the third party:

- to hold patient all patient information in strict confidence
- to use the information only to perform the third party's obligations under the contract
- to disclose only to the third party's employees who need access under the contract and who have signed a confidentiality agreement obligating them to hold all patient information in confidence
- to return the records in usable form upon request and upon termination of the contract

- to indemnify the provider for breaches of these obligations. It may not be possible to obtain such indemnification. However, the contract should not place any limits on the liability of the third party for breaches of its obligations.

Some outside computer services or data organizations analyzing a provider's patient data may wish to obtain the provider's patient data for purposes not in keeping with the provider's duty to preserve patient confidentiality. It is not uncommon for an outside computer service or data organization to attempt to obtain a provider's patient data to create databases or other proprietary information products. Such third parties will seek to own and control the information products and will want the right to distribute them freely. Such distribution will generally not accord with the provider's confidentiality obligations, unless the information product cannot be used directly or indirectly to identify individual patients. All contracts with such outside computer and data services should address whether the service will be permitted to use patient information in its information products and establish the precautions the service will be required to observe concerning patient confidentiality if the contract permits the use of patient information in the organization's information products.

When patient information is transmitted over public channels of communication, including telephone lines, radio waves, microwaves, etc., as in the case of wide-area networks, protecting the information from outside access becomes more difficult and requires additional precautions. As communications protocols become more standard, the potential for unauthorized tapping of such communication channels will increase. One possible response to this confidentiality problem is to encrypt information communicated over such channels of communication.

An additional threat to patient confidentiality results from the computer's capacity for mass storage and copying of records. One possible safeguard against the mass breach of confidentiality that would occur if numerous records are improperly accessed or disclosed is to restrict use of software functions that permit copying of multiple records at one time.

Computer Sabotage

Computerized patient record systems make possible widescale alteration or destruction of patient data through computer sabotage. Viruses and other forms of sabotage, such as worms, bombs, and trojan horses, can jeopardize both the integrity and accessibility of information on the system by causing the system to slow or crash. Although both inside and outside users of the system potentially can commit sabotage, the biggest threat to computer security is often internal. Disgruntled employees may pose a substantial threat of sabotage.[19]

The risk of sabotage by outside parties is present whenever there is any networking or electronic datasharing with outside parties, or disks or other storage media from outside sources are used on the system. It may be impractical to control this risk by eliminating networking and datasharing with outside computers and by not using any disk or other storage medium from an outside source, since connections with outside facilities and other databases may be essential for clinical, research, or other purposes. Joint Commission standards specifically address the need for hospital information systems to link up with external databases and bodies of clinical, administrative, and research knowledge.[20] Antivirus software, which assists in detecting and/or blocking computer viruses, is a useful means of reducing this risk. It is advisable to check all disks and similar media from outside sources for viruses prior to using them on a patient record system.

Hospitals should also be sensitive to the risk of sabotage from software vendors. In isolated cases, software vendors have sabotaged or threatened to sabotage a system after a provider withheld payment as permitted under the system contract, because the system fails to meet contractual standards. This form of sabotage involves the insertion of a virus or keylock into system software, which enables the vendor to lock or shut the system down in the event of a payment dispute. Contracts for the purchase, lease, license, or maintenance of a CPR system should obligate the vendor and its agents to refrain from inserting viruses or keylocks into the system. Contracts should also provide that the vendor will indemnify the provider for any and all losses and damages resulting from insertion of viruses or keylocks by the vendor or its agents.

While no computer security technology and methods available to the provider can totally guarantee that no breaches of system security will occur, it is important to employ system security technology and techniques that are at least reasonable by current standards. Nevertheless, the need to preserve the confidentiality and ensure the integrity of patient records will have to be balanced against the practical constraints on achieving perfect computer security.

---

[19]A. Waller, Legal Aspects of Computer-based Patient Records, *The Computer-based Patient Record: An Essential Technology for Health Care* (Washington, D.C.: National Academy Press, 1991).

[20]Joint Commission on Accreditation of Healthcare Organizations, *Accreditation Manual for Hospitals* (Oakbrook Terrace, Ill., 1994), Standards IM 2.2.2 and 2.3.

Preserving Access to Computerized Records

Delivering quality patient care requires that medical records be readily available. Federal reimbursement regulations,[21] state hospital licensure requirements,[22] and Joint Commission accreditation standards all require that medical records for current hospital patients be readily accessible and stored so as to be promptly retrievable.[23] Thus, a CPR system must make records readily accessible and provide for prompt retrieval of the records. When a system crashes or experiences downtime, computerized records become inaccessible. It is, therefore, imperative that a system be designed and maintained to minimize downtime and that adequate backup mechanisms be available. Patient record system downtime may hinder patient care and result in negligence liability. Excessive system downtime may also violate applicable licensure requirements and accreditation standards.

There are several precautions that can assist in preserving accessibility of computerized patient records. First, it is important that system hardware be properly maintained and that system software be tested, debugged where necessary, and maintained appropriately. When considering acquisition of a particular system, it may be wise to inquire as to other users' experience with the system relative to downtime and the time required to bring the system back up quickly. Any agreement for acquisition of a computerized record system or any component thereof should contain performance standards, as well as warranties of reliability and covenants to provide ongoing maintenance and support. It is also important to take appropriate precautions against sabotage of the system to prevent a computer virus from locking up or crashing the system. It is also important that a provider conduct adequate backup procedures. A provider's disaster or emergency plan should include planning for emergency capabilities for the patient record system.

Durability Concerns

Computerized patient records must be durable to meet state licensure requirements, to be available as evidence in malpractice and other litigation involving

---

[21]42 C.F.R. § 482.24 (1992).

[22]See, e.g., Mass. Regs. Code, tit. 105, § 130.200 (1993); Utah Admin. Code R., 432-100-7.402 (1993); Cal Code Regs., tit 22, § 70751 (1994).

[23]Joint Commission on Accreditation of Healthcare Organizations, *Accreditation Manual for Hospitals* (Oakbrook Terrace, Ill., 1994), Standard IM 5, which requires that the transmission of data and information be timely and accurate. See also, Standard IM 7, which requires that the information management function provide for the definition, capture, analysis, transformation, transmission, and reporting of individual patient-specific information related to the processes and outcomes of the patient's care.

the care received by a patient or the patient's medical condition, and to provide data for research. When medical records are computerized, the problem of durability becomes more complex than is the case with paper records. There are two preconditions for durability of computerized records. The first is that the medium on which the information is stored must last for at least the minimum time a provider is required to retain medical records. The second is that the provider must be able to access old records created or maintained on older, and perhaps obsolete, technology.

Changes in technology can render a computer system obsolete before the need for records stored on the system has ended. Frequently old and new systems do not interact, making the older records inaccessible through the newer system. Equipment may need to be maintained in good working order long after it is obsolete and another record system is in use. If an old and new system are able to interface, copying patient records from one system to the others can be problematic. Prior to copying such records, providers should check with knowledgeable legal counsel to ascertain whether such copied records will be considered original records for evidentiary purposes and whether retention of the copies in lieu of the originals complies with state licensure requirements. When records are copied from one system to another, it is important to preserve evidence of the chain of copying. When copying records, it is also important to verify that both the medium onto which the record will be copied and the copying process comply with applicable state licensure requirements.

Before selecting a medium for creation and storage of computerized patient records, the long-term durability of the medium should be investigated. Only media with proven durability should be utilized for patient record storage. It is important to note that the durability of some storage media, such as certain types of optical disks, has yet to be proven.[24]

Some state licensure regulations address medical record storage and retention requirement in general terms, stating that hospitals must store records to provide easy retrieval and security.[25] A few states have promulgated more elaborate requirements for record storage.[26] Some states specify acceptable storage media for medical records.[27] A provider that adopts a method for storing computerized records should verify in advance that the method complies with state licensure requirements for record retention (for a more detailed discussion of retention of medical records, see Chapter 1).

---

[24]See P. Zachary, Compact Disks Aren't Forever, It Turns Out, The *Wall Street Journal*, October 6, 1991.

[25]See, e.g., Kan. Admin. Regs. 28-34-9a (1992).

[26]See, e.g., Cal. Code Regs. tit. 22, § 70751(a) through (f) (1993).

[27]Or. Admin. R. 333-505-050 (1990) (paper, microfilm, electronic, or other media are acceptable).

Accuracy Issues

Computerized patient records, like paper records, must be completed in a timely and accurate fashion.[28] Maintaining a complete and accurate record is essential not only for compliance with licensure and accreditation requirements but also to establish that appropriate care was provided to each patient (for a more extensive discussion of medical record entries, see Chapter 2).

Error in computerized medical records can result from defective performance of either the hardware or the software or from human or machine input. In complex systems with open architecture, errors can result from unanticipated interactions among programs. To minimize the risk of error, a provider should have regular maintenance and performance checks conducted, and the results should be documented. The provider should also have a system to review human input for accuracy and should document that such review has occurred. Joint Commission standards require that an organization review the completeness, accuracy, and timeliness of medical record entries at least quarterly. At a minimum, the review must be performed by the medical staff in cooperation with nursing, the health information or medical record department, management and administrative services, and representatives of other departments, or services as appropriate.[29]

In addition, all laboratory and other types of equipment that generate input for a computerized records system should be well maintained and should be tested and calibrated periodically to minimize machine input errors.

The use of bar codes and other programmed codes can also raise accuracy concerns. Optical scanning of bar codes is used to monitor services and supplies provide to patients and to enter clinical data, such as temperature, pulse, blood pressure, and respiration. Bar codes can also be applied to a patient's wrist band and to packages of supplies. The use of such codes allows providers to create medical records much faster than is possible if data are charted by hand or entered through a computer keyboard. Optical scanning equipment should be tested periodically and the test results recorded. There should be a mechanism for confirming input generated from bar codes or other programmed codes either visually or otherwise.

STATE LICENSURE REQUIREMENTS

Many states impose specific requirements for medical records in statutes and regulations governing qualification for licensure as a hospital or other health

---

[28]JCAHO standards require that data be collected in a timely and efficient manner and with the degree of accuracy, completeness, and discrimination necessary for their intended use. Joint Commission on Accreditation of Healthcare Organizations, *Accreditation Manual for Hospitals* (Oakbrook Terrace, Ill., 1994) Standard IM 3.2.

[29]JCAHO, *Accreditation Manual for Hospitals*, Standard IM 3.2 (1994).

care facility. Many of these licensure requirements were formulated when paper records were the rule rather than the exception. Because state law is changing so rapidly in this area, this chapter will not include a detailed discussion of specific state requirements. It is important, nevertheless, for a provider automating its medical records to check applicable state requirements to ensure that the record system and the records will meet applicable requirements with respect to the creation, authentication, and retention of patient records, as well as requirements for record content (see discussion in Chapter 2).

REIMBURSEMENT REQUIREMENTS AND ACCREDITATION STANDARDS

It is important that a health care provider's records meet applicable governmental reimbursement standards and accreditation standards. A more detailed discussion of reimbursement and requirements and accreditation standards applicable to medical records can be found in Chapter 1. Both the Health Care Financing Administration (HCFA) and the Joint Commission permit computerization of patient records.

Medicare Conditions of Participation

To participate in the Medicare program, a provider must meet the applicable Medicare conditions of participation. The conditions of participation for hospitals include requirements for medical records but do not include an express restriction on permissible media for creating and storing such records.[30] Medicare conditions of participation for hospitals permit authentication of patient records by signature, written initials or computer entry.[31]

Accreditation Standards

In theory, the Joint Commission is a voluntary organization administering a voluntary accreditation process. However, its accreditation standards are incorporated in some state hospital licensure requirements, at least in part, and a hospital is deemed to meet certain of the Medicare conditions of participation if it is accredited by the Joint Commission.[32] The Joint Commission's accreditation requirements applicable to medical records are primarily found in the standards concerning management of information.[33] The Joint Commission clearly con-

---

[30]42 C.F.R. § 482.24.

[31]42 C.F.R. § 482.24(c)(1)(ii).

[32]See 42 U.S.C. § 1395 bb.

[33]Joint Commission on Accreditation of Healthcare Organizations, *Accreditation Manual for Hospitals* (Oakbrook Terrace, Ill., 1994), Management of Information.

templates that hospitals may record a portion or the whole medical records on computer. For example, the accreditation standards provide that authentication of patient record entries may be by written signatures or initials, rubber-stamp signature or computer key.[34] The Joint Commission also requires that a practitioner utilizing a computer key signature sign a statement that the practitioner alone will use the code for the computer key.[35]

Auto-Authentication

Both the Joint Commission and the Medicare conditions of participation require that medical records be authenticated by the responsible practitioner.[36] Authentication involves signature or another approved means of identifying the practitioner responsible for a medical record entry and accepting responsibility for the contents of the entry. Often, however, health professionals do not enter information directly into a computerized record system; rather, the information is dictated into a digital dictation system. Some hospitals have been using what is referred to as "auto-authentication," which refers to a process whereby physicians sign on to a digital dictation system with a computer key and then dictate record entries. The dictated record entries are then transcribed. The dictated entry is sent to the dictating physician, who is given a stated time period in which to make changes. If the physician fails to return corrections within this time period, the physician is deemed to have approved the record entry for accuracy, completeness, etc.

Both HCFA and the Joint Commission have expressed concern that auto-authentication does not meet their respective standards. In particular, HCFA does not believe that auto-authentication complies with the Medicare conditions of participation, because physicians often do not authenticate the final record entry. The Joint Commission has also taken the position that an auto-authentication process does not conform with its accreditation standards for hospitals.[37]

---

[34]Joint Commission on Accreditation of Healthcare Organizations, *Accreditation Manual for Hospitals* (Oakbrook Terrace, Ill., 1994), Standard IM.7.9.1.

[35]Joint Commission on Accreditation of Healthcare Organizations, *Accreditation Manual for Hospitals* (Oakbrook Terrace, Ill., 1994), Standard IM.7.9.2.

[36]Joint Commission on Accreditation of Healthcare Organizations, *Accreditation Manual for Hospitals* (Oakbrook Terrace, Ill., 1994), Standard IM.7.9.1 (1994); 42 C.F.R. § 482.24(c)(1).

[37]In addition, at least one state Department of Health has taken the position that auto-authentication of medical records without requiring physicians to verify information in record entries after transcription is unacceptable. Specific auto-authentication procedures, such as those involving sharing of the physician's access code with transcriptionists or others, may violate the hospital licensure requirements of several states.

AUTOMATED MEDICAL RECORDS AS EVIDENCE

In addition to enabling providers to respond properly to the medical needs of patients, medical records serve as a diary of a provider's actions. It is, therefore, important that the information contained in a record be admissible as evidence in court when the care received by the patient or the patient's medical condition is an issue. Because of the widespread computerization of general business records, courts have developed standards for judging the trustworthiness of computerized records.

The Rule against Hearsay

One barrier to introduction of any medical record as evidence in court is the rule against hearsay. Hearsay is generally defined as a statement made out of court by a declarant and proffered as evidence to prove the truth of the matter asserted in that out-of-court statement. Courts exclude hearsay from evidence, unless one of the exceptions to the hearsay rule applies. Since all medical records, regardless of form, are written statements made outside the courtroom, they are classed as hearsay if offered as evidence to prove the truth of any matter asserted in the record.

One important exception to the hearsay rule is the business records exception. Although the statement of this rule may vary from jurisdiction to jurisdiction, generally, to come within the business records exception, records must be kept regularly in the ordinary course of business and must not have been prepared specifically for trial. The business record exception applies only to record entries made at or near the time of the event recorded. In addition, the identity of the person making or recording the entry must be captured in the record, and the record must have been prepared by a person with firsthand knowledge of the event recorded or from information transmitted by such a person. The person making the record or transmitting the information for the record must be acting in an ordinary business capacity at the time the record is made.

A computerized record made in the ordinary course of a provider's business should meet the requirement that the record be kept regularly and in the ordinary course of business. An automated record system should record the date and time of each entry and update to a patient record so that the time of the entry or update and its timeliness can be shown in court. The identity of the person who makes each entry or update should be captured by the system. If employees or health professionals share passwords or make entries under an identifier that is not their own, it will be impossible to ensure that the system's record of the identity of the person making the entry is accurate.

It is important that errors in computerized records be corrected appropriately. The system should preserve both the original entry and the correction and should record the identities of the persons making each original entry or correction so as not to create an appearance that the record has been altered or that records on the system are not reliable and trustworthy as evidence.

Write-once, read-many (WORM) or nonerasable compact disk, read-only memory (CD-ROM) technology may be attractive in this context, because records cannot be altered once information is recorded. Another method of preserving records in their original form is write-protecting the portions of computer disks on which patient information is stored so that the integrity of records is protected. Nevertheless, if a system uses reliable software and preserves erroneous entries, tracking the history of each entry and correction, the provider should be able to demonstrate the reliability of the record in court.

It is advisable for the provider to have an employee or technical consultant who can testify concerning the reliability of the system's identification and entry-dating features and the trustworthiness of the system as a whole, including system security features and procedures.

Records created and stored on a properly designed and maintained computer-based record system should come within the business record (or a similar exception applicable to medical records) to the hearsay rule if the procedures described above are followed. Under the business record exception to the hearsay rule, statements contained in such computerized records may also be admissible if made by providers or staff acting in the ordinary course of business. Statements contained in such computerized records may also be admissible if made by the declarant for "purposes of medical diagnosis or treatment and describing medical history, or past or present symptoms, pain, or sensations, or the inception or general character of the cause or external source thereof insofar as reasonable pertinent to diagnosis or treatment.[38]

Best Evidence Rule

Another evidentiary rule relevant to the admissibility of computerized medical records is the best evidence rule. The best evidence rule expresses a judicial preference for the original of a writing if the contents of a writing are in dispute. In the context of computerized records, a question arise as to whether a hard copy of the contents of the record is an "original" for purposes of the best evidence rule. The Federal Rules of Evidence state the requirements for data stored on a computer or similar device. Rule 1001(3) states that "[i]f data are stored in a computer or similar device, any printout or other output readable by sight, shown to reflect the data accurately, is an 'original.' " The Federal Rules of Evidence also provide that duplicates are admissible to the same extent as originals, unless a genuine issue of authenticity of unfairness arises.[39]

---

[38]Federal Rules of Evidence, Rule 803(4). This exception to the rule against hearsay is known as the medical records exception.

[39]Federal Rules of Evidence, Rule 1003.

Some states' evidentiary rules also provide that computerized documents shall be accepted as originals.[40] Other states permit admission of reproductions into evidence when the reproductions are made in the regular course of business and satisfy other criteria for trustworthiness.[41] The trustworthiness of a record created on a computerized system refers to the reliability of system hardware and software, the use of proper procedures for creating and storing records, the assurance that entries are made by adequately trained personnel, and the prevention of unauthorized access to the records and of tampering with the system.

FACSIMILE TRANSMISSION OF MEDICAL RECORDS AND MEDICAL RECORD ENTRIES

The widespread use of facsimile (fax) machines to transmit information, including medical records, from one location to another has created a new threat to confidentiality and may, in some circumstances, call into question the integrity or authenticity of orders and other medical record entries transmitted by fax. Both paper and computerized records can be sent via fax machines; in addition, the use of a fax modem on a computer makes possible transmission of a computerized records from one computer to another without generating any hard copy of the record as a necessary by-product of the transmission. In either case, fax transmissions to external parties generally travel over telephone networks or other public channels of communication. Because there is a significant risk that fax transmissions will be misdirected, use of facsimile machines to transmit confidential medical record information is risky and is extremely risky if highly sensitive patient information is involved.

These risks can be reduced, however, if proper maintenance and security techniques are used and if proper procedures are followed in transmitting medical record by fax. Nevertheless, it is probably never prudent to send via fax highly sensitive health information, except in encrypted form or over nonpublic channels of communication that are highly secure (e.g., a local area network within a facility). The American Health Information Management Association recommends use of the Fax machine to transmit patient health information only when the original document or mail-delivered photocopies will not serve.[42]

A provider sending confidential information by fax offsite should verify that the recipient is authorized to receive it. Some, but by no means total, protection against unauthorized access to a fax transmission can be obtained by calling the recipient before sending the transmission, alerting the recipient to stand by for

---

[40]See, e.g., Fla. Sta. Ann. § 90.951.

[41]See, e.g., Cal. Evid. Code § 1270-1272.

[42]See, Practice Bulletin: Guidelines for Faxing Patient Health Information. *Journal of AMRA*, June 1991, p. 29.

the transmission and verifying that the fax number to which the transmission will be directed is the correct number. The cover sheet on the document should also include a confidentiality legend, emphasizing the nature of the information contained in the transmission and requesting that the recipient contact the sender if the fax is received by someone other than the recipient shown on the cover sheet. Encrypting faxed information is another method of protecting its confidentiality. However, this process generally requires that the receiving fax machine or computer be equipped to disencode the encrypted information, and this will often not be the case. When sending faxes offsite, a provider should retain a record of each fax transmission (including the number of the receiving fax machine) and the contents of the fax.

When receiving orders or other medical record information from outside the facility, a provider should also take special precautions. If caller identification is available, the receiving fax machine should be equipped with a mechanism for recording the number of the telephone from which the fax transmission originated. The personnel operating the fax machine should have a list of telephone numbers from which medical staff members transmit orders and should verify that the telephone number identified on the fax machine appears on that list.[43] A hospital may also treat faxed orders like verbal orders and require authentication of the order by the appropriate medical staff member within the time period permitted for authentication of verbal orders. Nevertheless, with the advent of computer fax boards, with their attendant opportunities for electronic manipulation, may make it difficult to establish the accuracy and authenticity of a faxed order in court, if either is disputed by the originating practitioner.[44] In the context of computer fax boards and fax modems, use of cryptography for message authentication may be advisable.[45]

Nevertheless, providers should refer to state rules of evidence to determine if, and under what circumstances, facsimile transmissions that become part of a patient record are admissible in court. Fax machines used to transmit orders internally should also be equipped to print the date, time, and address of the originating fax machine to help support the authenticity of internally faxed documents. The original of each such fax transmission should be retained.

---

[43]It is important to note that a number generated by the fax machine originating the transmission and printed on the fax may not be a correct number, since some fax machines can be programmed to transmit a number other than that of the originating telephone.

[44]For a discussion of the possibility of such manipulation, see F. Sommers, Is a Fax a Legal Document? *Banking Law Review*, Fall 1991.

[45]See also AHIMA's recommendations for both releasing and receiving patient information by Fax, *supra*, n. 42 at pp. 31–32.

7

Courtroom Disclosures of Medical Records Information

INTRODUCTION

Medical records have become increasingly important in the prosecution and defense of legal actions at trial and in administrative proceedings before government regulatory agencies. Success in a Workers' Compensation claim, personal injury action, or professional negligence suit often depends upon the information contained in those records. Consequently, patients and other parties in the litigation seek every record that may be relevant to their controversy and demand access to patient medical records, hospital and medical staff quality assurance and other committee records, and hospital incident reports. Whether these records are discoverable or admissible may significantly affect the outcome of the legal action. The manner in which the records are created and maintained will have an important effect on their value as legal documents and their discoverability and admissibility.

At the outset, it is important to distinguish between the discoverability and admissibility of evidence. Discoverability involves access to documents or witnesses; admissibility concerns whether documents, objects, or testimony may be admitted formally into evidence in a trial. Something may be discoverable but, under the applicable rules of evidence, may not be admissible into evidence. In many jurisdictions, discoverability is not dependent upon admissibility. The court or administrative hearing officer or panel, applying applicable evidentiary rules, will determine whether a record is discoverable or admissible. Since these rules vary from state to state, it is extremely important for hospitals to refer questions on this subject to their legal counsel. The institutions' counsel will interpret applicable rules and help the hospitals prepare appropriate arguments for or against discoverability or admissibility.

ADMISSIBILITY OF MEDICAL RECORDS

Although historically there was a diversity of opinion as to the admissibility of medical records in judicial and quasi-judicial proceedings, and although the decisions may vary based on the particular facts, the rules of evidence, the type of proceeding, and numerous other factors, most modern courts hold medical records to be admissible into evidence.[1] Whether the records are admissible is of primary importance to the hospital in its own defense, since they may contain information damaging to the institution. For example, if the hospital is being sued in a medical malpractice suit, a medical record that clearly shows that a hospital nurse incorrectly administered a medication would be damaging to the hospital's defense. The record also might show that the physician improperly prescribed the medication, a fact that might help the hospital's case. Whether such a record is discoverable and admissible, therefore, will be significant to the hospital.

The admission of records in proceedings in which the hospital is not a party should be of less concern to the institution as long as it discloses the medical records in accordance with the law.

HEARSAY AND THE BUSINESS RECORDS EXCEPTION

Hearsay is a statement made out of court, introduced into a court proceeding for the purpose of proving the truth of the facts asserted in that statement.[2] Under traditional rules of evidence, a patient care record is hearsay. Generally, hearsay is not admissible into evidence because the person who actually made the statement is not there to be cross-examined. Consider the example of a nurse who has made an entry regarding the patient's blood pressure. The following problems may result if the record is admitted into evidence as proof of that blood pressure: (1) The opposing side cannot ask the nurse about mistakes the individual may have made in transcribing the record. (2) The jury cannot observe the nurse's demeanor and judge the nurse's veracity. (3) The jury will be unable to check the records as it would if the record were part of the nurse's testimony in the courtroom.

Because hearsay is not admissible into evidence unless it falls within one of the exceptions discussed below, medical records historically have been inadmis-

---

[1]See generally Annotations. 10 A.L.R. 4th 552; 69 A.L.R. 3d 104; 69 A.L.R. 3d 22; 10 A.L.R. Fed. 858; 44 A.L.R. 2d 553; 38 A.L.R. 2d 778; 175 A.L.R. 274, 286; see also 6 *Wigmore*, Evidence § 1707 (Chadbourn rev. 1976 & Supp. 1991). See 40 *Am. Jur.* 2d. Hospitals and Asylums § 43 (1968 & Supp. 1993).

[2]See McCormick, *Evidence* 3d ed. (1984) Supp. 1987 § 313.

sible.[3] However, now medical records may be admitted into evidence on a variety of other grounds.

In states that have enacted laws permitting admissibility of business records, medical records are admissible when they qualify as business records, defined as documents that are made in the regular course of business at or within a reasonable time after the event recorded occurred and under circumstances that reasonably might be assumed to reflect the actual event accurately.[4] Documents that summarize hospital records and are kept in the regular course of business, such as discharge summaries and record extracts, also may be admitted into evidence as business records.[5]

In federal courts, medical records may be admissible as business records under the Federal Rules of Evidence.[6] The Federal Rules allow the admission of a record of an event made at or near the time of the event by a person with knowledge of the event, if the record is made in the regular course of business, and if it is the regular practice of the business to keep such a record. In addition, the method or circumstances of preparation must be trustworthy. The trial court is given great latitude in determining the circumstances that indicate trustworthy or untrustworthy preparation.[7] Improper alteration of a record, for example, suggests a lack of trustworthiness.[8] Courts generally favor the admission of evidence under the Federal Rules.[9]

Application of the business records exception to the hearsay rule is not unlimited, however. Information in the medical record may be inadmissible as a business record to the extent that it is not relevant to the patient's diagnosis or treatment. For example, a New York appeals court held that a statement by an unidentified person as to how a patient's accident occurred did not qualify as part of a business record.[10]

Thus, a medical record may be held inadmissible because it contains objectionable conclusions or opinions. However, observations in a patient care record that physicians are trained to make and that they routinely make in the course of

---

[3]See *Chernov v. Blakeslee*, 111 A. 908 (Conn. 1921); *Jordan v. Apter*, 105 A. 620 (1919); *Piccarreto v. Rochester Gen. Hosp.*, 108 N.Y.S.2d 717 (App. Div. 1951); *Sauer v. Weidel*, 218 N.Y.S. 888 (App. Div. 1926); *A.A. v. State*, 252 N.Y.S.2d 800 (Ct. Cl. 1964).

[4]See, e.g., Fla. Stat. ch. § 90.803 (1993); N.D. Cent. Code § 31-08-01 (1993); Okla. Stat., tit. 12, § 2803 (1994); McCormick, *Evidence,* 2d ed. (1984 & Supp. 1987) § 313.

[5]*Sandegren v. State*, 397 So. 2d 657 (Fla. 1981).

[6]Fed. R. Evid., 803 (6).

[7]*Mississippi River Grain Elevator v. Bartlett & Co. Grain*, 659 F.2d 1314, 1315 (5th Cir. 1981).

[8]*Hiatt v. Groce*, 523 P.2d 320 (Kan. 1974).

[9]See *In re Ollag Constr. Equip. Corp.*, 665 F.2d 43 (2d Cir. 1981).

[10]*Mikel v. Flatbush Gen. Hosp.* 370 N.Y.S.2d 162 (App. Div. 1975). See also *Davies v. Butler*, 602 P.2d 605 (Nev. 1979), in which an unattributed statement in the medical record regarding the source of liquid on a patient's clothing was held inadmissible.

treating patients may be admissible. In one case, for example, a physician's observation that the patient was intoxicated on arrival at the hospital was held admissible.[11] However, it is clear that a record that stated that the patient was injured by a car that ran a red light would not be admissible to prove the color of the traffic light. In another case, a court ruled that a medical record that concluded that a patient's injuries were caused by inhalation of insect poisoning was inadmissible.[12] The court said that "this conclusion of causation is not one that all persons skilled in the art would likely reach. . . . It is a conclusion not based upon directly observable fact or well-known tests."[13]

Even if not found to be a business record, a medical record may be admissible if it qualifies under some other exception to the hearsay rule. For example, declarations against interest, spontaneous exclamations, dying declarations, and admissions of a party all may be admissible as exceptions to the hearsay rule if recorded by a person with personal knowledge.[14] Because these statements generally are considered to be free of the untrustworthiness and inaccuracy that underlie most untested assertions by a third party, when the person making the statements is unavailable to testify in court (because of death or other causes), courts will admit such statements into evidence. For example, if a person makes a statement of facts that is against that individual's own interest, it is assumed the statement is true. Statements made in a moment of surprise or in immediate response to an unexpected event usually are considered trustworthy because the person had no time to fabricate a false statement.

A wide variety of statutes provide for the admission of hospital records into evidence because such records are public or official records. This is especially true when state statutes require public hospitals to keep records. The rationale is that the requirement that the record be kept ensures that the information in the record will be reliable. Hospital records also may be admissible under Workers' Compensation laws. Under Illinois law, for example, medical records, certified as true by a hospital officer and showing medical treatment given to an employee in the hospital, are admissible as evidence of the medical status of the Workers' Compensation claimant.[15]

Under the hospital lien laws of most states, the person being sued is permitted to examine the hospital records pertaining to the treatment of the injured person if the hospital claims a lien. The Illinois law also requires any hospital claiming a lien under the act to furnish any party to an action in court or the clerk of the

---

[11]*Rivers v. Union Carbide Corp.*, 426 F.2d 633, 637 (3d Cir. 1970).

[12]*Skogen v. Dow Chem. Co.* 375 F.2d 692, 704 (8th Cir. 1967).

[13]*Id.*, at 705.

[14]*Skillern & Sons, Inc. v. Rosen*, 359 S.W.2d 298 (Tex. 1962); see also 5 *Wigmore*, Evidence ch. 48. (Chadbourn rev. 1974 & Supp. 1991).

[15]820 Ill. Comp. Stat. Ann. 305/16 (1993).

court with a written statement of the injuries and treatment of the injured person as shown by the hospital records.[16]

Before a hospital record may be admitted in evidence under an exception to the hearsay rule, it must meet the tests of relevancy, materiality, and competency. Although these three terms often are used as synonyms, they have distinct meanings.[17] Relevancy refers to the logical relationship between the proposed evidence and a fact to be established. Materiality refers to whether a fact or proposition is an important factor in the particular dispute. Competency refers to what the very nature of "the thing to be proved" requires as fit and appropriate proof in the circumstances. Evidence must be relevant, material, and competent before it can be admitted.

DISCOVERABILITY OF MEDICAL RECORDS

Discovery procedures involve pretrial access to either witnesses or documents, which allow parties to a suit to discover facts and possible evidence in the case. Discovery may be conducted by obtaining the oral deposition or questioning of a party or a witness, or by obtaining court permission to examine documents or other objects. The use of discovery procedures may result in testimony or other information that may be introduced as evidence at trial. In a patient's suit against a hospital, for instance, the hospital may interrogate the patient or seek to obtain access to all the patient's medical records at the discovery stage. Similarly, a hospital may seek to discover the medical records of other members of the injured patient's family to establish that the injuries result from genetic defects and not medical negligence.[18]

The issue of whether a patient is entitled to assert a privilege that would prevent disclosure of medical record information is raised frequently at the discovery stage, although it should be emphasized that the existence of a privilege also would govern the admissibility of such information as evidence at trial. Most states have confidential communications statutes that protect communications between a patient and a physician from disclosure in judicial or quasi-judicial proceedings under circumstances specified in the law. The purpose of this privilege is to protect the confidentiality of the physician-patient relationship in order to encourage the patient to tell the physician all the

---

[16]770 Ill. Comp. Stat. Ann. 35/3 (1993).

[17]*Am. Jur.* 2d Evidence § 251 (1967).

[18]See, e.g., *Dierickx v. Cottage Hosp. Corp.*, 393 N.W.2d 564 (Mich Ct. App. 1986), in which the court ruled that health care providers could not discover the medical records of siblings of a child whose parents were suing for malpractice, even though the child's injuries were consistent with genetic defects.

information necessary for treatment, no matter how embarrassing.[19] Statutory provisions vary as to the scope and extent of the patient's privilege to prevent disclosure by the physician, the extent to which the physician may exercise the patient's privilege, and the nature of the proceeding in which the privilege may be raised.[20]

Several concepts must be kept in mind in applying the patient-physician privilege. First, this privilege usually does not exist unless it is created by statute.[21] Second, if a statute exists, it generally will apply only to statements made to general practitioners and those whose business comes fairly within the definition of "physician."[22] Today, the privilege has been extended to communications between a patient and a psychiatrist, psychologist, or other psychotherapist.[23] The patient-physician privilege will not apply to matters that fall outside the physician-patient relationship.[24] The privilege is created to protect the patient's privacy, not the physician's.[25] Finally, when patients put their health in issue (e.g., by suing for injuries sustained in the course of treatment) or otherwise consent to disclosure, the privilege does not apply.[26]

The Illinois and Virginia confidential communications statutes are typical. Illinois law prohibits any physician or surgeon from disclosing information acquired while attending to a patient in a professional relationship necessary to enable the physician to treat the patient.[27] This statute limits the application of the privilege in a number of situations, including homicide trials, civil or criminal malpractice actions, and patient consent. When the patient brings an action in which the individual's physical or mental condition is at issue, the court may find that the patient implied consent to the admission of the record.

Virginia's privilege statute protects the information a licensed practitioner of any branch of the healing arts acquires in treating a patient in a professional capacity if the information is necessary to treat the individual.[28] However, the Virginia law states that when the physical or mental condition of a patient is at issue, or when the court decides disclosure is necessary "to the proper administration of justice," the information will not be privileged.

---

[19]See Annotation 10 A.L.R. 4th 552, at 557.

[20]See, e.g., 735 Ill. Comp. Stat. Ann. 5/8-802 (1993); N.J. Stat. § 2A:84A-22.2 (1993); *Osterman v. Ehrenworth*, 256 A.2d 123 (N.J. Super. Ct. Law Div. 1969).

[21]81 *Am. Jur.* 2d, Witnesses § 437 (1992).

[22]*Id.*, § 451.

[23]*Id.*, § 452.

[24]*Id.*, § 477.

[25]*Id.*, § 438; *People v. Bickham*, 431 N.E.2d 365 (Ill. 1982).

[26]*Am. Jur.* 2d supra, n.21 at §§ 490, 506.

[27]735 Ill. Comp. Stat. Ann. 5/8-802 (1993).

[28]Va. Code Ann. § 8.01-399 (1993).

The patient may waive this privilege expressly or by failing to assert it. Courts often disagree on what constitutes a waiver, as well as the extent of such a waiver.[29] Most courts hold that the act of bringing a suit that places the party's physical or mental health in issue constitutes an implied waiver of the privilege.[30] In one case, a question arose as to the monetary loss suffered by the mother of a person who had died.[31] The court ruled that the medical records of the mother's kidney treatment were relevant in determining her life expectancy, reasoning that she had waived any privilege by bringing her suit and putting her health into issue.

Further, confidential communications statutes generally state that the privilege is waived if the injured party brings a suit in which the person's physical condition is at issue.[32] However, the mere fact that a trial involves an issue of the patient's physical condition does not result in a waiver of the privilege. For example, in an Arizona case, results of a urinalysis were held inadmissible in a prosecution for drunk driving.[33] The tests were not performed at police request, and the court held that the patient had not waived his privilege.

A number of courts have ruled that no waiver of the privilege occurs, unless it is evident that the patient intended to waive it.[34] Similarly, some courts have held that to waive the privilege requires a clear, unequivocal act showing such waiver. In one case, a court found that the patient had not waived his privilege by turning his records over to his insurer because that act was not so unequivocal as to demonstrate an intention to abandon the privilege.[35] Rather, it was an act consistent with the intention to reveal confidential information only to the extent necessary to obtain treatment and payment.

Although confidential communications statutes have been held to apply to confidential matters appearing in patient care records, they affect the hospital directly only in cases in which the hospital is a litigant. In suits between the patient and others, it is not the hospital's concern or right to assert the privilege, or to oppose a records subpoena. However, the court may order the hospital to permit examination of medical records without disclosing confidential communications.[36] For example, in a New York case, a hospital was ordered to furnish all information on the treatment, care, and maintenance of the injured person to a party liable for a hospital lien.[37] This information was necessary to evaluate the

---

[29]See generally Annotation 10 A.L.R. 4th 552, at 558.

[30]*Carr v. Schmid*, 432 N.Y.S.2d 807 (Sup. Ct. 1980).

[31]*McCluskey v. United States*, 562 F. Supp. 515 (S.D.N.Y. 1983).

[32]See, e.g., 735 Ill. Comp. Stat. Ann. 5/8-802 (1993).

[33]*State of Arizona v. Santeyan*, 664 P.2d 652 (Ariz. 1983).

[34]*Schaffer v. Spicer*, 215 N.W.2d 134 (S.D. 1974).

[35]*State ex rel. Gonzenbach v. Eberwein*, 655 S.W.2d 794 (Mo. Ct. App. 1983).

[36]See *In re D.M.C., R.L.R., Jr.*, 331 N.W.2d 236 (Minn. 1983); *Application of Larchmont Gables, Inc.*, 64 N.Y.S.2d 623 (Sup. Ct. 1946).

[37]*Application of Larchmont Gables*, 64 N.Y.S.2d 623.

reasonableness of the hospital's charges yet did not disclose confidential communications concerning the diagnosis and treatment of the patient. In general, whether the privilege should be asserted and whether it will be applied are issues for the courts and the parties involved.

When the hospital is a party to a suit, but neither the patient nor the physician is a party, the hospital may be able to assert the physician-patient privilege on behalf of the patient. While the effectiveness of the hospital's assertion depends on the requirements of the applicable statute, several court decisions have permitted a party to assert the privilege on behalf of a patient who was not a party to the action.

The Pennsylvania Supreme Court, for example, held that a hospital properly asserted the physician-patient privilege on behalf of a patient in refusing to submit the original records of certain tissue specimens.[38] A hospital may assert this privilege when the personal nature of the records results in an obligation on the part of the hospital to maintain the confidentiality of the information by limiting access to the records to authorized personnel. More generally, a hospital that asserts the privilege for a patient who is not a party to the action is acting consistently with its interest in protecting its patient's confidentiality, and the court will decide when the privilege applies. Unless applicable law requires hospitals to disclose medical records information in these circumstances, they should attempt to assert the confidential communications privilege on behalf of the patient if the patient is not a party to the lawsuit.

Some courts have held that the physician-patient privilege may give way to an overriding public interest.[39] For example, when dealing with a child care or custody case, courts often find that the interest of the child outweighs the parents' interest in keeping medical records confidential.[40] The Illinois confidential communications statute specifically provides that the privilege does not apply in civil or criminal actions arising out of the filing of a report under Illinois' Abused and Neglected Child Reporting Act.[41] In this situation, a court may protect the physician-patient privilege, in part, by allowing a private examination of medical records by the court and other parties.

The interest of the state in a grand jury investigation also may override the physician-patient privilege. In a New York case, a trial court ruled that a hospital under investigation for Medicare violations was required to turn over the billing

---

[38]*In re The June 1979 Allegheny County Investigating Grand Jury,* 415 A.2d 73 (Pa. 1980); see also *Parkson v. Central DuPage Hosp.*, 435 N.E.2d 140 (Sup. Ct. 1982).

[39]*People v. Doe*, 435 N.Y.S.2d 656, 658 (Ill. App. Ct. 1981).

[40]See, e.g., *Bieluch v. Bieluch*, 462 A.2d 1060 (Conn. 1983); *In re Baby X*, 293 N.W.2d 736 (Mich. Ct. App. 1980); *In re Doe Children*, 402 N.Y.S.2d 958 (Fam. Ct. 1978); but see *In re Adoption of H.Y.T.*, 436 So. 2d 251 (Fla. Dist. Ct. App. 1983).

[41]735 Ill. Comp. Stat. Ann. 5/8-802(7) (1993).

and medical records of 96 former patients to the grand jury.[42] Noting that "the privilege was never intended to prevent disclosure of evidence of a crime," the court refused to grant the hospital's request to quash the grand jury's subpoenas.[43]

While the physician-patient privilege is a creation of statute, a few courts in jurisdictions in which no statutory privilege exists have by their decisions created such a privilege and have extended it to hospital records.[44] Federal courts have declined to create a privilege in the absence of congressional legislation.[45] A federal court also may decline to apply the state's physician-patient privilege statute. In one case, a United States court of appeals held that Illinois' privilege statute did not apply in a federal civil action under the Sherman Antitrust Act.[46]

In some cases, the privilege may be defeated. In negligence actions against health care providers, it is a general rule that evidence of similar acts or omissions is not admissible. However, if the admission of such evidence is sought to prove a fact of the case on trial—for example, to rebut a contention that it was impossible for the accident to happen in the manner claimed—the evidence will be admissible.[47] Under these exceptions, the medical records of persons other than the individual suing may be admitted into evidence. For example, in a Georgia case, the court allowed the introduction of evidence as to orthodontic treatment provided by the dentist to patients other than the person suing.[48] Here, the court stated that the evidence was admissible on the question of malice or wanton misconduct and to contradict any possible testimony by the dentist that in similar cases, similar treatment had not resulted in the same unfortunate results.

HOSPITAL AND MEDICAL STAFF RECORDS

Hospitals are required by a variety of authorities to establish and maintain programs to monitor and improve the quality of the patient care they provide. Included in these quality assurance programs are certain committees of the medical staff, each of which may collect data and generate records on the

---

[42]*People v. Doe*, 435 N.Y.S.2d 656 (Sup. Ct. 1981).

[43]*Id.*, 435 N.Y.S.2d at 658. See also *In re Pebsworth*, 705 F.2d 261 (7th Cir. 1983).

[44]See 10 A.L.R. 4th 552.

[45]See, e.g., *U.S. v. Moore*, 970 F.2d 48 (5th Cir. 1992); *General Motors Corp. v. Director of Nat'l Inst. for Occupational Safety & Health*, 636 F.2d 163 (6th Cir. 1980).

[46]*Memorial Hosp. for McHenry County v. Shadur*, 664 F.2d 1058 (7th Cir. 1981).

[47]*Chastain v. Fuqua Indus., Inc.*, 275 S.E.2d 679 (Ga. Ct. App. 1980); *Gunthorpe v. Daniels*, 257 S.E.2d 199 (Ga. Ct. App. 1979).

[48]*Gunthorpe v. Daniels*, 257 S.E.2d 199 (Ga. Ct. App. 1979).

performance of individual physicians practicing in the hospital or the treatment of hospital patients. Attorneys pursuing negligence actions against practitioners and hospitals have shown an increasing interest in the proceedings, records, and reports of these committees as a source of important evidence. Peer review committees have the responsibility of monitoring and evaluating the quality of care provided at the hospital.

The number and type of medical staff committees varies from facility to facility. The only committee the Joint Commission on Accreditation of Healthcare Organizations (Joint Commission) requires hospital medical staffs to create is an executive committee.[49] According to the Joint Commission, this committee makes recommendations to the governing body regarding the structure of the medical staff; the mechanism used to review credentials and to delineate individual clinical privileges; individuals seeking medical staff membership; delineated clinical privileges for each eligible individual; the organization of the quality assessment and improvement activities of the medical staff as well as the mechanism used to conduct, evaluate, and revise such activities; the mechanism by which membership on the medical staff may be terminated; and the mechanism for fair-hearing procedures.[50] The executive committee receives and acts on reports and recommendations from medical staff committees, clinical departments/services, and assigned activity groups.[51]

The Joint Commission also requires that the medical staff provide effective mechanisms to monitor and evaluate the quality of patient care and the clinical performance of individuals with delineated clinical privileges.[52] Its standards also specify that there must be a surgical case review, drug usage evaluation, medical record review, blood usage review, pharmacy, and therapeutics function.[53] The medical staff also is required to participate in other review functions, including infection control, internal and external disaster plans, hospital safety, and utilization review.[54]

Hospital medical staffs generally have a medical executive committee, a credentials committee, and various performance evaluation committees to carry out their functions. The potential value of records generated by such committees to a person suing for negligence is clear, and the demand for access to them has created a substantial body of statutory and case law. A hospital should be familiar with the applicable statutes and court decisions in its state before it establishes procedures for creating and maintaining hospital and medical staff

[49]Joint Commission on Accreditation of Healthcare Organizations, *Accreditation Manual for Hospitals* (1994): MS. 4.1.

[50]*Id.*

[51]*Id.*

[52]*Accreditation Manual*, MS. 5; PI.4.2; PI.4.2.1 (1994).

[53]*Id.* at PI.3.4.2; PI.3.4.2.2; IM.3; PI.3.4.2.3; PI.3.4.2.2.

[54]*Id.* at PI.3.4.2.4.

committee records. (For a discussion of the rules applicable in each state, see Appendix B.)

DISCOVERABILITY OF COMMITTEE RECORDS

Authorities do not agree on whether hospital and medical staff committee records should be discoverable. Some courts hold that, if quality assurance programs are to work properly, they must be conducted confidentially and the records therefore are not discoverable. Other courts give greater weight to the patients' need for information vital to their cases than to policy considerations in favor of confidential committee proceedings. In response to decisions declaring those records to be discoverable, many state legislatures have enacted statutes protecting the records from discovery to varying degrees, although the extent of protection varies.

Some laws provide that such records generally are not subject to subpoena, discovery, or disclosure; others state specifically that such committee records, proceedings, and reports are not discoverable or describe such material as confidential or privileged. A common exception to nondiscovery statutes allows physicians to discover records of staff privilege committees when contesting the termination, suspension, or limitation of their staff privileges. Nondiscovery statutes also typically provide that the laws are not to be construed as protecting from discovery information, documents, and records that otherwise are available from original sources. Persons who testify before committees are not immune from discovery, but they may not be asked about their testimony before the committee. (For a discussion of statutes applicable in each state, see Appendix B.)

The California nondiscovery statute is typical:

> Neither the proceedings nor the records of organized committees of medical [or] medical-dental staffs in hospitals having the responsibility of evaluation and improvement of the quality of care rendered in the hospital or medical . . . review . . . committees of local medical . . . societies shall be subject to discovery. . . . [No] person in attendance at a meeting of any such committee shall be required to testify as to what transpired thereat.[55]

Although most statutes provide protection only to medical staff committee activities and records, a few are broad enough to include other hospital review committees.[56]

---

[55]Cal. Evid. Code § 1157 (1984). See also *West Covina Hosp. v. Superior Court*, 200 Cal. Rptr. 162 (Ct. App. 1984).

[56]See statutes of Idaho, Louisiana, Minnesota, Tennessee, and Texas discussed in the state-by-state analysis, Appendix B.

Federal statutes governing Professional Review Organizations (PROs) prohibit disclosure of any data or information acquired by any PRO in the exercise
of its duties, except under circumstances provided for by regulation or to federal
or state agencies in connection with investigations of fraud or abuse, for
licensure and certification of providers, or to assist such agencies responsible for
identifying cases or patterns involving risks to the public health.[57] (For a
discussion of the confidentiality of PRO records, see Chapter 5.)

Courts that have prohibited discovery of hospital and medical staff committee
records have found an overwhelming public interest in holding hospital quality
assurance committee meetings on a confidential basis. In a case arising in the District
of Columbia, a professional negligence action in which a patient's estate sought the
minutes and reports of staff committees concerning the individual's death in the
hospital, the court reasoned that constructive professional criticism cannot occur
when committee members fear that their comments might be used against a
colleague in a malpractice suit.[58] The court held that, absent a showing of extraordinary circumstances, the minutes and records of staff committees are privileged.[59] It
did not elaborate on what would constitute extraordinary circumstances.

In a subsequent case in the District of Columbia, the court did address the
question of extraordinary circumstances.[60] It found that peer review records
indicating a physician's substandard surgical practice in the performance of
open heart surgery were discoverable in a medical malpractice suit. A hospital
conducting a peer review of several open heart surgeries found a pattern of
substandard surgical practice by a physician, and withdrew his privileges. The
physician's suit against the hospital to have his privileges restored ended in a
settlement that provided that the hospital would remove certain materials from
his file, including the complaint of the hospital's medical review board and other
materials relating to the suspension. The terms of the settlement were to be kept
private. Six years later, the widower of a patient who had undergone open heart
surgery with the physician sued him for malpractice after learning in a newspaper article about the peer review proceedings. The trial court allowed discovery
of the hospital's peer review records relating to the physician, finding that
extraordinary necessity justified granting access to the records.

The appeals court agreed. The hospital's use of the peer review process to
detect substandard care and subsequently withholding information relating to

[57]42 U.S.C. § 1320c-9 (1993).

[58]*Bredice v. Doctor's Hospitals, Inc.*, 50 F.R.D. 249 (D.D.C. 1970).

[59]See also *Mennes v. South Chicago Community Hosp.*, 427 N.E.2d 952 (Ill. App. Ct. 1981); *Posey
v. District Court*, 586 P.2d 36 (Colo. 1978); *Oviatt v. Archbishop Bergan Mercy Hosp.*, 214 N.W.2d 490
(Neb. 1974); *Texarkana Mem. Hosp. Inc. v. Jones*, 551 S.W.2d 33 (Tex. 1977); *Jenkins v. Wu*, 468
N.E.2d 1162 (Ill. 1984); see also *Kappas v. Chestnut Lodge, Inc.*, 709 F.2d 878 (4th Cir. 1983).

[60]*Scott v. Jackson*, 596 A.2d 523 (D.C. Ct. App. 1991).

inadequate care were in themselves "extraordinary," the court declared. In addition, ten years had elapsed since the incident of alleged malpractice, and the peer review records were perhaps the most reliable evidence available. The appeals court concluded that because the facts of the case constituted "extraordinary circumstances," the peer review records were discoverable.

Several courts have recognized that there are public policy considerations in favor of confidential committee proceedings, especially where nondiscovery is mandated by statute, and these courts, therefore, will interpret such laws to promote that public policy. In a Connecticut case, in ruling against discovery, the court said "[t]he overriding importance of these review committees to the medical profession and the public requires that doctors have unfettered freedom to evaluate their peers in an atmosphere of complete confidentiality. No chilling effect can be tolerated if the committees are to function effectively."[61]

It is important to consider how broadly the courts will interpret the protection of the relevant nondiscovery statute. The Colorado Supreme Court found that a nondiscovery statute that prohibited the subpoena of review committee records "in any suit against the physician" barred the subpoenaing of records in any civil suit, including one against a hospital.[62] In interpreting the same statute in another case, that court also denied discovery of review committee records by a physician seeking damages due to the suspension of staff privileges.[63] In interpreting Georgia law, that state's supreme court held that the statute that prohibited the discovery of the "proceedings and records" of review committees included the records of a medical review committee relating to the care of patients other than the person suing.[64] In a 1993 case, a California court ruled that under the state peer review legislation the identities of hospital medical staff review committee members cannot be discovered in a medical malpractice case.[65]

In a Maryland case, the court interpreted the statute broadly.[66] A person suing for malpractice sought to discover the transcripts of staff conferences on patients' care and treatment, claiming that the statute protected only medical review committees in the area of peer review and disciplinary review. The Maryland law provided that "[t]he proceedings, records, and files of a medical review committee are neither discoverable nor admissible into evidence in any civil action arising out of matters which are being reviewed and evaluated by the

---

[61]*Morse v. Gerity,* 520 F. Supp. 470, 472 (D. Conn. 1981), at 472.

[62]*Posey v. District Court,* 586 P.2d 36 (Colo. 1978).

[63]*Franco v. Dist. Court,* 641 P.2d 922 (Colo. 1982).

[64]*Hollowell v. Jove,* 279 S.E.2d 430 (Ga. 1981); see also *Morse v. Gerity,* 520 F. Supp. 470 (D. Conn. 1981).

[65]*Cedars-Sinai Medical Ctr. v. Superior Court,* No. B066187 (Cal. Ct. App. 1993); see also *Hollowell v. Jove, supra,* note 64.

[66]*Kappas v. Chestnut Lodge, Inc.,*709 F.2d 878 (4th Cir. 1983).

committee."[67] The statute defines medical review committees generally as committees formed and approved by the hospital's governing board, whose function was to evaluate the performance and quality of health care. The court observed that staff conferences are roundtable discussions on individual cases, attended by a cross-section of hospital staff and personnel. Although these conferences do not involve formal peer evaluation or discipline, they provide a less structured method of reviewing the care being provided at the hospital. Based on this observation, the court found that the staff conferences fell within Maryland's broad definition of a medical review committee whose proceedings are protected from discovery by the statute.[68]

However, other courts have interpreted the scope of the nondiscovery statutes more narrowly and have permitted the discovery of hospital and medical staff records that fell outside the scope. For example, a California court held that while credentials committee records may be privileged statutorily, hospitals' administration records were not covered by the state's nondiscovery law.[69] Further, where the statute protected only the records of a specific hospital committee, such as the utilization review or peer review committee, the records of other hospital or staff committees were held discoverable.[70] A law that protects information "collected for or by individuals or committees assigned [a quality] review function" does not protect data obtained by physicians on their own initiative and later presented to a review committee.[71]

The Arizona Supreme Court, interpreting a state statute that allowed the trial judge to determine what may be disclosed, held that:

> the proper demarcation is between purely factual, investigative matters and materials which are the product of reflective deliberation or policymaking processes. Statements and information considered by the committee are subject to subpoena for the determination of the trial judge, but the reports and minutes of the medical review committees are not.[72]

Courts are likely to find committee records discoverable if they fall within a statutory exception to a nondiscovery rule[73] or if they are sought by persons not

---

[67]*Id.* at 880.

[68]*Id.;* see also *Murphy v. Wood,* 667 P.2d 859 (Idaho Ct. App. 1983).

[69]*Matchett v. Superior Court for County of Yuba,* 115 Cal. Rptr. 317 (Ct. App. 1974).

[70]*Id;* see also *Davidson v. Light,* 79 F.R.D. 137 (D. Colo. 1978); *Young v. King,* 344 A.2d 792 (N.J. Sup. Ct. Law Div. 1975); Coburn v. Seda, 677 P.2d 173 (Wash. 1984) (*en banc*).

[71]*Marchand v. Henry Ford Hosp.,* 247 N.W.2d 280 (Mich. 1976).

[72]*Tucson Medical Ctr., Inc. v. Misevch,* 545 P.2d 958, 961 (Ariz. 1976).

[73]*Roseville Community Hosp. v. Superior Court for Placer County,* 139 Cal. Rptr. 170 (Ct. App. 1977); *Auld v. Holly,* 418 So. 2d 1020 (Fla. Dist. Ct. App. 1982), *quashed in part,* 450 So. 2d 217 (Fla. 1984); *Good Samaritan Hosp. Ass'n v. Simon,* 370 So. 2d 1174 (Fla. Dist. Ct. App. 1979).

specifically prohibited from access to such records.[74] Moreover, some courts have prohibited questioning of review committee members concerning the proceedings, records, actions, and recommendations of the committee but have interpreted protective statutes as allowing those members to be called as expert witnesses and asked hypothetical questions based on facts in evidence that are obtained from nonprivileged sources.[75]

In federal cases, state-enacted statutory privileges may not apply.[76] A federal court in California ruled that a physician suing a hospital for federal antitrust damages after it had terminated his staff privileges could discover the records of the peer review that led to his termination.[77] The hospital's Executive Credentials Committee had upheld the recommendation of a lower body to terminate a gynecologist's surgical privileges. The physician sued the hospital and two staff physicians under federal antitrust law for conspiring unlawfully to eliminate him as a competing obstetrician/gynecologist. The physician sought broad discovery of hospital information, including peer review records generated by the committee that had made the final recommendation to terminate his privileges. The hospital argued that a federal peer review privilege precludes discovery of these records.

The court ordered the hospital to surrender the committtee records to the physician, observing that federal courts have not created a general medical peer review privilege. Although federal courts have denied discovery of peer review records in medical malpractice suits, the court determined that such records are discoverable in physicians' antitrust suits against hospitals because the information contained in them is essential to the physician's claim. The court also observed that the Health Care Quality Improvement Act, while affording physicians immunity from liability for participation in legitimate peer review actions, does not preclude discovery of peer review records to determine whether the review was conducted for illegitimate purposes. Finally the court concluded that while California's peer review privilege could be interpreted to prohibit discovery in this case, such an interpretation would conflict directly with federal law allowing discovery, and said it therefore is obligated to resolve the conflict pursuant to federal law. The court held that the need for relevant evidence outweighed the need for confidentiality in hospital staff committees.

Similarly, the U.S. Court of Appeals for the Seventh Circuit allowed discovery in a federal antitrust case brought by a physician who alleged restraint of trade

---

[74]See *Unnamed Physician v. Commission on Medical Discipline of Md.*, 400 A.2d 396 (Md. Ct. App. 1979), *cert. denied*, 100 S. Ct. 142 (1979), statute prohibiting discovery of committee records "by any person" does not prevent review by a state agency.

[75]*Eubanks v. Ferrier*, 267 S.E.2d 230 (Ga. 1980).

[76]Fed. R. Evid. 501.

[77]*Pagano v. Oroville Hosp.*, 145 F.R.D. 683 (E.D. Cal. 1993). See also *Ott v. St. Luke Hosp. of Campbell County, Inc.*, 522 F. Supp. 706 (E.D. Ky. 1981); *Robinson v. Magovern*, 83 F.R.D. 79 (W.D. Pa. 1979).

by a group of competing physicians who he alleged had misused a hospital's committee apparatus to exclude him from the medical staff.[78] The court explained that Illinois confidentiality law was not binding because the case was brought under federal law. Further, even though the federal courts should consider the state's interest in granting confidentiality, that interest did not outweigh the "public interest in private enforcement of federal antitrust law." The court was influenced by the fact that denying the physician access to the requested documents would prevent him from suing altogether, since his complaint centered on the proceedings of the committee.[79]

Some federal courts have permitted discovery of peer review committee records when violation of a federal constitutional right is alleged. For example, when a female physician requested access to peer review records to prove that a hospital had violated federal law by sexual discrimination, a federal court allowed access despite a state law mandating absolute confidentiality of peer review records.[80] The female physician alleged that a hospital had denied her staff privileges because of her sex. Although the court already had granted her access to her own peer review materials, the physician claimed she needed access to peer review reports of male physicians applying for staff privileges to compare the standards used in the decision-making process. Pointing out that a federal court need not follow state law when a constitutional violation is involved, the court ruled that the federal interest in protecting citizens from unconstitutionally disparate treatment takes precedence over the state statute's policy of promoting candid and conscientious evaluations of clinical practices. The court observed that the physician's sexual discrimination charge would be extremely difficult to argue without access to the male physicians' records. Besides, the court concluded, the state's interests could be preserved adequately by an appropriate protective order over the documents.

In another case involving a constitutional claim, a federal court in Kentucky ruled that the peer review committee records were discoverable even though a state statute specifically prohibited discovery of such records.[81] A physician claimed that a public hospital had denied him due process in the rejection of his application for staff privileges. He contended that peer review committee meetings were held without giving him notice or the opportunity to be heard, and that the committee had employed constitutionally improper considerations and ulterior motives in denying him staff privileges.

Although the federal court recognized that a state statute specifically granted peer review committee records privileged status, it noted that it was not bound

---

[78]*Memorial Hosp. for McHenry County v. Shadur,* 664 F.2d 1058 (7th Cir. 1981).

[79]*Id.*

[80]*Dorsten v. Lapeer County Gen. Hosp.,* 88 F.R.D. 583 (E.D. Mich. 1980).

[81]*Ott v. St. Luke Hosp. of Campbell County, Inc.,* 522 F. Supp. 706 (E.D. Ky. 1981).

by state law in deciding a federal question, and therefore declined to rule on the basis of the statute. Instead, the court held that although the peer review committee probably understood that its communication would not be disclosed, and although the relationship among the members of the committee is one to be fostered, there was no evidence that its functions would be impaired substantially by a denial of privilege. "Indeed," the court ruled, "the true efficiency of such committees may be fostered by an atmosphere of openness, in that they may be less likely to rely on hearsay or information tainted by bias or prejudice in making their decisions. . . ."[82] The court said it believed that it would not be able to evaluate the physician's constitutional claims effectively if the records were kept confidential.

The courts that have permitted discovery of committee records in the absence of nondiscovery laws have emphasized the benefit to the litigation process of liberal discovery rules. A Kentucky appeals court, for example, specifically rejected qualified privilege for committee records.[83] The court found no public policy in favor of protecting such records from discovery where it could be shown that the information sought was "relevant to the subject matter involved in the pending action" and held that confidentiality of staff committee proceedings must give way to discovery of truth.

The Wisconsin Supreme Court also has expressed doubt as to whether the public interest in maintaining the confidentiality of committee records was compelling enough to warrant the judicial creation of a nondiscovery rule.[84] The court refused (1) to apply retroactively, to hospital committee records, Wisconsin's nondiscovery statute, (2) to find a privilege at common law, or (3) to extend the statutory privilege granted to records that are required by law to be kept.

ADMISSIBILITY OF COMMITTEE RECORDS

While courts generally adhere to liberal rules of discovery in the absence of nondiscovery statutes, they are inclined to find hospital and medical staff quality assurance committee records inadmissible as hearsay. Unlike medical records, committee minutes and reports often do not meet the formal requirements of the business records exception to the hearsay rule. Hospital committees do not generate records at or reasonably soon after the time at which the events discussed occurred. Moreover, committee records usually contain conclusions or opinions that generally are inadmissible.[85]

---

[82]*Id.* at 711.

[83]*Nazareth Literary and Benevolent Inst. v. Stephenson*, 503 S.W.2d 177 (Ky. 1973).

[84]*Davison v. St. Paul Fire & Marine Ins. Co.*, 248 N.W.2d 433 (Wis. 1977).

[85]See, e.g., Florida, Minnesota, Montana, and Oregon statues in the state-by-state analysis, Appendix B.

A party who is unable to overcome these barriers to admissibility still may be able to have committee records admitted into evidence under rules of evidence that allow an expert witness to express an opinion based, in part, on information "perceived by or made known to him at or before hearing."[86] If counsel succeeds in obtaining the records and allows the expert witness to review them before trial, that witness may be able to testify as to the content of the records. Further, an expert witness may be able to testify concerning the contents of medical records even though the records are found to have been admitted improperly.[87]

HOSPITAL POLICIES ON COMMITTEE RECORDS

Since state statutes and court decisions on protection of peer review and quality assurance activities from discovery vary considerably, hospitals should review carefully and understand thoroughly the applicable law. Institutions should organize and operate peer review and quality assurance activities in a manner designed to obtain the greatest possible protection available. While arguments may be made in support of the discoverability of committee records, hospitals generally can operate with greater flexibility and efficiency and with less risk if peer review and quality assurance records carry some degree of protection.

Once the hospital has developed its policies for committee records, all hospital and medical staff personnel involved in committee activities should be educated as to the importance of following those policies meticulously. Peer review and quality assurance activities should be identified as such and documented in a manner that reinforces their official peer review status and thereby is likely to qualify them for maximum protection under state law.

All peer review committee minutes and reports should be prepared carefully and should demonstrate that the hospital performed an objective, considered review. In most states, committee minutes should document primarily actions taken on the matter discussed and not the details of the actual discussion or personal comments made by committee members. The hospital should limit distribution of and access to committee minutes and reports to as few individuals and files as possible.

In all matters relating to developing policies on the creation and use of peer review and quality assurance materials, hospitals should consult with their legal counsel, especially in states in which rules of discoverability are ambiguous or in which courts have construed protection statutes narrowly. Hospitals should

---

[86]Fed. R. Evid. 703.

[87]See, e.g., *Wilson v. Clark*, 417 N.E.2d 1322 (Ill. 1981), *cert. denied*, 102 S. Ct. 140 (1981).

instruct counsel to advise them of changes in applicable laws as they occur and to review these policies at least annually.

HOSPITAL INCIDENT REPORTS

An incident is ". . . any happening which is not consistent with the routine operation of the hospital or the routine care of a particular patient. It may be an accident or a situation which might result in an accident."[88] A hospital generates incident reports to document promptly the circumstances surrounding an incident, to alert its insurer or defense counsel to a potential liability situation, and to create data with which to monitor the number and type of incidents occurring in the institution. Incident reports are an essential part of good hospital risk and claims management programs and, like other hospital records, can be a fertile source of information for parties in litigation involving hospitals.

In many states, incident reports are protected from discovery primarily under the attorney-client privilege and the attorney's work product rule.[89] Where legal advice is sought from an attorney acting as such, communications between the attorney and the client relating to such advice are privileged and therefore may not be disclosed by the attorney unless the client waives the privilege.[90] Therefore, an incident report made to an attorney for purposes of obtaining legal advice based thereon may not be discovered.[91] In one case, however, the court held that incident reports not prepared exclusively for the hospital's attorney were not protected by the attorney-client privilege.[92] In that case, a nurse who allegedly was negligent completed the reports, placed a copy in the patient's medical record, and gave copies to the hospital administrator and director of nursing.

An Illinois court ruled that a report written by a coordinator in a hospital's risk management department that contained summaries of statements from people she had interviewed is not discoverable in a malpractice suit against the hospital.[93] The court observed that the hospital had submitted evidence indicating that it relied on the coordinator's advice and opinions in its decision to settle or litigate matters she investigated. The coordinator therefore was a member of

---

[88]American Hospital Association and National Safety Council, *Safety Guide for Health Care Institutions* 33 (Chicago: 1972).

[89]But see *In re Application To Quash Subpoena Duces Tecum in Grand Jury Proceedings*, 446 N.Y.S.2d 382 (App. Div. 1982).

[90]See McCormick, *Evidence*, 3d ed. (1984 & Supp. 1987): § 87-97.

[91]See *Sierra Vista Hosp. v. Superior Ct. for San Luis Obispo County*, 56 Cal. Rptr. 387 (Ct. App. 1967).

[92]*Bernardi v. Community Hosp. Ass'n*, 443 P.2d 708 (Colo. 1968).

[93]*Mlynarski v. Rush Presbyterian-St. Luke's Medical Ctr.*, 572 N.E.2d 1025 (Ill. Ct. App. 1991).

a control group of hospital employees who were entitled to the protection of a privilege when they communicated with hospital counsel.

Conversely, the Arizona Supreme Court ruled that the attorney-client privilege did not protect interviews with employees concerning an alleged incident of malpractice that were obtained by the hospital's legal department.[94] A child suffered neurological impairment after a cardiac arrest during surgery at a hospital. Shortly after the surgery, at the direction of the hospital's legal department, a nurse paralegal interviewed three nurses and a scrub technician about what they had witnessed in the operating suite. The paralegal wrote summaries of the interviews and the legal department retained possession of them. The child and her parents later sued the hospital and the surgeons, and attempted to discover the interviews.

The Arizona Supreme Court held that the patient should have access to the documents, ruling that the attorney-client privilege was not applicable. When an employee does not initiate communication with counsel, a factual communication is privileged only if it concerns the employee's own conduct within the scope of that individual's employment and is made to assist the attorney in assessing or responding to the legal consequences for the corporate client. In this case, although the employees were present during the operation, which was a function of their corporate employment, they had no other connection to the incident. Because the employees were only witnesses to the event, their statements were not entitled to the attorney-client privilege.

Incident reports made by hospital staff to the hospital's insurer in connection with anticipated settlement or defense of a negligence action are protected by the attorney's work product rule and are not discoverable[95] unless the party seeking the reports can demonstrate to the court that the information sought is or might lead to admissible evidence, is material to the trial preparation, or for some other reason is necessary to promote the ends of justice.[96]

In a New York case, a federal court ruled that a state confidentiality law did not prevent discovery of hospital incident reports in a civil rights lawsuit involving the kidnapping of an infant on hospital premises.[97] The parents sued the hospital under federal civil rights laws and sought to discover incident reports that the hospital had prepared about the kidnapping. The court ordered the hospital to release the information. It acknowledged that under state law, incident reports are protected from release in medical malpractice lawsuits.

---

[94]*Samaritan Found. v. Goodfarb*, No. CV-92-0282-PR (Ariz. Nov. 16, 1993).

[95]See *Sligar v. Tucker*, 267 So. 2d 54 (Fla. Dist. Ct. App. 1972); *Verini v. Bochetto*, 372 N.Y.S.2d 690 (App. Div. 1975). But see *Kay Laboratories, Inc. v. District Court for Pueblo County*, 653 P.2d 721 (Colo. 1982); *Shibilski v. St. Joseph's Hosp. of Marshfield, Inc.*, 266 N.W.2d 264 (Wis. 1978).

[96]See *Peters v. Gaggos*, 249 N.W.2d 327 (Mich. Ct. App. 1976).

[97]*White v. New York City Health and Hosp. Corps.*, No. 88 Civ. 7536 (S.D.N.Y. Mar. 19, 1990).

Despite that statutory protection, the court ruled that the hospital's interests in safeguarding the confidentiality of the incident reports must give way when violations of constitutional law are involved.

Even when a state statute expressly prohibits discovery of incident reports, the courts often are nonetheless willing to permit discovery if the information is vital to the person's lawsuit and no other source of information is available. The Iowa Supreme Court, for example, ruled that statements prepared by nurses shortly after an incident and in anticipation of litigation were discoverable because two years had elapsed between the incident and the nurses' depositions and the nurses were able to recall very little of the event.[98]

In another case, a New York court would not extend the state's statute to prohibit discovery of postincident investigation reports.[99] The patient was misdiagnosed as having cancer. In her suit against the hospital, she attempted to discover statements and records relating to a retrospective investigation of her case. The court found that the reports were not protected from discovery within the New York statute prohibiting disclosure of "proceedings [and] records relating to performance of medical review functions." Although peer review investigations clearly are not discoverable under the statute, the hospital could not establish that the incident reports constituted a medical review function and, therefore, was ordered to produce the records.

Since incident reports constitute hearsay, they are inadmissible in evidence unless they fall into one of the exceptions to the hearsay rule.[100] The hearsay exception most frequently cited for the purpose of admitting incident reports into evidence is the business records exception, particularly where the party seeking the reports can show that the report was made in the routine course of business at or near the time of the occurrence reported under circumstances that would indicate a high degree of trustworthiness.[101] Although some courts have interpreted "business" narrowly, the trend is toward admitting incident reports that meet the requirements of the business record exception.

Although it is becoming difficult in some jurisdictions to prevent discovery and admission of incident reports, a hospital that has established incident-reporting procedures should take specific actions to protect its reports. It should:

1. treat incident reports as confidential documents, clearly marked as such
2. limit strictly the number of copies made and the distribution of the reports in the institution

---

[98]*Berg v. Des Moines Gen. Hosp. Co.*, 456 N.W.2d 173 (Iowa 1990).

[99]*Wiener v. Memorial Hosp. for Cancer and Allied Diseases*, 453 N.Y.S.2d 142 (Sup. Ct. 1982).

[100]McCormick, *Evidence* 3d ed. (1984): §§ 246, 306.

[101]See *Fagan v. Newark*, 188 A.2d 427 (N.J. Super. Ct. 1963); *Burt v. St. John's Episcopal Hosp.*, N.Y.L.J., Oct. 30, 1981, at 15, col. 1 (N.Y. Sup. Ct., Oct. 29, 1981).

3. not place a copy of the report in the patient's medical record or in a file on the patient care unit; however, it may retain copies with other quality assurance records

4. limit the content of the report to facts, not conclusions or assignment of blame; analyses of the cause of an incident should be placed in a separate document

5. address the report and any separate analysis of an incident to the hospital's attorney or claims manager by name

6. train hospital personnel to complete incident reports with the same care used in completing a medical record

7. treat incident reports generally as quality assurance records and subject them to the same stringent policies as are applied to other quality assurance records

8

Liability for Improper Disclosure of Medical Records

INTRODUCTION

A release of medical records information that has not been authorized by the patient or that has not been made pursuant to statutory, regulatory, or other legal authority may subject the hospital and its staff to civil and criminal liability. States may impose criminal or professional disciplinary sanctions for violation of statutory confidentiality requirements. In addition, three possible civil liability actions are available to patients who show injury as a result of a disclosure of information in their medical records by hospitals or physicians: defamation, invasion of privacy, and breach of contract.

PENALTIES FOR IMPROPER DISCLOSURE

State statutes may impose both criminal sanctions and civil liability on health care providers that improperly disclose medical records information in an unauthorized manner. The Tennessee law, for example, addresses both forms of liability:

> A willful violation of the provisions of [the Medical Records Act] is a Class C misdemeanor. . . . No hospital, its officers, employees, or medical and nursing personnel practicing therein, shall be civilly liable for violation of [the Medical Records Act] except to the extent of liability for actual damages in a civil action for willful or reckless or wanton acts or commissions constituting such violation. Such liability shall be subject, however, to any immunities or limitations of liability or damages provided by law.[1]

---

[1]Tenn. Code Ann. § 68-11-311 (1993). See also Hawaii Code Ann. § 324-34 (1993).

Unlike a criminal proceeding, which is initiated by state officials, a civil lawsuit must be instituted by a private individual. The Illinois Mental Health and Developmental Disabilities Confidentiality Act is more specific as to civil remedies available to the patient: "Any person aggrieved by a violation of this Act may sue for damages, an injunction, or other appropriate relief. Reasonable attorney's fees and costs may be awarded to the successful plaintiff in any action under this Act."[2]

In some states, statutes impose specific penalties for revealing particular medical records information, such as whether a patient is HIV-positive. For example, in Wisconsin, an individual who negligently discloses a patient's HIV status may be liable for actual damages and costs, as well as $1,000 in exemplary, or punitive, damages. An individual who intentionally discloses such information may be liable for up to $5,000 in exemplary damages. If the disclosure causes bodily or psychological harm to the patient, the individual who disclosed the information may be fined up to $10,000 and sentenced to nine months in jail.[3] In Virginia, the penalties for disclosing an individual's HIV-status are more lenient. A person who willfully or through gross negligence discloses such information may be subject to a fine up to $5,000, to be paid into a state fund. The patient also may recover actual damages or $100 (whichever is greater) and attorney's fees and court costs.[4]

DEFAMATION

Defamation is one legal theory on which patients may base lawsuits for improper disclosure of medical records information. Defamation may be defined as a written or oral communication to someone other than the person defamed of matters that concern a living person and tend to injure that person's reputation.[5] If the individual bringing the defamation suit is a public official or public figure, the individual will recover only if the speaker knew the statement was false or acted with reckless disregard of its truth or falsity.[6]

There are two types of defamation. Traditionally, libel is the written form of defamation, while slander is oral. Libel is actionable without proof of actual damages, although slander suits ordinarily require special or actual damages. Medical records may contain information that is inaccurate and that, if published, would affect a person's reputation in the community adversely, causing

---

[2]740 Ill. Comp. Stat. Ann. 110/15 (1993).

[3]Wis. Stat. Ann. § 252.15(8) (1993).

[4]Va. Code Ann. §§ 32.1-36.1(B), (C) (1993); see also Colo. Rev. Stat. § 25-4-1409(2)(1993).

[5]Prosser & Keeton, *The Law Of Torts*, 5th Ed. (1984 & Supp. 1988): 773-784.

[6]See, e.g., *New York Times Co. v. Sullivan*, 376 U.S. 254 (1964); *McKinnon v. Smith*, 275 N.Y.S.2d 900 (N.Y. Sup. Ct. 1966).

special damages. Thus, oral disclosure by a hospital to an unauthorized person could result in an action for defamation.

However, the possibility of a patient's obtaining a recovery against a hospital for defamation for release of medical records information is slight. Medical records entries ordinarily are true and, as a general rule, truth of the published statement is an absolute defense to a civil cause of action for libel or slander, irrespective of the publisher's motive. Although the rule has been modified in some states to allow application of the defense only where the publisher's motive was good, the traditional rule, even as modified, provides substantial protection for hospitals.

Patients who sue health care providers for defamation first must show that the statement that is the basis of the suit was published—that is, that it was revealed to someone other than the patient or health care provider. For example, a state appeals court affirmed a judgment in favor of two physicians when the allegedly libelous statement was contained in a letter that the physicians mailed to the patient.[7] The physicians prepared a letter containing the results of a patient's physical examination, including a statement that the patient had had gonorrhea in 1985, during the patient's marriage. In fact, the patient had had gonorrhea years before he was married. When the letter arrived at the patient's home, the patient's wife opened it and read it to him over the telephone. The patient and his wife sued the physicians for libel, claiming that the defamatory contents of the letter caused marital discord. The court rejected the patient's suit because the letter was sealed and addressed only to the patient. The letter was not published to the patient's wife, except by the patient, who had asked her to read it to him over the phone.

Moreover, the law recognizes two privileges that may preclude liability upon publication of even false statements that are injurious to the subject's reputation. These are absolute privilege and qualified privilege. Publications made in legislative, judicial, and administrative proceedings are absolutely privileged, and thus do not give rise to a cause of action in defamation. Disclosure of defamatory medical records information in a court therefore would not be actionable. In *Gilson v. Knickerbocker Hospital*,[8] for example, a patient sued a hospital for libel, claiming that, by complying with a lawful subpoena, the hospital maliciously had allowed the publication of false and defamatory matter in the individual's medical record. The record contained an observation that the plaintiff was under the influence of alcohol. The court denied the patient's claim, stating that the defendant's act was absolutely privileged because it was acting pursuant to lawful judicial process.[9]

---

[7]*Dowell v. Cleveland Clinic Found.*, No. 59963 (Ohio Ct. App. 1992).

[8]116 N.Y.S.2d 745 (App. Div. 1952).

[9]See also *O'Barr v. Feist*, 296 So. 2d 152 (Ala. 1974) (letter from physician to probate judge absolutely privileged); *Bond v. Becaut*, 561 F. Supp. 1037 (N.D. Ill. 1983), *aff'd* 734 F.2d 18 (7th Cir. 1984) (letter from psychologist relevant to custody proceedings and within judicial privilege).

There are limits to the scope of absolute privilege, however. One court has stated that a physician who discloses medical records information in connection with a court proceeding may lose the protection of absolute privilege upon disclosing information unrelated to the court action.[10]

The second type of privilege, known as conditional, or qualified, privilege provides protection from liability if the communication was made in good faith, without actual malice, with reasonable or probable grounds for believing them to be true, on a subject matter in which the author of the communication has an interest, or in respect to which he has a duty, public, personal or private, either legal, judicial, political, moral, or social, made to a person having a corresponding interest or duty.[11]

For example, a hospital was not liable for defamation for indicating on an insurance claim form that an unmarried 14-year-old was pregnant because the institution had acted within its qualified privilege.[12] The hospital was required to provide a diagnosis to the insurance company in order to receive compensation for its services. Although the diagnosis of pregnancy was incorrect, the court ruled that the hospital was not liable because it had fulfilled the elements necessary to claim the protection of a qualified privilege. Specifically, the hospital had acted in good faith and in pursuit of its valid business interest in obtaining compensation. In addition, the statement was limited in scope to the proper purpose, occasion, manner, and parties, having been disclosed only as required on the standard insurance claim forms.

As demonstrated above, where a hospital is serving its own interests, as in its efforts to procure payment from a third party, its disclosure of medical records information may be protected by a qualified privilege because it satisfies the requirement that the material be disclosed in the pursuit of a valid interest.[13] Also, in instances in which a public interest is being served, such as protecting the community from highly contagious diseases, it may be proper to inform those persons who potentially might be affected. For example, in an early case, the Nebraska Supreme Court, ruling on the question whether a physician had violated a statute that prohibited out-of-court disclosure of confidential communications, held the physician not liable for disclosing to the owner of a boardinghouse the fact that his patient had a venereal disease.[14] In addition to intimating that the diagnosis was incorrect, the court reasoned that the rules of qualified

---

[10]*Moses v. McWilliams*, 549 A.2d 950 (Pa. Super. Ct. 1988).

[11]C.J.S. *Libel and Slander* § 59 (1987).

[12]*Edwards v. University of Chicago Hosp.*, 484 N.E.2d 1100 (Ill. App. Ct. 1985).

[13]*Id.*.

[14]*Simonsen v. Swenson*, 177 N.W. 831 (Neb. 1920); see also *Shoemaker v. Friedburg*, 183 P.2d 318 (Cal. Ct. App. 1947).

privilege, under the law of defamation, would govern this case. The physician was held to have had a moral or legal duty to disclose his diagnosis to those persons who might be endangered by this contagious disease. While this case involved an action for violation of a professional confidence, the court used the same standard that is used in measuring a qualified privilege in an action for defamation. In spite of the holding in this case, health care providers should be wary of revealing information regarding a patient's contagious status to third parties. Many states now have statutes specifying when and to whom such information may be revealed (see Chapter 4) and case law is continuing to develop in this area (see "Invasion of Privacy" and "Breach of Confidentiality," below).

The interested party who receives the information need not be in danger for a qualified privilege to apply. In *Quarles v. Sutherland*,[15] a customer sued a store owner for injuries sustained in the store. The store's physician examined the injured customer and gave the medical report to the store's attorney. The court held that the release of this report was a true communication made in good faith to an interested party and, as such, was subject to a qualified privilege. (See "Breach of Confidentiality," below.)

A more difficult question regarding whether a qualified privilege exists is presented when neither the interest of the hospital nor that of the general public is involved directly. Such cases may arise when medical records information is disclosed to employers, insurance companies, litigating parties, news media, etc. For example, an insurance company was sued by one of its insured after the company had informed an agency subscribed to by other life insurance companies that the insured had a heart condition. The court dismissed the suit, holding that the insurance company's disclosure was qualifiedly privileged.[16] Because the company did not act with malice, it was within the privilege and not liable for the disclosure. In a later case based on virtually identical facts, a court found that a qualified privilege to exchange medical information was supported by the insurer's and agency's business interest in the information, as well as the public's interest in the insurance industry.[17] One court has held specifically that, in an action under that state's privacy statute, a qualified privilege protects parties who disclose medical information where the disclosure is reasonably necessary to protect or further a legitimate business interest.[18]

---

[15]389 S.W.2d 249 (Tenn. 1965).

[16]*Mayer v. Northern Life Ins. Co.*, 119 F. Supp. 536 (N.D. Cal. 1953).

[17]*Senogles v. Security Benefit Life Ins.*, 536 P.2d 1358 (Kan. 1975); see also *Hauge v. Fidelity Guaranty Life Ins. Co.*, No. 91-C-20033 (N.D. Ill. 1992).

[18]*Bratt v. International Business Machines Corp.*, 467 N.E.2d 126 (Mass. 1984). See also *Hauge, supra*, n.17.

The extent of the qualified privilege is uncertain and impossible to reduce to a formula. The disclosure must be justified by the importance of the interest served, and it must be called for by a legal or moral duty, or by generally accepted standards of decent conduct. In any action brought for defamation, the court will determine whether the prerequisites of qualified privilege have been met.

A request for information by a totally disinterested party, however, never can create a qualified privilege. For a disclosure to be privileged, the party to whom it is made must have a valid interest in obtaining the information. Whether or not the information was requested or volunteered will help to determine whether the publisher acted in good faith or had a moral duty to communicate. Moreover, it is important to remember that the qualified privilege can be lost if it is abused or if the publication is found to be malicious.[19]

Even in the absence of a privilege, a health care provider will not be liable for the release of medical information if the patient has consented to the release. A person who knowingly consents to the release of medical records is barred from bringing a defamation suit when those records subsequently are released. In *Williamson v. Stocker*,[20] for example, a pilot submitted to a chemical dependency evaluation at the request of his employer, the results of which indicated that he was an alcoholic. Before the analysis, the pilot had signed a number of forms, including consent forms for the release of information relating to his evaluation and treatment. The records, which contained the diagnosis of alcoholism, were released to the pilot's employer and the employer's insurance company. When the pilot subsequently was grounded, and then fired (apparently for an unrelated reason), he brought suit against the facility where the test was performed and the chemical dependency counselor. The pilot alleged that they had defamed him with their diagnosis of episodic excessive drinking and acute and chronic chemical dependency, and that their diagnosis of early stages of alcoholism had an inadequate factual basis and resulted from a lack of diligence in ascertaining the truth. Although the pilot admitted that he had signed release forms, he contended that he did not consent to the release of the defamatory statements because either they were not in existence or their contents were not known to him at the time he signed the forms. However, the court found that there was no indication that the pilot did not know the implications of the forms that he signed, and that there was no evidence of fraud or malice on the part of those who prepared the reports in the released records. Citing the principle that "one who agrees to submit his conduct to investigation knowing that its results will be published consents to the publication of the honest finding of the investigators," the court concluded that the pilot could not sue for defamation.

---

[19]Prosser & Keeton, *Law of Torts*, 849-868, *supra*, n.5.

[20]*Williamson v. Stocker*, No. 4-79-335 slip op. (D. Minn. Dec. 21, 1982); see also *Clark v. Geraci*, 208 N.Y.S.2d 564 (Sup. Ct. 1960).

Health care providers should take care, however, not to exceed the scope of a patient's consent to release medical records information. If the disclosure of the record exceeds the scope of the authorization given by the patient or other appropriate person, the disclosure will be unauthorized and therefore unprotected in the event of a defamation suit.

To avoid defamation cases, hospitals are well advised to take the conservative approach and withhold medical records information unless they find exceptionally good reasons to disclose it. They should establish appropriate reasons for disclosure with the help of their legal counsel and should set forth those reasons in their medical records policies.

INVASION OF PRIVACY

A second legal theory upon which a patient could base a suit for improper release of medical records information is invasion of privacy. Releasing patient information to unauthorized individuals, agencies, or news media may make a hospital liable to the patient for an invasion of privacy. A cause of action for invasion of privacy can be sounded in either state common law (as developed by the courts), state or federal constitutional law, or state statutory law.

In the common law, an invasion of an individual's right of privacy has been defined as an unwarranted appropriation or exploitation of that individual's personality, the publication of the person's private concerns in which the public has no legitimate interest, or a wrongful intrusion into the person's private activities.[21] However, the right of privacy is not an absolute right. The purpose of the right is to protect the individual from mass dissemination of information concerning private, personal matters. To give rise to an action for damages, this exploitation, publication, or intrusion must be done in a way that would cause outrage or mental suffering, shame, or humiliation to a person of ordinary sensibilities.[22] Some courts have held that an oral publication alone cannot constitute an invasion of privacy.[23]

There is some overlap between the theories of defamation and common law invasion of privacy. However, several factors distinguish the two causes of action. First, truth of the information published is not a defense to an invasion of privacy suit, although it often is a defense to an allegation of defamation. Thus, an unauthorized disclosure even of accurate medical information could subject

---

[21]*Restatement (Second) of Torts*, § 652A (1981).

[22]Prosser & Keeton, *Law of Torts*, 849-868, *supra*, n.5.; *Restatement (Second) of Torts*, § 652D and cmt. c, *supra*, n.21.

[23]*Pangallo v. Murphy*, 243 S.W.2d 496 (Ky. Ct. App. 1951); *Melvin v. Reid*, 112 Cal. App. 285, 297 P. 91 (1931); *Brents v. Morgan*, 221 Ky. 765, 299 S.W. 967 (1927); Annotation. 19 A.L.R. 1318.

a hospital to liability for invasion of a patient's privacy. Second, to recover for an invasion of privacy, the plaintiff need not prove special damages, unlike the plaintiff in a defamation action, who often must prove that the disclosure actually harmed the individual. Third, the two theories provide redress for different types of injury arising from the unauthorized disclosure of personal information. A cause of action for invasion of privacy looks to the harm a disclosure has caused to the plaintiff's feelings.[24] Thus, a plaintiff in an action for invasion of privacy may recover even for the disclosure of favorable information. Defamation, on the other hand, focuses on the injury to the plaintiff's reputation. Fourth, although an action for invasion of privacy often involves publication, it is not a necessary element for recovery. Thus a single human agency can invade an individual's privacy. The law of defamation normally requires publication to a second person.

Defamation and common law invasion of privacy resemble one another in that the public interest places similar restrictions on the right to recover for both causes of action. Thus, a disclosure entitled to protection by the qualified privilege in a defamation action also often is protected if the action is based on invasion of privacy.

Common law invasion of privacy can be divided into four categories: (1) appropriation of plaintiff's name or likeness for the defendant's benefit, (2) intrusion upon the plaintiff's solitude or private concerns, (3) public disclosure of embarrassing private facts, and (4) publicity that places the plaintiff in a false light in the public eye.[25] Because medical records are highly personal, improper disclosure of patient information can expose hospitals and physicians to liability for invasion of privacy.

Constitutional invasion of privacy claims occur less frequently. A patient who brings a claim for improper disclosure of medical records information based on the federal or state constitution typically must show that the individual had a "reasonable expectation of privacy" in the information that was disclosed.[26] Courts will consider factors such as the content of the disclosure and the circumstances under which the patient provided the information to the health care worker.[27]

Finally, a patient may sue a health care provider under a state statute creating a right to sue for certain invasions of privacy. For example, the Massachusetts statute states that, "A person shall have a right against unreasonable, substantial, or serious interference with his privacy."[28]

---

[24]Prosser & Keeton, *Law of Torts*, 849-868, *supra*, n.5.

[25]*Id.*

[26]See, e.g., *Urbaniak v. Newton*, 226 Cal. App. 3d 1128 (Ct. App. 1991).

[27]*Id.*

[28]Mass. Gen. L. ch. 214 § 1B (1993).

The patient who expressly consents orally or in writing to disclosure of private information cannot complain later that the disclosure was an invasion of privacy. The patient's consent protects the hospital if the individual wanted the information disclosed for personal benefit and the hospital disclosed the information in the manner the patient authorized.[29] Therefore, hospitals should endeavor to obtain the patient's written consent to the disclosure of information. If a patient authorized a disclosure but refused to sign an authorization form, hospital personnel should note that consent on the form, properly sign and date the note, and insert the form in the patient's medical record. Teaching hospitals, especially, should be certain their patients understand that they will be participating in the education and training of medical, nursing, and other students who may observe or assist in treatment.

Hospitals should establish and enforce strict rules against permitting lay persons to observe patient treatment without express patient consent. Hospital policy should include safeguards against the use of patient-authorized photographs or videotape in an unauthorized manner or for an unauthorized purpose. The policy should require that patient authorization include specific language describing permitted uses of the materials and should prohibit uses not authorized by the patient. The hospital also should be careful not to draft a policy on confidentiality that is too vague.[30]

Photographs

Courts have held health care providers liable for the first type of invasion of privacy—an improper appropriation of the plaintiff's likeness for the defendant's benefit, primarily where the provider exploited the patient for commercial benefit. However, courts also have imposed liability in situations where a health care provider used a patient's name or likeness for a noncommercial benefit by applying the theory of intrusion upon solitude invasion of privacy. This theory can lead to liability even if the photographs were not published. In *Clayman v. Bernstein*,[31] for example, the court prohibited a physician from using photographs of a patient's facial development in connection with medical instruction. The court found that even taking the picture without the patient's express consent was an invasion of privacy; it was not necessary to show that the

---

[29]See, e.g., *Clark v. Geraci*, 208 N.Y.S.2d 564 (Sup. Ct. 1960). Patient had authorized physician to disclose incomplete information about his illness; plaintiff therefore was estopped from claiming that he had not consented to the disclosure of the underlying cause of the illness—alcoholism.

[30]See, e.g., *Group Health Plan, Inc. v. Lopez*, 341 N.W.2d 294 (Minn. Ct. App. 1983).

[31]38 Pa. D. & C. 543 (1940).

physician had used the photographs improperly or shown them to others to establish liability. A court reached a similar conclusion in *Estate of Berthiaume v. Pratt*,[32] in which a physician photographed a terminally ill patient shortly before his death. The court allowed the case to proceed to trial, rejecting the physician's argument that his scientific interest in having a full photographic record of the patient's case justified taking the picture. The court held that unauthorized photography under such circumstances would constitute an invasion of privacy, whether or not the photographs were published.

Publication of photographs also may subject health care providers to liability under the type of invasion of privacy known as public disclosure of embarrassing private facts. For example, a court ruled that a physician had invaded a patient's privacy by using "before-and-after" photos of her face to demonstrate the effects of a face lift on television and at a department store presentation.[33] The use of the photographs publicized the fact that the patient had had a face lift, which she found embarrassing and distressing. The court held that the patient's right to privacy outweighed the public's general interest in plastic surgery and held the physician liable.[34]

Hospital medical records policies should establish the circumstances under which the institution will permit the patient to be photographed for any reason. Photographs taken in connection with scientific research should be part of a research protocol approved by appropriate committees of the medical staff. All other photographs of patients should be taken in accordance with hospital policy. In general, these policies should require approval of such photography by an appropriate hospital representative.

Invasion of Privacy within the Hospital

Courts have found an unwarranted intrusion upon the plaintiff's solitude or private concerns where the defendant bugged the plaintiff's telephone or bedroom, invaded the plaintiff's house, or in other ways intruded in an objectionable manner into the plaintiff's concerns.[35] Monitoring a patient's telephone conversations from the hospital may subject an institution not only to liability for

---

[32]365 A.2d 792 (Me. 1976). For a discussion of taking unauthorized photographs as invasion of privacy in this and other contexts, see Annotation, 86 A.L.R. 3d 374.

[33]*Vassiliades v. Garfinkel's, Brooks Bros.*, 492 A.2d 580 (D.C. 1985).

[34]When an individual's name or likeness is published in connection with a newsworthy event, the person does not have an action for invasion of privacy. (See discussion under "Disclosure to the News Media," below.) *Siegel v. Esquire, Inc.*, 167 N.Y.S.2d 246 (App. Div. 1957); *Gilbert v. Medical Economics Co.*, 665 F.2d 305 (10th Cir. 1981) (newsworthiness of physician's psychiatric history precludes liability for disclosure).

[35]Prosser & Keeton, *Law of Torts*, 849-868, *supra*, n.5.

invasion of privacy, but also to liability under federal statutes prohibiting the interception of private communications.[36] Also, when nonmedical personnel are allowed to witness medical procedures or to examine a patient without the latter's consent, the invasion of the patient's privacy may be actionable.[37]

Insurance Carriers

It is unlikely that a hospital or individual health care provider will be held liable for invasion of privacy upon releasing medical records information for the purpose of obtaining reimbursement. Court decisions have established that publication of information to an extent reasonably calculated to serve the legitimate interests of the publisher does not constitute a common law invasion of privacy.[38] This restriction is similar to the qualified privilege in defamation actions. Thus, release or disclosure of information in the medical record to private individuals, such as attorneys or insurance company representatives, for purposes of reimbursement ordinarily would not constitute an invasion of the common law right of privacy.[39] However, the privilege may not protect health care providers from invasions of privacy actions based on state constitutions.[40] (For a discussion of disclosure of medical records information to an attorney for litigation purposes, see Chapter 7.)

Disclosure to the News Media

Perhaps the hospital practice most likely to give rise to questions of invasion of privacy is the release of information concerning patients to news entities. A hospital has no legal obligation whatsoever to disclose medical records information to news media. In some states, statutes limit the dissemination of medical records information to certain entities or individuals that the state has deemed to

---

[36]*Gerrard v. Blackman*, 401 F. Supp. 1189 (N.D. Ill. 1975).

[37]See *Knight v. Penobscot Bay Medical Ctr.*, 420 A.2d 915 (Me. 1980). The viewing of plaintiff's delivery of child by nurse's husband was found, under the circumstances, not to be an invasion of privacy. For a discussion of liability arising from an entry in a hospital medical record, see *Behringer v. Medical Ctr. at Princeton*, under "Breach of Confidentiality," below.

[38]See generally *Voneye v. Turner*, 240 S.W.2d 588 (Ky. Ct. App. 1951); *Patton v. Jacobs*, 78 N.E.2d 789 (Ind. Ct. App. 1948); *Lewis v. Physicians & Dentists Credit Bureau*, 177 P.2d 896 (Wash. 1947).

[39]*Pennison v. Provident Life & Accident Ins. Co.*, 154 So. 2d 617 (La. Ct. App. 1963) (disclosure to plaintiff's insurance company not an invasion of privacy); *Edwards v. University of Chicago Hosp.*, 484 N.E.2d 1100 (Ill. App. Ct. 1985) (no liability where hospital publishes diagnosis in standard insurance claim form to obtain payment). But see *Estate of Urbaniak v. Newton*, discussed under "Invasion of Privacy," *supra*, n. 26.

[40]See, e.g., *Heller v. Norcal Mutual Ins. Co.*, 17 Cal. App. 4th 127 (Ct. App. 1993) (statutory privilege does not overcome state constitutional right to privacy).

have a legitimate interest in the information.[41] However, where not prohibited by statute, hospitals may release such information under certain circumstances. Announcements simply of patient admissions, discharges, or births may pose no problem unless the hospital specializes in the care of patients with specific diseases that are considered shameful in the public mind.[42] To publicize the fact that Mrs. Jones gave birth to a normal healthy boy may not ordinarily be considered overstepping the bounds of propriety, but to publicize the fact that Mrs. Jones gave birth to a child conceived through artificial insemination might be actionable.

A hospital that discloses medical records information to the news media may be sued for common law invasion of privacy under two theories: (1) publication of private facts that cause embarrassment to the plaintiff or (2) publicity that places the patient in a false light in the public eye. The leading case in the hospital industry is *Bazemore v. Savannah Hosp.*[43] This case recognized a hospital's duty to prevent unauthorized persons from invading its patients' privacy. Parents brought an invasion of privacy suit against a hospital, a photographer, and a newspaper to recover damages and to enjoin the unauthorized publication of pictures of their deceased child.[44] The Supreme Court of Georgia held that the parents were entitled to sue the hospital that had cared for the child, as well as the photographer and newspaper responsible for publishing the picture. The parents' suit specifically alleged a duty on the part of the hospital:

> upon the arrival of said child, to properly care for and administer to it such skill, comforts, and protection as would safely protect it . . . from an invasion of an unauthorized person or persons, whereby its monstrosity and nude condition would be likely to be exposed to any person, and particularly to the general public. . . .[45]

Thus, by allowing the suit to go forward, the court implicitly recognized that the hospital had a duty to protect the privacy of its patients. Although *Bazemore* dealt with the practice of photographing patients, its holding is broadly applicable. A hospital also could be liable for an invasion of privacy if it improperly disclosed information in its patients' medical records.

---

[41]See, e.g., *Cal. Civ. Code* § 56.10 (1993).

[42]See *Koudsi v. Hennepin County Medical Ctr.*, 317 N.W.2d 705 (Minn. 1982).

[43]155 S.E. 194 (Ga. 1930).

[44]Courts are "usually unsympathetic" to claims of invasion of privacy brought on behalf of a deceased person, although those in a few jurisdictions have permitted such actions. Annotation. 18 ALR 3d 873 §§ 3–5.

[45]*Bazemore, supra*, n. 43.

However, a health care provider will not be liable for invasion of privacy if the information disclosed to the news media is newsworthy or is a matter of legitimate public interest. If the patient is a public figure, the person's prominence, in itself, makes virtually all of the patient's doings of interest to the public and therefore not subject to invasion of privacy actions.[46] Relatively obscure people voluntarily may take certain actions that bring them before the public, or they may be victims of newsworthy occurrences, such as accidents, crimes, etc., thus making them of interest to the public. The latitude extended to the publication of the personal matters, names, photographs, etc., of public figures varies. Public figures may not complain if their lives are given some publicity, and this may be true long after they have ceased to be in the public eye.[47]

Ordinary citizens who voluntarily adopt a course of action that is newsworthy cannot complain if the event is reported along with their names and pictures. For example, a patient who filed a $38 million lawsuit against an emergency room physician was not entitled to sue the physician later for invasion of privacy when the physician informed a newspaper reporter that the patient carried the AIDS virus.[48] The court held that medical malpractice lawsuits, particularly those for large monetary sums, were a matter of legitimate public interest. By filing such a suit, the patient was precluded from later claiming that his privacy had been invaded by the physician's public comments regarding the allegations. The physician revealed the HIV status to explain why the patient had not been diagnosed accurately at the outset. Because the information was related directly to the newsworthy malpractice case, the physician was not liable.[49]

A strange illness or an accident also may be a newsworthy event. Courts have held that the name and photograph of the victim of a circumstance that itself is newsworthy may be published.[50] However, the court may distinguish between the newsworthiness of the event and the newsworthiness of the identity of the

---

[46]*Cason v. Baskin*, 30 So. 2d 635 (Fla. 1947); Annotation. 57 A.L.R. 3d 16.

[47]For example, in *Estate of Hemingway v. Random House, Inc.*, 296 N.Y.S. 2d 771 (N.Y. 1968), Ernest Hemingway's widow was unable to recover for invasion of privacy against a young author who had written a memoir describing her personal feelings and relationship with her husband. As the widow of a major literary figure and author of magazine articles on her relationship with her husband, she was a public figure.

[48]*Lee v. Calhoun*, 948 F.2d 1162 (10th Cir. 1991), *cert. denied*, 112 S. Ct. 2940 (1992).

[49]See also *Metter v. Los Angeles Examiner*, 95 P.2d 491 (Cal. Ct. App. 1939). (Suicide of someone's wife is a newsworthy event; the husband could not prevent publication of her picture.)

[50]*Bremmer v. Journal-Tribune Publishing Co.*, 76 N.W.2d 762 (Iowa 1956) (publication of mutilated dead boy's picture); *Kelly v. Post Publishing Co.*, 98 N.E.2d 286 (Mass. 1951) (publication of automobile accident victim's picture); *Jones v. Herald Post Co.*, 18 S.W.2d 972 (Ky. 1929) (publication of picture of murder victim's wife who had struggled with her husband's assailants). See also Annotation, 30 A.L.R. 3d 203.

individual involved. One court has ruled that, even when a particular medical condition is of interest to the public, hospitals that reveal the identity of individuals with such a condition are subject to invasion of privacy actions.[51] In that case, a married couple who participated in a hospital's in vitro fertilization program and subsequently attended the hospital's private social function for in vitro participants sued the hospital for invasion of privacy for disclosing to the media the couple's attendance at the function. The husband and wife attended a fifth anniversary party for the in vitro program after being assured by the hospital that the event would not be publicized. At the hospital's invitation, however, a television news reporting crew was present. The couple refused an interview and avoided the crew, but appeared on a televised news report nonetheless. The court ruled that the couple was entitled to sue the hospital, reasoning that although in vitro fertilization may be of interest to the general public, individual involvement in such a program is a private matter. The court also ruled that the couple had not waived the right to privacy by attending the event, but had consented to selected disclosure, not disclosure to the general public.

Similarly, in *Barber v. Time, Inc.*,[52] the court held that a magazine could be liable for invasion of privacy when it published the name and picture of a patient in a story titled "Starving Glutton" concerning the patient's hospitalization to treat her constant desire to eat, possibly caused by pancreatic dysfunction. The magazine's employees had obtained the patient's picture by surreptitious means and over her express objections. In holding that the patient was entitled to recover, the court said:

> certainly if there is any right of privacy at all, it should include the right to obtain medical treatment at home or in a hospital for an individual personal condition (at least if it is not contagious or dangerous to others) without personal publicity. . . . Whatever the limits of the right of privacy may be, it seems clear that it must include the right to have information given to or gained by a physician in the treatment of an individual's personal ailment kept from publication which would state his name in connection therewith without such person's consent.[53]

The court found that while the patient's ailment was of some interest to the public, her identity was not. Publishing her name and picture, which conveyed no medical information, thus was an invasion of her privacy.[54]

---

[51] *Y.G. v. Jewish Hosp. of St. Louis*, 795 S.W.2d 488 (Mo. Ct. App. 1990).

[52] 159 S.W.2d 291 (Mo. 1942).

[53] *Id.* at 295.

[54] See also *Vassiliades v. Garfinkel's, Brooks Bros., supra*, n. 33. (A patient who underwent plastic surgery was entitled to expect that the photos would not be published, even though plastic surgery is a matter of general public interest.)

Further, as time passes, the identity of the participant in such an event loses importance and action for invasion of the right of privacy then may be allowable.[55] However, the publisher need not prove that the event was "currently newsworthy" or published contemporaneously.[56] Courts will consider the length of time that has passed between the "event" and publication, along with other factors such as community standards and the importance of the matter published in determining whether the matter publicized is of legitimate public interest.[57]

More recently, invasion of privacy issues have arisen in cases involving the disclosure of information regarding whether a patient is HIV-positive or has AIDS. Many states have statutes containing specific confidentiality rules with respect to AIDS patients, reflecting the importance of protecting this type of medical information from disclosure. (See a more detailed discussion of AIDS Patients' Records in Chapter 4.)

In California, for example, a patient who, for the purpose of alerting a health care provider to take necessary precautions, informed the provider that he was HIV-positive, may sue the provider based on the state's constitutional right to privacy for disclosing his HIV status, an appeals court in that state held.[58] After receiving treatment for injuries at work, a patient brought a Workers' Compensation claim against his employer. During a medical examination with a physician selected by the employer's insurance carrier, the patient told the physician's nurse to be careful because he was HIV-positive. The patient claimed he made it clear to the nurse that he was disclosing the information in confidence. The physician's report mentioning AIDS as a possible source of the patient's symptoms was sent to the insurance company's attorney, who in turn sent copies to the patient's attorney, the insurance carrier, and the Workers' Compensation Appeals Board. The court concluded that the disclosure by the patient was protected under the constitutional right to privacy, holding that when a patient makes clear that he is communicating the fact that he is HIV-positive solely for the purpose of protecting medical professionals, the communication is entitled to constitute privacy.

Although a hospital should be reluctant to release patient information to the news media, the institution may determine in some cases that release of

---

[55]*Bernstein v. National Broadcasting Co.*, 129 F. Supp. 817 (D.D.C. 1955); *Mau v. Rio Grande Oil Inc.*, 28 F. Supp. 845 (N.D. Cal. 1939) (plaintiff, victim of an armed robbery, could sue for invasion of privacy a broadcasting company that named plaintiff in a dramatization of the robbery 18 months after it occurred); *Melvin v. Reid*, 297 P. 91 (Cal. Ct. App. 1931) (plaintiff, former prostitute who had married and led a quiet life for seven years, had an action for invasion of privacy against the producers of a movie that depicted her life and used her maiden name).

[56]*Montesano v. Donrey Media Group*, 668 P.2d 1081, 1086 (Nev. 1983), *cert. denied*, 104 S. Ct. 2172 (1984); *Romaine v. Kallinger*, 537 A.2d 284 (N.J. 1988).

[57]*Montesano v. Donrey, supra*, n. 56.

[58]*Estate of Urbaniak v. Newton, supra*, n. 26.

information of legitimate news value may be appropriate. In such circumstances, the risk of liability is dependent on the specific nature of the disclosure. Merely releasing the status of the patient's condition may not create liability exposure, but disclosing more detailed information or a photograph without the individual's consent should be avoided. While the patient's participation in a newsworthy event may protect the hospital that releases specific information about the person from an invasion of privacy action, the best policy the institution can adopt is to refuse to release any information (other than the status of the patient) without the patient's consent. The fact that the patient is newsworthy does not require the hospital to disclose information; it simply may protect the hospital if it chooses to disclose the information. The best approach is to protect the patient's confidentiality, if possible.

Blood Donor Records

A number of cases involving claims by patients who contracted AIDS through blood transfusions have raised the issue of the rights of privacy of blood donors. Such cases generally involve malpractice claims against a hospital or blood supplier or both, in which a patient attempts to discover the identity of the donor who provided the contaminated blood. The patient frequently alleges that access to the blood donor's identity is necessary to establish whether the hospital or supplier used proper screening and testing procedures when they accepted the blood.

Courts are divided on the issue of whether a donor's right to privacy outweighs an individual patient's need to prove negligence on the part of a health care provider in a malpractice suit. Some courts that have considered the issue have refused to order blood collection facilities to reveal the identities of donors. The Florida Supreme Court ruled in *Rasmussen v. South Florida Blood Service*,[59] for example, that the privacy interests of donors and society's interest in maintaining a strong volunteer blood donation program outweigh a patient's need to prove the source of his AIDS contamination in a personal injury suit. The court ruled that the release of the blood donor's records would result in an undue invasion of privacy, and added that discovery should be denied so that donors would not be deterred from donating blood for fear that someone would be able to inquire into their private lives by obtaining their blood records. Similarly, a federal trial court in South Carolina ruled that a patient who sued a blood bank after she acquired HIV from a blood transfusion was not entitled to discover the identity of

---

[59]500 So. 2d 533 (Fla. 1987).

the donor because the donor's interest in privacy and public interest in protecting voluntary blood programs outweighed the patient's interest in the case.[60] However, other courts have held that the patient's interest in discovering the identity of the donor outweighs the donor's privacy rights. The Louisiana Supreme Court allowed a patient who tested HIV-positive after a blood transfusion to discover the identity of a donor who tested HIV-positive.[61] The court ruled that the patient's interest in discovering the identity of the donor outweighed both the donor's privacy interest and public policy considerations favoring nondisclosure. The court emphasized that the donor already had tested HIV-positive, that the patient sought only to identify the donor of one specific unit of blood, and that the patient needed to identify the donor to evaluate the blood center's screening process. The patient's need to discover the donor's identity therefore is great, the court reasoned, because the individual otherwise would not be able to determine whether the blood center had followed its own procedures at the time of this donation. Accordingly, the court concluded that the patient's interest outweighs both the donor's privacy interests and any public interest justifying nondisclosure.[62] One court has allowed a patient to sue a blood donor identified through information inadvertently provided by the Red Cross.[63] The court held that the patient's right to litigate her claim against the donor substantially outweighed the individual privacy rights and public interest in maintaining a safe and adequate blood supply, especially in light of evidence suggesting donor misconduct.

Some courts have resolved blood donor cases by allowing, but limiting, disclosure, such as by requiring the blood collection agency to reveal the name of the infected donor to the court, which then relays relevant communications between the patient and the donor.[64] One court that adopted this method also directed that communications between the donor and that person's lawyer and the court be maintained with redacted signatures in a sealed envelope marked "Confidential."[65] One court that permitted discovery of donors' identities ordered the plaintiff not to communicate with the donors or undertake further discovery.[66]

---

[60]*Doe v. American Red Cross Serv.*, 125 F.R.D. 646 (D. S.C. 1989).

[61]*Most v. Tulane Medical Ctr.*, 576 So. 2d 1387 (La. 1991).

[62]See also *Sampson v. American National Red Cross*, 139 F.R.D. 95 (N.D. Tex. 1991); *Mason v. Regional Medical Ctr. of Hopkins County*, No. 87-0123-0 (CS) (W.D. Ky. July 25, 1988) (patient's interest in discovering identity of donor outweighs donor's constitutional right to privacy); *Tarrant County Hosp. Dist. v. Hughes*, 734 S.W.2d 675 (Tex. Ct. App. 1987), *cert. denied*, 108 S. Ct. (1988); *Long v. American Red Cross*, 145 F.R.D. 658 (S.D. Ohio Feb. 26, 1993).

[63]*Coleman v. American Red Cross*, 979 F.2d 1135 (6th Cir. 1992).

[64]*Belle Bonfils Memorial Blood Ctr. v. District Court in and for the City and County of Denver*, 763 P.2d 1003 (Colo. 1988). See also, *Watson v. Lowcountry Red Cross*, 974 F.2d 482 (4th Cir. 1992).

[65]*Watson v. Lowcountry, supra*, n. 64.

[66]*Tarrant County Hosp. Dist. v. Hughes, supra*, n. 62.

BREACH OF CONFIDENTIALITY

Yet another legal theory under which a patient may sue a health care provider who improperly discloses medical records information is breach of confidentiality, also known as breach of physician-patient privilege. In some states, the parameters of the privilege and the manner in which it can be waived are governed by statute.[67] In other states, the privilege was developed through common law. Most courts that have considered the question have held that a physician who violates the physician-patient privilege is liable to the patient for damages.[68] Several courts have concluded that public policy favors the protection of the confidential relationship between doctor and patient. These courts have found evidence of this public policy in state testimonial privileges, unprofessional conduct statutes, physician licensing statutes, and statutes limiting the availability of medical records.[69] Other courts have applied such statutes more directly, finding that a physician who breaches such standards by improperly disclosing medical records information may be liable for breach of contract to the patient.[70]

A New Jersey hospital was liable for failing to protect the confidentiality of a diagnosis of AIDS in a staff physician who had been treated at the facility in *Behringer v. Medical Center at Princeton*.[71] In that case, a physician became ill and was hospitalized at the facility where he held staff privileges. A bronchoscopy and a blood clot test subsequently revealed that he had AIDS. While the treating physician and the laboratory personnel initially preserved the confidentiality of

---

[67]Annotation. 21 A.L.R. 3d 912.

[68]See, e.g., *Anker v. Brodnitz*, 413 N.Y.S.2d 582 (Sup. Ct. 1979) *aff'd*, 422 N.Y.S.2d 887 (App. Div. 1979), *appeal dismissed*, 411 N.E.2d 789 (N.Y. 1980); *Alberts v. Devine*, 479 N.E.2d 113 (Mass. 1985); *Horne v. Patton*, 287 So. 2d 824 (Ala. 1973); *Stempler v. Speidell*, 495 A.2d 857 (N.J. 1985). But see *Collins v. Howard*, 156 F. Supp. 322 (Ga. 1957); *Quarles v. Sutherland*, 389 S.W.2d 249 (Tenn. 1965); *Bower v. Murphy*, 444 S.W.2d 883 (Ark. 1969); *Neese v. Neese*, 161 S.E.2d 841 (N.C. Ct. App. 1968). For an overview of which states have recognized this cause of action, see Annotation. 48 ALR 4th 668.

[69]*Id.*, see also *Bryson v. Tillinghast*, 749 P.2d 110 (Okla. 1988); *Stempler v. Speidell*, 495 A.2d 857 (N.J. 1985); *Geisberger v. Wiluhn*, 390 N.E.2d 945 (Ill. App. Ct. 1979); *Schaffer v. Spicer*, 215 N.W.2d 134 (S.D. 1974); *Horne v. Patton*, 287 So. 2d 824 (Ala. 1973); *Hammonds v. Aetna Casualty and Surety Co.*, 243 F. Supp. 793 (N.D. Ohio 1965); *Hague v. Williams*, 181 A.2d 345 (N.J. 1962); *Clark v. Geraci*, 208 N.Y.S.2d 564 (Sup. Ct. 1960); *Berry v. Moench*, 331 P.2d 814 (Utah 1958).

[70]*Hammonds v. Aetna Casualty and Surety Co.*, 237 F. Supp. 96 (N.D. Ohio 1965), 243 F.Supp. 793 (N.D. Ohio 1965); *Doe v. Roe*, 400 N.Y.S.2d 668 (Sup. Ct. 1977). More recently, a Minnesota appeals court allowed a patient to sue a physician for breach of contract for publishing "before" and "after" pictures in a publicity brochure. The court ruled that an implied contract can exist between a patient and a physician, and one of the implied terms of such a contract is the physician's duty not to disclose medical information without the patient's consent. See *Stubbs v. North Memorial Medical Ctr.*, 448 N.W.2d 78 (Minn. Ct. App. 1989).

[71]592 A.2d 1251 (N.J. Super. Ct. 1991).

the diagnosis, the test results were placed in the physician's medical chart, which was kept at the nurses' station on the floor where the physician was an inpatient. There were no restrictions on access to the record. Within hours of the diagnosis, the physician's condition was widely known within the hospital. Soon thereafter, several of the physician's patients learned of his condition and many refused to seek further treatment from him. The physician sued the hospital, claiming that it had breached its duty of confidentiality.

The New Jersey court held that the hospital was negligent in failing to take reasonable precautions regarding access to the physician's record, finding a strong tradition in favor of the physician-patient privilege in that state, as evidenced by case law and statutory law. The court ruled that a physician may not reveal confidential medical information unless disclosure is required by law or necessary to protect an individual or the community. The court rejected the argument that the hospital was not liable because the method of charting is a decision for physicians, not the hospital. According to the court, the issue is not the charting itself, but the accessibility of the chart. When the impact of such accessibility is so clearly foreseeable, the hospital, as custodian of the chart, must take reasonable measures necessary to ensure confidentiality. Accordingly, the court concluded, the hospital was liable for failing to take such steps in this case.

In an interesting case involving the newspaper publication of a patient's photograph that was taken in a hospital's AIDS clinic waiting room, a New York appeals court ruled that a patient could sue a hospital and treating physician for breach of privilege because he had consented to the picture only after they had assured him that he would not be recognizable. When the photograph was published, a friend recognized the patient. Although the court ruled that the hospital had not violated the privilege simply by allowing the media to be present in the waiting room of its infectious disease unit, it held that the physician-patient privilege protects the identity of a patient, as well as the treatment provided. The court concluded that the hospital and physician had possibly breached the privilege by making such assurances and by not informing the patient that the photographer was with the local media.[72]

While courts have acknowledged physicians' legal duty to maintain their patients' confidentiality, they also have recognized two possible defenses for a physician charged with breaching that duty: privilege and waiver. As in defamation and invasion of privacy cases, a privilege will protect a health care provider from liability for disclosing medical records information when failure to disclose information about the patient would jeopardize the health or safety of third

---

[72]*Anderson v. Strong Memorial Hosp.*, 542 N.Y.S.2d 96 (N.Y. App. Div. 1989), *aff'g.* 531 N.Y.S.2d 735 (Supp. Ct. 1988).

persons or of the patient.[73] For example, in *Bryson v. Tillinghast,* the Supreme
Court of Oklahoma held that a patient cannot sue for breach of the physician-
patient privilege when a physician reveals medical information to police,
leading to the patient's arrest for rape.[74] A patient sought treatment at a hospital
for a bite wound on his genitals. A physician who treated the patient later learned
that police were looking for a suspected rapist with injuries similar to those of the
patient. The physician provided the police with information regarding the
patient, leading to his arrest. The patient, who was convicted of rape, later sued
the physician, alleging breach of the doctor-patient privilege as well as breach of
contract. The court dismissed the suit, holding that the state's statutory physician-patient privilege regarding in-court testimony was not designed to protect
criminals from apprehension. The court ruled that a public policy exception
allows physicians to reveal otherwise confidential medical information when the
information will benefit the public. In this case, the apprehension of a suspected
rapist benefited the public, absolving the physician of liability for disclosing
information to the police. Similarly, the breach of contract claim was precluded
by the public policy in favor of apprehending accused rapists.[75]

In several jurisdictions, a patient waives the physician-patient privilege,
foreclosing any claims for breach of the privilege, by putting information
exchanged within the privilege at issue in a lawsuit—for example, a medical
malpractice lawsuit.[76] However, courts disagree as to the scope of the waiver. In
Street v. Hedgepath, the District of Columbia Court of Appeals held that a
patient's physician could communicate with attorneys defending a medical
malpractice suit brought by the patient's surviving husband against a second
physician.[77] After a patient died as a result of thyroid cancer, her husband sued
a former physician who had failed to detect the cancer. Attorneys for the
defending physician consulted with the physician who had treated the cancer and
called the treating physician to testify. The patient's husband sued the treating
physician, alleging that the participation in the medical malpractice suit was a
breach of physician-patient confidentiality. The court dismissed the suit, holding
that by filing a medical malpractice suit, the husband had waived the privilege
between his wife and her treating physician. The waiver was equivalent to a
consent to disclosure of medical information, the court reasoned, precluding any
later claims that the physician had breached his duty of confidentiality. Simi-

---

[73]See, e.g., *Horne v. Patton,* 287 So. 2d 824, 830 (Ala. 1973).

[74]749 P.2d 110 (Okla. 1988).

[75]See also *Horne v. Patton, supra,* n. 73; *Mull v. String,* 448 So. 2d 952 (Ala. 1984).

[76]See, e.g., *Fedell v. Wierzbieniec,* 485 N.Y.S.2d 460 (Sup. Ct. 1985). For a discussion of which
jurisdictions have adopted this view, see Annotation. A.L.R. 3d 912; see also Annotation. 40 A.L.R. 4th.

[77]607 A.2d 1238 (D.C. 1992).

larly, in Alabama, patients who sue any individual other than their own physician waive the physician-patient privilege as to any information that would be legally discoverable in that suit.[78]

A much narrower view of the waiver defense was adopted by the court in *Schaffer v. Spicer*.[79] A psychiatrist disclosed extensive information concerning a patient's state of health to her husband's attorney in the course of lengthy divorce and custody proceedings, during which the patient herself had testified that she had consulted a psychiatrist. The patient's testimony indicated that she had only consulted and been diagnosed by the psychiatrist. The testimony did not relate to the nature and extent of her illness or treatment, nor did it relate to any communications with the psychiatrist. As a result, the court found that the patient's testimony did not amount to a waiver of the confidential relationship. Furthermore, even if the patient's statement had constituted a waiver of the testimonial privilege, it did not completely release the doctor from his duty of secrecy and loyalty to his patient.[80]

A patient who successfully sues for breach of the physician-patient privilege is entitled to consequential damages, that is, compensation for harm caused indirectly by the disclosure, such as deterioration of a marriage, the loss of a job, and emotional distress.[81]

---

[78]*Mull v. String, supra*, n. 75.

[79]215 N.W.2d 134 (S.D. 1974).

[80]See also *Canfield v. Sandock*, 563 N.E.2d 526 (1990) (filing auto accident suit does not waive physician-patient privilege as to all medical records, only records containing information relevant to the suit); *Davis v. Superior Court of Kern County*, 7 Cal. App. 4th 1008 (Ct. App. 1992) (plea for pain and suffering damages in personal injury suit does not waive constitutional right to privacy).

[81]*MacDonald v. Clinger*, 446 N.Y.S.2d 801 (App. Div. 1982).

9

Documentation of Patient Consent in the Medical Record

INTRODUCTION

Health care providers must obtain proper authorization before performing diagnostic or therapeutic procedures on a patient. In most circumstances, the express or implied consent of the patient, or the patient's representative if the individual is incapacitated in some way, constitutes authorization to diagnose or treat. In most instances the law requires that the patient be given sufficient information concerning the nature and risks of the recommended and alternative treatments so that the consent given is an informed consent. Generally, if the patient decides not to consent, the examination or procedure cannot be performed. In some circumstances, however, the law overrides the patient's decision and provides authorization for involuntary treatment, such as in emergencies and in compulsory treatment situations for certain conditions such as mental illness. Patient consent cannot be used to authorize procedures that are prohibited by law.

Physicians and other independent practitioners have the primary responsibility for obtaining informed consent for treatment. Hospitals generally are not liable for failing to obtain the patient's informed consent unless it is a hospital employee who is performing the procedure. However, the hospital frequently assists members of its medical staff in obtaining written confirmation of the patient's consent when the physician is unable to do so. Thus, hospital administrators, medical record administrators, and individual health care providers must be familiar with the legal principles on patient consent and the proper documentation of consent.

The consent requirement, the decision-making roles of patients and their representatives, the exceptions to the consent requirement, and the function of the medical record in the patient consent process are discussed in this chapter.

DIFFERENT TYPES OF CONSENT

The common law long has recognized the right of persons to be free from harmful or offensive touching. The intentional harmful or offensive touching of another person without authorization is called battery. The earliest medical consent lawsuits arose in England in the eighteenth century. In those early cases, when surgery was done without consent, the courts found the surgeons liable for battery. Modern courts still find the physicians liable for battery if they do not obtain patient consent.

On the other hand, there are cases in which the patient consents to the procedure but does not have sufficient information to make an informed decision. Today, nearly all courts have adopted the position that although failure to disclose the necessary information does not constitute a battery, it does constitute negligence, for which the provider can be held liable.

Express and Implied Consent

Consent may be either express or implied. Express consent is consent that is given by direct words, either orally or in writing. There are a few procedures, particularly those involving reproduction, for which some states require written consent. With the exception of those procedures, either oral or written consent can be legally sufficient authorization where express consent is necessary. However, because it often is difficult to prove oral consent, providers should seek written consent.

Implied consent includes consent that is inferred from the patient's conduct and consent that is presumed in certain emergencies. When a patient voluntarily submits to a procedure with apparent knowledge of the nature of the procedure, the courts usually will find implied consent. For example, in *O'Brien v. Cunard S.S. Co.*[1] the court found that a woman had given her implied consent to being vaccinated by extending her arm and accepting the vaccination without objection. In a 1983 case, a patient who revoked his express written consent to a surgical procedure, but thereafter silently acquiesced to preoperative medication and submitted to surgery, was held to have impliedly consented to the operation.[2]

Consent also is presumed to exist in medical emergencies, unless the health care provider has reason to believe that consent would be refused. If the patient previously had refused treatment, consent could not be implied by an emergency requiring such treatment. This emergency exception to the consent requirement

---

[1]28 N.E. 266 (Mass. 1891).
[2]*Busalacchi v. Vogel*, 429 So. 2d 217 (La. App. 1983).

clearly applies when there is an immediate threat to life or health. In an early Iowa case,[3] the court found implied consent to the removal of a patient's mangled limb that had been run over in a train accident. The court accepted the physician's determination that the amputation was necessary to save the patient's life. Courts have disagreed on whether pain is enough justification to find implied consent. A New York court[4] held pain to be a significant factor in establishing a finding of implied consent, while a South Dakota court ruled that pain was not a sufficient emergency because the danger to the patient's health was not immediate and the patient was conscious and able to make an informed decision.[5]

Some courts have found implied consent to extensions or modifications of surgical procedures beyond the scope specifically authorized when unexpected conditions arise, and when the extension or modification is necessary to preserve the patient's life. Many surgical consent forms include explicit authorization of extensions or modifications to preserve the patient's life or health. These provisions minimize disagreements over the scope of authorization by providing an opportunity for the patient to forbid specific extensions or modifications.

Some courts have addressed whether a patient impliedly has authorized the substitution of one practitioner for another. Generally, unless an emergency or other special circumstance occurs, hospitals should assume that the patient's consent includes express authorization for a particular practitioner to perform a procedure and any deviation from that authorization may invalidate the consent. If the patient refuses to consent to treatment by a certain caregiver, then that caregiver is prohibited from engaging in treatment. Likewise, if the primary physician chooses an assistant to whom the patient objects, that assistant is precluded from participating in the procedure.[6] For example, an Illinois court determined that there was a material issue of fact concerning whether a patient had consented to treatment administered by an "on-call" physician.[7] The court stated that the general consent form the patient signed did not indicate either the on-call arrangement or the fact that another physician might perform the procedure.

Both express consent and implied consent must be obtained voluntarily. A consent secured through coercion or undue inducement probably would be void if challenged.

There are some exceptions to the requirement of consent in which the law authorizes treatment despite the refusal of the patient or the patient's representative. These exceptions are discussed later in this chapter.

---

[3]*Jackovach v. Yocom*, 237 N.W. 444 (Iowa 1931).

[4]*Sullivan v. Montgomery*, 155 Misc. 448, 279 N.Y.S. 575 (N.Y. City Ct. 1935).

[5]*Cunningham v. Yankton Clinic*, 262 N.W.2d 508 (S.D. 1978).

[6]See, e.g., *Kenner v. Northern Illinois Medical Ctr.*, 517 N.E.2d 1137.

[7]*Johnson v. McMurray*, 461 So. 2d 775 (Ala. 1984).

Informed Consent

The courts have developed two standards for determining the adequacy of the information the physician has given the patient to obtain the patient's consent: (1) the reasonable physician standard and (2) the reasonable patient standard. In states using the first standard, the physician has a duty to provide the information that a reasonable medical practitioner would offer under the same or similar circumstances.[8]

The second and more modern standard has been adopted by an increasing number of states. Under the reasonable patient standard, the extent of the physician's duty to provide information is determined by the information needs of the patient, rather than by professional practice. Information that is material to the decision must be disclosed. In *Canterbury v. Spence,*[9] the court defined a risk to be material "when a reasonable person, in what the physician knows or should know to be the patient's position, would be likely to attach significance to the risk or cluster of risks in deciding whether or not to forgo the proposed therapy."

Generally a physician or other health care provider must disclose the following categories of information to a patient: (1) diagnosis, (2) nature and purpose of the proposed treatment, (3) risks and consequences of the proposed treatment, (4) probability that the proposed treatment will be successful, (5) feasible treatment alternatives, and (6) alternatives and prognosis if the proposed treatment is not given. Although this is the generally accepted list of items that should be discussed, under the more modern rule the list may be expanded to include all information that the physician knows or reasonably should know would be material to the patient's decision-making process.[10]

Most of the cases concerning informed consent involve allegations that the provider failed to reveal sufficient information as to the risks and consequences of the procedure. Not all risks need to be disclosed. For example, risks that are very remote and improbable generally can be omitted.[11] (Note, however, that the test still will be whether the information would be material to a reasonable patient.) Similarly, some risks with a very high probability could be considered to be so commonly known that the physician is not required to speak of them. If the physician can document that the patient had certain knowledge of risks and consequences from other sources, such as from a prior course of treatment or from discussions with the physician's associate, the physician may be able to demonstrate that the patient gave an informed consent.

---

[8]See, e.g., *Natanson v. Kline*, 350 P.2d 1093, 1106 (Kan. 1960).

[9]464 F.2d 772, 787 (D.C. Cir. 1992), *cert. denied*, 409 U.S. 1064 (1972).

[10]See, Consent to Medical and Surgical Procedures, *Hospital Law Manual* (1994): Sec. 2-3.

[11]See, e.g., *Lemke v. U.S.*, 557 F. Supp. 1205 (D.N.D. 1983).

In *Hales v. Pittman*, the patient told the physician that preserving his ability to work was crucial in determining a course of treatment.[12] The court ruled that the physician should have informed the patient of the risks that could affect his ability to work. That case illustrates that when the patient indicates the need for additional information, there may be a duty to provide it.

There also has been litigation concerning the consequences of the patient's refusal to have the proposed treatment. In California, the courts have extended the informed consent doctrine to require informed refusal. In the California case that established this concept, the court ruled that a physician could be liable for a patient's death from cancer of the cervix based on the physician's failure to inform the patient of the risks of not consenting to a recommended Pap smear.[13] The Pap smear probably would have led to discovery of the patient's cancer in time to begin treatment that would have extended her life. The California informed consent rule also requires the primary physician to disclose the risks of not consulting a specialist.[14]

The most difficult element for the patient to prove in an informed consent case is causation. The patient must show a link between inadequate informed consent and the injury, proving that the individual would not have given consent if the risk that occurred had been disclosed. The courts have developed two standards for this proof. Some jurisdictions apply an objective standard to determine what a reasonable person in the patient's position would have decided if informed of the risk.[15] Other courts apply a subjective standard, which requires the plaintiff to prove that the individual would have refused to consent to the procedure if informed of the risk.[16] Either of these standards provides substantial protection for the conscientious physician who discloses the major risks, and whose patient suffers from a more remote risk. A patient who consents to a procedure knowing of the risk of death and paralysis will find it difficult to convince a court that knowledge of a minor risk would have led to refusal.

Medical Experimentation and Research

Patients consenting to treatment ordinarily consent to procedures and treatments that are used customarily. If innovative or experimental procedures are to be used, the physician must disclose the pertinent information to the patient and obtain appropriate consent. Federal, state, and local laws on human experimen-

---

[12]576 P.2d 493 (1978).

[13]*Truman v. Thomas*, 611 P.2d 902 (1980).

[14]*Moore v. Preventive Medicine Medical Group, Inc.*, 223 Cal. Rptr. 859 (1986).

[15]*Canterbury v. Spence*, 464 F.2d 772 (D.C. Cir.), *cert. denied*, 409 U.S. 1064 (1972).

[16]*Wilkinson v. Vesey*, 295 A.2d 676 (R.I. 1972).

tation and the protection of human subjects contain guidelines that hospitals must be aware of and comply with as applicable. These laws contain specific safeguards for research subjects and guidelines for obtaining informed consent.

Exceptions to the Informed Consent Requirement

The courts have recognized four situations in which consent is required, but informed consent, i.e., adequate disclosure, is not necessarily required: emergencies, the therapeutic privilege, patient waiver, and treatment required by law.

Emergencies

In emergencies in which consent is implied, there is a modification of the disclosure requirement. When there is no time to obtain consent, there clearly is no time to provide the information required for an informed consent. In a New Mexico case, the patient suffered from a snake bite that required immediate treatment.[17] The court recognized that even when there is time to secure consent, certain emergency situations may allow only an abbreviated disclosure of information as to the required treatment.

Therapeutic Privilege

Many courts recognize an exception to the informed consent doctrine, called therapeutic privilege, that permits a physician to withhold information when disclosure of information poses a significant threat of detriment to the patient. In addition, many state consent statutes contain a therapeutic privilege provision.[18] Courts have carefully limited the therapeutic privilege by making it inapplicable when the physician fears only that the information might lead the patient to forgo needed therapy. Instead, physicians should rely on this privilege only when they can document that a patient's anxiety is significantly above the norm. In *Lester v. Aetna Casualty & Surety Co.*, the court ruled that when the therapeutic privilege is applied to prevent the patient from receiving information, the information must be disclosed to a relative.[19] While it may be sound practice for the health care provider to discuss the proposed treatment with the spouse when information is kept from the patient, a court in Hawaii in *Nishi v. Hartwell* ruled that no disclosure to relatives was required because the duty to make full disclosure arises from the physician-patient relationship and is owed only to the patient.[20]

---

[17]*Crouch v. Most*, 432 P.2d 250, 254 (N.M. 1967).

[18]See, e.g., Del. Code Ann., tit. 18 § 6852(b)(3) (1992).

[19]240 F.2d 676 (5th Cir.), *cert. denied*, 354 U.S. 923 (1957).

[20]473 P.2d 116, 112 (Haw. 1970).

Patient Waiver

Some cases have indicated that a patient can waive the right to be informed before giving consent.[21] However, it is doubtful that courts will accept a waiver initiated by a treating physician. A prudent physician should not suggest a waiver but instead should encourage reluctant patients to be informed. If the patient persists, the waiver should be documented in the patient's medical records and carefully witnessed. The documentation should describe the patient's waiver and the physician's effort properly to inform the patient.

Treatment Required by Law

In some instances the police or certain laws require health care providers to perform various tests or procedures ranging from blood or urine tests to more invasive procedures. These situations arise most frequently in cases of criminal suspects, mental illness, and communicable diseases. Theoretically, a hospital or health care provider might be held liable for performing a nonconsensual procedure even when there was a police request or order, but there are no reported cases to that effect. It seems reasonable that medical personnel should be entitled to rely on a police officer's determination of legal authority. On this reasoning, recovery against medical personnel acting in good faith would be likely to be limited to nominal damages unless the procedures were blatantly unreasonable or if the patient were injured because the procedure had been performed negligently. In some states, health care providers are protected by state laws that grant them immunity when acting on the request of a police officer.[22]

There have been several cases addressing the appropriateness of procedures ordered by police officers or courts, such as pumping of a suspect's stomach to recover drugs,[23] blood tests performed despite patient refusal,[24] and bullet removal from a suspect's body.[25] However, those cases do not address the liability of the health care provider; rather, they involve the constitutional rights of the patient and evidentiary concerns.

WHO CAN GIVE CONSENT

The person who makes the consent decision must be legally and actually competent to make the decision and must be informed, unless one of the

---

[21]*Putensen v. Clay Adams, Inc.*, 91 Cal. Rptr. 319, 333 (Ct. App. 1970).

[22]See, e.g., N.Y. Veh. & Traf. Law § 1194 (1993).

[23]*Rochin v. California*, 342 U.S. 165 (1951).

[24]*Schmerber v. California*, 384 U.S. 757 (1966).

[25]*Winston v. Lee*, 105 S. Ct. 1611 (1985).

exceptions applies. Competent adults and some mature or emancipated minors make decisions regarding their own care. Someone else must make the decisions for incompetent adults and other minors.

Competent Adults

The age of majority is established by the legislature of each state. In most states, legal majority is now 18 years of age. In some states, a person can be considered an adult before the statutory age of majority by taking certain actions, such as by getting married or serving in the armed forces.

An adult is competent if (1) a court has not declared the person incompetent, and (2) the individual generally is capable of understanding the consequences of alternatives, weighing the alternatives by the degree they promote the person's desires, and choosing and acting accordingly. There is a strong legal presumption of continued competence. For example, in one case a court found a woman competent to refuse a breast biopsy even though she has been committed to a mental institution with a diagnosis of chronic schizophrenia and two of her three reasons for refusal were delusional.[26] In another case, a court found a woman competent to refuse the amputation of her gangrenous leg even though her train of thought sometimes wandered, her conception of time was distorted, and she was confused on some matters.[27] The fact that her decision was medically irrational and would lead to her death did not demonstrate incompetence. The court believed she understood the alternatives and the consequences of her decision. The Texas Supreme Court, in a 1986 case, held that physicians have a duty to disclose to the mentally ill information that a reasonable person desires.[28]

Competence is not necessarily determined by psychiatrists. A practical assessment of competence should be made by the physician who obtains the consent or accepts the refusal. When it is difficult to assess competence, consultation with a specialist should be considered. If the physician suspects underlying mental retardation, mental illness, or disorders that affect brain function, the consultant should be a psychiatrist or other appropriate specialist.

Competent adults have the right and capacity not only to consent to medical treatment, but also to refuse such treatment. This refusal must be honored regardless of the basis on which it is grounded.

Some patients refuse treatment on religious grounds. The religious beliefs of Jehovah's Witnesses, for example, prohibit them from receiving blood transfu-

---

[26]*In re Yetter*, Pa. D. & C. 2d, 169 (Pa. C. Pl., Northampton County, 1973).

[27]*Lane v. Candura*, 376 N.E. 2d 1232 (Mass. Ct. App. 1978).

[28]*Barclay v. Campbell*, 704 S.W.2d 8 (Tex. 1986).

sions. The majority of courts have ruled that such patients have the right to refuse blood transfusions even if such refusal will lead to their death.[29] Some courts consider whether the patient's right to refuse treatment is outweighed by the need to prevent the abandonment of minor children in the event of the patient's death. Several courts have ruled, however, that even when minor children are involved, the patient's right to refuse treatment predominates when the family is capable and willing to provide for the children if the patient dies.[30]

In these sensitive situations, hospitals and physicians should seek the advice of legal counsel if the patient's refusal is a serious threat to health, as long as the delay involved in seeking that guidance would not further endanger the patient's life.

Terminally ill competent adult patients constitute another category of those who may refuse consent to treatment. Documentation of their wishes in a hospital's medical record is addressed in detail in Chapter 3.

Incompetent Adults

The patient's guardian or, if no guardian exists, the representative of the incompetent adult patient makes consent decisions on the patient's behalf. Representatives of patients, such as family members or friends, or an agent designated by a durable power of attorney, have a narrower range of permissible choices regarding that person than they would have concerning their own care. In addition, the known wishes of the patient should be considered in reaching decisions about treatment.

When a court rules that a person is incompetent, it designates a person to be the incompetent individual's guardian. The guardian has the legal authority to make most of the decisions regarding the incompetent person's care.

Because some patients who actually are incompetent never have been determined to be incompetent by a court, they have no legal guardians. When decisions must be made concerning their care, it is common practice to seek a decision from the next of kin or others who have assumed supervision of the patient. In many states, statutes[31] or court decisions support that practice.[32]

If the incompetence is temporary, the medical procedure should be postponed until the patient is competent and capable of making the decision, unless the postponement presents a substantial risk to the patient's life or health, in which case consent will be implied from the emergency.

---

[29]See, e.g., *In Melideo*, 390 N.Y.S. 2d 528 (1976); *In re Brown*, 478 So. 2d 1033 (Miss. 1985).

[30]See, e.g., *Norwood Hospital v. Munoz*, 564 N.E.2d 1017 (Mass. 1991); *Fosmire v. Nicoleau*, 551 N.Y.S.2d 876 (N.Y. 1990).

[31]See, e.g., Miss. Code Ann. §§ 41-41-3 and 41-41-5 (1991).

[32]*Farber v. Olkon*, 254 P.2d 520 (1953).

When a patient expresses wishes concerning treatment before becoming incompetent, those wishes should be considered seriously in choosing a course of treatment. If a patient was aware of the condition and available treatment alternatives when those wishes were expressed, the wishes usually should be followed. When there is significant unanticipated change in the patient's condition or in available treatments, there is more latitude for the individual's representative or guardian to reach a decision that departs from the person's wishes.

Any person acting on behalf of an incompetent adult has a responsibility to act in the best interests of the adult. Certain procedures, such as sterilization and organ donation, require special consideration. Traditionally, the general rule is that neither the courts nor a guardian can authorize involuntary sterilization of incompetent minors or adults without specific statutory authority.[33] However, several state courts have held that courts have inherent authority to order the sterilization of incompetents.[34] Hospitals should not perform sterilization procedures on incompetents without appropriate legislative authority, case law authority, or a court order.

As for organ transplants involving incompetents as donors, the courts generally examine the situation to establish whether the procedure is in the best interest of the incompetent person. In some cases, courts have concluded that operations, such as kidney transplants, are not in the patient's best interest.[35] In one case, a court ruled that it would not be in the best interest of three-year-old twins for the court to order them to participate in a bone marrow harvesting procedure for the benefit of their 12-year-old half brother who was suffering from a life-threatening disease.[36] Other courts, however, have been willing to find indirect benefit to the incompetent sufficient to support consent to the procedure. Some courts have upheld the right of a guardian to authorize kidney donations because of the close relationship between the donor and the proposed recipient, the emotional injury to the donor if the recipient were to die, and the reasonable motivations of the patient and the patient's parent or guardian.[37]

Minors

Parental or guardian consent should be obtained before treatment is given to a minor unless (1) the patient requires emergency treatment, (2) a statute grants

---

[33]See, e.g., *Hudson v. Hudson*, 373 So. 2d 310 (Ala. 1979).

[34]See, e.g., *In re C.D.M.*, 627 P.2d 607 (Alaska 1981); *In re Grady*, 426 A.2d 467 (N.J. 1981).

[35]See, e.g., *In re Guardianship of Pescinski*, 226 N.W.2d 180 (1975).

[36]*Curran v. Bosze*, 566 N.E.2d 1319 (Ill. 1991).

[37]See, e.g., *Strunk v. Strunk*, 445 S.W.2d 145 (Ky. 1969); *Hart v. Brown*, 289 A.2d 386 (1972).

the minor the right to consent, or (3) a court or other legal authority orders treatment.[38]

Emergency Care

As with adults, consent for treatment of a minor is implied in medical emergencies when an immediate threat to the patient's life or health exists. Most states have statutes addressing this issue. If the health care provider believes that the patient's parents would refuse consent to emergency treatment and if time permits, the provider should seek court authorization for treatment or notify the appropriate government agency responsible for seeking court authorization. If the patient requires immediate treatment, the provider in most cases should treat the minor, even if the parents object. The hospital, with the help of its legal counsel, should establish policies for responding to these situations.

Emancipated Minors

Emancipated minors may consent to their own medical care. Minors are considered emancipated when they are married or otherwise no longer subject to parental control or regulation and are not supported by their parents. The specific factors necessary to establish emancipation usually are set forth in a statute and vary from state to state. Some states require that the parent and child agree on the emancipation, so that a minor cannot become emancipated in those states simply by running away from home. In some states, the doctrine of emancipation is established by the courts, and no statutory definition of emancipation exists. Because the doctrine of emancipation is unsettled in many states, hospitals should try to obtain the consent of a parent in addition to that of the minor, or find another basis upon which to treat a minor without parental or guardian consent. A hospital policy established with the advice of legal counsel will help guide practitioners confronted with this issue.

Mature Minors

Mature minors may consent to some medical care under common law and constitutional principles and under the statutes of some states. Many states have treatment of minors statutes that authorize older minors to consent to any medial treatment. The age limits and scope of treatments to which a minor may consent vary from state to state. Many states have special laws concerning minors'

---

[38]See, e.g., *In re Eric B.*, 235 Cal. Rptr. 22 (1987), in which a California court allowed the state to order the monitoring of a child's condition when the parents refused to do so on religious grounds.

consent to treatment for venereal or other communicable diseases and substance abuse without regard to age.

Most courts reject chronological age as the sole factor in determining maturity, and tend to balance a number of factors.[39] In one case the Illinois Supreme Court ruled that a mature minor has the right to refuse life-sustaining medical treatment if state interests in preserving life, protecting third party interests, preventing suicide, and maintaining the ethical integrity of the medical profession do not outweigh this right.[40] In that case, a 17-year-old patient needed blood transfusions to treat leukemia, but both she and her mother refused consent on religious grounds. The court held that the mature minor had the right to refuse medical treatment. The court pointed out that although the age of majority is 18, other statutes grant certain rights to minors and allow them to exercise those rights autonomously. Because no rigid age restriction exists to limit a minor's rights in some areas, the court declared that mature minors may possess and exercise the same rights regarding medical care that state common law grants adults.

Since the U.S. Supreme Court's decision in *Webster v. Reproductive Health Services*, the states have been allowed greater latitude in legislating consent requirements for minors for decisions concerning abortion.[41] The law varies from state to state, and currently is in a state of flux. In 1993, the Supreme Court let stand a Mississippi statute that requires the consent of both parents (if available within a reasonable amount of time) for an abortion procedure on a minor.[42] State statutes usually provide that a minor can avoid the necessity of parental consent by proving to a court that she is a mature minor capable of making such a decision on her own.

Generally, when treating a minor it is prudent to urge that the minor involve the person's parents in making consent decisions. When a mature minor refuses to permit parental involvement, the health care provider can give the necessary care without substantial risk based on the minor's consent alone, unless there is likelihood of harm to the minor or others that can be avoided only through parental involvement. When the likelihood of such harm arises, parents usually should be involved, unless state law forbids notifying them.

Parental or Guardian Consent

Either parent can give legally effective consent for treatment of a minor child, except when the parents are legally separated or divorced. While it is not

---

[39]See, e.g., *Cardwell v. Bechtol*, 724 S.W.2d 739 (Tenn. 1987).

[40]*In re E.G.* No. 66089 (Ill. 1989).

[41]190 S. Ct. 3040 (1989).

[42]See *Barnes v. Mississippi*, No. 92-7264 (5th Cir. May 26, 1993), *cert. denied*, No. 93-314 (U.S. Nov. 15, 1993).

necessary to determine the wishes of both parents, if a provider knows or suspects that one parent objects, the provider should use caution and seek the advice of its legal counsel. When the parents are legally separated or divorced, usually only the consent of the custodial parent must be obtained unless there is an agreement between the parents that both must agree. This often is specified in state statutes. The provider should rely upon the parent or parents to provide information that substantiates the authority of one or both of them to consent to the minor's care.

RESPONSIBILITY FOR OBTAINING CONSENT

It is the physician's responsibility to provide the necessary information to the patient concerning the individual's condition and proposed treatment and to obtain informed consent before proceeding with diagnostic and therapeutic procedures. Other independent practitioners who order procedures have a similar responsibility concerning those procedures. The hospital generally is not liable for the failure of the physician or other independent practitioner to obtain informed consent unless the physician is an employee or otherwise acting on behalf of the hospital.[43] Some states have codified this principle in their statutes. For example, Ohio law states: "No hospital, home health agency, or provider of a hospice care program shall be held liable for a physician's failure to obtain an informed consent from his patient prior to a surgical or medical procedure, unless the physician is an employee of the hospital, home health agency, or provider of a hospice care program."[44]

In one of the earliest court decisions addressing physician liability for operating without consent, the court observed that while the hospital generally is not liable for operations without consent by physicians who are independent contractors, it may be liable for failing to intervene when it has actual knowledge that the procedure is being performed without required informed consent.[45]

The courts have ruled overwhelmingly that hospitals do not have an affirmative obligation to monitor the content of disclosures given by nonemployed health care practitioners to patients being treated within the hospital's facilities to ensure that consent is informed.[46]

---

[43]See, e.g., *Fiorentino v. Wenger*, 227 N.E. 2d 296 (1967).

[44]Ohio Rev. Code Ann. § 2317.54 (1993).

[45]*Schloendorff v. Society of N.Y. Hosp.*, 105 N.E. 92 (1914).

[46]See, e.g., *Petriello v. Kalman*, 576 A.2d 474 (Conn. 1990); *Pauscher v. Iowa Methodist Medical Ctr.*, 408 N.W.2d 355 (Iowa 1987); *Kershaw v. Reighert*, 445 N.W.2d 16 (N.D. 1989). But see *Magana v. Elie*, 439 N.E.2d 1319 (Ill App. 1982), in which an Illinois appeals court ruled that a hospital may have a duty to its patients to ensure that independent medical staff physicians inform them of the risks of and alternatives to surgery.

Another issue that may arise is which provider has the duty to disclose when there is more that one provider involved in rendering care. The trend in court decisions is to hold that if a primary treating physician remains active in the patient's treatment, that physician must obtain informed consent.[47] Responsibility for disclosure also may depend on whether the primary treating physician has asked for a consultation with another physician or whether the patient has been referred to a second physician. For example, the highest court in Maine has ruled that a primary physician who sends a patient to a surgeon for a consultation has a duty to disclose to the patient the risks and benefits of surgery and the option of doing nothing, even if the surgeon obtains the patient's informed consent to surgery, because the primary physician is responsible for treatment of the patient's condition.[48]

Medical records practitioners can determine that documentation is in the patient's medical record substantiating informed consent; they cannot judge the adequacy of the consent. Hospital administration and medical staff officers should make certain that medical staff bylaws clearly place the responsibility of obtaining informed consent on the treating physician. Hospital employees (e.g., nurses and resident physicians) should assist the physician in accordance with a carefully prepared institutional policy. It is generally recognized that it is not feasible for the hospital to be responsible for the adequacy of information a physician gives a patient for that individual to make an informed decision. The monitoring necessary to enforce such a rule could destroy the physician-patient relationship. However, the hospital can be held liable for failing to intervene if it knew the physician's disclosure was not adequate.

There is disagreement as to the appropriate role of hospital employees in the consent process. Some hospitals permit nurses to obtain the required signature of the patient on the consent form once the physician has informed the patient of proposed procedures and obtained the patient's verbal authority to proceed with treatment. Other hospitals permit nurses to provide some or all of the information necessary for the patient to give an informed consent. Although both of these approaches provide the patient with some or all of the information necessary for an informed consent, they could impair the physician-patient relationship by reducing the opportunity for adequate communication and negotiation. These practices also could shift the liability for inadequacies of the information the patient receives to the hospital as the employer of the nurse. To avoid those adverse consequences, some hospitals prohibit nurses from obtaining consents. In hospitals where this limitation on the nurses' role is not practical, nurses who secure signatures on consent forms should not attempt to answer patient ques-

---

[47]See, e.g., *Jones v. Philadelphia College of Osteopathic Medicine*, 813 F. Supp. 1125 (E.D. Pa. 1993); *Ritter v. Delaney*, 790 S.W.2d 29 (Tex. Ct. App. 1990).

[48]*Jacobs v. Painter*, 530 A.2d 231 (Me. 1987). See also *Kashkin v. Mount Sinai Medical Ctr.*, 538 N.Y.S.2d 686 (1989).

tions concerning the procedure. If the patient seeks additional information or expresses reluctance to consent, the nurse should contact the physician rather than attempting to convince the patient to sign the form.

Although participation of hospital nurses in the consent process is permissible under the laws of most states, hospitals should use caution in establishing consent procedures that involve nurses. The soundest approach is to require the person recommending the treatment to provide sufficient information for making an informed decision but to permit nurses to document the physician's consent conference with the patient by obtaining the patient's signature on the hospital's consent form.

The routine use of a standard consent form before performing certain procedures may protect the hospital from the risk of liability based on lack of consent. A battery consent form described later in this chapter will fulfill this purpose. The purpose of the standard consent form, therefore, is twofold: (1) to document that the physician discussed the information required by state law for informed consent, and (2) to protect the hospital from an action in battery for treating without consent.

The role of hospital employees in completing a consent form should be limited to (1) screening for completion of the form or alternative authorization to ascertain that the hospital has documented the patient's consent in accordance with established hospital policy, and (2) informing the responsible physician when the patient has concerns or questions about the consent form, seems to be confused about the proposed treatment, or has withdrawn or retracted consent given previously. The patient may withdraw consent at any time, even if the individual already has signed a consent form. If the physician does not respond appropriately, medical staff and hospital officials should be notified in order to determine whether intervention is necessary.

DOCUMENTATION

Consent is not merely a form, despite common belief to the contrary. The patient and all involved with providing health care services should understand clearly that obtaining the patient's consent means obtaining the patient's authorization for diagnosis and treatment. Once the patient has authorized the proposed care, it is important to document that authorization in the patient's medical record. Most attorneys who represent physicians and hospitals agree that the best way to document informed consent is to obtain the signature of the patient or the patient's representative on an appropriate form. If there is a prior form signed by the appropriate person, the courts usually accept the form as proof of consent, unless the plaintiff can prove that special circumstances required that the form be disregarded. A few attorneys disagree with the desirability of a form signed by the patient and recommend that the physician write a note in the medical record concerning the discussion of consent with the patient or the patient's representative. These attorneys are concerned that courts will view a consent form as all the information given to the patient and not believe the physician's testimony that additional information was provided. Hospitals using consent forms should indicate that the form does not contain all the information provided by the physician.

The Joint Commission accreditation standards on medical records require evidence of appropriate informed consent for procedures or treatments for which it is required by hospital policy.[49] The Joint Commission does not specify the procedures or treatments and does not require the consent to be documented by the signature of the patient or the patient's representative. Although several accredited hospitals do not require the patient's signature on a progress note or consent form, the more prudent practice is for the hospital or its medical staff to require the appropriate practitioner to obtain a consent on a standard form or in a progress note signed by the patient before certain procedures or treatments are performed.

A hospital's consent policy should require that the patient or the patient's representative provide a signed consent for certain types of procedures, including (1) major or minor invasive surgery, (2) all procedures that involve more than a slight risk of harm, (3) all forms of radiological therapy, (4) electroconvulsive therapy, (5) all experimental procedures, and (6) all procedures for which consent forms are required by statute or regulation. The hospital and its medical staff should outline more specifically in hospital policy the treatments for which a signed consent is required.

In developing or applying a policy on the use of consent forms, hospitals should be aware that the actual process of providing information to the person giving consent and of determining the person's decision is more important than the consent form. The form is only evidence of the consent process and is not a substitute for the consent process. Hospitals should designate a senior administrator or medical staff officer to determine that actual consent exists even when the form has been lost or inadvertently not signed before treatment, or when other circumstances make it difficult to obtain the necessary signature. In all cases, the information on a consent form must be consistent with the information given the patient by the physician. If the physician provides information different from that on the standard consent form, the doctor should revise the form before the patient signs it.

CONSENT FORMS

There are three basic types of consent forms: (1) the blanket consent form, (2) the battery consent form, and (3) the detailed consent form.

---

[49]Joint Commission, *Accreditation Manual for Hospitals* (1994), IM Standard 7.2.10.

Blanket Consent Forms

In the past, many hospitals provided consent forms that authorized any procedure the physician wished to perform. Some courts have ruled, however, that these blanket consent forms are not evidence of consent to major procedures because the procedure is not specified on the form.[50] While some attorneys recommend the continued use of a blanket admission consent form to cover the procedures for which individual special consent is not sought, most believe those admission forms provide no more protection than the implied consent that is inferred from admission and submission to minor procedures. Moreover, because they show a failure to document proper consent for major procedures, blanket admission consent forms used for such procedures can be harmful to the hospital's and physician's positions in defense of a malpractice lawsuit arising from such procedures.

Battery Consent Forms

For major procedures, most hospitals now use consent forms that provide space for the name and description of the specific procedure. In addition, the form states that (1) the person signing has been told about the medical condition, consequences, risks, and alternative treatments; and (2) all the person's questions have been answered to the individual's satisfaction. This type of consent form usually will defeat a claim of battery if the proper person signs the form and the procedures described in the form are the ones performed on the patient. Following the procedures concerning the use of the form provides strong support for the hospital's position that the person who signed was informed adequately. It also provides support for the physician's assertion that the patient was informed. However, it still is possible that the person who signed a battery consent form could convince a court that the individual did not receive information as to consequences, risks, and alternatives to the treatment, especially if someone other than the physician obtained the patient's signature.

Detailed Consent Forms

Some physicians use forms that include written detail describing the medical condition, procedure, consequences, risks, alternatives to treatment, and alternative treatments. Such forms have been mandated for federally funded sterilizations and research involving human subjects. It is much more difficult for the patient to prove that the information in the form was not disclosed. However, detailed consent forms can be costly and time consuming to prepare for each

---

[50]See, e.g., *Rogers v. Lumbermens Mut. Casualty Co.,* 119 So. 2d 649 (La. Ct. App. 1960).

individual procedure, and the risks and alternatives they describe change so that the forms can become obsolete. Thus, some physicians who use detailed consent forms use them only for procedures such as cosmetic surgery for which there is a higher risk of misunderstanding and unsatisfactory results.

Challenges to Consent Forms

Although consent forms are strong evidence of informed consent, they usually are not conclusive. The person challenging the adequacy of the consent process will have an opportunity to convince the court that informed consent was not actually obtained. For example, the person who signed the form may prove he or she was not competent as a result of the effects of medication. Thus, it is important that the explanation be given and the signature be obtained at a time when the consenting party is capable of understanding the decision being made. Consent forms may be challenged on the basis that the wording was too technical or that the form was written in a language the patient could not understand. Although persons are presumed to have read and understood documents they have signed, courts will not apply this presumption when the document is too technical or is written in a language not understood by the patient.

As a result, it is important that forms are understood by the person signing them. If the person has difficulty understanding English, someone, preferably a hospital employee capable of understanding the technical information, should translate the form. It usually is not necessary to have forms in other languages, although it is advisable to have them in the primary languages used by a substantial portion of the patients served by the hospital. It usually is sufficient to have the form translated orally and have the translator certify that the form and discussion of the procedure have been translated orally for the person signing the form. If a patient refuses to sign a consent form but is willing to give oral consent after receiving an adequate explanation of the procedures, the fact of oral consent and the reason for the patient's refusal to sign should be documented on the consent form, along with the witnessed signature of the person obtaining the verbal consent.

A consent form also may be challenged on the ground that the signature was not voluntary. Because the person signing would have to prove that there had been some threat or undue inducement to prove that the signature was coerced, it is difficult to prove coercion. However, if a physician misrepresents the probability of death or injury involved in refusing to undergo the proposed procedure, the patient or the patient's representative might be successful in showing coercion and thereby invalidate the patient's prior consent.

Exculpatory Clauses

Some providers have included exculpatory clauses in their consent forms stating that the person signing the form waives the right to sue for injuries or agrees to limit any claims to not more than a specified amount. Courts will not enforce exculpatory clauses in lawsuits brought by patients against health care providers. For example, in one case, a court refused to enforce a $15,000 limit on liability in an agreement the patient had signed before surgery.[51] Moreover, courts may invalidate the entire consent form together with such clauses. Courts are hostile to exculpatory language, especially where it is imposed on an individual by a large organization.

Period of Validity of Consent Forms and Withdrawal of Consent

Unless specified by statute, there is no absolute limit on the period of validity of a consent or the documentation of that consent by a signature on a consent form. If the patient's condition or the available treatments change significantly, the earlier consent no longer is valid, and a new consent should be obtained. Otherwise, the consent is valid until it is withdrawn.

Whenever a patient refuses to consent to or withdraws consent for treatment, the attending physician should be notified, and written acknowledgment of the refusal or withdrawal should be obtained after the physician has discussed the implications of the refusal or withdrawal with the patient. These steps generally will protect the hospital from liability. If the patient refuses to sign a form releasing the hospital from responsibility for the consequences of refusal or withdrawal of consent, these facts should be documented thoroughly in the medical record.

Because a claim that consent was withdrawn becomes more credible as time passes, some hospitals obtain a new consent each time the patient is admitted. The consent may be obtained in the physician's office before the admission, provided that the time between the consent and the admission is not too long. Some hospitals use a guideline that consent forms should be signed no more than 30 days before the procedure; others require new consents periodically, especially in outpatient treatment settings. Carefully prepared hospital policy should establish guidelines governing the validity of patient consent.

Impact of Statutes

Some states have passed statutes concerning consent forms that must be considered when developing forms for use in those states. Several statutes provide that, if the consent form contains certain information and is signed by the appropriate person, it is conclusive evidence of informed consent[52] or creates a presumption of

---

[51]*Tatham v. Hoke*, 469 F.Supp. 914 (W.D.N.C. 1979), *aff'd*, 622 F.2d 584, (1980).

[52]Nev. Rev. Stat. § 41A.110 (1991).

informed consent.[53] Such statutes indicate how the courts will treat forms containing only the information specified in the statute. The statutes do not apply to forms containing different information. Although it is not a violation of these statutes to use a form that contains different information or to forgo the use of a form completely in states that make certain forms conclusive evidence of informed consent, hospitals should be sure that a decision to use forms that do not meet the statutory requirements is based on careful consideration of the risks. In any case, hospitals should not adopt such forms without the advice of their legal counsel.

SUPPLEMENTS TO DOCUMENTATION

Some physicians supplement their explanations to patients of proposed treatment with other educational materials, such as booklets and videos. For example, some physicians are making audiovisual recordings of the consent process to supplement or even substitute for written consent. Some give their patients tests or have them write their own consent forms to determine and document the level of understanding. None of these steps is required legally, but they should be given serious consideration whenever controversial procedures are proposed.

The hospital should adopt policies for the use of these supplemental materials and should specify how the materials became part of the patient's medical record. If the materials and procedures are used in the hospital, the institution should require that a copy of them be made available to the hospital and, if possible, be made a part of the patient's permanent medical record.

INSTITUTIONAL POLICY ON CONSENT

Hospital administration can take several steps to make sure the consent process works to the advantage of the patient, the physician, and the hospital.

First, the hospital administrative staff can develop adequate policies that explain consent: what it is, when it is necessary, who must obtain it, and when, and in what manner it should be documented. At the same time, administration should make certain such policies are reviewed and updated routinely, with particular attention paid to:

- identifying policies that are not being followed so that appropriate action can be taken
- recognizing when changes in the law, regulations, and licensing and accreditation requirements necessitate a change in policies

---

[53]Iowa Code § 147.137 (1992).

- reviewing consent forms to be sure they conform to current requirements and include preprinted descriptions of risks of or alternatives to the proposed procedures that are consistent with current medical knowledge

When the risk or alternatives change, so should the forms. The review of consent forms should include a review of the procedures and instructions for their use to make sure they are adequate and accurate.

Second, as procedures are developed to implement consent policy, care should be taken to make hospital procedures conducive to patients' understanding of the consent they are being asked to give and their right to refuse to give consent and to obtain answers to questions before giving consent or signing a consent form. This means that employees involved in obtaining a patient's signature on a consent form must be educated in current consent concepts and how to carry out their responsibilities. Of particular concern should be the attitude the employees project to the patient when carrying out this function, since that attitude will reflect positively or negatively on the organization and its approach to the consent process.

Third, a single person should be assigned primary responsibility within the organization to obtain timely and helpful responses to questions concerning consent. If the facility has in-house legal counsel, an attorney may be that person. Otherwise, it should be an individual who has the ability to determine when a situation is such that an attorney's assistance is needed and who then can translate the advice obtained into appropriate action within the facility.

10

Medical Records and Hospital Risk Management/ Quality Assurance

INTRODUCTION

Hospital risk management and quality assurance (QA) programs depend in large measure on medical records and medical records practitioners for information necessary to identify potential risks. Medical records practitioners, therefore, can contribute significantly to the success of risk management and quality assurance programs; but to do so, they must have a good working knowledge of risk management principles, risk management and quality assurance program objectives, and how medical records information affects management of potential risk.

This chapter discusses generally the relationship between hospital quality assurance programs and risk management, the definition and components of hospital risk management programs, and the use of medical records in risk management and quality assurance, including the role of medical records departments.

NATURE AND PURPOSE OF A HOSPITAL RISK MANAGEMENT PROGRAM

While large industrial corporations, the insurance industry, and other industries have had substantial experience developing and implementing risk management and quality control programs, the hospital industry's experience with risk management principles and techniques is relatively new. Hospitals were slow to recognize the importance of risk management, partly because the doctrine of charitable immunity[1] protected their industry in many states from

---

[1] A discussion of the doctrine of charitable immunity, see Chapter 12.

negligence liability actions. With the abolition of the doctrine, hospitals' exposure to medical malpractice claims expanded enormously. Other departments also have fostered this recognition of risk management, including the malpractice crisis of the mid 1970s and the imposition of the requirement, beginning in 1980 and continuing to the present, that all hospitals accredited by the Joint Commission have in place comprehensive quality assurance programs.[2] In 1989, the Joint Commission began requiring "operational linkages between risk management functions and quality assurance functions, and access of quality assurance functions to risk management information useful in identifying and correcting potential risks in patient care and safety."[3] Despite this delayed recognition, risk management has become recognized as an essential part of health care administration in recent years.[4]

RELATIONSHIP BETWEEN QA AND RISK MANAGEMENT

The purposes of hospital risk management and quality assurance programs often are viewed as complementary.[5] The patient safety aspect of risk management— preventing events most likely to lead to patient injury—is the area of greatest interaction between quality assurance and risk management. Poor quality of care that creates a risk of injury to patients poses financial risk both to health care practitioners and to health care facilities. Logically, identification and resolution of problems in patient care will prevent events that may result in patient injury and consequently reduce the potential risk of liability to the health care provider.

In addition to the common aim of ensuring patient safety, quality assurance and risk management use similar methodologies. Both depend on the establishment of screening criteria, collection and analysis of data pertaining to those criteria, and correction of identified problems through improvements in the system and individual practices.

Risk management has additional responsibilities to the institution beyond patient safety. Quality assurance may deal with improvements in hospital

---

[2]See, e.g., Joint Commission, *Accreditation Manual for Hospitals* (1994), LD.4. In the 1994 edition, the Joint Commission integrated the quality assessment and improvement requirements into other sections of the Manual rather than keeping QA as a separate section. The former QA standards were recast to focus on improving individual and organizational performance.

[3]Joint Commission, *Accreditation Manual for Hospitals* (1989), Appendix B, MA. 1.8 through MA. 1.8.3.

[4]A. Kuhn, Introduction to Risk Management, in B. Youngberg, *The Risk Manager's Desk Reference*, (Gaithersburg, Md.: Aspen Publishers, Inc., 1994), 1.

[5]This section is adapted from I. Winer and C. Krizek, Integrating Quality Assurance and Risk Management, in B. Youngberg, *The Risk Manager's Desk Reference* (Gaithersburg, Md.: Aspen Publishers, Inc., 1994) 5–12.

systems that lead to better, more efficient patient care but will not necessarily reduce the rate of adverse occurrences.

The sources of data relied on by each of these disciplines are substantially similar, and the data may be obtained in a more cost-effective manner if coordinated properly. Nevertheless, quality assurance and risk management differ in at least one significant respect related to the perspective each brings to the analysis of data. Quality assurance generally approaches the identification and analysis of patient care problems and issues from the perspective of goals of what should occur in the hospital, whereas risk management tends to approach these tasks from the perspective of what should not occur in the hospital. Quality assurance often looks at patterns of activity, while risk management concentrates on specific incidents.

DEFINITION OF RISK MANAGEMENT

Risk management can be defined as "a systemic program designed to reduce preventable injuries and accidents and to minimize financial loss to the institution."[6] Exposure to financial loss or risk is generated by the hospital's property, personnel, and activities.

Whether a risk management program can undertake effective prevention of all preventable financial risks, however, is questionable. In practice, hospital risk managers seldom take responsibility for the financial risk associated with a business failure, which is more likely the responsibility of the institution's chief financial officer. Risk management programs, like other hospital activities, must exist in the complex political structure of the hospital. If the program takes on more than it can manage or more than institutional politics will tolerate, its effectiveness will suffer.

Moreover, although an ideal risk management program eventually would eliminate all risks and all possibility of exposure to financial loss, such a goal is impossible for hospitals to achieve, since the provision of medical care unavoidably is accompanied by the potential for injury. Thus, the definition of risk management must be tempered by reality; the cost of preventing risks must not exceed the cost of the risk itself.

COMPONENTS OF A HOSPITAL RISK MANAGEMENT PROGRAM

Understanding and appreciating the elements of loss exposure is essential to comprehending the scope and depth of the risk management process. Risk management theory states that any given loss exposure has three elements:

---

[6]American Society for Healthcare Risk Management, *Self Assessment Manual* (Chicago: American Hospital Association, 1991), 1.

1. The subject of a loss includes assets or any tangible owned thing of value, as well as the income produced therefrom.
2. The cause of a loss includes natural, human, and economic forces causing losses, such as, for example, fire, theft, medical malpractice, unemployment, etc.
3. The value of a loss includes the relative financial effect on the organization, such as, for example, the percentage of hospital assets lost or committed to payment for the loss.[7]

Consequently, hospital risk management programs should be designed to permit monitoring of all of the institution's financial resources as well as any actual or potential threats to those resources.[8] That does not mean, however, that the risk management program should take responsibility for the institution's financial and personnel departments. It means that information concerning those areas should be available to the risk manager, and all departments of the hospital should coordinate their efforts to reduce loss risks.

The structural process that most hospitals have designed to identify and minimize the economic threats arising from these loss exposures typically includes six identifiable components:

1. identification
2. evaluation
3. elimination
4. reduction
5. transfer of liability
6. insurance

Prospective, concurrent, and retrospective identification of loss exposure is the most important component of any hospital risk management program and the most difficult element for any risk manager to master. Tools that help identify loss exposure include checklists or inventories of assets and important resources, operational flow charts and financial statements, patient incident or unusual occurrence reports, medical audits, interdisciplinary risk management or quality assurance committees, and constant communication among hospital staff members and physicians about patient complaints and problems.

After a loss exposure has been identified, efforts are focused on evaluating it to determine its economic threat to the hospital. Evaluation of loss exposure is based on three predictive factors:

---

[7]Schmitt, Risk Management—It's More Than Just Insurance, *Health Care Financial Management* (March 1983), 11.

[8]*Id.*

1. loss frequency, or the number of times the incident giving rise to the loss is likely to occur
2. loss severity, or the estimated dollar loss of each individual incident
3. loss dispersion, or the range in estimated dollar losses for similar incidents[9]

Individuals responsible for risk management in hospitals, using these three factors, rely on hospital-specific and industrywide data of documented past experience with identified incidents to evaluate the loss exposure. Included in this process is the use of probability theory, both formal (using the laws and principles of probability theory) and informal (using the experience and judgment of the risk manager with respect to past hospital experience and community standards).

Emerging from and included in the evaluation process is a risk classification system based on the economic consequences of the occurrence of specific individual risks. Classification systems vary, but they generally break down into the following categories:

1. *Prevented risks:* These are risks whose cost of occurrence is higher than their cost of management and whose occurrence may result in the assessment of additional legal sanctions (e.g., punitive damages) against the hospital. Included in this class are intentional torts and injuries determined to have been caused by gross negligence.
2. *Normally prevented risks:* These are risks whose cost of occurrence is greater than the cost of their management but whose occurrence will be considered to be the result of negligent conduct. Included in this class are more negligent injuries (e.g., medical malpractice) and most types of product liability actions.
3. *Managed risks:* These are risks whose cost of occurrence is only slightly greater than their cost of management. Injuries that occur as the result of a risk in this class usually require the injured party to prove that the defendant owed a special duty to the injured party, a duty that was breached by the defendant.
4. *Unprevented risks:* These are risks whose cost of occurrence is less than their cost of management.
5. *Unpreventable risks:* These are risks whose occurrence is unmanageable.[10]

Proper and accurate classification of a risk or loss exposure into one of these classes is difficult but very important, as the class of a risk determines how much

---

[9]*Id.* at 16.

[10]*Id.*

effort must be expended to prevent it from occurring.[11] Misclassification of a risk can result in large financial losses to an institution. Consequently, classification of risks should be reviewed periodically to "determine if the cost of the risk-taking behavior has changed, thereby altering the classification."[12] The remaining four components essentially are loss control techniques that are designed to "change loss exposures by reducing the frequency, financial seriousness, or variation of losses."[13] The technique used depends, in substantial part, on the class to which the risk or loss exposure has been assigned.

Elimination of a loss exposure or risk, once it has been identified and evaluated, is mandatory for prevented risks and may be appropriate for certain normally prevented risks. For example, a hospital may choose to avoid a risk altogether by not recruiting physicians whose practice is associated with very high risk surgical procedures because it does not consider it prudent to invite such exposure to potential loss.

Risks that cannot be eliminated should be reduced. They include normally prevented risks and many managed risks. A substantial amount of a risk manager's time and effort typically is devoted to reducing normally prevented risks and many managed risks. It is clear that the legal liability that arises from a normally prevented risk is linked inextricably with the risk management efforts devoted to preventing such risks.[14] That is, the greater and the clearer the legal liability associated with a normally prevented risk, the greater the risk manager's effort to prevent its occurrence. Many of the precautions commonly thought of as forming the standard of care, e.g., sterile technique, sponge counts, and proper diagnostic tests and workups, are part of the risk management prevention strategy, and "the explicit description and documentation of the precautions taken can prevent many malpractice suits from being filed."[15]

The fifth component of the risk management process, transfer of liability, does not change the actual loss exposure, as is true with efforts directed toward eliminating or reducing risks. Rather, a transfer of liability is a loss financing technique designed to provide funds for paying losses incurred as the result of some normally prevented risks, managed risks, and a few unprevented risks. Exculpatory agreements limiting legal liability are the primary tools used to transfer liability. Examples include having patients sign an agreement releasing the hospital from liability and responsibility for theft of personal property not

---

[11]E. Richards III & K. Rathbun, *Medical Risk Management* (Gaithersburg, Md.: Aspen Publishers, Inc., 1983), 25.

[12]*Id.*

[13]Schmitt, Risk Management, 17.

[14]Richards & Rathbun, *Medical Risk*, 29.

[15]*Id.*

left in the hospital's safe, and the use of warranties and hold harmless and indemnification agreements with manufacturers and suppliers of drugs, equipment, and services to the hospital.

The last component of the risk management process is utilized for unpreventable risks and for all the other classes of risk as a safeguard against both anticipated and unanticipated losses. Insurance is another loss financing technique that does not alter the actual loss exposure but simply funds the losses that occur as a result of the risk. Insurance utilized by hospitals is not limited to malpractice insurance—it also covers general liability, fire, business interruption, officers and directors liability, and other types of insurance. In addition to commercial insurance, many hospitals have established planned programs of funded risk retention (or self-insurance) as a more cost-effective method for insuring against loss than commercial carriage.

The importance of hospital risk management programs to the effective delivery of quality medical care has been acknowledged by the federal government[16] and more than half of the states that have either malpractice statutes or licensing statutes requiring hospitals to have risk management programs. Many of the state statutes establish minimum requirements for such programs, which are similar to those discussed. The Rhode Island statute is typical:

> Every hospital licensed in this state and its insurance carrier shall cooperatively, as part of their administrative functions, establish an internal risk management program which shall include at least the following components:
>
> (1) an in-hospital grievance or complaint mechanism designed to process and resolve as promptly and effectively as possible grievances by patients or their representatives related to incidents, billing, inadequacies in treatment, and other factors known to influence medical malpractice claims and suits. Such mechanism shall include appointment of a representative accountable to the hospital administration who shall anticipate and monitor on a day-to-day basis such grievances and administer said mechanism;
>
> (2) the continuous collection of data by each hospital with respect to its negative health care outcomes (whether or not they give rise to claims), patient grievances, claims suits, professional liability premiums, settlements, awards, allocated and administrative costs of claims handling, costs of

---

[16]*Medicare and Medicaid Guide* (CCH) ¶ 5999x-32 (1983). This section requires that a provider have an adequate risk management program to examine the cause of losses and to take action to reduce the frequency and severity of losses in order to be reimbursed for self-insurance.

patient injury prevention and safety engineering activities, and other relevant statistics and information;

(3) medical care evaluation mechanisms, which shall include but not be limited to tissue committees or medical audit committees, to review the appropriateness of procedures performed, to periodically assess the quality of medical care being provided at an institution, and to pass on the necessity of surgery;

(4) education programs for the hospital's staff personnel engaged in patient care activities dealing with patient safety, medical injury prevention, the legal aspects of patient care, problems of communication and rapport with patients, and other relevant factors known to influence malpractice claims and suits.[17]

It is evident that medical records form an essential part of the data used in risk management, and that the medical records department in all hospitals is an integral part of the risk management and quality assurance process.[18]

MEDICAL RECORDS IN RISK MANAGEMENT

The medical record is the basic document for all quality assurance and risk management activities. The Joint Commission minimum requirements for a medical record are discussed in Chapter 1 and are not reviewed at length in this chapter. Nevertheless, certain Joint Commission requirements that are important from the perspective of quality assurance and risk management are highlighted here. Particular attention is focused on reviewing potential problems in record management, some of the uses of medical records in quality assurance audits, and recommendations for a simple risk management program in a medical records department itself.

The medical records department and its personnel occupy an important position in ensuring that hospital staff members who have either the authority to make entries in the medical record or the right to examine the record do so in accordance with applicable laws, regulations, and accreditation standards. For Joint Commission-accredited hospitals, the accreditation standards recognize several purposes for maintaining medical records, which also are important to the proper functioning of a risk management and quality assurance program.

The 1994 Joint Commission Scoring Guidelines for the management of information standards related to patient-specific data/information, state that:

---

[17]R.I. Gen. Laws § 23-17-24 (1992).

[18]Joint Commission, *Accreditation Manual for Healthcare Organizations* (1994), PPI.1; IM.7.

The information management function provides for the use of patient-specific data/information to facilitate patient care, serve as a financial and legal record, aid in clinical research, and support decision analysis. Patient-specific data/information also provide a basis for professional and organizational performance improvement. This information is provided and used by a heterogeneous group-administrative staff, ancillary departments/services, and direct care providers. The system can recall historical data about a specific patient as well as access data about current encounters. To facilitate consistency and continuity in patient care, very specific data/information are required, as outlined in the standards.

The environment in which patient-specific information is provided supports timely, accurate, secure, and confidential recording and use of patient-specific information.[19]

As is evident from the excerpt above, a complete and accurate medical record is necessary to fulfill several important functions: (1) It chronicles the history of a patient's care and will reveal both the positive and negative aspects, if any, of that patient's dealings with health care providers. (2) It will be used for both risk management and quality assurance purposes, to evaluate the quality of the care rendered, and to identify potential problems with either the system of delivering care or with the providers who deliver it.

The medical records department's role in the risk management program of a hospital should include the following components:

- supervising of data gathering, with documentation of the data produced at all levels
- training of clerical personnel engaged in locating the most useful sources of required information
- determining the incidence of relevant data requested for the use of committees and individuals
- screening of medical records for compliance with established clinical criteria and designated exceptions or equivalents as established by the medical staff
- participating in the selection and design of forms used in the medical record and in the determination of the sequence and format of the contents of the medical record

---

[19]*Ibid.*, Volume II, Scoring Guidelines, IM.7 through IM.7.2.23, p. 21.

- suggesting to the professional staffs methods of improving the primary source data that will facilitate their retrieval, analysis, tabulation, and display
- performing continuing informational surveillance of practice indicators or monitors for medical staff review
- ensuring the provision of a mechanism to protect the privacy of patients and practitioners whose records are involved in quality assessment activities
- reviewing all requests for access to or copies of medical records by patients and third parties to determine their validity under applicable state law
- reviewing all medical records for which requests for access to or copies have been received from, in particular, patients, attorneys, and court orders or subpoenas, to determine whether it is apparent from the medical record that the hospital has potential exposure to liability; medical records personnel should confer closely with the hospital's risk manager and legal counsel in this function, as the early identification of potential claims can greatly enhance and facilitate the hospital's defense to any claim that may be brought against it.

Each of these components of a risk management program in the medical records department should be evaluated with respect to the needs of the institution and available personnel and resources so that the most effective program may be implemented in the hospital.

11

Introduction to the American Legal System

INTRODUCTION

The law affects many of the judgments that health record administrators, health professionals, and technical staff members must make each day. Their decisions may have significant potential legal consequences. Since it is impractical, if not impossible, to obtain professional legal advice before making every decision, medical records administrators must develop an understanding of the medical records law so they will be able to exercise judgment consistent with applicable law and to identify problems that require expert legal counsel.

This chapter sets forth general information about law, including the mechanics of the American legal system and the roles of the branches of government in creating, administering, and enforcing it.

THE NATURE OF LAW

According to most definitions, law is, in essence, a system of principles and processes by which people who live in a society deal with their disputes and problems, seeking to solve or settle them without resort to force. Law governs the relationships among private individuals, organizations, and government. Through law, society establishes standards of behavior and the means to enforce those standards. Law that deals with the relationships between private parties is called private law, while public law deals with the relationships between private parties and government. The increasing complexity of society and life in the United States has been accompanied by a broadening of the scope of public law, and the regulation of private persons and institutions has become more pervasive.

Private law is concerned with the recognition and enforcement of the rights and duties of private individuals and organizations. Legal actions between private parties are of two types: tort and contract. In a tort action, one party asserts that wrongful conduct on the part of the other party has caused harm and seeks compensation for the harm suffered. In a contract action, one party asserts that, in failing to fulfill an obligation, the other party has breached the contract, and the party seeks either compensation or performance of the obligations as a remedy.

An important part of public law is criminal law, which proscribes conduct considered injurious to the public order and provides for punishment of those found to have engaged in such conduct. Public law consists also of an enormous variety of regulations designed to advance societal objectives by requiring private individuals and organizations to follow specified courses of action in connection with their activities. While there are criminal penalties for those who do not abide by the regulations, the purpose of public law is to secure compliance with and attain the goals of the law, not to punish offenders.

The formulation of public policy concerning health care has thrust hospitals into the arena of legislative debate about containment of health care costs, quality of care, medical device safety, research with human subjects, confidentiality of patient information, labor relations, employment policies, facility safety, and other important issues. The object of public law at both the federal and state level is to deal with societal problems of a broad nature.

Law serves as a guide to conduct. Most disputes or controversies that are covered by legal principles or rules are resolved without resort to the courts. Thus, each party's awareness of the law and of the relative likelihood of success in court affects its willingness to modify its original position and reach a compromise acceptable to both sides.

SOURCES OF LAW

The four primary sources of law are federal and state constitutions, federal and state statutes, the decisions and rules of administrative agencies, and the decisions of the courts.

The Constitution

The Constitution of the United States is the supreme law of the land. It establishes the general organization of the federal government, grants certain powers to the federal government, and places certain limits on what the federal and state governments may do.

The Constitution establishes and grants certain powers to the three branches of the federal government—legislative, executive, and judicial. The Constitution also is a grant of power from the states to the federal government. The federal government has only the powers granted to it by the Constitution. These powers are both express and implied. The express powers include, for example, the power to collect taxes, declare war, and regulate interstate commerce. The Constitution also grants the federal government broad implied powers to enact laws "necessary and proper" for exercising its other powers. When the federal government establishes law, within the scope of its powers, that law is supreme. All conflicting state and local laws are invalid.

The Constitution also places certain limits on what the federal and state governments may do. The most famous limits on federal power are the first ten amendments to the Constitution—the Bill of Rights. The basic rights protected by the Bill of Rights include the right to free speech, free exercise of religion, freedom from unreasonable searches and seizures, trial by jury, and the right not to be deprived of life, liberty, or property without due process of law. State powers are limited by the Fourteenth Amendment, as follows: ". . . nor shall any state deprive any person of life, liberty or property, without due process of law; nor deny to any person within its jurisdiction the equal protection of the laws." These clauses of the Fourteenth Amendment frequently are referred to as the due process clause and the equal protection clause. The right to privacy is another constitutional limitation on both state and federal governmental power that frequently affects hospitals and health care professionals.

Due Process of Law

The due process clause imposes restrictions and duties only on state action, not on private action. Actions by state and local governmental agencies, including public hospitals, are considered to be state actions and must comply with due process requirements. Actions by private individuals at the behest of the state also can be subject to the requirements. In the past, private hospitals were considered to be engaged in state action when they were regulated or partly funded by governmental agencies. Today it is rare for private hospitals to be considered engaged in state action on that basis.

The due process clause applies to state actions that deprive a person of "life, liberty or property." In that context, a position or a particular status can be considered property. For example, a physician's appointment to the medical staff of a public hospital and a hospital's institutional licensure by the state are considered property rights. Thus, in the first example, the public hospital must provide due process to the medical staff applicant, while in the second the state and local governmental agencies provide due process to the hospital.

The process that is due varies somewhat depending on the situation. Due process consists primarily of two elements: (1) the rules being applied must be reasonable and not vague or arbitrary; and (2) fair procedures must be followed in enforcing the rules. Two fundamental procedural protections must be offered:

(1) notice of the proposed action and (2) an opportunity to present evidence as to why the disputed action should not be taken. The phrase "due process" in the Fourteenth Amendment also has been interpreted by the United States Supreme Court to include nearly all of the rights in the Bill of Rights. Thus, state governments may not infringe on those rights.

Equal Protection of the Laws

The equal protection clause also restricts state action. The concept of equal protection is intended to ensure that like persons are treated in like fashion. As a result, the equal protection clause is concerned with the legitimacy of the classification used to distinguish persons for various legal purposes. The determination of whether a particular difference between persons can justify a particular difference in rules or procedures can be difficult. In general, courts require that the government agency justify the difference with a rational reason. The major exception to this standard is the strict scrutiny courts apply to distinctions based on particular "suspect classifications," such as race.

Right of Privacy

In *Griswold v. Connecticut*,[1] the United States Supreme Court recognized a constitutional right of privacy. The Court has ruled that the right of privacy limits governmental authority to regulate contraception, abortion, and other decisions affecting reproduction. Several state courts have ruled that the right of privacy permits terminally ill patients and those acting on their behalf to choose to withhold or withdraw medical treatment.[2]

State Constitutions

Each state also has its own constitution. The state constitution establishes the organization of the state government, grants certain powers to the state government, and places certain limits on what the state government may do.

Statutes

Another major source of law is statutory law, which is the law enacted by a legislature. Legislative bodies include the United States Congress, state legisla-

---

[1]381 U.S. 479 (1965).
[2]See, e.g., *Satz v. Perlmutter*, 379 So. 2d 359 (Fla. 1980).

tures, and local legislative entities, such as city councils and county boards of supervisors. Congress has only the powers delegated by the Constitution, but those powers have been interpreted broadly. State legislatures have all powers not denied by the United States Constitution, by federal laws enacted under the authority of the federal government, or by their state constitutions. Local legislative bodies have only those powers granted by the state. Through statutes or constitutional amendments, some states have granted local governments broad powers authorizing home rule.

When federal and state law conflict, valid federal law supersedes. In some cases, federal law may preempt an entire area of law, so that state law is superseded even if it is not in direct conflict. In some law, such as bankruptcy law, Congress explicitly preempts dual state regulation. In other areas of the law, the courts find that preemption is implied from the aim and pervasiveness of the federal scheme, the need for uniformity, and the likelihood that state regulation would obstruct the full goals of the federal action. Preemption is not always implied, especially when the state is exercising its police power to protect the public health. In *Huron Portland Cement Co. v. Detroit*,[3] the United States Supreme Court ruled that the extensive federal regulation and licensure of shipping did not preempt a city ordinance concerning smoke emissions. Therefore, a federally licensed vessel could be prosecuted for violating the ordinance. When state law and local government rules conflict, valid state law supersedes. In some cases, state law may preempt an entire area of law, so that local law is superseded even if it is not in direct conflict. For example, in *Robin v. Incorporated Village of Hempstead*,[4] the court ruled that New York had preempted the regulation of abortions. Therefore, additional regulation by local authorities was prohibited.

Decisions and Rules of Administrative Agencies

The decisions and rules of administrative agencies are other sources of law. Legislatures have delegated to numerous administrative agencies the responsibility and power to implement various laws. The delegated powers include the quasi-legislative power to adopt regulations and the quasi-judicial powers to decide how the statutes and regulations apply to individual situations. The legislature has delegated these powers because it does not have the time or expertise to address the complex issues involved in many areas that it believes need to be regulated. Examples of administrative agencies that have been

---

[3]362 U.S. 440 (1960).
[4]285 N.E.2d 285 (N.Y. 1972).

delegated these powers include the Food and Drug Administration (FDA), the National Labor Relations Board (NLRB), and the Internal Revenue Service (IRS).

The FDA has the power to promulgate regulations and apply them to individual determinations involving the manufacture, marketing, and advertising of foods, drugs, cosmetics, and medical devices. The NLRB has the power to decide how national labor law applies to individual disputes, and the IRS has the power to promulgate regulations and apply them to individual disputes concerning federal taxation. Many administrative agencies, such as the NLRB, seek to achieve some consistency in their decisions by following the position they adopted in previous cases involving similar matters. That is similar to the way the courts develop the common law, discussed later in this chapter. When dealing with these agencies, it is important to review the body of law that has evolved from their previous decisions.

Administrative rules and regulations are valid only to the extent that they are within the scope of the authority granted by legislation to the agency that has promulgated them. The Constitution also limits delegation by the legislature. The legislature must retain ultimate responsibility and authority by specifying what regulations the administrative body may make. In the past, courts often declared delegations to be unconstitutional unless there was considerable specificity. Today the courts interpret the Constitution as permitting much broader delegation, but the general area of law still must be specified.

Congress and many state legislatures have passed administrative procedure acts. These specify the procedures administrative agencies must follow in promulgating rules or reaching decisions in contested cases, unless another law specifies different procedures. Generally, these laws provide that most proposed rules be published to allow individuals an opportunity to comment before the rules are finalized. Many federal agencies must publish both proposed and final rules in the *Federal Register*. Many states have comparable publications of the proposed and final rules of state agencies. Those involved with hospitals should monitor proposed and final rules through these publications, their professional or hospital associations, or other publications. Administrative agencies often rely on the public and the industries regulated by the agencies to alert agency personnel to the potential implications of agency proposals through this comment process.

Court Decisions

The judicial decision is the fourth source of law. In the process of deciding individual cases, the courts interpret statutes and regulations, determine whether specific statutes and regulations are permitted by state or federal constitution, and create the common law when deciding cases not controlled by statues, regulations, or a constitution.

Disagreements over the application of statutes or regulations to specific situations arise frequently. In some situations, an administrative agency has the initial authority to decide how they shall be applied. That agency's decision usually can be appealed to the courts. However, courts generally defer to the decisions of administrative agencies in discretionary matters and limit their review to whether the delegation to the agency was constitutional and whether the agency acted within its authority, followed proper procedures, had a substantial basis for its decision, and acted without arbitrariness or discrimination.

Whether or not an administrative agency is involved, the court still may have to interpret the statute or regulation or decide which of two or more conflicting statutes or regulations apply. Courts have developed several rules for interpretation of statutes. In some states, a statute specifies rules of interpretation. These rules or statutes are designed to help determine the intent of the legislature in passing the law.

The courts also determine whether specific statutes or regulations violate the Constitution. All legislation and regulations must be consistent with the Constitution. The case of *Marbury v. Madison*[5] established the power of the courts to declare legislation invalid when it is unconstitutional.

Many of the legal principles and rules applied by the courts in the United States are the product of the common law developed in England and, subsequently, in the United States. The term "common law" is applied to the body of principles that evolves from court decisions resolving controversies. Common law continually is being adapted and expanded. During the Colonial period, English common law applied uniformly. After the American Revolution, each state provided for the adoption of part or all of the then existing English common law. All subsequent common law in the United States has been developed on a state basis, so common law may differ from state to state.

Statutory law has been enacted to restate many legal rules and principles that initially were established by the courts as part of the common law. However, many issues, especially those pertaining to disputes in private law, still are decided according to common law. Common law in a state may be changed by enactment of legislation modifying it or by later court decisions that establish new and different common law.

In deciding specific controversies, courts for the most part adhere to the doctrine of *stare decisis*, which frequently is described as following precedent. By referring to similar cases decided previously and applying the same rules and principles, a court arrives at the same ruling in the current case as in the

---

[5]5 U.S. 137 (1803) (1 Cranch).

preceding one. However, slight differences in the situations presented may provide a basis for recognizing distinctions between precedent and the current case. Even when such differences are absent, a court may conclude that a particular common law rule no longer is in accord with the needs of society and may depart from precedent.

One clear example of this departure from precedent in the law affecting hospitals was the reconsideration and elimination in nearly every state of the principle of charitable immunity, which had provided nonprofit hospitals with virtual freedom from liability for harm to patients resulting from wrongful conduct. In state after state over a period of 30 years, courts found justification to overrule precedents that had provided immunity and, thereby, to allow suits against nonprofit hospitals.

Another doctrine that courts follow to avoid duplicative litigation and conflicting decisions is *res judicata*, which means a thing or matter settled by judgment. When a legal controversy has been decided by a court and no more appeals are available, those involved in the suit may not take the same matters to court again. This is different from *stare decisis* in that *res judicata* applies only to the parties involved in the prior suit and the issues decided in that suit. The application of the doctrine of *res judicata* can be complicated by disagreements over whether specific matters actually were decided in the prior case.

GOVERNMENTAL ORGANIZATION AND FUNCTION

This section focuses on the structure of the three branches of government—the legislative, executive, and judicial branches—and the manner in which their functions interrelate. In a simplified summary of the functions of the three branches, the legislature makes the laws, the executive branch enforces the laws, and the judiciary branch interprets the laws. The three branches of government exist under a vital concept in the constitutional framework of the United States government and of the various state governments: the separation of powers. Essentially, separation of powers means that no one of the three branches of government is clearly dominant over the other two; however, in the exercise of its functions, each may affect and limit the activities, functions, and powers of the others.

The concept of separation of powers, which may be referred to as a system of checks and balances, is illustrated by the involvement of the three branches in the federal legislative process. Specifically, when a bill to create a statute is enacted by Congress and signed by the president, a representative of the executive branch, it becomes law. If the president should veto the bill, a two-thirds vote of each house of Congress can override the veto. Finally, the president can prevent a bill from becoming law by not taking any action while Congress is in session.

Thus, by his veto the president can prevent a bill from becoming law temporarily and possibly prevent it from becoming law at all if later sessions of Congress do not act favorably on it. A bill that has become law ultimately may be declared invalid by the United States Supreme Court, an agency of the judicial branch of government, if the Court decides that the law is in violation of the Constitution.

Another example of the relationship among the branches of government involves the selection of federal court judges. Individuals nominated by the president for appointment to the federal judiciary, including the United States Supreme Court, must be approved by the United States Senate. Thus, over time, both the executive and legislative branches can affect the composition of the judicial branch of government.

In addition, while a Supreme Court decision may be final with regard to the specific controversy before the Court, Congress and the president may generate revised legislation to replace the law previously held unconstitutional. The processes for amending the Constitution, while complex and often time consuming, also can serve as a method for offsetting or overriding a Supreme Court decision.

Each of the three branches of government has a different primary function. The function of the legislative branch is to enact laws. This process may involve creating new legislation or amending or repealing existing legislation. It is the legislature's responsibility to determine the nature and extent of the need for new laws and for changes in existing laws. By means of a committee system, legislative proposals are assigned or referred for study to committees with specific areas of concern or interest. The committees conduct investigations and hold hearings, at which persons may present their views, in order to assist the committee members in their consideration of the bills. Some bills eventually reach the full legislative body where, after consideration and debate, they may be either approved or rejected. The Congress and every state legislature except Nebraska consist of two houses. (Nebraska has only one house.) Both houses must pass identical versions of a legislative proposal before it can be presented to the chief executive.

The primary function of the executive branch is to enforce and administer the law. However, the chief executive, either the governor of a state or the president of the United States, has a role in the creation of law through the power either to approve or veto a legislative proposal. The exception is North Carolina, where the governor has no veto power. If the chief executive accepts the bill through the constitutionally established process, it becomes a statute, a part of the enacted law. If the chief executive vetoes the bill, it can become law only if the process for overriding the veto by the legislature is successful.

The executive branch of government is organized into departments. The departments have responsibilities for different areas of public affairs and each enforces the law within its assigned area of responsibility. Much of the federal law affecting or pertaining to hospitals is administered by the Department of Health and Human Services. In most states there are separate departments with responsibility over health and welfare matters, and those departments administer and enforce most laws pertaining to hospitals. Other departments and government agencies also affect hospital affairs, however. On the federal level, for example, laws relating to wages and hours of employment are enforced by the Department of Labor.

The judicial branch of government is responsible for adjudicating and resolving disputes in accordance with law. Many types of disputes involving hospitals go before the courts. For example, suits against hospitals by patients seeking compensation for harm allegedly suffered as the result of wrongful conduct by hospital personnel are decided by the courts. Hospitals resort to the courts to challenge exercises of authority by government agencies and departments, to have legislation concerning hospitals declared invalid, to collect unpaid hospital bills, and to enforce contracts.

Although many disputes and controversies are resolved without resort to the courts, in many situations there is no way to end a controversy without submitting to the adjudicatory process of the courts. A dispute taken before a court is decided in accordance with the applicable law; this application of the law is the essence of the judicial process.

ORGANIZATION OF THE COURT SYSTEM

It is necessary to understand the structure of the court system to understand the effect of court decisions as precedents and to understand the judicial branch of government. There are more than 50 court systems in the United States, including the federal court system, each state's court system, the District of Columbia court system, and those of Puerto Rico and the territories. These courts do not all reach the same decisions on specific issues. Frequently, a majority approach and several minority approaches exist on each issue. Thus, careful review is necessary to determine which court's decisions apply to an individual hospital and, if no decisions are specifically applicable, to predict which approach the courts are likely to adopt.

The federal court system and many state court systems have three levels of courts—trial courts, intermediate courts of appeal, and a supreme court. Some states have no intermediate courts of appeal.

State Court System

The trial courts in some states are divided into special courts that deal with specific issues, such as family courts, juvenile courts, probate courts, and limited courts that deal only with lesser crimes, such as misdemeanors, or with civil cases involving limited amounts of money. Each state has trial courts of general jurisdiction that may decide all disputes not assigned to other courts or disputes barred from the courts by valid federal or state law.

At the trial court level, the applicable law is determined and the evidence is assessed to determine the facts. The applicable law then is applied to those facts. It is the judge's role to determine what the law is. If there is a jury, the judge instructs the jury as to the law, and the jury determines the facts and applies the law. If there is no jury, the judge also determines the facts. In either case, the determination of the facts must be based on the evidence properly admitted during the trial, so the facts as heard by the decision maker may not necessarily be what actually happened.

In some cases, everyone agrees on the facts and the only issues presented to the court concern what the law is. In other cases, everyone agrees what the law is, but there is disagreement over the facts. To determine the facts for purposes of deciding the case, the credibility of the witnesses and the weight to be given other evidence must be determined. Many cases involve both questions of law and questions of fact. The judge has significant control over the trial even when a jury is involved. If the judge finds that insufficient evidence has been presented to establish a factual issue for the jury to resolve, the judge can dismiss the case or, in civil cases, direct the jury to decide the case in a specific way. In civil cases, even after the jury has decided, the judge can rule in favor of the other side.

Most state court systems have an intermediate appellate court. Usually, this court decides only appeals from trial court decisions. In some states, there are a few issues that can be taken directly to the intermediate appellate court. When an appellate court decides an appeal, it does not accept additional evidence. It uses the evidence presented in the record from the trial court. Appellate courts almost always accept the determination of the facts by the jury or judge in the trial court because they saw the witnesses and therefore can judge their credibility more accurately. Usually, the appellate court bases its decision on whether proper procedures were followed in the trial court and whether the trial court properly interpreted the law. However, an appellate court occasionally will find that a jury verdict is so clearly contrary to the evidence that it will either reverse the decision or order a new trial.

Each state has a single court at the highest level, usually called the supreme court. In some states the name is different. For example, in New York the highest court is the Court of Appeals, while trial courts are called supreme courts. The highest level court in each state decides appeals from the intermediate appellate courts or, in states without such courts, from trial courts. The highest level court frequently has other duties, including adopting rules of procedure for the state court system and determining who may practice law in the state, which includes disciplining lawyers for improper conduct.

Federal Court System

The federal court system has a structure similar to state court systems. The federal trial courts are the United States district courts and special purpose courts, such as the Court of Claims, which hears certain claims against the United States. Federal trial courts are fundamentally different from state trial courts because the federal courts have limited jurisdiction. A federal suit must involve either a question of federal law or a dispute between citizens of different states. In many cases, the controversy must involve at least $10,000. Federal questions include cases involving possible violations of federal law or of rights under the United States Constitution. When a federal trial court decides a controversy between citizens of different states, it is acting under what is called its diversity jurisdiction, using federal court procedures but applying the law of the applicable state.

Sometimes federal trial courts will decline to decide state law questions until they have been ruled on by a state court. That is called abstention. It is designed to leave states' issues for state courts and to minimize the workload of the federal courts. Federal courts generally will not abstain when there also are important federal questions not affected by the state law question. Some states have procedures by which the federal courts can ask a state court directly to decide a particular question of state law when it is important to the decision of a case before the federal court.

Appeals from the federal trial courts go to a United States court of appeals. The United States is divided into 12 areas, called circuits, numbered 1 through 11, plus the District of Columbia circuit court.

The highest court in the United States is the United States Supreme Court, which decides appeals from the United States courts of appeals. Decisions of the highest state courts also may be appealed to the United States Supreme Court if they involve federal laws or the United States Constitution. When the courts of appeals or the highest state courts decline to review a lower court decision, the decision sometimes can be appealed directly to the United States Supreme Court.

The United States Supreme Court has the authority to decline to review most cases. With only a few exceptions, a request for review is made by filing a petition for a *writ of certiorari*. If the Supreme Court grants *certiorari*, the record for the lower court decision is transmitted to the Supreme Court for review. In most cases, the Supreme Court denies the *writ of certiorari*. Such a denial does not indicate approval of the lower court decision; it merely means the Supreme Court declines to review the decision.

Stare Decisis

The preceding description illustrates the complexity of the court system in the United States. When a court is confronted with an issue, it is bound by the doctrine of *stare decisis* to follow the precedents of higher courts in the same court system that have jurisdiction over the geographic area where the court is located. Each appellate court, including the highest court, generally is bound also to follow the precedents of its own decisions, unless it decides to overrule the precedent due to changing conditions.

Thus, decisions from equal or lower courts or from courts in other court systems do not have to be followed. One exception occurs when a federal court decides a controversy between citizens of different states and must follow the state law as determined by the highest court of the state. Another exception is when a state court decides a controversy involving a federal law or constitutional questions and must follow the decisions of the United States Supreme Court. Another situation that may force a court to alter its prior position is a change in the applicable statutes or regulations by the legislature or an administrative agency.

When a court is confronted with a question that is not answered by applicable statutes or regulations and the question has not been addressed by its court system, the court usually will examine the judicial solutions reached in the other systems to decide the new issue. When a court decides to reexamine its position on an issue it has addressed, it often will examine the judicial decisions of the other systems to decide whether to overrule its position. A clear trend in decisions across the country can form a basis for a reasonable legal assessment of how to act even when the courts in a particular area have not decided the issue. However, a court is not bound by decisions in other systems, and it may reach a different conclusion.

Thus, there can be a majority approach to a certain issue that many state court systems follow and several minority approaches that other states follow. State courts show more consistency on some issues than on others. For example, nearly all state courts have completely eliminated charitable immunity. However, while nearly all states require informed consent to medical procedures, many states determine the information that must be provided to patients by reference to what a patient needs to know, while several states make the determination by reference to what other physicians would disclose. A few states have not yet decided what reference to use.

Differences in applicable statues and regulations between states may force courts in different states to reach different conclusions on certain questions. For example, numerous states have enacted statutes that protect hospital and medical staff review committee records from discovery, although the extent of protection varies. Some statutes provide that such records generally are subject to subpoena, discovery, or disclosure; other statutes state specifically that such committee records, proceedings, and reports are not discoverable or describe such material as confidential or privileged. There also are common exceptions to the nondiscovery statutes, allowing physicians to discover records of staff privilege committees when contesting the termination, suspension, or limitation of their staff privileges. As a result of these variations, courts throughout the country have construed nondiscovery statutes with varying results.

In summary, while it is important to be aware of trends in court decisions across the country, legal advice should be sought before taking actions based on decisions from court systems that have no jurisdiction over the geographic area in which the hospital is located.

12

Principles of Hospital Liability

INTRODUCTION

Since the abolition of the doctrine of charitable immunity in the mid-1960s, hospitals have been confronted with significant increases in the number of malpractice lawsuits brought against them for alleged instances of negligent treatment of patients. In contrast, for well over 100 years physicians have voiced their concern at the increase in the number of malpractice claims brought against them. For example, in 1847, one surgeon wrote: "Legal prosecutions for malpractice in surgery occur so often that even a respectable surgeon may well fear for the results of his surgical practice."[1] While the perception that malpractice lawsuits are continuing to escalate at an uncontrolled rate is fairly universal and is of concern to all individuals involved in delivering health care services, it nevertheless is true that a malpractice suit remains an infrequent occurrence.

In 1975, at the beginning of the malpractice crisis, when professional liability insurance premiums increased so dramatically, one commentator noted that "[s]tatistically, only about one out of every 226,000 patient visits to doctors results in a malpractice action, and the majority of hospitals, no matter how large, go through an entire year without having a single claim filed against them."[2] Still, when a medical malpractice lawsuit is brought against a hospital, the role of the medical records practitioner and the medical record of the patient are of great importance because the medical record becomes a legal document and evidence of the care that was provided, which may or may not demonstrate that the care was negligent. Moreover, the ability of the patient to bring a lawsuit

---

[1]Annas, The Rights of Hospital Patients 198 (1975), quoting Burns, Malpractice Suits in American Medicine before the Civil War, 43 *BULLETIN OF HISTORICAL MEDICINE* (1969): 41, 52.

[2]Annas, *supra*, n. 1, at 199, citing *Medical Malpractice: Report of the Secretary's Commission on Medical Malpractice*, U.S. Department of Health, Education & Welfare, DHEW Pub. No. (OS) 73-88 (Washington, D.C.: U.S. Government Printing Office, 1973), Stock #1700 00114), at 12.

against a hospital within the time allowed by law has a significant bearing on the record retention policies developed by each medical records practitioner.

Chapter 11, in introducing the nature and services of law and the structure of the American legal system, distinguishes between public law, which is concerned primarily with regulating and enforcing individual conduct (principally criminal law), and private law, which is concerned either with the enforcement of agreements among individuals (contract law) or the enforcement of duties and rights between and among individuals in their conduct toward one another (tort law). This chapter reviews the principles of private law, specifically tort law, that govern the circumstances under which, and the determination of when, hospitals, through the conduct of their employees, agents, or medical staff, will be held liable for the payment of money damages to individuals who claim to have suffered an injury as the result of their conduct. This chapter does not address the principles underlying hospital violations of criminal law, nor does it specifically review instances in which hospitals have been held liable for the actions or conduct of their medical records personnel, as that is the subject of Chapter 8. Rather, the purpose of this chapter is to provide a foundation for understanding the circumstances under which the courts will impose liability on hospitals for the negligent conduct of their employees, agents, or medical staff.[3]

NEGLIGENCE DEFINED

Defining negligence in theory is relatively simple, and the legal literature has propounded many definitions,[4] but most essentially state that it is "a matter of risk—that is to say, of recognizable danger of injury. . . . Against this probability, and gravity of the risk, must be balanced in every case the utility of the conduct in question."[5] Stated another way, negligence is conduct society considers unreasonably dangerous and is classified as such because "first, the [individual] did foresee or should have foreseen that it would subject another or others to an appreciable risk of harm, and second, the magnitude of the perceivable risk was such that the [individual] should have acted in a safer manner."[6]

---

[3]This chapter illustrates the principles of hospital liability by discussing conduct considered by courts to be negligent; that is, conduct that is considered to be not as safe as society is entitled to expect from individuals under the circumstances. Intentional torts, for example, such as invasion of privacy, defamation of character, false imprisonment, etc., are not specifically considered, as several other chapters in the book discuss such causes of action. Moreover if negligence theory and its principles are understood, the analysis of intentional torts conceptually is not difficult to understand and appreciate.

[4]Possner, A Theory of Negligence, 1 *Journal of Legal Studies* (1972): 29; Restatement (Second) of Torts § 282 (1965); Terry, *Negligence,* 19 *Harvard Law Review* (1915): 40.

[5]See W. Prosser, *Handbook of the Law of Torts,* 4th ed. (1971), 145–149.

[6]Keeton, Medical Negligence—The Standard of Care, *Speciality Law Digest: Health Care* (March 1980), at 3.

In practice, however, defining negligence can be much more difficult because such theoretical definitions do not offer a standard of care by which conduct may be evaluated and determined to be unreasonably dangerous. This has led to the adoption of the reasonable person standard, which asks a jury, for example, to evaluate the conduct of the parties involved in a lawsuit in light of the general experience and background of each member of the jury. Thus, no special knowledge is required to determine whether a driver who failed to stop at a stop sign and injured another party was negligent. Professional liability cases are different in this respect because the average jury member typically does not possess the special knowledge that would be needed to determine whether the professional against whom a lawsuit was brought used the skill and care required. This is particularly true, for example, in claims brought against hospitals for medical malpractice, because the perceivable danger that should have been avoided (that is to say, the risk or hazard related to the delivery of medical treatment) typically is not commonly known or understood. Consequently:

> [t]he standard by which a professional is to be judged in determining the amount of danger that he should have perceived from alternative [courses] of action must be one that takes into account that the [individual] has held himself out as possessing technical skill and knowledge above that which is commonly known. . . .[7]

PRINCIPLES OF HOSPITAL LIABILITY

The Doctrine of Charitable Immunity

It is important to realize that not-for-profit hospitals only comparatively recently have been held liable for the negligent conduct of their employees. Before the late 1950s and early 1960s, many not-for-profit hospitals were held by courts to be immune from liability for the negligent conduct of their employees under the doctrine of charitable immunity. The doctrine of charitable immunity was premised on the assumption that not-for-profit institutions, like hospitals, depend solely on the income from their property and the endowments and gifts of benevolent persons for funds to carry out the charitable purposes for which they were organized.

Over time, however, the impracticality of the doctrine of charitable immunity was recognized, and exceptions to its blanket exemption from liability were created. For example, the Illinois Supreme Court held in one case that "the sole object of the doctrine . . . was to protect the trust funds of charities from depletion

---

[7]*Id.* at 5.

through the tortious conduct of their employees and agents"[8] and concluded that "the exemption or immunity which has been afforded a charitable institution should go no further than to protect its trust funds from being taken to satisfy its liability for the tortious acts of its agents or servants."[9] Subsequently, in a decision of national importance, the Illinois Supreme Court held, in the case of *Darling v. Charleston Community Memorial Hospital,* that

> the doctrine of charitable immunity can no longer stand. [A] doctrine which limits the liability of charitable corporations to the amount of liability insurance that they see fit to carry permits them to determine whether or not they will be liable for their torts and the amount of that liability, if any. Whether or not particular assets of a charitable corporation are subject to exemption from execution in order to satisfy a judgment does not determine liability. No such issue arises until liability has been determined.[10]

With the doctrine of charitable immunity thus cast aside, the exposure of hospitals to liability claims increased dramatically, based on a number of legal theories.

Elements of a Negligence Claim against a Hospital[11]

To prevail in a suit alleging hospital negligence, the patient must prove the existence of four elements: First, that the hospital had a duty to act in accordance with a standard of reasonable care so as to prevent injury to a patient. Second, that the hospital's conduct failed to conform to the applicable standard of care. This element is referred to as the breach of duty. Third, that the hospital's breach of duty proximately caused the patient's injury; proximate cause is a factual determination typically decided by a jury based on the evidence introduced and accepted at trial and is not discussed at length here. It should not be concluded, however, that proximate cause is a simplistic issue. Determining whether an event or action proximately caused the event or action that led to the patient's injury has challenged the thinking of some of the foremost jurists of the United

---

[8]*Moore v. Moyle,* 92 N.E. 2d 81(Ill. 1950), overruled in *Darling v. Charleston Community Memorial Hospital, infra* note 10.

[9]*Id.* at 86.

[10]211 N.E.2d 253 (Ill. 1965), *cert. denied,* 383 U.S. 946 (1966).

[11]For an excellent and lengthy discussion of the principles of hospital liability, see *Hospital Law Manual,* Principles of Hospital Liability, Attorney's Volume 11B (Gaithersburg, Md.: Aspen Publishers, Inc., 1994).

States over the years as they have struggled with the problems of "intervening events," "transferred negligence," and "foreseeability."[12] Last, that the individual suffered actual harm or injury as a result of the hospital's negligent conduct, for which the patient may request money damages.

The patient may recover damages for all physical pain and suffering caused by the negligent act, as well as for any emotional distress accompanying the injury. The patient also may seek compensation for any reduction in the quality of life, such as loss of consortium. Out-of-pocket costs, past and future medical costs, and past and future wage losses all are compensable as actual damages. Recovery of those damages may be limited, or even barred, by the doctrines of comparative negligence or contributory negligence, discussed later in this chapter.

Two different theories of negligence generally are used in support of liability actions against hospitals for alleged negligent conduct. Under the more traditional and older theory, the hospital, as a separate entity that can be sued in its own right, is recognized as an entity that can act or function only through the individuals it employs. As a result, the negligent actions of the hospital's employees over whom it has control are imputed to the hospital under the doctrine of *respondeat superior,* or the doctrine of agency.

The second theory, more recent in origin, holds the hospital liable for its own independent acts of negligence. This theory, known as corporate negligence, imposes on the hospital the responsibility for monitoring the activities of the independent and nonemployed individuals functioning within its facilities. The doctrine of corporate negligence has had a significant effect on hospital–medical staff relationships since its application to hospitals can and does result in their liability for the negligent conduct of physicians on their medical staffs. Under either theory, the four elements of a negligence action just discussed must be proved.

The Hospital's Duty

Upon the initiation of treatment or the admission of the patient to the hospital, the duty arises to provide services in accordance with the applicable standard of care. The scope of the hospital's duty with respect to the quality of treatment has been expanded greatly in court decisions through reliance on the doctrine of *respondeat superior* and on the theory of liability premised on corporate negligence. Correspondingly, the standard of care against which hospitals' conduct will be measured has become more demanding, and they have been held

---

[12]See, e.g., Justice Benjamin N. Cardozo's opinion in *Palsgraf v. Long Island R.R. Co.,* 162 N.E. 99, *rehearing denied,* 164 N.E. 564 (N.Y. 1928).

more directly responsible for the quality of medical care provided by their independent staff physicians who are not employees.

Unquestionably, the leading court decision in this area is *Darling v. Charleston Community Memorial Hospital*,[13] an Illinois Supreme Court ruling that is significant in three respects. First, it abolished the doctrine of charitable immunity in Illinois, consistent with the nationwide trend to abrogate that doctrine.[14] Second, the court held, in a proposition subsequently adopted by courts in several other states,[15] that state licensing requirements for hospitals, standards of the Joint Commission on the Accreditation of Hospitals (now the Joint Commission on Accreditation of Healthcare Organizations), and the hospital's own bylaws, policies, rules, and regulations could be introduced as evidence of the duty or standard of care the institution owed to its patients. Third, the *Darling* decision has been cited frequently as authority for imposing an independent legal duty on a hospital to monitor and provide overall surveillance of the quality of patient care services provided in its facility and to intervene when inadequate or inappropriate care is rendered to a patient. The patient in the *Darling* case suffered immediate complications and the eventual amputation of his leg following the negligent application of a leg cast by a Dr. Alexander, who was on duty in the emergency department of the hospital. Although it is not known from the court's opinion whether Dr. Alexander was an employee of the hospital or an independent nonemployed physician on the medical staff of the hospital, the court concluded:

> The conception that the hospital does not undertake to treat the patient, does not undertake to act through its doctors and nurses, but undertakes instead simply to procure them to act upon their own responsibility, no longer reflects the fact. Present-day hospitals, as their manner of operation plainly demonstrates, do far more than furnish facilities for treatment. They regularly employ on a salary basis a large staff of physicians, nurses and interns, as well as administrative and manual workers, and they charge patients for medical care and treatment, collecting for such services, if necessary, by legal action. Certainly, the person who avails himself of "hospital facilities" expects that the hospital will attempt to cure him, not that its nurses or other employees will act on their own responsibility.[16]

---

[13]211 N.E. 2d 253 (1965), *cert. denied*, 383 U.S. 946 (1966).

[14]See also, *President and Directors of Georgetown College v. Hughes*, 130 F.2d 810 (D.C. Cir. 1942); *Bell v. Presbytery of Boise*, 421 P.2d 745 (Idaho 1966); *Adkins v. St. Francis Hosp.*, 143 S.E. 2d 154 (W.Va. 1965).

[15]See, e.g., *Lucy Webb Hayes Nat'l. Training Sch. v. Perotti*, 419 F.2d 704 (D.C. Cir. 1969); *Niblack v. U.S.*, 438 F. Supp. 383 (D. Colo. 1977); *Johnson v. Misericordia Community Hosp.*, 301 N.W. 2d 156 (Wis. 1981).

[16]*Darling*, 211 N.E.2d, 253, 257, *citing Bing v. Thunig*, 143 N.E.2d 3, 8 (N.Y. 1957).

. . .[O]n the basis of the evidence before it the jury could reasonably have concluded that the nurses did not test for circulation in the leg as frequently as necessary, that skilled nurses would have promptly recognized the conditions that signaled a dangerous impairment of circulation in the plaintiff's leg, and would have known that the condition would become irreversible in a matter of hours. At that point it became the nurses' duty to inform the attending physician, and if he failed to act, to advise the hospital authorities so that appropriate action might be taken. As to consultation, there is no dispute that the hospital failed to review Dr. Alexander's work or require a consultation; the only issue is whether its failure to do so was negligence. On the evidence before it the jury could reasonably have found it was.[17]

Subsequent Illinois court decisions[18] interpreting *Darling* have concluded that it was not meant as new law to be generally used to impose liability upon hospitals for all negligent treatment by an attending physician. However, other courts citing *Darling* have expanded significantly the scope of the hospital's duty to check properly a physician's credentials upon application to the medical staff,[19] or to obtain information on prior negligent conduct of an applicant to the medical staff.[20] *Darling* at the very least supports the proposition, with respect to the hospital's obligation to a patient for the treatment provided by an attending physician, that where a patient received negligently administered treatment in the facility and the hospital knew or reasonably should have known that the treatment was negligent, the hospital is negligent for failing to intervene to require further review or consideration of the treatment. Other courts have interpreted *Darling* similarly, holding that a hospital is liable for injuries caused by the negligence of a staff physician where it can be shown that the institution had actual or constructive notice of the physician's prior incompetent efforts at performing a comparable medical task,[21] or that the hospital, through the exercise of reasonable care, could have acquired such knowledge and acted on it to prevent the patient's injury but failed to do so.[22]

---

[17]*Id.* at 253, 258.

[18]*Lundahl v. Rockford Memorial Hosp. Ass'n*, 235 N.E.2d 671 (Ill. App. Ct. 1968); *Collins v. Westlake Community Hosp.*, 299 N.E.2d 326 (Ill. App. Ct. 1973), *rev'd on other grounds*, 312 N.E.2d 614 (Ill. 1974).

[19]See, e.g., *Johnson v. Misericordia Community Hosp.*, 301 N.W.2d 156 (Wis. 1981); *Rule v. Lutheran Hosp. & Homes Soc'y of Am.*, 835 F.2d 1250 (8th Cir. 1987); *Blanton v. Moses H. Cone Memorial Hosp., Inc.*, 354 S.E.2d 455 (N.C. 1987).

[20]See, e.g., *Elam v. College Park Hosp.*, 183 Cal. Rptr. 156 (Ct. App. 1982); *Joiner v. Mitchell County Hosp. Auth.*, 186 S.E.2d 307 (Ga. Ct. App. 1971), *aff'd*, 189 S.E.2d 412 (Ga. 1972).

[21]See, e.g., *Purcell v. Zimbelman*, 500 P.2d 335 (Ariz. Ct. App. 1972).

[22]See, e.g., *Gonzales v. Nork*, Cal. App. Dep't. Super. Court Mem. of Dec. No. 228566 (Nov. 19, 1973), *retransferred on other grounds* to Ct. App., 573 P.2d 458 (Cal. 1978); *Thompson v. Nason Hosp.*, 535 A.2d 1177 (Pa. Super Ct. 1988).

The Health Care Quality Improvement Act of 1986 requires hospitals to query a national database identifying physicians who have been disciplined professionally or subject to malpractice verdicts or settlements whenever considering a physician for staff privileges, and every two years thereafter. The duty to check physicians' credentials that was evolving through case law now has been established through this law.[23]

Breach of Duty

After the standard of care or the hospital's duty has been established, evidence must be offered to prove the hospital's conduct amounted to a breach of that duty. Generally, the standard of care required of a hospital depends on the circumstances of the particular case. The most common means for determining the standard of care typically has involved the testimony of experts. However, as the *Darling* case demonstrated, the standard of care may be determined by examining the criteria outlined in statutes, regulations, accreditation standards, and hospital bylaws, rules, regulations, and policies. The importance of this statement to medical records practitioners cannot be overlooked because it suggests a cautious and realistic approach to drafting hospital policies, rules, and regulations, and demands that the medical records practitioner be generally familiar with applicable laws, regulations, and court decisions on the creation, maintenance, and security of medical records. Following is a review of each of the more frequently employed means of proving the standard of care and ascertaining whether it was breached.

Community Standards

Perhaps the most common method of establishing the applicable standard of care in a particular case and demonstrating a breach of that duty is by showing a violation of community standards. Expert testimony typically is required to establish the standard of care recognized in medical and hospital communities.[24] Certain exceptions to this rule are recognized where, for example, the reasonableness of the hospital's conduct may be evaluated on the basis of the common knowledge and experience of a lay person.[25] For example, in one case a Florida court held that expert testimony was not required when a confused patient fell

---

[23]Health Care Quality Improvement Act, 42 U.S.C.A. § 11101 (1987).

[24]See, e.g., *Walker v. North Dakota Eye Clinic, Ltd.*, 415 F. Supp. 891 (D. N.D. 1976); *Krause v. Bridgeport Hosp.*, 362 A.2d 802 (Conn. 1975).

[25]See, e.g., *Newhall v. Central Vt. Hosp., Inc.*, 349 A.2d 890 (Vt. 1975).

from a bed with no siderails.[26] A related issue in proving liability based on a showing of a violation of community standards is whether the community is local, state, or national. The traditional rule, favorable to hospitals, required that their conduct conform to the standards of others in the same locality.[27] This rule subsequently was expanded to include practices common to hospitals in the same or similar communities,[28] and the modern trend has been for courts to evaluate a hospital's conduct against a standard that is not necessarily the same as for that of the others in the area in which the hospital in question is located.[29]

Statutes and Regulations

Statutes and regulations may be used as evidence of common practice. Under certain circumstances, courts will consider a statute or regulation as establishing a standard of care, the violation of which will result in hospital liability to the patient if the patient and the injury suffered fall within the class of persons and harms that the statute or regulation was designed to safeguard and the injuries that it was designed to prevent.[30] Similarly, accreditation standards, particularly those of the Joint Commission, strongly suggest the standard of care required of a hospital.[31] Consequently, medical records practitioners, in particular, should recognize the liability risk that is inherent in the violation of these standards.

Hospital Policies

A hospital's internal rules, as contained in protocols, policies, procedure manuals, and bylaws, can be and frequently are used as evidence of the standard of care required in a particular case.[32] Many times a hospital's rules simply embody a standard of conduct already imposed by other regulatory or accrediting bodies. All too frequently, however, hospitals establish rules that set an internal standard of care greater and more demanding than that required by regulatory or accrediting standards, or even that expected in the community.

An example is the case of *Johnson v. St. Bernard Hosp.,* an Illinois appellate court decision.[33] In *Johnson,* the court held that the requisite standard of care

---

[26]*Stepien v. Bay Memorial Medical Ctr.,* 397 So. 2d 333 (Fla. Dist. Ct. App. 1981), *petition dismissed,* 402 So. 2d 607 (Fla. 1981).

[27]See, e.g., *Mason v. Geddes,* 154 N.E. 519 (Mass. 1926).

[28]See, e.g., *Wood v. Miller,* 76 P.2d 963 (Or. 1938); *Weintraub v. Rosen,* 93 F.2d 544 (7th Cir. 1937).

[29]See, e.g.. *Chandler v. Neosho Memorial Hosp.,* 574 P.2d 136 (Kan. 1977).

[30]*Darling, supra,* n. 10.

[31]*Id.*

[32]*Id.*

[33]399 N.E.2d 198 (Ill. App. Ct. 1979).

applicable to the hospital included a self-imposed obligation to assist staff members in obtaining consultations. The court examined two provisions of the hospital's bylaws, one of which provided that "urgent consultation shall be answered within 24 hours from the time requested and all other consultations shall be answered within 48 hours. After 48 hours, if consultation is not answered, administration shall be notified."[34] The other bylaw provision authorized the hospital to take corrective action against staff physicians whenever necessary to enforce the standards of the medical staff or "in the best interests of patient care."[35] Rejecting the hospital's claim that obtaining a consultation was a medical decision solely within the province of the attending physician, the court stated:

> [w]e believe that the hospital bylaws impose a duty upon the hospital to use reasonable efforts to assist physicians or its staff in obtaining consultations from other staff physicians. This conclusion does not require the hospital administration to engage in the practice of medicine. . . . It requires not medical expertise, but administrative expertise, to enforce rules and regulations which were adopted by the hospital to ensure a smoothly run hospital, routine and adequate care, and under which the physicians have agreed to operate.[36]

The message of this case is clear. For anyone likely to be involved in drafting hospital bylaws or rules and policies, "care should be taken to avoid creating a self-imposed standard of conduct that is either impossible to satisfy or infeasible because of practical constraints."[37] Certainly, each hospital's risk management and quality assurance programs should include procedures for identifying hospital policies that are not being followed so that careful evaluation of the need for the policy can be conducted. Obviously, out-of-date or inappropriate policies should be revised. (For a general discussion of hospital risk management and quality assurance programs and activities, see Chapter 10.)

Res Ipsa Loquitur

An exception to the general principle that a patient must prove negligence in order to establish the hospital's liability is the doctrine of *res ipsa loquitur* (literally, the thing speaks for itself). This doctrine is applicable where a court determines, as a matter of law, that "the occurrence is such as in the ordinary

---

[34]*Id.* at 201.

[35]*Id.* at 205.

[36]*Id.*

[37]*Aspen Hospital Law Manual, supra,* n. 11, at 20.

course of things would not have happened if the party exercising control or management had exercised proper care."[38]

The elements that must be established for the doctrine to apply are the following: (1) the defendant must have had exclusive control over the thing that produced the injury, (2) the injurious occurrence ordinarily would not have occurred in the absence of the defendant's negligence, (3) the injury must have been one that could not have occurred from any voluntary action by the plaintiff, and, in some states, (4) the defendant must have had superior knowledge of the course of the accident.[39]

For example, in a District of Columbia case, the patient underwent abdominal surgery and, following the operation, the patient's evidence showed she still had a surgical sponge inside her abdominal cavity.[40] The court held that there was evidence that the physician's initial surgery had caused the problem (i.e., the physician had had exclusive control over the devices that caused the injury), that the condition would not normally have occurred in the absence of negligence, and that the injury did not occur as a result of any voluntary action by the patient as she was under anesthesia.

CONTRIBUTORY AND COMPARATIVE NEGLIGENCE

Proof of hospital negligence does not mean the institution is exclusively liable for the patient's injuries. Two related doctrines of negligence law—contributory negligence and comparative negligence—operate to reduce or eliminate a hospital's ultimate liability to the patient who has established the hospital's negligence.

Contributory negligence is an absolute bar or defense to a plaintiff's claim for damages. Specifically, if a defendant whose negligence has been established can prove that the plaintiff's conduct breached that individual's duty of self-protection and contributed to the injury, the plaintiff's claim for damages will be denied. Essentially, the elements that a defendant must establish to prove the plaintiff's negligence parallel those the plaintiff must prove to establish the negligence of the defendant.[41]

Under the comparative negligence doctrine, the fault of the plaintiff is compared with that of the defendant in determining the amount of damages to be awarded to the plaintiff. In practice, a percentage is assigned to the respective negligence of each party, which thereafter is used to reduce the recovery

---

[38]*Walker v. Rumer*, 381 N.E.2d 689, 691 (Ill. 1978). For a statutory recodification of the doctrine of *res ipsa loquitur*, see 735 Ill. Comp. Stat. Ann. 5/2 1113 (1993).

[39]*Id.*

[40]*Burke v. Washington Hosp. Ctr.*, 475 F.2d 364 (D.C. Cir. 1973).

[41]See, e.g., *Borus v. Yellow Cab Co.*, 367 N.E.2d 277 (Ill. App. Ct. 1977).

according to the plaintiff's relative degree of fault. Varying forms of comparative negligence have been adopted. The pure form of comparative negligence permits the plaintiff to recover damages for the portion of the injury attributable to the defendant's negligence, irrespective of which party was at greater fault.[42] Under the approach used in a majority of the states that have adopted the doctrine of comparative negligence, a modified comparative negligence is applied, and the plaintiff whose negligence is determined to have exceeded that of the defendant's is barred from recovering any damages.[43]

STATUTES OF LIMITATION

State statutes, commonly referred to as statutes of limitation, are an important limitation on the liability of hospitals. As a matter of public policy, all states have established prescribed periods of time after which a plaintiff may not sue a defendant, so that a defendant does not face unending exposure to liability for any actions.

Typically, claims against hospitals for injuries caused by the negligence of the facilities or their employees have been classified as personal injury actions. Usually the statute of limitation applicable to such claims is two years; that is, a person has two years from the date of the injury in which to sue the party whose negligent conduct allegedly caused the injury. Failure to file suit within the prescribed time period bars the patient from suing the hospital for that injury.

A growing number of jurisdictions has specific statutes of limitation applicable to medical malpractice actions that supersede the more common and traditional personal injury time period.[44] These statutes vary as to the period of limitation and the types of health care providers affected. The two primary issues in this area of the law of concern to medical records practitioners and all other health care professionals are (1) the computation of the statutory time period, and (2) the circumstances in which the time period for filing suit is deferred or tolled by law for reasons of public policy.

Ordinarily, the statutes of limitation applicable to negligence actions begin to run when the injury occurs.[45] However, claims against hospitals often involve considerations, not found in common personal injury negligence claims, that affect the ability of the patient to know when there had been an injury. The classic example, of course, is the foreign object left inside the patient after surgery. The patient usually does not learn of the problem until some time after the injury occurred. Under traditional statutes of limitation rules, the time period

---

[42]See, e.g., *Alvis v. Ribar*, 421 N.E.2d 886 (Ill. 1981).

[43]See, e.g., Wis. Stat. § 895.045 (1991-1992).

[44]See, e.g., Mass. Gen. Laws. Ann., ch. 260, § 4; 735 Ill. Comp. Stat. Ann. § 5/13-212 (1993).

[45]See, e.g., *Hawks v. DeHart*, 146 S.E.2d 187 (Va. 1966).

would begin to run from the date of the injury, whether or not the patient knew of any injury, thereby seriously jeopardizing and possibly even barring the individual's right to file a claim against the person who committed the injury. In many states, rules have been adopted to mitigate the harshness of this general principle. The most straightforward of these rules is known as the discovery rule, which states that the statute of limitation does not begin to run until the wrongful act was or reasonably should have been discovered.[46] In an effort to minimize any undue prejudice to hospital defendants that could result from the application of the discovery rule, several states have limited its applicability solely to claims arising from foreign objects left in the body.[47]

Extensive application of the discovery rule has greatly increased hospital and physician exposure to liability and has resulted in a concomitant inability of professional liability insurers to predict accurately their potential financial obligations. This, together with the proliferation of medical malpractice claims in the 1970s, resulted in huge increases in medical malpractice insurance premiums. In an effort to balance the interests of both parties in these circumstances, many states have adopted another limitation on the discovery rule, known as the double time limit. This statute permits an action to be brought within a prescribed time period after discovery, but it also sets a maximum time period for action, dating from the cause of the injury, that bars any claim irrespective of when discovery of the injury occurs. In Illinois, for example, a person may bring a medical malpractice lawsuit two years after discovering the injury but no more than eight years after the event that caused the injury.[48]

A final departure from the discovery rule is the continuous treatment rule. Under this rule, the time of injury and the time of discovery are immaterial. The rule is premised on the theory that patients will not change their physician or hospital unless and until they become aware that they are being treated negligently. The statutes of limitation begin to run when the relationship between the patient and the hospital or physician terminates.[49] The practical effect of such a rule is potentially to extend indefinitely the period of time during which a patient can bring a malpractice action.

The last issue of importance in determining when the statute of limitation period begins to run involves the circumstances under which, by law and for reasons of public policy, the limitation period does not start when it otherwise would normally begin to run. This is known as an event that tolls the running of the statute of limitation.

---

[46]See Prosser, *Handbook of the Law of Torts*, 144; *Oliver v. Kaiser Community Health Found.*, 449 N.E.2d 438 (Ohio 1983).

[47]See. e.g., Mo. Rev. Stat. § 516.105 (1993).

[48]735 Ill. Comp. Stat. Ann. § 5/13-212 (1993).

[49]See, e.g., N.Y. Civ. Prac. L. & R. § 214-A (1993).

A majority of jurisdictions provides that, in the event of a patient's mental incompetence or minority, the limitation period will not begin to run until the person is declared competent or reaches the age of majority.[50] The rationale underlying these rules is that mental incompetence and minority are legal disabilities affecting the individual's ability to know of the existence of an injury and a corresponding right to sue for damages.

In some states, the statutes of limitation also may be tolled where a fiduciary relationship (e.g., the existence of a guardian of a disabled person, the trustee of a trust, etc.) is determined to exist between the hospital and the injured party. Fraud, constructive fraud, and fraudulent concealment are encompassed within such circumstances, and courts may find that the hospital had a duty to disclose information and that it had breached that duty.[51] A good example of fraudulent concealment is a hospital's refusing to give patients access to their medical records. In one case, for example, the patient alleged that his leg had to be amputated because of the failure of physicians at a Veterans Administration hospital to order certain tests and follow-up laboratory reports reasonably promptly and to administer proper antibiotics for control of the infection.[52] He argued that he should not be barred by the statute of limitations because the hospital had failed to give him access to his medical records, thereby delaying his ability to discover the acts of negligence causing his injury and precluding him from bringing his cause of action within the statutory time period. The court agreed, holding that his claim was not barred by the statute of limitation.[53]

---

[50]See, e.g., Ariz. Rev. Stat. § 12-502 (1993); Cal. Civ. Proc. Code § 352 (1993); Mich. Comp. Laws § 600.5851 (1992). See also *Perez v. Espinola*, 749 F. Supp. 732 (E.D. Va. 1990).

[51]See, e.g. *Nutty v. Universal Engineering Corp.*, 564 F. Supp. 1459 (S.D. Ill. 1983); *Garcia v. Presbyterian Hosp. Ctr.*, 593 P.2d 487 (N.M. Ct. App. 1979).

[52]*Waits v. United States*, 611 F.2d 550 (5th Cir. 1980).

[53]*Id.* at 553; see also *Emmett v. Eastern Dispensary and Casualty Hosp.*, 396 F.2d 931 (D.C. Cir. 1967); *Harrison v. United States*, 708 F.2d 1023 (5th Cir. 1983).

Appendix A

List of Statutes Concerning Medical Records

This appendix contains a list of state statutes concerning medical records that are cited in this book. Some states publish statutes in more than one form. As a result, the citations found here are from the publications following the name of each state. Since state legislatures revise their statues constantly, laws not listed here may appear from time to time. Therefore, this appendix should be used as a general guide to the statutory treatment of medical records in the various states.

ALABAMA: *Alabama Code*

§12–21–5.	Copy of hospital records, admissibility.
§12–21–6.	Same, Subpoena duces tecum; inspection; form; weight; cost.
§22–8A–4.	Written declaration, requirements, form.
§22–11A–1.	Reporting Notifiable diseases.
§22–50–9.	Department—Powers generally.
§22–50–10.	Same, Termination of Alabama mental health board; transfer of authority to department.
§22–50–11.	Same—Additional and cumulative powers.
§26–10–5.	Recordation, inspection, etc., of petition, orders, etc., in adoption proceedings; effect of final order of adoption as to legal rights, obligations, etc., of natural parents, adopting parents, and child generally; visitation rights of natural grandparents; annulment, avoidance, etc., of final adoption order.
§34–24–58.	Decisions, opinions, etc., of utilization review committee privileges.
§38–7–13.	Records to be kept by child care facility; use and disclosure information.

ALASKA: *Alaska Statutes*

§18.20.085.	Hospital records retention.
§18.20.090.	Information confidential.

279

| §18.23.030. | Confidentiality of records of review organization. |
| §18.23.065. | Patient access to records. |

ARIZONA: *Arizona Revised Statutes Annotated*

§12–2235.	Doctor and patient.
§36–151.	Definitions.
§36–339.	Reproduction of records.
§36–340.	Disclosure of records, violations.
§36–341.	Copies of and data from vital records.
§36–343.	Persons required to keep records.
§36–445.01.	Confidentiality of information; conditions of disclosure.
§36–445.02.	Immunity for serving on or furnishing information to review committees.
§36–509.	Confidential records.

ARKANSAS: *Arkansas Code Annotated*

§16–46–105.	Records of, and testimony before, committees reviewing and evaluating quality of medical or hospital care.
§16–46–106.	Access to medical records.
§16–6–302.	Furnishing copies of records in compliance with subpoenas.
§16–63–219.	Fee for discovery of medical records.
§20–9–304.	Use of records for medical research.
§20–9–913.	Confidentiality.
§20–46–103.	Records of State Board of Health, hospitals, etc., confidential—Exceptions and liability.
§20–46–104.	Records of State Hospital confidential.
§25–19–105.	Examination and copying of public records.

Uniform Rules of Evidence

| Rule 503. | Physician- and psychotherapist-patient privilege. |

CALIFORNIA: *California Evidence Code Annotated*

§994.	Physician-patient privilege.
§1156.	Records of medical-dental study of in-hospital staff committee.
§1156.1.	Medical or psychiatric studies undetaken by quality assurance committee.
§1157.	Exemption from discovery of proceedings and records of specified committees and bodies.
§1157.5.	Proceedings or records of nonprofit medical care foundation or professional standards review organization.
§1157.6.	Proceedings and records of mental health quality assurance committees.
§1157.7.	Proceedings and records of committee reporting on specialty health care services.

DELAWARE: *Delaware Code Annotated*

Tit. 10, §8116.	Savings for infants or persons under disability.
Tit. 19, §2321.	Minimum duration of incapacity.
Tit. 19, §2322.	Medical and other services and supplies as furnished by employer.
Tit. 19, §2323.	Selection of physician, surgeon, dentist, optometrist, or chiropractor by employee.
Tit. 24, §1768.	Immunity of boards of review; confidentiality of review board records.
Tit. 25, §4301.	Liens in favor of charitable hospitals.
Tit. 25, §4302.	Establishment of lien, notice of claim.
Tit. 25, §4303.	Attachment of lien to judgment.
Tit. 25, §4304.	Release as effective, liability of person making payment, limitation.
Tit. 25, §4305.	Recording of liens, fees.
Tit. 25, §4306.	Examination of hospital records.
Tit. 29, §7202.	Records.

Delaware Rules of Evidence

Rule 503.	Physician- and Psychotherapist-Patient Privilege.

DISTRICT OF COLUMBIA: *District of Columbia Code*

§6–2002.	Disclosures prohibited; exceptions.
§6–2011.	Disclosures by client authorization.
§6–2016.	Authority of mental health professional to limit authorized disclosures.
§6–2041.	Right to access.
§6–2042.	Authority to limit access.
§6–2422.	Declaration: execution, form.
§6–2805.	Confidentiality of medical records and information.
§14–307.	Physicians and mental health professionals.

FLORIDA: *Florida Statute Annotated*

§63.162.	Hearings and records in adoption proceedings, confidential nature.
§§90.101–90.958.	Florida Evidence Code.
§395.016.	Patient records, form and content.
§395.017.	Patient records, copies, examination.
§395.018.	Criminal and administrative penalties, injunctions, emergency orders, moratoriums.
§415.511.	Immunity from liability in cases of child abuse or neglect.
§766.101.	Medical review committee, immunity from liability.

GEORGIA: *Georgia Code Annotated*

§24–7–8.	Proving medical records or reproductions.
§24–9–40.	When medical information may be released by physician, hospital, health care facility, or pharmacist; immunity from liability; waiver of privilege; psychiatrists and hospitals excepted.

HAWAII: *Hawaii Revised Statutes Annotated*

IDAHO: *Idaho Code*

ILLINOIS: *Illinois Annotated Statutes*

Illinois Compiled Statutes Annotated

Ch. 805, §§410/1—   Uniform Preservation of Private Business Records
   410/6.   Act.
Ch. 820, §305/16.   Rules and orders—Depositions—Subpoenas—
                        Hospital Records— Court reporter—Fees and
                        charges.

INDIANA: *Indiana Statutes Annotated*

§16–1–14–5.	Who is incompetent.
§16–39–4–2.	Provision of information.
§16–39–4–3.	Provision of information upon written request.
§16–41–2–2.	Reporting of information required by rules.
§16–41–2–3.	Reporting of HIV infectious cases.
§16–41–2–4.	Waiver of patient privilege.
§16–41–2–5.	Duties under IC 16–41–7–3 not satisfied.
§16–41–2–6.	Good faith reports not subject to liability.
§16–41–2–7.	False reports—Liability.
§16–41–2–9.	Reckless violation—Failure to comply—Penalty.
§16–41–7–2.	When carrier is serious and present danger to the health of others—Reporting—Immunity from liability—False reports.
§16–41–7–3.	Physician to inform patient of patient's duty— Information provided to patient—Physician immune from liability—Waiver of patient privilege.
§34–3–15.5–1 et seq.	Hospital medical records.
§34–4–12.6–1.	Definitions.
§34–4–12.6–2.	Confidentiality and privilege.

IOWA: *Iowa Code Annotated*

§22.7.	Confidential records.
§135.40.	Collection and distribution of information.
§135.41.	Publication.
§135.42.	Unlawful use.
§147.137.	General provisions regulating practice professions, malpractice, consent in writing.
§622.10.	Communications in professional confidence, exceptions, application to court.

KANSAS: *Kansas Statutes Annotated*

§59–2928.	Restraints and seclusion.
§59–2929.	Rights of patients.
§60–245(d).	Subpoenas, service.
§60–427.	Confidential communications statute.
§65–177.	"Data" defined; Study of diseases and deaths from maternity causes, confidentiality, use, admissibility as evidence, reports, contents.
§65–504.	Licenses; contents; limitations; posting; inspections; temporary permits; access to premises; temporary licenses; denial or revocation of license; procedure.

| §65–2423. | Adoption cases. |

KENTUCKY: *Kentucky Revised Statutes Annotated*

§311.377.	Waiver of claim for damages by applicant for or grantee of staff privileges, records, confidentiality, exceptions.
§311.595.	Causes for denial, probation, suspension, or revocation of licenses and permits.
§422.300.	Use of photostatic copies of medical records, originals held available.
§422.305.	Subpoena of records, certification of copies, personal delivery.
§422.310.	Personal attendance of custodian of hospital records, when.
§422.315.	Patient may ask to prohibit or limit use of his medical records.
§422.320.	Return of medical records to court clerk.
§422.325.	Proper procedure for obtaining records required.
§422.330.	Privileges not waived.

LOUISIANA: *Louisiana Revised Statutes Annotated*

§13:3714.	Charts or records of hospital, admissibility of certified copy.
§13:3715.	Court order for chart or record of state-operated health care facilities, certified copy as sufficient compliance.
§13:3715.1.	Subpoena duces tecum to a health care provider for patient records; reimbursement for records produced.
§28:94.	Transfer of patients between institutions.
§44:7.	Hospital records.
§44:39.	Microfilm records; use as evidence.

MAINE: *Maine Revised Statutes Annotated*

Tit. 10, §3412.	Notice.
Tit. 10, §3413.	Duration.
Tit. 16, §101.	Subpoenas for witnesses.
Tit. 16, §357.	Hospital records and copies of records.
Tit. 22, §1711.	Patient access to hospital medical records.
Tit. 32, §3296.	Records of proceedings of hospital medical staff review committees confidential.
Tit. 34A, §3003.	Confidentiality of information.
Tit. 34B, §1207.	Confidentiality of information.
Tit. 34B, §3803.	Patients' rights.

MARYLAND: *Maryland Code Annotated Health-General Article*

§4–301.	Definitions.
§4–302.	Confidentiality and disclosure generally.
§4–303.	Disclosure upon authorization of a person in interest.

MASSACHUSETTS: *Massachusetts General Laws Annotated*

MICHIGAN: *Michigan Compiled Laws Annotated*

MINNESOTA: *Minnesota Statutes Annotated*

§41–41–13.	Physician treating minor for venereal disease need not obtain parental consent.
§41–63–3.	Certain medical and dental information may be furnished for evaluation and improvement of quality and efficiency of medical or dental care.
§41–63–9.	Discoverability and admissibility into evidence of proceedings and records of review committees.

MISSOURI: *Missouri Statutes Annotated*

§287.140.	Employer to provide medical and other services, transportation, artificial devices, refusal of treatment, effect, medical evidence, division, commission responsibilities.
§491.060.	Persons incompetent to testify.
§491.110.	Subpoenas, by whom served.
§516.140.	What actions within two years.
§537.035.	Members of certain professional standards boards or committees exempt from action for damages, when.

MONTANA: *Montana Code Annotated*

§26–1–805.	Doctor-patient privilege.
§27–12–302.	Content of application—Waiver of confidentiality of medical records.
§33–19–301.	Access to recorded personal information.
§50–5–106.	Records and reports required of health care facilities.
§50–16–202.	Committees to have access to information.
§50–16–203.	Committee information and proceedings confidential and privileged.
§50–16–204.	Restrictions on use or publication of information.
§50–16–205.	Data confidential, inadmissible in judicial proceedings.
§50–16–502.	Legislative findings.
§50–16–525.	Disclosure by health care provider.
§50–16–526.	Patient authorization to health care provider for disclosure.
§50–16–527.	Patient authorization—Retention—Effective period—Exception.
§50–16–528.	Patient's revocation of authorization for disclosure.
§50–16–529.	Disclosure without patient's authorization based on need to know.
§50–16–530.	Disclosure without patient's authorization—Other bases.
§50–16–531.	Immunity of health care providers pursuant to written authorization—Form required.
§50–16–535k.	When health care information available by compulsory process.
§50–16–541.	Requirements and procedures for patient's examination and copying.

§50–16–542.   Denial of examination and copying.

NEBRASKA: *Nebraska Revised Statutes*
§25–12, 120.   Hospital records, examination and inspection,
                   hospital medical staff committee, utilization
                   review committee.
§25–12, 121.   Hospital records, hospital medical staff committee,
                   utilization review committee, recommendations,
                   not liable for damages.
§27–504. Rule 504. Physician-patient privilege, definitions, general rule
                   of privilege, who may claim privilege, exceptions
                   to the privilege.
§71–2048.   Communications; privileged; waiver.
§71–3401.   Information, statement, data, furnish without
                   liability.

NEVADA: *Nevada Revised Statutes Annotated*
§41A.110.   Consent of patient, when conclusively established.
§49.025.   Required reports privileged by statute.
§49.215.   Definitions.
§49.225.   General rule of privilege.
§49.235.   Who may claim privilege.
§49.245.   Exceptions.
§51.125.   Hearsay exceptions: recorded recollection.
§51.135.   Hearsay exceptions: records of regularly conducted
                   activity, affidavit of custodian or medical records.
§52.325.   Subpeonaed records: Delivery of authenticated copy
                   by custodian; order for return of record; form of
                   affidavit of authentication.
§108.640.   Hospital records, examination; copying.
§629.021.   "Health care records" defined.
§629.041.   Provider of health care to report persons having
                   certain injuries.
§629.045.   Provider of health care to report persons having
                   certain burns.
§629.051.   Health care records: retention.
§629.061.   Health care records: inspection; use in public
                   hearing; immunity from civil action.
§629.065.   Health care records relating to test of blood, breath,
                   or urine: Availability to district attorney and
                   agencies of law enforcement; use as evidence;
                   immunity of certain persons from civil action for
                   disclosure.

NEW HAMPSHIRE: *New Hampshire Revised Statutes Annotated*
§126–A:4–a.   Medical and scientific research information.
§329:26.   Confidential communications.
§§337–A:1—A:6.   Preservation of private business records.

NEW JERSEY: *New Jersey Statutes Annotated*

§2A:44–45.	Statement of hospital charges; examination of hospital records.
§2A:82–41.	Person against whom claim is asserted, right of examination.
§2A:84A–22.1.	Definitions.
§2A:84A–22.2.	Patient and physician privilege.
§2A:84A–22.8.	Utilization review committees of certified hospital or extended care facility, exceptions.
§26:8–5.	Institutional records.

NEW MEXICO: *New Mexico Statutes Annotated*

§14–6–1.	Health information, confidentiality, immunity from liability for furnishing.
§14–6–2.	Hospital records, retention.
§14–7–1.	Requiring notice of intent to gain access to records of financial institutions.
§24–1–15.	Reporting of contagious diseases.
§24–1–20.	Records confidential.

NEW YORK: *New York Consolidated Laws Annotated*

New York Education Law Article

§6527.	Special provisions.

New York Mental Hygiene Law Article

§31.09.	Powers of the department regarding investigation and inspections.
§31.11.	Certain duties of providers of services.
§31.13.	Powers of subpoena and examination.
§31.17.	Formal hearings, procedure.

New York Lien Law Article

§189.	Liens of hospitals.

New York Public Health Law Article

§17.	Release of medical records.
§201.	Functions, powers, and duties of the department.
§2801.	Definition.
§2803.1(a).	Commissioner and council, power and duties.
§2805–g.	Maintenance of records.
§4160.	Fetal deaths, registration.
§4161.	Fetal death certificates, form and content, physicians, midwives, and hospital administrators.
§4165.	Persons in institutions, registration.

New York Civil Practice Law and Rules Article

§2306.	Hospital records, medical records of department or bureau of a municipal corporation or of the state.

§2307.   Books, papers, and other things of a library,
                         department, or bureau of a municipal corporation
                         or of the state.
§4504.   Physician, dentist, podiatrist, chiropractor, and
                         nurse.

New York Penal Law Article
§265.25.   Certain wounds to be reported.

NORTH CAROLINA: *North Carolina General Statutes*
§8–44.1.   Copies of medical records.
§8–53.   Communications between physician and patient.
§14–118.3.   Acquisition and use of information obtained from
                         patients in hospitals for fraudulent purposes.
§48–25.   Recordation and information not to be made public,
                         violation a misdemeanor.
§58–2–105.   Confidentiality of medical records.
§58–39–45.   Access to recorded personal information.
§90–410.   Definitions.
§90–85.35.   Availability of patient records.
§130A–12.   Confidentiality of records.
§130A–143.   Confidentiality of records.
§130A–212.   Confidentiality of records.
§130A–374.   Security of health data.
§131E–87.   Reports of disciplinary action, immunity from
                         liability.
§131E–90.   Authority of administrator, refusal to leave after
                         discharge.
§131E–95.   Medical review committee.
§143B–139.6.   Confidentiality of records.

NORTH DAKOTA: *North Dakota Century Code Annotated*
§23–01–02.1.   Hospital utilization committees, internal quality
                         assurance review committee, reports, immunity.
§23–01–12.   Hospital records to be kept at direction of state
                         health officer.
§25–03.1–43.   Confidential records.
§25–03.1–44.   Records of disclosure.
§25–03.1–45.   Expungement of records.
§23–16–09.   Information confidential.
§31–08–01.   Admissibility in evidence of business records, term
                         "business records" defined, exception.

North Dakota Rules of Evidence Annotated
Rule 503.   Physician- and psychotherapist-patient privilege.

OHIO: *Ohio Revised Code Annotated*
§2305.24.   Information disclosed to a hospital utilization review
                         committee, immunity from liability.
§2305.251.   Confidentiality of review committee proceedings.
§2317.02.   Privileged communications and acts.

§3701.261.	Cancer incidence surveillance system; establishment.
§3721.01.	Definitions and classification; restrictions on facilities.
§3721.02.	Inspection; investigations; licensing; renewal; fees.
§3721.04.	Rules; standards.
§3721.26.	Rulemaking powers.
§3727.01.	Definitions.
§3727.02.	Certification or accreditation requirements for hospitals.
§3727.03.	Proof to department of health.
§3727.04.	Inspections.
§3727.05.	Injunctions.
§3727.06.	Admission and supervision of patients.
§3727.07.	Maternity and Psychiatric units.
§5122.31.	Disclosure of information.

OKLAHOMA: *Oklahoma Statutes Annotated*

Tit. 12, §§2101—3103.	Evidence code.
Tit. 12, §2503.	Physician and psychotherapist-patient privilege.
Tit. 59, §509.	Unprofessional conduct, definition.
Tit. 63, §1–1709.	Information concerning condition and treatment of patients—Restrictions—Exemption from liability—Review committees.
Tit. 67, §§251—256.	Uniform preservation of private business records act.
Tit. 76, §19.	Access to medical records, copies, waiver of privilege.

OREGON: *Oregon Revised Statutes*

§41.675.	Inadmissibility of certain health care facility and training data.
§192.525.	State policy concerning medical records.

Oregon Rules of Evidence

Rule 504.	Psychotherapist-patient privilege.
Rule 504–1.	Physician-patient privilege.

Oregon Rules of Civil Procedure

Rule 55(H).	Hospital records.

PENNSYLVANIA: *Pennsylvania Consolidated Statutes Annotated*

Tit. 35, §7309.	Health and exposure records.
Tit. 35, §7607.	Confidentiality of records.
Tit. 42, §6152.	Subpoena of records.
Tit. 42, §6153.	Receipts.
Tit. 42, §6154.	Affidavit of none or partial possession.
Tit. 42, §6155.	Rights of patients.
Tit. 42, §6156.	Opening of sealed envelopes.
Tit. 42, §6157.	Retention of records.

§44–115–40.   Physician not to release records without express
               written consent.
§44–115–50.   Physician may rely on representations of insurance
               carrier or administrator as to patient authorization
               to release records; immunity from liability and
               disciplinary action.
§44–115–140.   Immunity from civil, criminal, and disciplinary
               liability for compliance with request to release
               information.

SOUTH DAKOTA: *South Dakota Codified Laws*
§19–2–3.   Physician-patient privilege deemed waived when
               health of person an issue.
§19–13–7.   Patient's privilege on confidential communication
[Rule 503][b].   with physician or psychotherapists.
§34–12–15.   Inmate records and statistics required of institutions,
               copy to patient on request, reproduction codes, no
               liability for compliance.
§36–4–26.   Hospital and society liability not affected by
               immunity.
§36–4–26.1.   Proceedings of professional committees confidential
               and privileged, availability to physician subject of
               proceedings.
§44–12–7.   Notice of hospital lien, copy mailed to insurance
               carrier by hospital, disclosure of name of carrier.
§44–12–8.   Persons liable for payment of hospital lien.
§44–12–9.   Examination of hospital records by persons liable
               for lien.

TENNESSEE: *Tennessee Code Annotated*
§33–3–104.   Rights of patients or residents.
§63–6–219.   Legislative policy declaration—Medical review
               committees—Immunity of members—
               Confidentiality of records—Short title.
§68–11–218.   Disciplinary action reports.
§68–11–219.   Payment to health care agency of assigned insurance
               benefits, insurer's duty to request information.
§68–11–301.   Medical records act.
§68–11–302.   Medical records act, definitions.
§68–11–303.   Hospital's duty to keep records.
§68–11–304.   Records property of hospitals, access, not public
               records.
§68–11–305.   Preservation of records for specified time, method of
               destruction.
§68–11–306.   Abstract prepared where required, photographic
               reproductions, reproduction considered original
               record.
§68–11–307.   Continued storage of records.
§68–11–308.   Records of closed hospitals retained.
§68–11–309.   Retirement of hospital business records.

Appendix B _____

Discoverability and Admissibility of Medical Staff Committee Records

This State-by-State Analysis consists of a listing of the applicable statutes and important cases dealing with the discoverability and admissibility of medical staff committee records in each state. The list of cases for each state is not exhaustive, and additional citations may be encountered in legal research. The State-by-State Analysis does not constitute an exhaustive treatment of statutory protection in each state.

ALABAMA

Statutory Provisions

Ala. Code § 34-24-58.

The decisions, opinions, actions, and proceedings of utilization review committees or committees of similar nature or purpose are privileged if they are rendered, entered, or acted on in good faith and without malice and on the basis of facts reasonably known or reasonably believed to exist.

ALASKA

Statutory Provisions

Alaska Stat. §§ 18.23.030 and 18.23.070.

All data and information acquired by a review organization in the exercise of its duties shall be held in confidence and shall not be disclosed to anyone except to the extent necessary to carry out the purposes of the review committee. Such data and information are not subject to subpoena or discovery. Records and proceedings of review organizations are not subject to discovery or introduction into evidence in civil actions against health care providers arising out of matters that are the subject of evaluation and review. However, information that is otherwise available from original sources is not immune from discovery and introduction into evidence simply because it was presented to a review committee. In addition, a person whose conduct or compe-tence has been reviewed by a committee may obtain information for purposes of appellate review of the committee's action. Similarly, discovery proceedings may be brought by a plaintiff who claims that (1) information provided to a review organization was false and (2) the person providing the information knew or had reason to know it was false.

ARIZONA

Statutory Provisions

Ariz. Rev. Stat. Ann. §§ 36-445, 36-445.01, 36-2403, and 36-2917.

All proceedings, records, and materials prepared in connection with committees that review the nature, quality, and necessity of care provided in a hospital and the preventability of complications and deaths occurring in a hospital, including all peer reviews of individual health care providers practicing in and applying to practice in hospitals, and the records of such reviews, are confidential and not subject to discovery. Discovery is allowable in proceedings before the board of medical or osteopathic examiners, or in an action by an individual health care provider against a hospital or its staff arising from discipline of that health care provider or refusal, termination, suspension, or limitation of that individual's privileges, or in proceedings initiated by state licensing or certification agencies.

Selected Cases

Tucson Medical Ctr., Inc. v. Misevch, 545 P.2d 958 (Ariz. 1976). Statement and information considered by a medical review committee are subject to subpoena, but reports and minutes of the committee are not.

Samaritan Health Serv. v. City of Glendale, 714 P.2d 887 (Ariz. Ct. App. 1986). Arizona hospitals have no duty to assert the physician-patient privilege when served with a search warrant for patients' medical records.

John C. Lincoln Hosp. and Health Ctr. v. Superior Court of County of Maricopa, 768 P.2d 188 (Ariz. Ct. App. 1989). Minutes of a hospital's trauma critical care committee were protected under the state peer review statute because they concerned operating room communications. A Quality Assurance Program Incident Report was discoverable, however, because it did not constitute discussion, exchange, opinions, or proceedings relating to reviews but contained only factual data.

ARKANSAS

Statutory Provisions

Ark. Code Ann. §§ 20-9-304 and 20-9-503.

All information, interviews, reports, statements, memoranda, and other data used by hospital staff committees and other committees in the course of medical studies, the purpose of which is to reduce morbidity and mortality, and any other findings or conclusions resulting from such studies, are privileged and may not be received in evidence in any legal proceeding. This statute does not apply to original medical records pertaining to patients.

The proceedings and records of peer review committees are not subject to discovery and are inadmissible in any civil action against a provider of health services arising out of matters that are the subject of evaluation and review. However, documents, information, and records that are otherwise available from original sources are not protected simply because they were presented during committee proceedings.

Selected Cases

Baxter County Newspapers v. Medical Staff of Baxter Gen. Hosp., 622 S.W.2d 495 (Ark. 1981). The state Freedom of Information Act (FOIA) was held to permit public access to medical review committee proceedings because such proceedings were not expressly exempted from the FOIA.

Hendrickson v. Leipzig, 715 F. Supp. 1443 (E.D. Ark. 1989). Peer review legislation prohibits disclosure of information regarding a hospital's revocation of a physician's medical staff privileges that a hospital provided to the state medical board. The information cannot be discovered in a patient's malpractice suit.

CALIFORNIA

Statutory Provisions

Cal. Evid. Code § 1157.

The proceedings and records of organized medical staff committees, the function of which is to evaluate and improve the quality of care rendered in a hospital, are not subject to discovery. In addition, no person in attendance at a committee meeting can be required to testify as to what occurred there. The prohibition relating to discovery, however, does not apply to statements made by a person who attended such a committee meeting and who is a party to an action or proceeding, the subject of which was reviewed at the meeting, or to any person requesting staff privileges. Other exceptions are noted.

Selected Cases

Matchett v. Superior Court for County of Yuba, 115 Cal. Rptr. 317 (Ct. App. 1974). Reports of various medical staff committees are immune from discovery in a malpractice suit, but records of hospital management administration are discoverable.

Schulz v. Superior Court, 136 Cal. Rptr. 67 (Ct. App. 1977). Discovery of reports of the hospital's medical advisory board was denied in a malpractice action.

Roseville Community Hosp. v. Superior Court, 139 Cal. Rptr. 170 (Ct. App. 1977). Statements by individuals at a committee meeting of the hospital's medical staff are discoverable by persons whose requests for hospital staff privileges were denied.

Henry Mayo Newhall Memorial Hosp. v. Superior Court, 146 Cal. Rptr. 542 (Ct. App. 1978). A hospital's filing of the transcript of a staff committee hearing in an unrelated administrative mandamus action does not constitute a waiver of immunity from discovery under § 1157 of the California Evidence Code.

County of Kern v. Superior Court, 147 Cal. Rptr. 248 (Ct. App. 1978). The court found the trial court's order granting a discovery motion in a malpractice action to be overbroad and violative of § 1157 of the California Evidence Code.

West Covina Hosp. v. Superior Court, 200 Cal. Rptr. 162 (Ct. App. 1984). The records and proceedings of a hospital committee are nondiscoverable, even if the physician who provided the care in question was a member of the committee when it was reviewing that individual's conduct.

West Covina Hosp. v. Superior Court, 226 Cal. Rptr. 132 (Cal. 1986). A committee member may testify voluntarily in court about the proceedings of a hospital medical staff committee meeting, but may not be required or compelled to do so.

Mt. Diablo Hosp. Medical Ctr. v. Superior Court, 204 Cal. Rptr. 626 (Ct. App. 1984). The records or proceedings of a hospital committee are nondiscoverable even if needed to hold a hospital accountable for the competency of its medical staff.

Saddleback Community Hosp. v. Superior Court, 204 Cal. Rptr. 598 (Ct. App. 1984). Hospital administration records are discoverable to the extent that they do not contain references to nondiscoverable medical staff committee proceedings. Private court review of requested records is necessary to protect immune information from discovery.

Snell v. Superior Court, 204 Cal. Rptr. 200 (Ct. App. 1984). Physician personnel records maintained by a hospital medical review committee are immune from discovery because they are not hospital administration records but are the nondiscoverable records of an organized medical staff committee.

Brown v. Superior Court, 214 Cal. Rptr. 266 (Ct. App. 1985). Whether a hospital, in fact, screened the competence of a staff physician is discoverable in a malpractice action, although the information contained in that evaluation is protected from disclosure.

Santa Rosa Memorial Hosp. v. Superior Court, 220 Cal, Rptr. 236 (Ct. App. 1986). Information concerning whether a patient's treatment was reviewed by an infection control committee is immune from discovery if the hospital can show that such review would not be undertaken as a matter of course, because disclosure would indicate a suspicion of dereliction. An infection control committee is considered a medical staff committee for the purposes of the state peer review confidentiality law, notwithstanding that the committee is composed of a majority of personnel who are not physicians or medical staff members. Information obtained by hospital administrators that does not derive from a medical staff committee investigation or evaluation is not rendered immune from discovery merely because it later is made known to or placed in the possession of a medical staff committee.

Mt. Diablo Hosp. Dist. v. Superior Court, 227 Cal. Rptr. 790 (Ct. App. 1986). The minutes of a hospital peer review committee are nondiscoverable even if they pertain to the evaluation and adoption of standards for new treatments and drug care and not to the evaluation of the past performance of physicians.

California Eye Inst. v. Superior Court of Fresno County, 264 Cal. Rptr. 83 (Ct. App. 1989). A physician who sued a medical center, alleging that it had wrongfully interfered with his medical staff privileges, could not discover records relating to the restriction of his privileges. Under California law, hospital committee records are immune from discovery, except for a person who is requesting staff privileges. At the time of the suit, the center had reinstated the physician's privileges and he therefore was not entitled to the records.

Teasdale v. Marin Gen. Hosp., 138 F.R.D. 696 (N.D. Cal. 1991). A physician who brought an antitrust suit attacking the rescission of hospital surgical privileges was entitled to discover information in the credential files of the physicians he was suing. The peer review committee's decisions with respect to other physicians who allegedly participated in the conspiracy could be the most important evidence in the suit.

People v. Superior Court of Cal. for Los Angeles, 286, Cal. Rptr. 478 (Ct. App. 1991). State legislation granting immunity from discovery to the proceedings of hospital peer review bodies does not provide immunity against discovery in proceedings against a physician for criminal negligence.

Cedars-Sinai Medical Ctr. v. Superior Court, 16 Cal. Rptr. 2d 253 (Ct. App. 1993). State peer review legislation protects the identities of peer review committee members from discovery.

COLORADO

Statutory Provisions

Colo. Rev. Stat. §§ 12-36.5-104 and 25-3-109.

The records of professional review committees, utilization review committees, quality control committees, peer review organizations, and governing boards are not subject to a subpoena or discovery and may not be introduced into evidence in a civil suit against the physician who is the subject of the records. A separate statute for hospitals states that records, reports, and other information that is part of a quality management program designed to reduce risk of patient injury or improve the quality of patient care are confidential. This information is not subject to subpoena and is not admissible in any civil or administrative proceeding. Individuals who collected or used the quality management information may not testify regarding the information unless they have independent knowledge of the information, or if other exceptions apply.

Selected Cases

Posey v. District Court, 586 P.2d 36 (Colo. 1978). Section 12-43.5-102 of the Colorado Revised Statutes is applicable to civil suits against hospitals as well as physicians.

Davidson v. Light, 79 F.R.D. 137 (D. Colo. 1978). Section 12-43.5-102 is designed to confer immunity on professional review committees, not on hospital infection control committees.

Franco v. District Court, 641 P.2d 922 (Colo. 1982). Records of peer review committees are not discoverable by a physician who seeks to compel a hospital to restore his surgical privileges.

Beth Israel Hosp. & Geriatric Ctr. v. District Court, 683 P.2d 343 (Colo. 1984). A physician seeking to compel the restoration of his surgical privileges may discover his patient's records even though they were reviewed by a hospital surgical committee. The records did not become immune from discovery as "records of a review committee" merely because the committee used them in its deliberations.

CONNECTICUT

Statutory Provisions

Conn. Gen. Stat. § 19a-17b.

Proceedings of peer review, utilization review, medical audit, and similar committees are not subject to discovery and are not admissible into evidence in any civil action arising out of matters that are the subject of committee evaluation and review, subject to four exceptions: (1) writings recorded independently of such proceedings, (2) testimony of any person concerning facts acquired through personal knowledge and independently of such proceedings, (3) use in any health care provider proceedings concerning the termination or restriction of staff privileges other than peer review, and (4) disclosure in any civil action of the fact that staff privileges were terminated.

Selected Cases

Morse v. Gerity, 520 F. Supp. 470 (D. Conn. 1981). Peer review documents are nondiscoverable regardless of whether they pertain to the subject matter of a lawsuit.

Connecticut Comm'r. of Health Serv. v. William W. Backus Hosp., 485 A.2d 937 (Conn. Super. Ct. 1984). Hospital peer review records may be discovered by the State Medical Examining Board when investigating physician medical misconduct because such investigations are not considered civil actions in which the records would be statutorily privileged.

DELAWARE

Statutory Provisions

Del. Code Ann. tit. 24, § 1768.

Records and proceedings of hospital and nursing home quality review committees are confidential, to be used only in the exercise of proper committee functions, are not public records, and are not available for court subpoena or subject to discovery.

Selected Cases

Register v. Wilmington Medical Ctr., Inc., 377 A.2d 8 (Del. 1977). Staff reports concerning performance of a resident physician are discoverable in a malpractice action.

Robinson v. LeRoy, No. 84-121 (D. Del. Nov. 16, 1984). Records of hospital committees that consider applications for staff privileges are not discoverable in a malpractice action because Delaware's peer review records confidentiality statute extends to the records and proceedings of such committees.

Dworkin v. St. Francis Hosp., Inc., 517 A.2d 302 (Del. Super. Ct. 1986). Peer review committee records pertaining to the termination of a physician's privileges in violation of hospital bylaws are discoverable by the physician because the statutory peer review privilege does not protect improper peer review activities.

DISTRICT OF COLUMBIA

Statutory Provisions

D.C. Code Ann. § 32-505.

Absent a showing of extraordinary necessity, the files, records, findings, opinions, recommendations, evaluations, and reports of a peer review committee are not subject to discovery or admissible into evidence in any civil or administrative proceeding, except for the limited purpose of adjudicating the appropriateness of any adverse action affecting a health professional's employment, membership, or association. This privilege does not extend to primary health records or to any oral or written statements submitted to or presented before a committee.

Selected Cases

Laws v. Georgetown Univ. Hosp., 656 F. Supp. 824 (D.D.C. 1987). A letter sent by a physician to the chair of the Anesthesia Department to explain complications a patient suffered during a Caesarean delivery is not subject to discovery in an ensuing medical malpractice suit because her letter was written to provide information at a medical staff meeting to review the incident.

Spinks v. Children's Hosp. Nat'l Medical Ctr., 124 F.D.R. 9 (D.D.C. 1989). District of Columbia law establishes privilege for hospital committee records unless an extraordinary necessity to obtain access to these records is demonstrated. A patient failed to demonstrate an extraordinary need to access the minutes from a Morbidity and Mortality Committee meeting by arguing that she was anesthetized when the injury occurred, that the only witnesses to the event were hospital employees, and that the information was relevant to her suit. In addition, the federal trial court ruled that while the handwritten notes that a physician relied on making his submission to the committee were not protected from discovery under the statute, a privilege nonetheless applies because disclosure would undermine the effectiveness of hospital committees and be contrary to the public interest.

Jackson v. Scott, C.A. No. 9954-89 (D.C. 1991). The peer review records of a physician, who was sued for malpractice ten years after the investigation were discoverable although the hospital had entered into a settlement with the physician to remove certain documents from his file.

FLORIDA

Statutory Provisions

Fla. Stat. ch. § 766.101.

The proceedings, investigations, and records of medical staff, peer review, and medical review committees are not subject to discovery or admissible into evidence in any civil action against a health care provider arising out of matters that are the subject of committee evaluation and review. However, material otherwise available from original sources is not immune from discovery or use in civil actions.

Selected Cases

Carter v. Metropolitan Dade County, 253 So. 2d 920 (Fla. 1971). Minutes of a hospital teaching session are inadmissible.

Good Samaritan Hosp. Ass'n v. Simon, 370 So. 2d 1174 (Fla. 1979). Discovery is allowed where plaintiff physician alleges that the medical review committee acted fraudulently and maliciously in denying him staff privileges.

Dade County Medical Ass'n v. Hlis, 372 So. 2d 117 (Fla. 1979). Discovery of ethics committee records in a context different from the civil action against a health care provider is prohibited on public policy grounds.

Segal v. Roberts, 380 So. 2d 1049 (Fla. 1979). Section 768.40 of the Florida statute is not applicable where the subject matter of the lawsuit is different from the subject considered by the medical review committee, but discovery of the committee's records is prohibited nevertheless on public policy grounds [Section 768.40 has been recodified at Fla. Stat. ch. 766.101].

Gadd v. News-Press Publishing Co., 412 So. 2d 894 (Fla. Dist. Ct. App. 1982). Minutes and documents of a public hospital's utilization review committee are subject to public inspection under the Florida Public Records Act because no specific exemption or confidentiality requirement for such files is provided by statute.

City of Williston v. Roadlander, 425 So. 2d 1175 (Fla. Dist. Ct. App. 1983). Florida's medical staff committee records confidentiality statute may not be circumvented by claiming that in a public hospital, medical review committee records are public records.

Holly v. Auld, 450 So. 2d 217 (Fla. 1984). Physician-applicant for staff privileges was not entitled to discover credential committee records to prove his allegations that he had been defamed. Florida's peer review records confidentiality statute is not limited to malpractice actions, but applies as well to defamation actions arising out of matters that are the subject of evaluation and review.

Palm Beach Gardens Community Hosp. v. Shaw, 446 So. 2d 1090 (Fla. Dist. Ct. App. 1984). Monthly reports of a hospital's infectious disease control committee are immune from discovery in a medical malpractice suit because Florida law provides a privilege from discovery for the records of a medical review committee.

Mercy Hosp. v. Department of Professional Regulation, Bd. of Medical Examiners, 467 So. 2d 1058 (Fla. Dist. Ct. App. 1985). Peer review committee reports and records may be obtained by the state Department of Professional Regulation (DPR) in connection with a disciplinary investigation. Florida's peer review record confidentiality law shields records from discovery only in a civil action, and a DPR investigation is an administrative disciplinary investigation to which the statute does not apply.

Suwannee County Hosp. Corp. v. Meeks, 472 So. 2d 1305 (Fla. Dist. Ct. App. 1985). The proceedings and records of a medical staff committee are not subject to discovery even if no peer review was conducted at a committee meeting. Florida law broadly protects from discovery the records of committees "formed to evaluate and improve the quality of health care rendered."

Davis v. Sarasota County Pub. Hosp. Bd., 480 So. 2d 203 (Fla. Dist. Ct. App. 1985). A public hospital's bills incurred for legal services rendered during peer review proceedings are exempt from discovery.

Burton v. Becker, 516 So. 2d 283 (Fla. Dist. Ct. App. 1987). A patient suing a physician for medical malpractice may not discover a hospital's peer review records relating to the physician, even when the information is essential to the patient's case.

Ruiz v. Steiner, 599 So. 2d 196 (Fla. Dist. Ct. App. 1992). An informal meeting of physicians to discuss a pathologist's autopsy report is not a peer review proceeding.

Cruger v. Love, 599 So. 2d 111 (Fla. 1992). The peer review confidentiality statute protects any document considered by the committee as part of its decision-making process. In this medical malpractice suit against a physician, the court accordingly concluded that the physician's application for staff privileges was protected from discovery.

GEORGIA

Statutory Provisions

Ga. Code Ann. §§ 31-7-131 through 31-7-133 and 31-7-143.

Records and proceedings of any panel, committee, or organization, the function of which is to evaluate and improve the quality of health care rendered by health care providers or reduce morbidity or mortality, are not subject to discovery or introduction into evidence against a provider of professional health care services arising out of matters that are the subject of evaluation and review, except in proceedings alleging violation of the peer review act itself. Review organizations include groups that furnish health care providers with professional liability insurance, thereby extending confidentiality to reviews conducted to evaluate claims against health care providers or to make underwriting decisions concerning health care liability insurance coverage. Peer review organizations also include the Joint Commission on Accreditation of Healthcare Organizations and other national accreditation bodies. However, information, documents, and records otherwise available from original sources are not immune from discovery or use in civil actions simply because they were presented to a committee.

Selected Cases

Hollowell v. Jove, 279 S.E.2d 430 (Ga. 1981). Medical review committee records concerning a physician's care of a particular patient, that physician's care of other patients, and even a listing of the persons who were present at those review meetings are totally exempt from discovery in Georgia.

Emory Clinic v. Houston, 396 S.E.2d 913 (Ga. 1988). The state peer review statute imposes an absolute bar on the use of all peer records in civil litigation. Prior newspaper reports containing information about a peer review committee's activities do not alter the prohibition on discovery.

HAWAII

Statutory Provisions

Hawaii Rev. Stat. § 624-25.5.

Proceedings and records of peer review committees of hospitals are not subject to discovery. However, this prohibition does not apply to the statements made by any person in attendance at a committee meeting who is a party to an action or proceeding, the subject of which was reviewed at such meeting, or to any person who has requested hospital staff privileges. Other exceptions are noted.

IDAHO

Statutory Provisions

Idaho Code §§ 39-1392 through 39-1392(d).

Written records of interviews, reports, statements, minutes, memoranda, charts, and materials of any hospital medical staff committee, the function of which is to conduct research concerning hospital patient cases or medical questions or problems arising from hospital patient cases, are neither discoverable nor admissible. This section does not affect or prohibit the use of documents in hospital proceedings, the dissemination of information for medical purposes, or the admissibility of any original patient records. Other exceptions are noted.

Selected Case

Murphy v. Wood, 667 P.2d 859 (Idaho Ct. App. 1983). The treatment recommendation of a hospital tumor board could not be admitted into evidence by physicians defending against a medical malpractice suit because Idaho law prevents disclosure of medical staff committee proceedings.

ILLINOIS

Statutory Provisions

735 Ill. Comp. Stat. Ann §§ 5/82101 and -2102.

Information, interviews, reports, statements, or other data of patient care audit, medical care evaluation, utilization review, and similar committees of hospitals or medical staffs are strictly confidential and are not admissible. However, the claim of confidentiality cannot be invoked in any hospital proceeding concerning a physician's staff privileges or in a judicial review of such a proceeding to prevent the physician from accessing the data on which the decision was based.

Selected Cases

Matviuw v. Johnson, 388 N.E.2d 795 (Ill. App. Ct. 1979). Plaintiff physician is permitted to discover and use medical staff committee data in a defamation action.

Walker v. Alton Memorial Hosp. Ass'n, 414 N.E.2d 850 (Ill. App. Ct. 1980). The hospital was ordered to submit peer review records to a judge for private examination to determine whether the material was inadmissible at trial.

Mennes v. South Chicago Community Hosp., 427 N.E.2d 952 (Ill. App. Ct. 1981). Private judicial examination of peer review committee material relating to the granting of physicians' privileges or reappointment is not necessary because such information is nondiscoverable, regardless of the content of such material.

Jenkins v. Wu, 468 N.E.2d 1162 (Ill. 1984). Constitutionality of state peer review records confidentiality statute reinstated after trial court erroneously declared law invalid. Such records are not discoverable or admissible in medical malpractice actions; exception for physicians defending their staff privileges is rationally related to state's interest in safeguarding the physicians' right to due process.

Gleason v. St. Elizabeth Medical Ctr., 481 N.E.2d 780 (Ill. App. Ct. 1985). Remedial actions taken by a hospital pursuant to peer review of a staff physician are not shielded from discovery. Only the peer review process itself is nondiscoverable.

Richter v. Diamond, 483 N.E.2d 1256 (Ill. 1985). Information concerning whether a physician's hospital staff privileges were restricted, as well as the specific restrictions imposed, may be discovered from a hospital by a patient suing for malpractice because such information is outside the scope of the state peer review confidentiality law.

Flannery v. Lin, 531 N.E.2d 403 (Ill. App. Ct. 1988). The peer review privilege was applied to protect a "Code Blue Evaluation Report" under the Medical Studies Act. The report was used for internal quality control and was not part of the patient's medical record. It had been prepared by the director of quality management, reviewed by a hospital committee, and its recommendations had been implemented by the hospital's medical officer.

Willing v. St. Joseph Hosp., 531 N.E.2d 824 (Ill. App. Ct. 1988). Records relating to a physician's application for staff privileges and to the granting or modifying of such privileges are not shielded from disclosure in medical malpractice actions under the Medical Studies Act.

Ekstrom v. Temple, 553 N.E. 2d 424 (Ill. App. Ct. 1990). A hospital's records relating to infection control were discoverable in a medical malpractice suit against the facility although documents reflecting investigations and deliberations of committees that monitor infection control were not discoverable under the Medical Studies Act. The hospital failed to provide any evidence regarding the nature and content of the documents and the court refused to apply the privilege to all the materials based on the claim that some of the materials might be privileged.

INDIANA

Statutory Provisions

Ind. Code Ann. §§ 34-4-12.6-1 and 34-4-12.6-2.

Records of the determinations of or communications to a peer review committee are not subject to discovery or admissible into evidence. Information otherwise discoverable or admissible from original sources is not immune from discovery or use simply because it was presented during committee meetings. In addition, any professional health care provider who is under investigation has the right to see any records pertaining to his or her personal practice. Other exceptions are noted.

Selected Cases

Parkview Memorial Hosp. v. Pepple, 483 N.E.2d 469 (Ind. Ct. App. 1985). Indiana's peer review confidentiality law applies not only to medical malpractice cases, but also to civil actions brought by physicians challenging private hospitals' decisions concerning staff privileges. A physician seeking judicial review of a private hospital's adverse recommendation concerning recredentialing was therefore prohibited from introducing evidence relating to the hospital's peer review committee proceedings.

Terre Haute Regional Hosp., Inc. v. Basden, 524 N.E.2d 1306 (Ind. Ct. App. 1988). Although peer review committee members are immune from liability only if they act in good faith, peer review information that is protected from disclosure does not become subject to disclosure due to lack of good faith on the part of the committee members.

Ray v. St. John's Health Care Corp., 582 N.E.2d 464 (Ind. Ct. App. 1991). A trial court should have conducted an in camera review of documents sought by physicians in a suit against a hospital to determine whether the peer review privilege applied. The hospital's labels for these documents and the chief executive officer's statements that they were privileged were not decisive.

IOWA

Statutory Provisions

Iowa Code Ann. § 147.135.

Peer review records are privileged and confidential; are not subject to discovery, subpoena, or other means of legal compulsion; and are not admissible in evidence in judicial or administrative proceedings, except when a licensee's competence or disciplinary status is at issue. A person shall not be liable as a result of filing a report with or providing information to a peer review committee or for disclosure of privileged matter to a peer review committee. A person present at a peer review committee meeting shall not be permitted to testify as to the findings or opinions of the committee in any judicial or administrative proceeding.

Selected Cases

Boger v. Lee, No. 49568 (D. Iowa, June 16, 1982). Information produced by the activities of a professional standards review organization or a hospital performing the function of a PSRO is not subject to subpoena or discovery in a civil action except to the extent that the hospital contemplates using the information at trial.

Hutchison v. Smith Lab. Inc., 392 N.W.2d 139 (Iowa 1986). The records of a medical staff peer review committee and evaluation reports of a drug-injection procedure performed on a patient are discoverable and not entitled to a privilege based on common law or public policy.

KANSAS

Statutory Provisions

Kan. Stat. Ann. § 65-4915.

Proceedings and records of peer review committees and officers are privileged and are not discoverable or admissible in evidence in any judicial or administrative proceeding. This privilege does not apply to proceedings in which a health care provider contests the denial or status of staff privileges or authorization to practice.

Selected Cases

Wesley Medical Ctr. v. Clark, 669 P.2d 209 (Kan. 1983). The records of medical peer review committee proceedings may be discovered in a medical malpractice action because no statutory privilege for such records exists in the Kansas evidence code. However, a court may limit disclosure if it determines that a hospital's interest in confidentiality outweighs the need for the evidence.

Fretz v. Keltner, 109 F.R.D. 303 (D. Kan. 1986). The Joint Commission functions as a peer review committee and therefore its accreditation documents are not discoverable.

Porter v. Snyder, 115 F.R.D. 77 (D. Kan. 1987). Kansas peer review legislation, protecting the reports of executive or review committees, does not protect hospital incident reports from discovery in a patient's malpractice suit. Incident reports are not reports made by a review committee, but rather are contemporaneous statements of fact relating to incidents that are reviewed by a committee.

Jiricko v. Coffeyville Memorial Hosp. Medical Ctr., 700 F. Supp. 1559 (D. Kan. 1988). Peer review activities in Kansas are not immune from scrutiny under federal antitrust law because the state does not actively supervise peer review decisions. When both state and federal antitrust claims are made, the question of privilege is controlled by federal law, rather than the state peer review statute. Peer review privilege will not be recognized when there is a claim that the peer review process was abused as part of the antitrust conspiracy, because to deny discovery in such circumstances would effectively prevent the physician from suing.

Hill v. Sandu, No. 89-1338-C (D. Kan. Jan. 24, 1990). A patient suing a physician for medical malpractice is entitled to discover documents submitted to a peer review committee relating to the physician's being granted staff privileges. The documents concerned the hospital's awarding of staff privileges to the physician and were not privileged simply because the committee had referred to them when reviewing the physician.

Herbstreith v. Baker, 815 P.2d 102 (Kan. 1991). Peer review records were not admissible in a medical malpractice case against a physician in which there were allegations relating to the physician's qualifications.

KENTUCKY

Statutory Provisions

Ky. Rev. Stat. § 311.377.

The proceedings, records, opinions, conclusions, and recommendations of any committee, board, commission, PSRO, or other entity, the purpose of which is to review and evaluate the credentials or competency of professional acts or conduct of other health care personnel, are confidential and privileged; they are not subject to discovery, subpoena, or introduction into evidence in any civil action, court, or administrative proceeding. This statute does not protect materials that are independently discoverable or admissible, nor does it restrict or prevent the presentation of records and other materials in any statutory or administrative proceeding relating to the functions of any committee or other review body. Other exceptions are noted.

Selected Case

Sweasy v. King's Daughters Memorial Hosp., 771 S.W.2d 812 (Ky. 1989). The supreme court in this state has ruled that peer review records created by hospital peer review committees are confidential only in suits against peer review entities and can be discovered in medical malpractice suits.

LOUISIANA

Statutory Provisions

La. Rev. Stat. Ann. §§ 44:7 and 13:3715.3.

The records and proceedings of public and private hospital committees, medical organization committees, or extended care facilities are not public records and are not available for court subpoena. The peer review committee records of group medical practices of more than 20 physicians, free-standing surgical centers, and health maintenance organizations are confidential and are not available for discovery in litigation except for proceedings relating to a physician's staff privileges. In such proceedings, only the physician or other health care professional who is the object of an adverse decision with respect to staff privileges may obtain the records.

A medical staff member whose privileges are affected adversely by a decision of any hospital committee, medical organization committee, or extended care facility committee may obtain the records forming the basis of the decision, notwithstanding the confidentiality provisions of § 44:7.

Selected Case

Kadan v. City of New Orleans, 596 So. 2d 1306 (La. 1992). Hospital peer review records are confidential under state law and not subject to subpoena or discovery in court cases.

MAINE

Statutory Provisions

Me. Rev. Stat. tit. 32, §§ 3296 and 92-A.

All proceedings and records of proceedings of mandatory medical staff review committees and hospital review committees are exempt from discovery. All records of proceedings concerning quality assurance activities of any emergency medical service quality assurance committee are exempt from discovery.

MARYLAND

Statutory Provisions

Md. Code Ann., [Health Occ.] § 14-501.

The proceedings, records, and files of a medical review committee are neither discoverable nor admissible into evidence in any civil action arising out of matters that are the subject of committee evaluation and review. A medical review committee is a committee of the medical staff or other committee, including any risk management, credentialing, or utilization review committee, of a hospital if the governing board forms and approves the committee or approves the written bylaws under which the committee operates.

Selected Cases

Unnamed Physician v. Commission on Medical Discipline, 400 A.2d 396 (Md. 1979). The proceedings, records, and other documents of medical staff committees are discoverable in physician disciplinary proceedings but not in civil suits.

Kappas v. Chestnut Lodge, 709 F.2d 878 (4th Cir. 1983), *cert. denied*, 104 S. Ct. 164 (1983). Transcripts of a psychiatric hospital's medical staff conferences that evaluated patient care and treatment were not admissible because they qualified as reports of "medical review committee" proceedings.

Baltimore Sun v. University of Md. Medical Ctr., 584 A.2d 683 (Md. 1991). Peer review confidentiality legislation does not prevent the press from accessing records that were introduced as evidence in a physician's staff privileges suit against the hospital.

MASSACHUSETTS

Statutory Provisions

Mass. Ann. Laws ch. 11, §§ 204(a) and 205(b).

Records that are necessary to comply with risk management and quality assurance programs and that are necessary to the work product of medical peer review committees, including incident reports required to be furnished to the board of medicine, are proceedings, reports, or records of medical peer review committees. Such records are confidential and are not subject to disclosure unless they have been disclosed in an adjudicatory proceeding of the board of medicine. No person shall be prevented from testifying as to matters known by such person independent of risk management and quality assurance programs. Reports and records of a medical peer review committee are confidential and are not discoverable or admissible in any judicial or administrative proceeding, except proceedings by the boards of registration in medicine, social work, or psychology.

Selected Case

Commonwealth v. Choate-Symmes Health Serv., Inc., 545 N.E.2d 1167 (Mass. 1989). The Massachusetts Board of Registration in Medicine does not have a right of access to peer review committee records when it is investigating a complaint concerning a physician's conduct. State legislation grants the Board access to these documents only within its administrative proceedings.

MICHIGAN

Statutory Provisions

Mich. Comp. Laws § 333.21075 and 333.21515.
The records, data, and knowledge collected for or by individuals or committees assigned a professional review function in a health facility or agency are confidential, shall be used only for the purposes that are legislatively authorized, are not public records, and are not subject to court subpoena.

Selected Cases

Marchand v. Henry Ford Hosp., 247 N.W.2d 280 (Mich. 1976). Information collected by individuals other than those sitting as a professional practices review committee is discoverable.

Monty v. Warren Hosp. Corp., 366 N.W.2d 198 (Mich. 1985). Hospital personnel files of staff physicians must be produced for a private, in camera court inspection when sought for discovery in a malpractice action. The court must determine whether the information therein is privileged under the state peer review record confidentiality law or whether the information may be discovered.

In re Petition of Attorney Gen., 369 N.W.2d 826 (Mich. 1985). A hospital cannot be required to disclose peer review committee records, data, and knowledge collected during a disciplinary investigation, notwithstanding that the information is sought in connection with an investigation by the state Department of Licensing and Regulation.

MINNESOTA

Statutory Provisions

Minn. Stat. §§ 145.61 through 145.65.
Data and information of quality assurance, mortality and morbidity, cost control, and similar committees are not subject to subpoena or discovery. The proceedings and records of these committees are not subject to discovery or introduction into evidence in any civil action against a health care professional arising out of matters that are the subject of evaluation and review. However, documents or records otherwise available from original sources are not immune simply because they were presented during the proceedings of a review organization. This statute does not apply to committees that function to grant or deny staff privileges.

Selected Cases

Kalish v. Mt. Sinai Hosp., 270 N.W.2d 783 (Minn. 1978). Guidelines of a hospital medical staff committee are discoverable but not admissible.

In re Proposed Suspension or Nonrenewal of Nursing Home Licenses of Parkway Manor Healthcare Ctr. and Innsbruck Healthcare Ctr., 448 N.W.2d 116 (Minn. Ct.

App. 1989). The court rejected claims that a nursing center's quality assurance records were privileged, finding that the quality assurance program was not a review organization within the meaning of the statute.

MISSISSIPPI

Statutory Provisions

Miss. Code Ann. § 41-63-9.
The proceedings and records of medical review committees are not subject to discovery or introduction into evidence in any civil action against a health care provider arising out of matters that are the subject of evaluation and review. However, information, documents, and records that are otherwise discoverable from original sources are not immune from discovery merely because they were presented to a committee. This statute does not apply to legal actions brought by a committee to restrict or revoke a physician's license or privileges, or in any action brought against a committee or its members for actions alleged to be malicious.

MISSOURI

Statutory Provisions

Mo. Ann. Stat. § 537.035.
The proceedings, findings, deliberations, reports, and minutes of peer review committees are not discoverable or admissible in any judicial or administrative action for failure to provide appropriate care. No person at any peer review committee proceeding may be permitted or required to disclose any information obtained. However, information otherwise discoverable from original sources is not immune from discovery merely because it was presented to a committee. This statute does not apply to legal actions brought by a committee to deny, restrict, or revoke a physician's privileges or license to practice. Further, the state health care licensing board may obtain confidential information from peer review committees within its jurisdiction.

Selected Case

State ex rel. Faith Hosp. v. Enright, 706 S.W.2d 852 (Mo. 1986). Even though a credentials committee is a peer review committee, its findings and deliberations are not exempt from discovery unless they specifically concern the health care provided to a patient.

MONTANA

Statutory Provisions

Mont. Code Ann. §§ 50-16-201, 50-16-203 through 50-16-205.
Data (written reports, notes, and records) of tissue committees and committees that function to assist in the training, supervision, and discipline of health care professionals are confidential and are not admissible in evidence in any judicial proceeding. This

statute does not affect the admissibility of records dealing with a patient's hospital care and treatment.

Selected Case

Sistok v. Kalispell Regional Hosp., 823 P.2d 251 (Mont. 1991). Records of a medical executive committee are absolutely privileged and are not discoverable in a medical malpractice suit by a patient alleging that the hospital negligently allowed him to perform surgery knowing he had a history of alcoholism.

NEBRASKA

Statutory Provisions

Neb. Rev. Stat. § 71-2046 and 71-2048.

The proceedings, records, minutes, reports, and communications of medical staff committees and utilization review committees are not subject to discovery except upon court order after a showing of good cause arising from extraordinary circumstances and waiver by the patient. This statute does not preclude or affect discovery of or production of evidence relating to the hospitalization or treatment of any patient in the ordinary course of hospitalization of such patient.

Selected Case

Oviatt v. Archbishop Bergan Mercy Hosp., 214 N.W.2d 490 (Neb. 1974). The proceedings of a hospital medical staff committee are privileged in the absence of a showing of good cause arising from extraordinary circumstances.

NEVADA

Statutory Provisions

Nev. Rev. Stat. Ann. § 49.265.

The proceedings and records of medical review committees and organized medical staff committees responsible for evaluating and improving the quality of care rendered in hospitals are not subject to discovery. However, this statute does not apply to any statement made by an applicant for hospital staff privileges; nor does it apply to any statement made by a person in attendance at a committee meeting who is a party to an action or proceeding the subject of which is reviewed at such meeting. Other exceptions are noted.

NEW HAMPSHIRE

Statutory Provisions

N.H. Rev. Stat. Ann. § 329:29.

All proceedings, records, findings, and deliberations of medical review committees are confidential and privileged and are not to be used, available for use, or subject to process in any other proceeding.

Selected Case

In re K., 561 A.2d 1063 (N.H. 1989). A report prepared by a nurse epidemiologist and submitted to a hospital's infection control committee relating to how a maternity patient contracted herpes is privileged under New Hampshire law. The statutory privilege that applies to quality assurance activities is not confined to a single committee.

NEW JERSEY

Statutory Provisions

N.J. Stat. § 2A:84A-22.8.

Information and data obtained by utilization review committees may not be revealed or disclosed in any manner or in any circumstances except to (1) a patient's attending physician, (2) the chief administrative officer of a hospital that such committees serve, (3) the medical executive committee of a hospital, (4) representatives of governmental agencies in the performance of their duties, or (5) insurance companies, under certain circumstances.

Selected Cases

Young v. King, 344 A.2d 792 (N.J. Super. Ct. Law Div. 1975). Section 2A:84A-22.8 applies to information and data of utilization committees, but not to information and data of medical records committees, tissue committees, or infection control committees.

Garrow v. Elizabeth Gen. Hosp. & Dispensary, 401 A.2d 533 (N.J. 1979). A physician is entitled to discover data used by a hospital medical staff in its decision to reject his application for staff privileges.

Bundy v. Sinopoli, 580 A.2d 1101 (N.J. Super. Ct. Law Div. 1990). Opinions, criticisms, and evaluations contained in peer review committee files are protected from discovery in medical malpractice suits.

NEW MEXICO

Statutory Provisions

N.M. Stat. Ann. §§ 41-9-2 and 41-9-5.

Data and information on cost control, quality assurance, mortality and morbidity, and similar committees are confidential and not subject to discovery. However, information, documents, and records otherwise available from original sources are not immune from discovery or use in any civil action merely because they were presented during the proceedings of a review organization. Material is not protected if it is sought to be used in a judicial appeal from an action of a review organization.

Selected Cases

University Heights Hosp., Inc. v. Ashby, No. 14284 (N.M. June 16, 1982). Constitutionality of state peer review act reinstated after a trial court erroneously invalidated the confidentiality provisions of the act.

Southwest Community Health Serv. v. Smith, 755 P.2d 40 (N.M. 1988). The court upheld the constitutionality of the state peer review statute but ruled that when a plaintiff is able to demonstrate that privileged information is critical to the case, the court may, in its discretion, declare such evidence admissible.

NEW YORK

Statutory Provisions

N.Y. Educ. Law § 6527(3).

Proceedings and records of utilization review, quality control, and similar committees are not subject to disclosure. This exception from disclosure does not apply to statements made by any person in attendance at a committee meeting who is a party to an action or proceeding, the subject of which was reviewed at the meeting. Other exceptions are noted.

Selected Cases

Gourdine v. Phelps Memorial Hosp., 336 N.Y.S.2d 316 (App. Div. 1972). The court will not compel disclosure of documents of medical staff meetings where it is apparent that no such documents exist.

Pinder v. Parke Davis & Co., 337 N.Y.S.2d 452 (Schoharie County Sup. Ct. 1972). Section 6527 does not protect statements of a person in attendance at a medical staff committee meeting who is a party to an action or proceeding, the subject of which was reviewed at such meeting.

Lang v. Abbott Lab., 398 N.Y.S.2d 577 (App. Div. 1977). Discovery of hospital records concerning quality of intravenous fluid is not barred by section 6527.

Lenard v. New York Univ. Medical Ctr., 442 N.Y.S.2d 30 (App. Div. 1982). Statements by members of a hospital's medical review committee are not discoverable if the hospital, by itself, is a party to a medical malpractice suit, but would be discoverable if a member of the committee were a party to the lawsuit.

DePaolo v. Wisoff, 461 N.Y.S.2d 893 (App. Div. 1983). Minutes of hospital staff meetings are not discoverable in a malpractice action, but statements made by individual parties to the suit and contained in the minutes may be obtained after the court's private inspection of the minutes and deletion of privileged material.

Daly v. Genovese, 466 N.Y.S.2d 428 (App. Div. 1983). Allegedly slanderous statements made in peer review proceedings are not discoverable in a defamation action. Only statements concerning the subject matter of peer review proceedings may be discovered.

Palmer v. City of Rome, 466 N.Y.S.2d 238 (App. Div. 1983). Pathology reports prepared for use in evaluating the clinical performance of a physician are immune from discovery in a medical malpractice action even though the reviewing physicians did not constitute a "committee" as defined by New York's medical review confidentiality statute.

Byork v. Carmer, 487 N.Y.S.2d 226 (App. Div. 1985). Hospital review committee confidentiality statute does not protect from discovery in a malpractice suit a hospital's knowledge of alleged prior negligent acts of staff physician because such knowledge may be acquired from sources who did not participate in privileged review committee meetings.

Lilly v. Turecki, 492 N.Y.S.2d 286 (App. Div. 1985). New York's peer review confidentiality law satisfies due process requirements because it is a reasonable means for promoting and improving the quality of medical care; hospital review committee documents sought by patient in malpractice suit must be submitted to malpractice panel's presiding justice for determination of discoverability.

Parker v. St. Clare's Hosp., 553 N.Y.S.2d 533 (App. Div. 1990). In a suit charging a hospital with negligent physician credentialing, documents pertaining to physician's initial application for privileges and renewal applications were protected from discovery.

St. Elizabeth's Hosp. v. State Board of Professional Medical Conduct, 579 N.Y.S. 457 (App. Div. 1992). A medical conduct review board could subpoena a hospital quality assurance committee's records to investigate professional misconduct.

NORTH CAROLINA

Statutory Provisions

N.C. Gen. Stat. §§ 131E-76 and 131E-95.

The records, proceedings, and materials considered or produced by a committee that evaluates the quality, cost, or necessity of hospitalization or health care services are not discoverable or admissible in a civil action against a provider of professional health services where the action arises out of matters that are the subject of evaluation and review by the committee, and are not public records.

Selected Case

Shelton v. Morehead Memorial Hosp., 322 S.E.2d 499 (N.C. Ct. App. 1985). The state's peer review confidentiality law prevents discovery of information from a hospital's former chief executive officer who participated in review committee proceedings, as well as from the review committee itself. The minutes of a hospital's board of trustees may be discovered, however, because the board is not charged with peer review functions.

NORTH DAKOTA

Statutory Provisions

N.D. Cent. Code § 23-01-02.1.

Any information, data, reports, or records made available to a mandatory hospital committee or internal quality assurance review committee are confidential and can be used only for the proper functions of the committees. Information, documents, or records that are otherwise discoverable will not be confidential merely because they were presented at a review committee hearing, nor can witnesses be prevented from testifying in a suit merely because they testified before the committee.

OHIO

Statutory Provisions

Ohio Rev. Code Ann. § 2305.24.

Proceedings and records of tissue, utilization review, peer review, and similar committees are confidential and are not subject to discovery or introduction into evidence in any civil action arising out of matters that are the subject of evaluation and review. However, information, documents, or records otherwise available from original sources are not immune from discovery or use merely because they were presented during committee meetings.

Selected Cases

Samuelson v. Susen, 576 F.2d 546 (3d Cir. 1978). The Ohio statute protecting committee records does not deprive a litigant of Fifth and Fourteenth Amendment due process rights.

Young v. Gersten, 381 N.E.2d 353 (Franklin County Ct. of Common Pleas 1978). The Ohio statute protecting committee records does not violate the Ohio constitution.

Rees v. Doctor's Hosp., No. CA-5226 (Ohio Ct. App. Feb. 6, 1980). Hospital incident reports are discoverable in a civil action against a hospital.

Gates v. Brewer, 442 N.E.2d 72 (Ohio App. 1981). When an individual attempts to prevent the discovery of information by asserting the privilege provided by the Ohio statute that prohibits the discovery of review committees' records, it is incumbent on the trial court to hold an in camera inspection of the information, documents, and records in question to ensure that all the material sought to be discovered is in fact protected under the statute.

Fostoria Daily Review Co. v. Fostoria Hosp. Ass'n, 541 N.E.2d 587 (Ohio 1989). A public hospital's Joint Advisory and Quality Assurance Committee was not covered by Ohio legislation that protects the records of hospital review committees from discovery in malpractice suits. The committee did not perform quality assurance reviews itself but instead received reports from a subsidiary quality assurance committee.

Lemasters v. Christ Hosp., 791 F. Supp. 188 (S.D. Ohio 1991). A physician was entitled to discover peer review information in her suit claiming sex discrimination against a hospital in its decision to suspend her privileges. The physician's right to sue for discrimination and her need for information to prove her allegations outweighed the hospital's claim to confidentiality.

OKLAHOMA

Statutory Provisions

Okla. Stat. Ann. tit. 63, § 1-1709.

All information, interviews, reports, statements, memoranda, findings, and conclusions of committees formed for the purpose of advancing medical research or medical education in the interest of reducing morbidity and mortality are not to be used, offered, or received in evidence in any legal proceeding.

Selected Case

City of Edmond v. Parr, 587 P.2d 56 (Okla. 1978). Records kept by a hospital infectious disease control committee and records pertaining to an investigation concerning infection in the hospital or among patients and employees are inadmissible in a malpractice action.

OREGON

Statutory Provisions

Or. Rev. Stat. § 41.675.
All data of tissue, utilization review, and similar committees are confidential and are not admissible in evidence in any judicial proceeding, except where a health care practitioner contests the denial, restriction, or termination of clinical privileges. This statute, however, does not affect the admissibility in evidence of records dealing with a patient's hospital care and treatment.

Selected Case

Straube v. Larson, 600 P.2d 371 (Or. 1979). Section 41.675 is applicable to medical staff disciplinary committees as well as to hospital tissue committees.

PENNSYLVANIA

Statutory Provisions

Pa. Stat. Ann. tit. 63, §§ 425.2 and 425.4.
The proceedings and records of peer review, utilization review, medical audit, claims review, and similar committees are not subject to discovery or introduction into evidence in any civil action against a professional health care provider arising out of matters that are the subject of evaluation and review. However, information, documents, or records otherwise available from original sources are not immune simply because they were presented during committee proceedings.

Selected Cases

Robinson v. Magovern, 83 F.R.D. 79 (W.D. Pa. 1979). Pursuant to Rule 501 of the Federal Rules of Evidence, records of hospital medical staff credentials and executive committees are discoverable in federal antitrust action and in a pendent state claim, despite § 425.4.

Hankinson v. Threshold, Inc., No. 1482 of 1992 (Pa. Ct. of Common Pleas, Westmoreland County, Aug. 19, 1992). The records of a committee that investigated the murder of one patient by another patient are not protected by peer review privilege. The committee in this case was appointed in response to the particular incident, and was not charged with evaluating and improving care.

RHODE ISLAND

Statutory Provisions

R.I. Gen. Laws §§ 5-37.3-7 and 23-17-25.

Proceedings and records of medical peer review committees are not subject to discovery or introduction into evidence. However, information otherwise discoverable or admissible from original sources is not immune simply because it was presented during committee proceedings. The statute does not prohibit discovery in legal actions brought by a medical review committee to restrict or revoke a physician's license or staff privileges or in legal actions brought by aggrieved physicians. Other exceptions are noted.

Selected Cases

Cofone v. Westerly Hosp., 504 A.2d 998 (R.I. 1986). A medical staff infection control committee is a "peer review board," as defined by the state peer review confidentiality law, and its proceedings therefore are not subject to discovery.

Moretti v. Lowe, 592 A.2d 855 (R.I. 1991). Peer review legislation does not protect discovery information that was otherwise available from original sources, even if information was presented at peer review committee meetings. Accordingly, the court ruled that the hospital should identify all persons who have knowledge of the alleged incident of malpractice regardless of whether the person sits on the peer review committee or has presented evidence to the committee.

SOUTH CAROLINA

Statutory Provisions

S.C. Code §§ 40-71-10 and 40-71-20.

All proceedings and all data and information acquired by committees formed to maintain professional standards are not subject to discovery, subpoena, or introduction into evidence except upon appeal from a committee's action. Also, information, documents, and records that are otherwise available from original sources are not immune from discovery or use simply because they were presented before a committee.

SOUTH DAKOTA

Statutory Provisions

S.D. Codified Laws Ann. § 36-4-26.1.

The proceedings, records, reports, statements, minutes, or other data of committees, the function of which is to review the quality, type, or necessity of care rendered by a health care provider, or to evaluate the competence, character, experience, and performance of a physician, are not subject to disclosure or introduction into evidence. However, the prohibition relating to discovery of evidence does not apply in situations in which a physician seeks access to information on which a decision regarding his or her staff privileges was based.

TENNESSEE

Statutory Provisions

Tenn. Code Ann. § 63-6-219.

All information, interviews, statements, or other data furnished to any medical review committee are confidential and are not available for subpoena or discovery. However, material that is otherwise available from original sources is not protected merely because it was presented before a committee. Other exceptions to the general rule of nondiscoverability are noted.

Selected Case

Patton v. Mishra, No. 83-24-11 (Tenn. Ct. App. Mar. 9, 1984). Suspension or other punitive action taken by a hospital against a medical staff member is protected from discovery by the peer review confidentiality statute.

TEXAS

Statutory Provisions

Tex. Rev. Civ. Stat. Ann. art. 4495b.

All proceedings and records of a medical peer review committee are confidential and all communications made to a medical peer review committee are privileged. However, if a judge makes a preliminary finding that such proceedings, records, or communications are relevant to an anticompetitive action or a civil rights proceeding brought under 42 U.S.C.A. § 1983, then such proceedings, records, and communications are not confidential to the extent they are deemed relevant.

Selected Cases

Jordan v. Court of Appeals, 701 S.W.2d 644 (Tex. 1985). The state peer review privilege protects from discovery documents prepared by or at the direction of a hospital committee for committee purposes. The deliberations of a hospital committee, minutes of committee meetings, correspondence between committee members relating to the deliberation process, and any final committee products, such as recommendations, are also not discoverable. However, documents that are gratuitously submitted to a committee or that have been created without committee impetus and purpose are not protected by the privilege and may be discovered.

Santa Rosa Medical Ctr. v. Spears, 709 S.W.2d 720 (Tex. Ct. App. 1986). The discovery privilege is waived only by voluntary disclosure or consent to a disclosure, not by an improper disclosure where the hospital did not have an opportunity to claim the privilege. The identity of committee members, however, is not privileged under the statute.

Northeast Community Hosp. v. Gregg, 815 S.W.2d 320 (Tex. Ct. App. 1991). A trial court abused its discretion by ordering production of peer review records specifically protected from discovery by statute without first inspecting the documents in camera.

Manthe v. VanBolden, 133 F.R.D. 497 (N.D. Tex. 1991). In a medical malpractice suit, a hospital's peer review records were privileged and not subject to discovery.

UTAH

Statutory Provisions

Utah Code Ann. §§ 26-25-1 and 26-25-3.
All information, interviews, reports, statements, memoranda, and other data of committees, the function of which is to reduce morbidity or mortality or to evaluate and improve the quality of hospital and medical care, are privileged and are not to be used or received into evidence in any legal proceeding.

VERMONT

Statutory Provisions

Vt. Stat. Ann. tit. 26, §§ 1441, 1443.
The proceedings, reports, and records of committees formed to evaluate and improve the quality of health care rendered by providers of health care services, or to determine whether services were professionally indicated and performed or whether their cost was reasonable, are neither discoverable nor admissible in any civil action against a health care provider arising out of matters that are the subject of evaluation and review. However, information, reports, or documents otherwise available from original sources are not immune from discovery or use in civil actions simply because they were presented before a committee.

Selected Case

Wheeler v. Central Vt. Medical Ctr., 582 A.2d 165 (Vt. 1989). In a patient's negligent credentialing suit against a hospital, the patient did not introduce any impermissible evidence from peer review records, and therefore the hospital was not entitled to present evidence from those records in its defense.

VIRGINIA

Statutory Provisions

Va. Code Ann. §§ 8.01-581.16 and 8.01-581.17.
The proceedings, records, minutes, reports, and oral and written communications of cost control, utilization review, quality control, peer review, and similar committees are privileged and are not discoverable except upon court order after a showing of good cause arising from extraordinary circumstances. This statute does not immunize hospital records kept with respect to any patient in the ordinary course of the business of operating a hospital.

WASHINGTON

Statutory Provisions

Wash. Rev. Code Ann. § 4.24.250.

The proceedings, reports, and written records of committees formed to evaluate the competence and qualifications of members of the health care profession are not subject to subpoena or discovery in any civil action, except actions arising out of a committee's recommendations.

Selected Cases

Coburn v. Seda, 677 P.2d 173 (Wash. 1984). The proceedings, reports, and written records of "regularly constituted" hospital quality review committees are immune from discovery in medical malpractice suits.

Anderson v. Breda, 700 P.2d 737 (Wash. 1985). Information concerning the suspension, termination, or restriction of a staff physician's hospital privileges is not privileged under the state peer review confidentiality law when discovered independently from a physician named in a malpractice action.

WEST VIRGINIA

Statutory Provisions

W. Va. Code § 30-3C-3.

The proceedings and records of peer review, utilization review, medical audit, claims review, and similar committees are privileged and are not subject to subpoena, discovery, or introduction into evidence in any civil action arising out of matters that are the subject of evaluation and review. However, documents, information, and records that are otherwise available from original sources are not protected simply because they were presented during committee proceedings. Further, material is available in civil actions to individuals whose activities are under committee scrutiny. Other exceptions are noted.

WISCONSIN

Statutory Provisions

Wis. Stat. Ann. § 146.38.

Records of organizations formed to review and evaluate the services of health care providers may not be used in civil actions against health care providers or facilities. However, information, documents, and records are not to be construed as immune from discovery or use in civil actions merely because they were presented to a committee. Information can be released for medical and other specified purposes as long as the names of patients are withheld.

Selected Cases

Jacobs v. Gallagher, No. F3-1471 (Wis. Cir. Ct.-Branch 1, La Crosse County, Sept. 16, 1983). The Wisconsin statue that bars discoverability and admissibility of medical staff peer review records is constitutional.

State ex rel. Good Samaritan Medical Ctr.-Deaconess Hosp. Campus v. Maroney, 365 N.W.2d 887 (Wis. Ct. App. 1985). Wisconsin hospital records confidentiality statute construed as applying only to a "review or evaluation of the services of a health care provider;" credentials committee records are subject to discovery.

Mallow v. Angove, 434 N.W.2d 839 (Wis. Ct. App. 1988). An amendment to the peer review statute extending statutory immunity to good-faith acts by hospital governing bodies does not bring the activities of those bodies within the confidentiality provisions of the statute. Therefore, a patient was entitled to discover information relating to a hospital's governing board's decision to suspend a physician's staff privileges.

WYOMING

Statutory Provisions

Wyo. Stat. §§ 35-2-601 and 35-2-602.

All reports, findings, proceedings, and data of hospital medical staff committees that are responsible for the supervision, discipline, admission privileges, or control of staff members, or that evaluate and report on patient care and treatment; research; reducing mortality; prevention and treatment of diseases, illnesses, and injuries; and utilization review are confidential and privileged.

FEDERAL LAW

Rules

Rule 501, Federal Rules of Evidence.

Federal common law is controlling with respect to discovery questions, except where state law supplies the rule of decision, in which case state laws governing privilege are controlling.

Selected Cases

Bredice v. Doctor's Hosp., Inc., 50 F.R.D. 249 (D.D.C. 1970). Minutes of a hospital medical staff committee are not subject to discovery without a showing of exceptional necessity.

Gillman v. United States, 53 F.R.D. 316 (S.D.N.Y. 1971). Minutes and reports of a committee inquiring into hospital procedures and behavior of hospital personnel are not discoverable in an action under the Federal Tort Claims Act.

Robinson v. Magovern, 83 F.R.D. 79 (W.D. Pa. 1979). Under Rule 501 of the Federal Rules of Evidence, hospital medical staff committee records are discoverable even though privileged under a state statute.

Schafer v. Parkview Memorial Hosp., 593 F. Supp. 61 (N.D. Ind. 1984). Minutes of a hospital psychiatric review committee are discoverable in a suit based on the federal Age Discrimination in Employment Act because the need for discovery outweighs the reasons underlying the privilege provided by the state peer review record confidentiality statute.

Mewborn v. Heckler, 101 F.R.D. 691 (D.D.C. 1984). The minutes, reports, or other documents of a peer review committee may not be discovered in an action under the Federal Tort Claims Act absent a showing of extraordinary necessity, especially when the raw factual data that are sought can be obtained from other hospital reports and records.

Whitman v. United States, 108 F.R.D. 5 (D.N.H. 1985). Federal law recognizes a privilege protecting hospital peer review records from discovery, but that privilege can be waived voluntarily. Therefore, in an action under the Federal Tort Claims Act, the records of a peer review committee hearing were discoverable because a physician disclosed in a deposition the identity of persons at the hearing and a specialist's statement that the surgery under review was performed improperly. The records were not protected by the attorney's work product rule because the material was not generated in preparation for litigation.

Table of Cases

Index

About the Authors

William H. Roach, Jr., M.S., J.D., is a partner of the law firm of Gardner, Carton & Douglas, a large multispecialty firm based in Chicago with an office in Washington, D.C. Mr. Roach's health law practice specialties include the formation of integrated delivery systems, mergers and acquisitions of health care providers, hospital affiliations, corporate restructuring, tax-exempt organizations, health finance, physician/hospital organizations, certificate of need, medical staff bylaws and contracts, health information and records, patient rights and responsibilities, health industry joint ventures, and legal audits. Before entering private practice, Mr. Roach was vice president for legal affairs at Rush-Presbyterian-St. Luke's Medical Center (1976–1980) and senior staff counsel at Michael Reese Hospital and Medical Center (1974–1976), both large Chicago teaching hospitals. He received an A.B. from Columbia College of Columbia University in 1966, a JD from Vanderbilt University in 1972, and an MS from the Health Law Training Program of the University of Pittsburgh in 1973. He is a special features editor of *Topics in Health Information Management* and a contributing editor of the *Hospital Law Manual*. Mr. Roach is a member of the editorial boards of *Medical Records Briefing* and *Medical Staff Briefing*, a former president and founding director of the Illinois Association of Hospital Attorneys, and is a member of the American, Illinois, and Chicago Bar Associations, the American Academy of Hospital Attorneys, and the National Health Lawyers Association.

Patricia Younger, J.D., Cynthia Conner, LL.L., and Kara Kinney Cartwright, J.D., are Health Law Center staff members at Aspen Publishers, Inc., where they are involved in extensive research and writing on health law issues. Among the publications these attorneys write for are the *Hospital Law Manual*, a multivolume looseleaf treatise on a full range of health law issues, such as medical records, medical staff, pharmacy, consents, reproductive issues, tax, and financial management; the *Health Care Labor Manual*, a three-volume looseleaf treatise on labor and employment issues of concern to health care providers; and the *Managed Care Law Manual*, a treatise on legal issues of concern in the managed care environment, such as antitrust, utilization management, taxation, and fraud and abuse. In addition, these attorneys work with outside authors in producing the *Laboratory Regulation Manual*, a four-volume looseleaf addressing legal issues of concern to clinical laboratories written by the law firm of O'Connor and Hannon; and the *Hospital Contracts Manual*, a three-volume treatise covering contracting issues relevant to health care providers edited by the law firm of Baker and Hostetler.